Deep Dive

Exploring the Real-world Value of Open Source Intelligence

Rae Baker

About the Author

Rae Baker is a senior OSINT Analyst on the Dynamic Adversary Intelligence team at Deloitte specializing in maritime intelligence, human intelligence, corporate reconnaissance, and U.S. sanctions research. With an extensive background in graphic design, Rae has a unique insight into imagery analysis and how perception plays a role with intelligence interpretation. These practical skills have played a key role in her volunteer positions as Executive Board Member of OSINT Curious, Team Lead at Operation Safe Escape, and volunteer at the National Child Protection Task Force. In addition, Rae is a licensed Private Investigator and owner of Kase Scenarios, an immersive training experience geared toward readying individuals for real-life OSINT work. Rae has presented at conferences around the world including DEFCON Recon Village and ICS Village, Shmoocon, Trend Micro's DECODE, and the SANS OSINT Conference. Rae also holds several prominent industry certificates including SANS GOSI, Associate of ISC2 (CISSP), AWS Solutions Architect and is a Trace Labs First Place Black Badge winner and Most Valuable OSINT award winner.

About the Technical Editor

Espen Ringstad is a Senior Intelligence analyst specializing in OSINT. Espen is known for starting and running the OSINT Curious Projects Discord community with over 10,000 members from all over the world. Espen is currently the CEO and owner of Kase Scenarios, an OSINT training company specializing in hands-on OSINT training.

Acknowledgments

It would be impossible to include everyone who deserves thanks for this book, but I will give it a hearty try. I would be remiss to not acknowledge the impact my time at Penn State University and more specifically the Technology Club had on my career. Being President of the Technology club allowed me to explore cybersecurity, make lifelong friends, and meet industry leaders that have continued to be a huge part of my success. Additionally, I want to thank Patrick Laverty and the Layer 8 Conference for sponsoring my ticket to attend their conference as a student and to Trace Labs for being my first introduction into the world of OSINT.

My voice in the OSINT community would not have been quite as loud without the OSINT Curious team taking a chance on me. When I was added to the board of OSINT Curious it felt as if I had finally made it. Thanks to Ritu Gill for reading through the book and providing countless hours of feedback and insight.

A very special thank you to my Deloitte team for being such brilliant and talented people who are always rooting for me and constantly teaching me new things. To Neal and J.P., I will never forget the life-changing opportunities and guidance you have provided. Anna and Justin M, I could never thank you enough for the many nights you read through my book and offered feedback in addition to the unwavering moral support for my wild ideas that you both provide.

I truly believe I would not have finished this book without the help of Espen Ringstad my technical writer, support person, and good friend. Espen spent an immeasurable amount of time reading my drafts, providing feedback, and just listening to me complain. While projects like this can be a strain on friendships, I believe that ours is stronger because of it.

The OSINT Community deserves a special thanks as well for being a safe space for people who want to learn and grow. You welcomed me with open arms and allowed me to share my love of OSINT, you became my friends, and for that I will always be grateful.

Even with all of my work, this book would still be a pipedream if not for the amazing Wiley team who made this process so easy including Jim Minatel who took a chance on my crazy idea for an OSINT book, Pete Gaughan for being an extremely supportive Editor, and Shannon Jade for your kind and insightful feedback along the way.

To all of my friends outside of the cyber and OSINT communities who have had to listen to me talk about OSINT and this book nonstop, I appreciate you. Kelly, you have offered so much of your time and energy to me throughout the years. Alex, Maddie, Angie, Lyndy, Katrien, Alicia, Chelsea, we may have met by chance but you have grown to be one of the most supportive forces in my life. To all those I missed, I apologize I am really tired after writing all of these pages.

Huge shoutout to my parents for allowing me to believe I can accomplish anything regardless of difficulty. Thanks, Dad, for spending time fostering my interest in electronics and computers. Mom, thank you for instilling a love for arts and being endlessly creative which seeps into everything I do.

Most importantly, I want to thank my husband who supports me without question, and my kids who graciously sacrificed their time with me in support of my dreams, which is something I will never forget. If these guys are proud of me, truly nothing else matters.

Contents at a Glance

Contents

Foreword

In a small town in Germany, an 18-year-old woman left her family, most of her possessions, and all she had known and struck out in search of a better life. She made her way to Hamburg, Germany, where she boarded the ocean liner *S.S. Manhattan* on January 17, 1939. The 705-foot-long steam ship carried 1,300 passengers and was headed for the United States. The ship's manifest captured the woman's name, age, profession, and abilities to read and write, and on January 26, 1939, she arrived at Ellis Island, New York.

Using the data easily discovered on the Internet, it is simple to follow the woman's journey through life as she married, raised children and grandchildren, and finally, after 98 years, passed away. That was my grandmother whose epic journey from Germany to the United States was recorded in official government and commercial sources that were digitized and put onto the Internet. These online records from 1939 to present day captured snapshots of her life and my family's past. This is just some of the power and depth of open-source intelligence (OSINT).

As you read *Deep Dive: Exploring the Real-world Value of Open Source Intelligence*, you will be learning and honing skills that will become incredibly helpful in your work and, most likely, your personal life. Rae Baker infuses every chapter with stories, examples, and practical applications to help you make mental connections between tools and when to use them.

For some in the OSINT world, genealogical data is core to their work. For others, the transportation data I mentioned may be important. Others of us in OSINT may focus on businesses, social media, and Dark Web resources. This book touches all those topics and much more. The OSINT field is rapidly growing as employers and the public begin to understand what many of us have known for a while: being able to locate, collect, and properly analyze online data are core skills in today's workplaces. This is why you will find this book useful: it presents you with real-world skills and experiences in an easy-to-consume format.

I am honored to have been chosen to write this forward and hope that you enjoy learning from Rae.

— Micah Hoffman
Founder, My OSINT Training

Preface

Who is this book for?

This book was developed to be a resource for Analysts in varying stages from entry level to advanced. The content is meant to not only appeal to those seeking to gain a basic understanding of Open Source Intelligence (OSINT) but those wishing to hone their current tradecraft through real-world examples and insight from the leading experts in OSINT.

My background is born from my experiences in visual arts, true crime, and cybersecurity, but I have intentionally written "Deep Dive" to be as inclusive as possible and to incorporate perspectives not only from the Intelligence Community (IC), Law Enforcement (LE), and Cybersecurity but alternative fields and organizations that may utilize OSINT capabilities. There is intrinsic value in viewing obstacles through a different lens, and my hope is that by the end of this book everyone will come away with fresh knowledge, ideas, and perspectives for developing their tradecraft.

What can you learn?

Reading this book should leave you with a basic understanding of the history of OSINT, how it is practiced at present, and predictions for the future. We will learn how to apply the phases of the Intelligence Cycle and how to use critical thinking and pivoting to enhance our analysis capability. Focusing extensively on the benefits of thinking like the adversary we learn how employing an adversarial mindset when approaching OSINT analysis can make us better Analysts.

Prior to learning tradecraft, we must first learn how to protect ourselves through basic Operational Security tactics and techniques for developing effective and safe research accounts.

Areas of Focus

Part I: Foundational OSINT

This section provides entry-level foundational OSINT skills through the learning phases of the Intelligence Cycle, how to apply critical thinking skills, Operational Security best practices, writing and disseminating reports, pivoting, mental health considerations, and learning to think like the Adversary.

Part II: OSINT Touchpoints

After building a solid bedrock of core OSINT skills in Part I, we will hone our tradecraft through advanced skills in the following areas of research:

- Chapter 5: Subject Intelligence
- Chapter 6: Social Media Analysis
- Chapter 7: Business and Organizational Intelligence
- Chapter 8: Transportation Intelligence
- Chapter 9: Critical Infrastructure and Industrial Intelligence
- Chapter 10: Financial Intelligence
- Chapter 11: Cryptocurrency
- Chapter 12: Non-fungible Tokens

Each chapter in this part will first introduce the research area, followed by outlining the fundamental concepts and expert tradecraft techniques, sprinkled with relevant case studies and stories that begin to pull the concepts together through real-world examples.

Subject Intelligence

Learn the methods that OSINT Analysts use to study, track, and identify humans online using their actions enriched through publicly available data and how to locate and pivot through unique subject identifiers. Then we will find out how, when, and why we should utilize public indexes.

Social Media Analysis

We will walk through various methods for how to identify selectors, collect data points, and pivot through social media data. Learn about misinformation and disinformation identification and analysis and how to verify that information is true or valid.

Business and Organizational Intelligence

Take a dive into the innerworkings of entities both big, small, and non-profit. Learn how to effectively identify an entity's structure, affiliations, contracts, and lawsuits. Combining organizational data with Subject Intelligence we will learn to utilize social media along with targeted browser searching to locate information leaks.

Transportation Intelligence

Transportation is the crux of society and the data gathered from investigating railways, planes, ships, cars, buses, and subways can be used to enrich many other areas of OSINT Analysis. We will walk through how to make Transportation Intelligence valuable and relevant in our investigations by tracking shipments, movements, and passengers. We will find out what illicit activity takes place in the ocean and ways to identify and analyze these cases using geolocation and pattern tracking. Finally, we will see how easy it is to integrate Transportation Intelligence with the other forms of Intelligence within this book.

Critical Infrastructure and Industrial Intelligence

In this chapter we will look at the public data vulnerabilities within critical industrial systems such as the power grid, water treatment plants, manufacturing, boilers, pipelines, etc. Then, determine what data can be gleaned from Industrial Control Systems (ICS) like Supervisory Control and Data Acquisition (SCADA) and Distributed Control Systems (DCS) and led to solutions by investigating what infrastructure is open to the Internet using Shodan and network enumeration techniques. Discover methods for locating IoT devices that are broadcasting to the Internet including sensors, gadgets, appliances, and cameras. We will learn about challenges with critical IoT devices and how to identify reportable vulnerabilities. Touching on some Signals Intelligence (SIGINT), we will learn to investigate wireless, Bluetooth, MIFI and LORAWAN networks and the related public disclosures.

Financial Intelligence

This chapter will provide an overview of financial open source data the organizations tasked with preventing financial crime. We will cover methods for analyzing and understanding transactions, fraudulent or illegal activity, transnational crime, and other data aligned with other public disclosures.

Cryptocurrency

This chapter introduces the basic concept of cryptocurrency and details how the various forms of cryptocurrency work. Then, we will walk through the ways that cryptocurrency can be used, both good and bad, and how we can use wallet and account information for finding the true owner of the accounts.

Non-fungible Tokens

Here we learn what non-fungible tokens are, how they are used, and how we as analysts can use them to gain a deeper understanding of the sellers and buyers.

Why learn OSINT skills?

OSINT is a great practical skill set that translates effectively across many career paths making each Analyst an asset. Many of the skills we use as Analysts also make us very resourceful in our day-to-day lives, in fact, we might already be using OSINT and not even know! Many people routinely research their new babysitters, house cleaners, or dates online using all publicly available resources. Volunteer organizations use OSINT techniques to prevent child exploitation or for researching a domestic violence victim's online footprint to develop safety plans. Businesses use OSINT Analysts to keep their organization and employees safe, and governments use OSINT for National Security. OSINT is not only an increasingly attractive career choice but it can also be extremely exciting.

Introduction

How I got started in OSINT

I wish I could say I had been bitten by the OSINT bug at an early age, but the truth is I had no idea what OSINT was until 2019. Unbeknownst to me, the knowledge, passion, and curiosity required in order to excel in this field were being instilled and cultivated within me through seemingly unrelated experiences throughout my life.

Having an Electrical Engineer for a father meant as a child I was constantly fiddling around with electronic toys like multimeters, resistors, capacitors, LEDs and of course, computers. We purchased our first computer, a Commodore 64, back in the late 80s when programs were stored on 16k cartridges and 51/4" floppy disks were the norm. I fondly remember learning how to boot up games in DOS to play Zork II and later, on our 1990's Gateway computer, unsuccessfully trying to code a ball to bounce across the screen. The interest and willingness to learn was there but the mathematical and coding competence was certainly not.

Due to a personal lack of confidence in my technology skills and the frequency with which I skipped High School, I ended up gravitating strongly towards art. Drawing and writing always came very naturally to me and with very little effort I achieved an Associate Degree in Visual Communications and worked in various roles as a Senior Graphic designer for nearly 15 years. Creating artwork day in and day out for years was becoming increasingly banal, and I was desperately seeking a new challenge. Between us, I always felt like I chose to become an artist because I was scared to fail in a technology field.

Going back to college was not an easy decision to make at 36 years old. At this point in my life, I was comfortable in my job as a Senior Designer and I had a 2-year-old son with another on the way, but I needed more income, more security, and more of a mental challenge. I promptly enrolled in Pennsylvania State University World Campus to learn Networking and Security and Risk Analysis becoming the President of the Technology Club in the process. While acting as President, I focused on bringing industry leaders in (virtually) to talk about their position in the field and give advice to students. This endeavor led to many talks with important leaders in the field of Information Security and was a great networking opportunity for me. Leveraging these connections, a few club members were graciously invited to attend the Layer 8 Social Engineering & OSINT Conference in Rhode Island where I would first learn what OSINT is.

It is at this point that I find it necessary to stray a bit outside the topic at hand to discuss. . . *murder*. Don't worry, I haven't killed anyone despite crime being a fundamental part of my story. You see, outside of school, work, and familial obligations, I have a bit of a dark hobby, I am an enormous True Crime fan. I listen to all the best true crime podcasts, have watched nearly every documentary in existence (I keep a spreadsheet), and even have a tattoo from Damien Echols of the West Memphis Three. I am unquestionably obsessed with true crime, but why? Like anyone else I am pulled into the drama of a good story, but beyond that I am deeply vested in the investigation and analysis of cases. I long to be an insider privy to the who, why, and how behind the scenes. I revel in the minutiae of following each juicy breadcrumb deep into the rabbit hole. This my friends, is why I find OSINT so appealing. For me, OSINT isn't just a job, it is a magnificent nexus between true crime investigation, visualization, and information security- an apex of all my personal life experiences that have tailored my skillset to this very position, a field of expertise I had never once heard of before this moment in 2019 at the Layer 8 Conference.

Following the conference, I was determined to focus all my efforts into OSINT and build a brand for myself, I have a marketing background after all so I should use it! Beginning with my first shaky OSINT presentation at BSides Harrisburg, I battled my ever-present fear of public speaking to deliver my thoughts around OSINT. I have since presented at a slew of conferences including DEFCON, Shmoocon, The SANS OSINT Summit, and my Layer 8 to name a few. In a single whirlwind year, I grew from a Graphic Design Manager to holding a position as Executive Board member of The OSINT Curious Project and working side by side with the top names in the OSINT community. Most importantly, I was hired into an OSINT position at Deloitte, one of the top four consulting firms in the country, to one of the most incredibly talented teams whom I learn from every day.

Everyone dreams about working in a career doing something they are passionate about and for me, OSINT is that thing. I look forward to being able to share with you what I have learned and ignite the same spark for OSINT that I found.

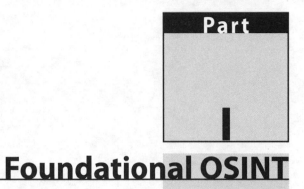

Part

I

Foundational OSINT

Open Source Intelligence

1.1   What Is OSINT?

Open-source intelligence (OSINT) is the production of intelligence through the collection and enrichment of publicly available information. When we talk about publicly available information, this means any data that is available for public access without the use of a secret clearance or intrusion into a system; however, it may also include data behind a paywall such as a newspaper subscription. This data may be gathered from the Internet, social media, mainstream media, publications and subscriptions, audio, imagery, videos, and geospatial/satellite information to name a few.

It is important to note that OSINT is a purely *passive* method of intelligence collection, meaning that we view information such as a person's credentials in a database, but we do not use those credentials to access anything or to log in. Using credentials or actively scanning/intruding into a system is *active* reconnaissance, which should be left to ethical hackers, penetration testers who have the legal authorization to do so, or law enforcement who have prior authorization and approved operational plans. Ultimately, we strive to collect information while making as little "noise" as possible to prevent detection.

OSINT may sound like a career path for only those with a military or intelligence background, but the field consists of a wide variety of experience and education levels. Many well-established analysts originate from different fields;

I held a 15-year career as a graphic design manager within a marketing team before pivoting toward investigations, developing blogs, and attending conferences related to OSINT. One of the most exciting parts of OSINT is that the field is broad and there is a myriad of specializations. Because OSINT is a relatively new field for many business and intelligence environments to include within their security structure, there are many opportunities to nurture your interests in a niche topic like I have in the field of maritime intelligence.

Many job descriptions and fields incorporate OSINT skills including the following:

- Journalism
- Intelligence (CIA, NSA, FBI, etc.)
- Government
- Armed forces
- Business
- Genealogy
- Education (training)
- Private investigation
- Security assessments

Additionally, several qualities would be advantageous for any OSINT analyst to possess. If I were to choose a single trait for every analyst to possess, it would unequivocally be curiosity. Technical, written, and critical thinking skills can all be taught, but if the analyst doesn't have the curiosity to dig deeper and to know more, they will struggle as an OSINT analyst. Curiosity is a driver for investigation and ultimately intelligence gathering. The following chart outlines several essential qualities of a great OSINT analyst. If none of these qualities sounds fitting, that does not necessarily mean you don't belong in OSINT. We don't need to be born natural investigators to become one; however, in that case it may require further training to learn those skills.

Qualities and Skills of a Great OSINT Analyst

Curious	Analytical	Active listening	Communication
Detail-oriented	Creative	Technical interest	Methodical
Structured	Self-motivated	Written/oral skills	Critical thinker
Organized	Tenacious		

Individuals interested in a career in OSINT might feel it isn't a possibility for them because they lack the technical skills needed to excel. It can be quite daunting from the outside watching top-tier OSINT analysts work. The good news is, because OSINT is a mindset, we don't need to get hung up on our proficiency (or lack thereof) with OSINT tools. Being methodical, detail-oriented, and curious will help us find new and innovative ways to look at challenges.

For example, in the following chart, we have two analysts, both tasked with finding an active email address associated with a subject.

Analyst 1 goes to the browser to search the subject's name in the format "firstname lastname." In the results she finds a blog called "Subject's Gamer Blog" and notices at the bottom of the page there is an email, `first.last@email.com`. Taking this email over to the web-based email verification tool `emailrep.io`, she can verify the last date it was used or when it was created.

Analyst 2 takes a different approach beginning with a LinkedIn search to find the company where the subject works. Once she knows the company, Analyst 2 quickly finds the domain name `company.com`. Analyst 2 then switches to her Linux machine and runs an advanced tool that cross checks the input email with all emails found in breaches. After the tool runs for a minute, Analyst 2 sees `first.last@company.com`, which matches the name of the subject. Just like the previous analyst, she verifies the last active date of the email in `emailrep.io`.

	ANALYST 1	ANALYST 2
■ Step 1	■ Searches in a browser for subject's name.	■ Uses LinkedIn to determine the subject's employer.
■ Step 2	■ Finds a blog related to the subject.	■ Locates the domain name for the employer: `company.com`.
■ Step 3	■ The subject's email is listed at the bottom of the blog.	■ Runs the domain in a Python tool in Linux to find all breached emails for `company.com`.
■ Step 4	■ Verifies the email is active with emailrep.io.	■ Sees subject's name as `first.last@company.com`.
■ Step 5		■ Verifies the email is active with `emailrep.io`.

Both analysts were able to find active emails with the subject's name as the original selector. Analyst 1 kept it simple, while Analyst 2 decided to use an advanced tool she was familiar with. Did one analyst do a better job at completing the task? No, they both completed the task and provided an active email in their report; the path they took to get there is irrelevant. The purpose of this exercise is to illustrate that each method accomplished the goal and that approaching a challenge using overly technical methods is not always the best option. Analyst 2 took an additional step to complete the goal and depending on the criticality of the initial ask, that time may be valuable. On the other hand, Analyst 1 lucked out finding an email with very little digging and could have spent more time finding a lead.

1.2   A Brief History of OSINT

In this section, I'll go over a brief history of OSINT (see Figure 1.1).

The Past

OSINT has been used in various forms by the U.S. intelligence community (IC) for more than 50 years. In 1941, President Roosevelt established the Foreign Broadcast Monitoring Service (FBMS). During World War II, the FBMS's primary task was recording, transcribing, and translating shortwave propaganda broadcasts for military reporting. After the attack on Pearl Harbor in December 1941, the FBMS grew in importance and was renamed the Federal Broadcast Information Service (FBIS). After World War II, Harry S. Truman created the Central Intelligence Group, and the FBIS was moved within it and renamed the Foreign Broadcast Information Service.

Up until the 1990s the FBIS was primarily used for monitoring and translating foreign news sources and analyzing propaganda. It provided critical information to the military during the Cuban Missile Crisis and all throughout the Cold War including the initial reporting on the Soviet removal of missiles from Cuba.

FBIS operated 20 worldwide bureaus to allow it to physically collect material for exploitation. Eighty percent of the information used to monitor the collapse of the Soviet Union was attributed to open sources.[1] In 1997, facing budget cuts and lack of funding, the FBIS neared dissolution but was saved by a public cry from the Federation of American Scientists who described the FBIS as "biggest bang for the buck in the American intelligence community."

Decades then passed with no major changes to OSINT; even during the U.S. terrorist attack on 9/11, nothing shifted until the social media boom of the mid-2000s. The FBIS collected what was at the time considered OSINT, but this open-source data was not collected or used the same as we do today.

The 2000s' iteration of OSINT looks vastly different than the OSINT we saw in 1941. This new version of OSINT was born from the breakneck growth and development of Internet usage, referred to as Web 2.0. This substantial shift from static web pages to user-generated content like social media completely transformed the practice of OSINT collection.

In 2005, the director of national intelligence (DNI) created the Open Source Center (OSC) and was entrusted with ensuring that open-source collection was effectively used and shared by the IC by providing training, developing tools, and testing new technologies. At this time, open source was seen by many as a less structured and decentralized form of collection discipline, and it was believed the IC wasn't fully aware of its potential and had no clear means of

---

[1] www.rand.org/content/dam/rand/pubs/research_reports/RR1900/RR1964/RAND_RR1964.pdf.

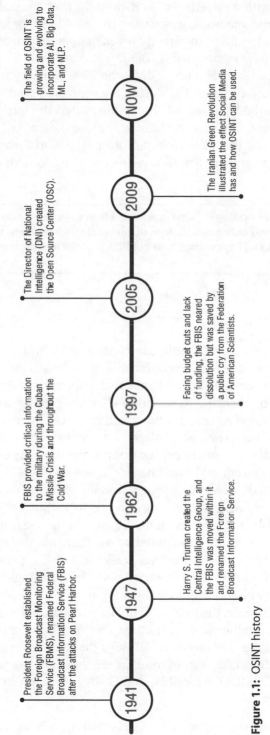

Figure 1.1: OSINT history

sharing the information effectively. Additionally, they grappled with under-standing sources and methods, evaluating the credibility of information, and protecting information that can directly reveal a person's identity, also known as *personally identifiable information* (PII).

Despite the IC's obstacles with OSINT, the 2009 Iranian Green Revolution (dubbed the Twitter Revolution) opposing the contested election of incumbent President Mahmoud Ahmadinejad clearly illustrated the importance of social media's inclusion in OSINT methodology. Despite the Iranian regime's forced media blackouts throughout the violent protests, the world was able to develop a full picture of the uprising through user-generated content on social media platforms.

> **"Individuals are making information available in ways that never existed before, including online expressions of personal sentiment, photographs of local places and happenings, and publicized social and professional networks."[2]**

The Present

As mobile phone and social media use continues to flourish, we have been afforded new and unique ways to harvest open-source data. The rise of plat-forms such as Instagram, TikTok, and Snapchat inspires users to upload copious amounts of data to our benefit. Maps and satellite imagery have grown exponen-tially more accurate and accessible allowing user access to previously classified technology. An emphasis has been placed on security and privacy leading to the mainstream adoption of encrypted communication methods like Signal, WhatsApp, and Telegram making it harder to obtain OSINT data. These data obstacles have created a need for uniquely developed tools that are often offered to the community by way of open-source repositories such as GitHub. OSINT communities are flourishing on social media, providing free training in the form of blog posts, videos, podcasts, and live streams. There are also several legitimate paid OSINT trainings and certifications available. Not-for-profit organizations are using crowdsourcing to combine analysis to tackle things such as humani-tarian rights issues and locating missing people.

With the Web 2.0 boom, the field of OSINT has expanded to cover more than just the traditional intelligence community. The lines between intelligence dis-ciplines are blurring as analysts develop skills that cross over into other collec-tion methods. Traditionally, within intelligence there are five main disciplines: HUMINT, SIGINT, IMINT, MASINT, and OSINT. Though in recent years, as

---

[2] www.rand.org/content/dam/rand/pubs/research_reports/RR1900/RR1964/RAND_RR1964.pdf.

technology capabilities increase, we are seeing techniques and disciplines along with the various INTs used within the community begin to blend.

The Five INTs[3]:

- HUMINT is the collection of information from human sources.
- SIGINT consists of the electronic transmissions that can be collected by ships, planes, ground sites, or satellites.
- IMINT or image intelligence includes geospatial intelligence (GEOINT).
- MASINT includes the advanced processing and use of data gathered from overhead and airborne IMINT and SIGINT collection systems.
- OSINT is a broad array of information and sources that are generally available, including information obtained from the media (newspapers, radio, television, etc.), professional and academic records (papers, conferences, professional associations, etc.), and public data (government reports, demographics, hearings, speeches, social media etc.).

Due to the advancements in satellite technology, analysts now have access to open-source satellite imagery at a resolution previously unseen by civilians. Supported by this newly available imagery, analysts can integrate *image intelligence (IMINT), geolocation*, and *geospatial intelligence (GEOINT)* tradecraft into their daily work. An example of this can be seen in organizations such as Bellingcat and the Centre for Information Resilience (CIR) where the analysts routinely identify people and places using imagery analysis techniques to illuminate human rights violations and war crimes.

Human intelligence (HUMINT) is another area where the lines of professional information gathering have grown hazy. Data brokers have made personal information cheap and easily accessible to the public, and social media usage has skyrocketed, allowing the tracking of individuals across the Internet. *Skip tracers* and *private investigators*, known for tracking down people who are hard to find, previously relied on locating an individual through face-to-face interviews with friends and family. Now, a person can be located just by hunting down posts, comments, likes, and check-ins online. The same private investigator could also use technology to track the individual's Bluetooth or Wi-Fi transmissions using *signals intelligence (SIGINT)* techniques enhanced by volunteer databases of unclassified wireless data collected from around the world.

Analysts today have access to a considerable supply of unclassified data repositories, the likes of which we have never seen. Because so much data is now available, we suddenly have to tackle the monstrous task of parsing through it all. Luckily, analysts have begun developing and collaborating on free open-source tools for the OSINT community that assist with making sense of the mountains

---

[3] https://usnwc.libguides.com/c.php?g=494120&p=3381426.

of new data. These parsing tools must be developed at the same rapid rate as the Internet and social media platform algorithms change, which has produced an innovative subgenre of OSINT analysts who are also developers.

It is incredible to think that there are individuals living today who have never known a life without the Internet, nor will they know the true pain of trying to connect to a dial-up connection. Right now, children are being born with a digital footprint, and some are even being signed up for email accounts while still in utero! The full impact of the "social media generation" remains to be seen, and because new forms of media seemingly pop up overnight, OSINT tradecraft continues to evolve to meet it; seemingly for us the Golden Age of OSINT still lies ahead.

The Future

In the coming years, there will be a shift from the present Web 2.0 to what is being called the Semantic Web or Web 3.0. The Semantic Web is meant to make Internet data machine readable through defining and structuring so that computers can make better interpretations of data.[4] Big Data, AI, NLP, and ML are just beginning to be applied to OSINT collection, analysis, and reporting. This new technology combined with the power of Web 3.0 will be crucial for enriching the phases of the intelligence life cycle.[5] The following are a few ways in which the life cycle may be enhanced and accelerated by these changes:

- **Planning and Requirements:** Planning and developing requirements at the stakeholder level will be better informed and targeted through sophisticated artificial intelligence (AI) and machine learning (ML) using cues aggregated from previous reporting.

- **Collection:** As Big Data continues to grow, collection will be further automated and streamlined through AI. ML and natural language processing (NLP) will be used to target collection sources more accurately, and ultimately analysts will be able to find and sort more data in less time.

- **Processing and Evaluation**: Facial and pattern recognition will grow more mainstream and facilitate analysts to determine suspects faster. NLP will review, measure, and interpret collected data for misinformation and disinformation to vet sources.

- **Analysis and Production:** Automated tools will provide more accurate analysis of collected information through correlation and clustering. AI

---

[4] www.w3.org/standards/semanticweb.
[5] www.recordedfuture.com/open-source-intelligence-future.

may be used to develop detailed graphs of associations enriched with personal and corporate data.

- **Dissemination and Consumption:** AI will automate and tailor near real-time alerts and reports for stakeholders and analysts so they can rapidly take the necessary actions. Increasing the speed in which intelligence is consumed will lead to faster response times.

As Big Data grows even bigger and data analytics and mining technology improve, one burgeoning research field to keep an eye on is *sentiment analysis*, or opinion mining. An overwhelming number of citizens across the globe use social media to discuss their opinions and feelings, and this collection of tone or sentiment can be analyzed using NLP, text analysis, and computational linguistics. Using these tools to analyze a sample of people, including how they speak, write, and use emojis and hashtags, it is possible to estimate the overall feeling of a population on a particular subject. We see this technology being used presently to analyze government elections and events such as citizen protests. In the case of the 2016 U.S. election, a study was performed to determine whether there was a political divide between urban and rural areas or between service and manufacturing zones.[6] Using the Twitter application programming interface (API), which allows a program to communicate with an application, researchers collected sentiment based on the geotagged locations within the tweet data called *metadata*. The results of this study determined that sentiment based on location did reflect the opinion of people on the ground and that this process may have tremendous benefits for predicting overall public opinion. In the future, the use of predictive analysis will become more prevalent within everyday OSINT analysis.

The 2016 election also illustrated how Internet content can sway user sentiment and public perception, and therefore more tools will need to be developed to combat the increasing assault of online propaganda, mis/disinformation, and deep fakes. This type of predictive analytic will be one facet used by the intelligence community and law enforcement for detecting and preventing crime.[7] The Tom Cruise movie *Minority Report* perfectly captured a future where crimes can be detected and prosecuted before they happen. In 2002, when this movie debuted, the concept of "pre-crimes" was unheard of, but now in 2022 we can see the beginnings of this type of predictive analysis being used widely today in law enforcement and criminal justice. While opinions differ on whether this technology actually reduces bias or whether it reinforces inequality and

---

[6] Ussama Yaqub, Nitesh Sharma, Rachit Pabreja, Soon Ae Chun, Vijayalakshmi Atluri, and Jaideep Vaidya. 2020. Location-based Sentiment Analyses and Visualization of Twitter Election Data. Digit. Gov.: Res. Pract. 1, 2, Article 14 (April 2020), 19 pages. https://doi.org/10.1145/3339909.

[7] Etter M, Colleoni E, Illia L, Meggiorin K, and D'Eugenio A. Measuring Organizational Legitimacy in Social Media: Assessing Citizens' Judgments With Sentiment Analysis. Business & Society. 2018;57(1):60-97. doi:10.1177/0007650316683926.

discrimination, it is no doubt here to stay and being augmented by facial recognition and object detection technologies.[8]

As detective and predictive analytics increase in popularity, people will become more adept at thwarting them. In 2019, during the Hong Kong protests over a controversial bill allowing extradition from Hong Kong to mainland China, protesters circumvented identification by using laser pointers, masks, and spray paint to block cameras using facial recognition software. According to reports, protesters had reason to be concerned as Hong Kong police were repeatedly accused of forcing citizens to use their face to unlock their phones and reveal their identities.[9] This battle between government and citizens on what negates a citizen's right to privacy and the protection of PII will continue to be a hot topic in the future, leading to new laws and training.

For the intelligence community and law enforcement, the future holds deeper and more practical OSINT training that will allow analysts to implement OSINT skills more effectively. Cases of the future will be enhanced through more robust OSINT databases and citizen collaboration.[10] While this type of crowdsourcing investigation can gather many leads, it is not without its challenges. Untrained citizens can and often do release the personal information of innocent people, ruin evidence, and even recklessly engage with suspects. As citizen investigations grow in popularity, the OSINT community will need to develop a more productive way to ingest, analyze, and visualize crowdsourced data. As OSINT concepts become more mainstream through movies, documentaries, and podcasts, we must be prepared to preach investigation ethics and passive-only collection to untrained citizens to maintain ethical standards.

Mark Twain famously referred to the industrial growth period in late 18th century America as the Gilded Age for being "an era of serious social problems masked in thin gold gilding."[11] This is not unlike the oncoming Gilded Age of OSINT that brims with technological advancements and growth underpinned by the tragedy of war, protests, loss of personal privacy, and civil unrest. Much of what drives the current advancements in OSINT technology are deeply rooted in politics and government. As analysts we have a duty to utilize all this exciting new technology to perform ethical investigations without the insertion of bias or politics. Unfortunately, with all this new technology have come many ethical "gray areas" we must address to remain ethical analysts.

---

[8] Shapiro, A. (2019). Predictive policing for reform? indeterminacy and intervention in Big Data policing. Surveillance & Society, 17(3), 456–472. Retrieved from `https://ezaccess`
`.libraries.psu.edu/login?url=www.proquest.com/scholarly-journals/`
`predictive-policing-reform-indeterminacy/docview/2290892716/`
`se-2?accountid=13158`.

[9] `www.nytimes.com/2019/07/26/technology/`
`hong-kong-protests-facial-recognition-surveillance.html`.

[10] J. Pastor-Galindo, P. Nespoli, F. Gómez Mármol, and G. Martínez Pérez, "The Not Yet Exploited Goldmine of OSINT: Opportunities, Open Challenges and Future Trends," in IEEE Access, vol. 8, pp. 10282-10304, 2020, doi: 10.1109/ACCESS.2020.2965257.

[11] Wuster, Tracy. "There's Millions in It!": The Gilded Age and the Economy of Satire." The Mark Twain Annual, vol. 11, 2013, p. 1–21. Project MUSE `muse.jhu.edu/article/526126`.

One area where the lines of ethics may become muddied is in the online crowdsourcing of investigations. *Crowdsourcing* is a relatively new method of analyst collaboration used as a way to tackle large and complex cases like cold cases and high-stakes, real-time events. Using team collaboration platforms and forums such as Discord, Slack, Teams, and Reddit, volunteers can participate in live ongoing investigations. Although this technique has proven useful for legitimate organizations such as The Centre for Information Resilience and Trace Labs, I would highly caution analysts from engaging in unvetted investigations.

Unofficial cases found in online forums often have no vetting process for members, and very little can be known about the backgrounds, ethics, and motives of the participants. From an ethical perspective, there are concerns that working on unofficial cases with untrained investigators has the potential to cause harm to the analyst as well as the friends and family of the victim or even the accuser. A perfect example of how crowdsourcing intelligence can have serious repercussions is the terrorist attack at the 2013 Boston Marathon.

On April 15, two explosions rocked the annual marathon in Boston, Massachusetts. Three people were killed in the blasts, and 264 were injured, including both participants and spectators near the finish line.[12] Soon, the FBI released a statement that they had located pieces of nylon, fragments of ball bearings, and nails at the scene, indicating a possible pressure cooker device was used in the bombing.[13] Over the next few days while the FBI worked tirelessly to locate the suspects in the bombing, the Internet began their own investigation.

The popular forum site Reddit hosts several news "subreddits" that began to unofficially crowdsource investigations into potential bombing suspects. A user in one of the subreddits suggested that a depressed man who had been reported missing since April 16 bore a resemblance to the suspect. The user unfairly decided that based on the way missing man Sunil Tripathi looked that this attack might be "religiously motivated." The post gained traction, and soon Sunil and his family were being harassed, and ultimately their personal information was released by these Internet sleuths.

A week after the bombing, on April 19, the real suspects, Dzhokhar Tsarnaev and Tamerlan Tsarnaev, were located by authorities. After a police manhunt, Tamerlan was shot and killed, and Dzhokhar was critically injured but captured and charged on April 22 of conspiring to use a weapon of mass destruction. After the arrest of Dzhokhar Tsarnaev, Reddit administrators issued an apology to Sunil's family for the misidentification and harassment of Sunil and his family.[14] Subsequently on April 23, Sunil's body was found in a river; the autopsy revealed he died by suicide.

---

[12] www.nbcnews.com/news/asian-america/
wrongly-accused-boston-bombing-sunil-tripathys-story-now-being-
told-n373141.

[13] www.bbc.com/news/av/world-us-canada-22179860.

[14] www.nytimes.com/2013/04/29/business/media/
bombings-trip-up-reddit-in-its-turn-in-spotlight.html.

1.3   Critical Thinking

Becoming a valuable OSINT analyst requires honing—said in my best Liam Neeson voice—"a particular set of skills." Critical thinking, or "the analysis of available facts, evidence, observations, and arguments to form a judgment[15]," is arguably the most important skill in our arsenal. Without the ability to think critically about the data we discover, we would be unable to make intelligent connections between data points or even to evaluate its legitimacy. Many journalists working in information verification on social media have become the front line in deciphering reality from fiction.

Users are bombarded by information at an alarming rate and left to determine on their own what is real versus fake. Intentional mis/disinformation is disseminated in a steady 24-hour stream through news, social media, and advertising. If that weren't enough, now we must consider the reality of synthetic AI media or *deep fakes* creating alternative false narratives. The verification of this onslaught of data requires critical thinking skills that allow us to evaluate and reflect on the information we consume. As analysts, being able to spot deception ultimately supports the effective collection of data and allows us to draw conclusions based on legitimate information.

"Critical thinking is not just about putting information together, finding a pattern, then choosing an answer, it is about reducing bias, considering all options available and presenting options to a decision-maker[16]."

Being able to think critically comes with experience and takes a fair amount of training and practice for it to feel natural. If critical thinking feels unnatural to you, don't get discouraged; everyone has periods of irrationality, and remember not even Sherlock Holmes thinks critically all the time. One way to jump-start your critical thinking is by applying David T. Moore's interpretation of Paul and Elder's Critical Thinking model to your investigations. The model is made up of eight main steps designed to help you look at a problem set using critical thinking[17]:

1. **Requirements**: Define the scope of data collection.

2. **Key Questions**: Define key questions the intelligence should answer.

3. **Considerations**: What evidence should we see? What effects would this evidence have?

---

[15] Edward M. Glaser. "Defining Critical Thinking." The International Center for the Assessment of Higher Order Thinking (ICAT, US)/Critical Thinking Community. Retrieved 16 May 2022.
[16] Moore, D. T. (2006). In Critical thinking and intelligence analysis (p. 76). essay, Center for Strategic Intelligence Research, Joint Military Intelligence College.
[17] Moore, D. T. (2006). In Critical thinking and intelligence analysis (p. 27). essay, Center for Strategic Intelligence Research, Joint Military Intelligence College.

4. **Inferences**: Determine evidence that is being inferred and any biases involved.

5. **Assumptions**: Determine what is being assumed about the evidence or any key questions that arise.

6. **Concepts**: Determine the reliability of evidence or the outcome of the collection method.

7. **Implications and Consequences**: Define the potential outcomes given correct/incorrect conclusions for key questions.

8. **Points of View**: Define other points of view on the situation.

Here is an example of critical thinking derived from David T. Moore's interpretation of Paul and Elder's Critical Thinking model[18]:

Requirements	Determine if vessels are illegally transferring oil to North Korea through ship-to-ship transfers to evade sanctions.
Key questions	Can we identify the tankers being used in the transfer of oil? Can we verify the locations with GPS and satellite imagery? Do we notice a pattern of identity obfuscation?
Considerations	If a ship-to-ship oil transfer is observed, what evidence should we see? If identity obfuscation is observed, what evidence should we see? What is not being seen?
Inferences	What is being inferred from the observed and collected evidence?
Assumptions	What is being assumed about the evidence? What is being assumed about the sources of evidence? What is being assumed about illegal oil transfers to North Korea?
Concepts	How does human analysis affect the observations? How reliable are the sources of evidence?
Implications and consequences	If conclusions are incorrect about the illegal ship-to-ship oil transfer to North Korea, what might happen? If conclusions are correct about the illegal ship-to-ship oil transfer to North Korea, what might happen?
Points of view	What other points of view exist on illegal ship-to-ship transfers to North Korea?

---

[18] Moore, D. T. (2006). In Critical thinking and intelligence analysis (p. 51). essay, Center for Strategic Intelligence Research, Joint Military Intelligence College.

By applying Paul and Elder's technique of breaking critical thinking down into eight steps, it is easy to see how this method can be applied to any investigation to inspire looking at things from a new and unique perspective. Effectively, what this technique has done is help us to develop pivot points for further analysis. Before we get too deep in the weeds with how to advance through pivot points, we must discuss the often overlooked topic of mental health.

1.4   Mental Health

The field of OSINT can be fast-paced, high-stakes, and overly stimulating at times. Analysts may be tempted to dive headfirst into a project without fully considering the detrimental effects it can have on mental health. OSINT case investigation can involve repeated exposure to graphic content in the form of human rights atrocities, murder, graphic digital material, victim accounts, torture, and sexual exploitation. Without properly considering the effects this material can have on the human mind, particularly repeated victimization, we cannot appropriately prepare to deal with it in a healthy way. Even the most seasoned OSINT analyst needs to maintain continuous awareness of possible mental health pitfalls associated with this line of work.

Through the volunteer positions I have held assisting domestic violence victims and preventing and exposing child exploitation, I have witnessed deeply graphic and traumatizing content firsthand. I am acutely aware of the many types of traumas and mental health compromises that may result from this type of work. For an analyst, mental health can seem like an afterthought when compared to the atrocities we are working to prevent; however, poor mental health can have a disastrous impact on not only the outcome of our cases but also on our personal and professional lives. It is important that we are able to recognize the different forms of trauma in ourselves and our friends and co-workers to help prevent further trauma. The following are some common forms of trauma that we may experience while working in the field of intelligence:

Vicarious trauma is trauma resulting from engaging empathically with survivors of trauma.

Secondary trauma results from hearing the firsthand trauma another individual has experienced.

Compassion fatigue is the emotional, physical, and psychological impact experienced through helping others.

Burnout is the emotional, physical, and mental exhaustion induced by high stress over an extended period of time often resulting in feeling emotionally drained and overwhelmed.

Post-traumatic stress disorder (PTSD) is a mental health condition that's triggered by experiencing or witnessing a terrifying event resulting in flashbacks, nightmares, and severe anxiety, along with uncontrollable thoughts about the event.[19]

The symptoms of trauma may vary from person to person as well as range from physical responses to emotional reactions. The physical symptoms of trauma can be alarming to the person experiencing it and might manifest as real and concerning as a physical injury. I have developed the following list of a few common symptoms of trauma to help you to recognize them in yourself and others:

- Shock
- Denial
- Anger
- Sadness
- Mood swings

- Irritability
- Paleness
- Lethargy
- Fatigue
- Racing heartbeat

The OSINT community has an obligation to bring attention and awareness to maintaining mental health, and we must strive to normalize self-care and self-assessment in the face of trauma. Analysts entering the field should feel supported and empowered to seek mental health assistance when necessary, and, in some cases, help should be routinely provided as a preventative measure.

If you feel you are experiencing a crisis, please contact a mental health crisis line near you.

- **United States:** Contact the National Institute of Mental Health by texting **HELLO** to 741741 for free and confidential support 24 hours a day throughout the United States.

- **United Kingdom:** Contact the Suicide Prevention line by texting **SHOUT** to 85258.

1.5   Personal Bias

Bias is defined as a prejudice in favor of or against one thing, person, or group compared with another, usually in a way considered to be unfair.[20] In other words, if we are so focused on a particular outcome or belief, our investigation could be swayed in favor of that outcome regardless of intention. Bias can lead

---

[19] www.mayoclinic.org/diseases-conditions/
post-traumatic-stress-disorder/symptoms-causes/syc-20355967.
[20] www.merriam-webster.com/dictionary/bias.

to false interpretations of the information we collect and analyze, which dissolves the impartiality necessary for a successful and valid investigation. An awareness of our personal biases allows us to openly challenge them by contemplating and then pushing them away. Once we realize everyone displays bias, we can more easily recognize our own. Looking often at our own biases and repeatedly asking ourselves "why" questions is a great way to flush out any beliefs we may have that could seep into our research.

"Why do I believe this is credible?"

"Why do I believe this is evidence?"

"Am I showing bias, and why do I feel this way?"

Indulge me for a moment and imagine that you are a huge Nicolas Cage fan. You enjoy his acting so much that you would argue that he is the best actor on the planet. Coincidentally you are then assigned to a team at work that is charged with investigating and determining who the best actor in the world is. Would you be able to perform this investigation as an impartial analyst, or would you knowingly (or unknowingly) sway the results toward the desired outcome? If the results of the investigation were swayed at all by your love for Nicolas Cage, that would be considered *confirmation bias*!

Confirmation bias does not necessarily have to be malicious or even intentional; humans tend to favor information that confirms our own beliefs. As analysts we need to be cognizant of confirmation bias when collecting and analyzing OSINT. The results of our research may have a much deeper impact than Nicolas Cage's career, although that's questionable. Evidence shows, even when trying to be subjective about our collection and analysis of information, we in fact, are still being influenced by our *perception biases*.[21]

On the front end of an investigation, analysts risk becoming exceedingly influenced by the first piece of data we are exposed to. This *first impression bias* may have a rippling effect throughout all proceeding data collection and analysis.[22] If a bias has tainted each piece of data we have collected, we have to question whether the information and subsequent analysis is sound.

If you have ever visited a casino and heard an excited guest proclaim they are "on a roll!" or they are "playing hot," this is called the *hot hand fallacy* or the *clustering illusion*.[23] This phenomenon causes us to see trends in clusters that are actually random events. One example would be assuming that a group of

---

[21] https://catalogofbias.org/biases/perception-bias/#:~:text=Perception%20bias%20is%20the%20tendency,influenced%20by%20perception%20biases%20unconsciously.

[22] Lim, K. H., Benbasat, I., & Ward, L. M. (2000). The Role of Multimedia in Changing First Impression Bias. Information Systems Research, 11(2), 115–136. www.jstor.org/stable/23015878.

[23] Gilovich, Thomas (1991). How we know what isn't so: The fallibility of human reason in everyday life. New York: The Free Press. ISBN 978-0-02-911706-4.

individuals hanging out together in a certain bar are gang members because the last three groups you investigated at that bar turned out to be gang members.

Outcome bias is where we base a decision on a previous outcome regardless of the factors causing us to reach that outcome.[24] This bias can lead to ineffective and inaccurate analysis because each data point is built upon previously incorrect data.

Blind spot bias is where we see ourselves as less biased than others, or we see more cognitive bias in other people.[25] Effectively, we have a "blind spot" regarding our own behavior within a situation.

Group think is defined by *Psychology Today* as being "a phenomenon that occurs when a group of well-intentioned people makes irrational or non-optimal decisions spurred by the urge to conform or the belief that dissent is impossible."[26] If you are performing research within a group of your peers and they make a claim that you disagree with but instead of arguing with them you choose to agree to maintain group harmony, this leads to group think. Group think can tarnish an otherwise great investigation with information that may not be validated or could be rife with bias.

The law of the hammer is a cognitive bias that involves an over-reliance on a familiar tool. Abraham Maslow said in 1966, "I suppose it is tempting, if the only tool you have is a hammer, to treat everything as if it were a nail."[27] This bias can be a common pitfall for OSINT analysts who focus their attention on new and shiny tools rather than taking the time to learn the methodology and the "why" behind the analysis we perform.

1.6   Ethics

Open-source intelligence often deals with complicated personal privacy concerns, regarding the privacy of the analyst, subject, and any third parties. Loss or invasion of privacy can be devastating not only physically to an individual but also emotionally and financially. As analysts, we often work in situations where the collection of personal information is part of the requirement, so we must be guided by strong morals and ethics to do the right thing. When an untrained individual intentionally violates an individual's privacy by disclosing personal information online (also known as *doxxing*), it can result in bullying,

---

[24] Gino, Francesca; Moore, Don A.; Bazerman, Max H. (2009). "No Harm, No Foul: The Outcome Bias in Ethical Judgments" (PDF). SSRN 1099464. Harvard Business School Working Paper, No. 08-080.

[25] https://dictionary.apa.org/bias-blind-spot.

[26] groupthink, 2022.

[27] Maslow, Abraham Harold (1966). The Psychology of Science: A Reconnaissance. Harper & Row. ISBN 978-0-8092-6130-7.

intimidation, loss of job, suicide, or physical harm. Amateur online investigators, like those who helped identify protesters in the January 6, 2022, U.S. Capital riot, have raised complex ethical questions with very few clear-cut answers.[28] The following are a few of the most prevalent ethical concerns we must consider when working in this field:

Who decides which individuals deserve the right to privacy?

In the United States, we have First Amendment rights to access and analyze open-source information, but individuals also have reasonable privacy rights. Unfortunately, in high-pressure cases, analysts can unintentionally make biased judgments about who is guilty, who is innocent, and who deserves to maintain their privacy.

Possible Outcome: Sometimes analyzing real-time events can be chaotic and what we think we see is not always clear. A rush to identify a suspect could lead to misidentification, loss of employment, and physical harm to you or the individual.

Is the use of breach data acceptable?

A *data breach* is an incident in which information is stolen or removed from a system without the knowledge or permission of the system owner. Because this data is stolen, it may be ethically unacceptable to possess or distribute this data.

Possible Outcome: By utilizing breach data, some would argue that we are perpetuating further breaches of data and rewarding the perpetrators. Ethics aside, if you work in a law enforcement field, using stolen data without permission could have dire consequences to your case.

Is it OK to doxx someone who we believe did something illegal?

Analysts may feel compelled to publicly expose bad actors and their crimes when they discover evidence of criminal activity such as fraud, pedophilia, and theft. Often the exposure comes by way of doxxing or publishing their personal information and crimes online for everyone to see. Some believe that because the data was discovered through open source, and it is being revealed for a good cause, that we have the right to expose this information.

Possible Outcome: We take a lot of risks when we find evidence of a crime and decide to take matters into our own hands instead of alerting the authorities. We are putting ourselves, the victims, and their families at

---

[28] www.technologyreview.com/2021/01/14/1015931/
how-to-be-an-ethical-online-investigator-activist.

risk, we are risking misidentifying and exposing the wrong people, and we are jeopardizing the cases that law enforcement may be building.

Can we use password knocking to attempt to garner information?

Password knocking is the process of resetting the password of an individual's account in an attempt to reveal all or part of their information, such as email address, username, contact information, etc. Depending on the platform, this reset attempt may trigger an email or notification sent to the account holder. An argument could be made that we may be crossing a line between passive OSINT and active hacking.

Possible Outcome: Because resetting a password for an individual's account requires physical contact with the account, it can be considered active involvement in some cases. Performing a password reset attempt on your case without prior stakeholder approval can jeopardize both the case and your job. Further, if the reset notifies the account owner that an attempt has been made against their account, it could thwart investigations or, worse, it could make you a target.

Like password knocking, much of OSINT can be considered an ethically challenging gray area because unlike other security and intelligence fields, there is no standard set of ethics to adhere to. Here, in an effort to develop and define a consistent set of OSINT ethics, I applied the Principles of Professional Ethics for the Intelligence Community set forth by the Office of the Director of National Intelligence (ODNI)[29]:

OSINT Ethics

- We seek the truth and obtain, analyze, and provide intelligence objectively.
- We uphold the highest standards of integrity, responsible behavior, and ethical conduct in investigation activities.
- We comply with laws, ensuring that we carry out our mission in a manner that respects privacy, civil liberties, and human rights obligations.
- We treat all people fairly and with respect, do not engage in harassment or discrimination, and avoid injuring others.
- We demonstrate integrity in our conduct, mindful that all our actions, whether public or not, should reflect positively on the OSINT community at large.

---

[29] www.dni.gov/index.php/how-we-work/ethics.

- We are responsible stewards of the public trust; we use intelligence authorities and resources prudently, report wrongdoing through appropriate channels, and remain accountable to ourselves and ultimately to the public.
- We seek to improve our tradecraft continuously, share information responsibly, collaborate with our colleagues, and demonstrate innovation.

"Communication intelligence gives insight into what is being said, planned and even considered by one's friends and enemies alike and is as close as one can come, from a distance, to reading another side's mind."[30]

—Mark Lowenthal

---

[30] Lowenthal, Intelligence: From Secrets to Policy, p.71.

CHAPTER 2

The Intelligence Cycle

2.1   What Is the Intelligence Cycle?

Originating from the intelligence community, the *intelligence cycle*, as practiced in the United States, is used as a guide for gathering and processing information in a reliable and repeatable way. The cycle typically consists of five key phases beginning with Planning and ending in Dissemination (see Figure 2.1). However, the former vice chairman of the National Intelligence Council, Mark Lowenthal, proposes in his book combining the Dissemination phase with Consumption and inserting a Feedback phase.[1] He suggests that key decision-makers or stakeholders would not always be inspired to consume and act upon provided intelligence and that adding a Feedback phase to the cycle would motivate stakeholders to read and provide feedback to analysts.

The cycle begins by first establishing the needs and requirements of the key stakeholders or consumers of the intelligence. Once the requirements are developed, listed, and prioritized, they are used to prompt the collection of data. The cycle ends with Feedback and restarting the cycle with any new questions derived at the end of the process.

---

[1] *Intelligence: from secrets to policy*/Mark M. Lowenthal.

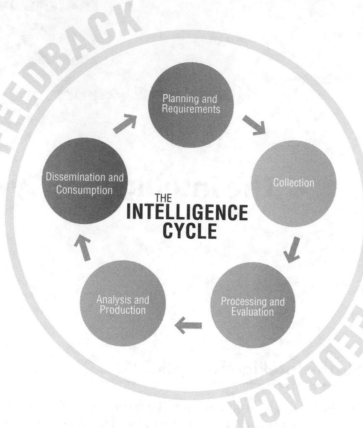

Figure 2.1: Intelligence cycle

According to Lowenthal, the cycle is made up of these six key phases:

1. Planning and Requirements
2. Collection
3. Processing and Evaluation
4. Analysis and Production
5. Dissemination and Consumption
6. Feedback

2.2 Planning and Requirements Phase

Planning the strategy for successfully investigating and producing a final product, identifying the requirements of stakeholders, and defining the intelligence questions we aim to answer through our collection and analysis are all key elements of the *Planning and Requirements phase*. Requirements should be set by the key stakeholders and consumers meant to receive our final reporting. More simply, we need to know the "who, what, why, and how" before beginning the investigation process, and we need that information to be decided by the people requesting the intelligence. As analysts, we may be inclined to hop directly into collection without gathering these key questions, but this could result in wasted time in the form of chasing unnecessary leads and poor unactionable intelligence.

After clearly defining the questions received from key stakeholders, we must develop a plan that spans the length of the Collection phase to the Feedback phase. This plan requires answering several fundamental questions including the following:

- How many analysts are required for this project?
- Do we require specialized analysts?
- How much time will be spent?
- What data sources will be used?
- Will we require mass data collection tools such as APIs?
- Are there any legal issues or sensitivities to be aware of?
- Where will the data be kept?
- Who will have access to the data?
- What security risks will the analysts encounter?
- How will we collaborate?
- In what format will we store notes (mind map, Word file, etc.)?
- What will the final report look like?
- Will the report be a presentation or a document?
- Once the stakeholders consume the report how will they provide feedback?

It is easy to see how the Planning and Requirements phase sets up the success for the rest of the process. If this phase is poorly developed and performed without stakeholder buy-in, a waterfall effect takes place leading to unnecessary data collection, unproductive analysis, and ultimately reporting on intelligence that is unusable and unactionable.

At this stage, it is important to define the intelligence discipline we are using to collect (HUMINT, OSINT, IMINT, SIGINT, MASINT) as this often determines how the information is evaluated by an analyst. This distinction also helps to determine if all-source or single-source intelligence is being used, which will affect the credibility and classification of products. Once you feel confident that the planning and requirements have been set for the investigation, you can move onto the next phase.

2.3   Collection Phase

At this point in the process, we should have successfully gathered intelligence questions and requirements from stakeholders and have developed and refined a plan for tackling the remaining phases. We may now move into arguably the most exciting phase of the cycle, the *Collection phase*. This is where the predetermined plan for collection is put into action and where we as analysts tend to thrive. The identified data sources should now be active and collecting information, APIs should be abuzz, and analysts should be head down scouring public data sources for applicable information. The amount of data collected in this phase as well as any legal limitations should be determined entirely by the pre-established requirements from the first phase and be in line with key stakeholder's needs.

Depending on the location where the data is being collected, we may run into compliance restrictions, and it's imperative we remain aware of the laws around collecting personal data within the country and even state we operate in. In the EU, laws and regulations like the *General Data Protection Regulations (GDPR)* can be confusing; for instance, personal and journalistic collection is mostly exempt from GDPR, and law enforcement follows a different framework from commercial collection entities.[2] Furthermore, laws may differ across EU countries making it hard to ascertain what exactly is legal. The GDPR provides some guidance for data collection, but before we begin collection, it is imperative to get legal advice to ensure no laws are being broken.

- A legal basis for processing personal data is required.
- Certain principles outlined in GDPR must be used when processing personal data.
  - Lawfulness, fairness, and transparency
  - Purpose limitation
  - Data minimization
  - Accuracy
  - Storage limitation
  - Integrity and confidentiality
  - Accountability
- The rights of the subject must be anticipated, understood, and honored.
- It must be determined if we are the data controller or data processor.

---

[2] https://eur-lex.europa.eu/eli/dir/2016/680/oj.

The methodology of data collection can vary across analysts and teams based on personal preference and requirements. Analysts may choose to begin researching from various starting points including Big Data collection, search engine results, and social media accounts. Whichever methodology we are using, the main technique of collection referred to as *pivoting* must be understood and integrated for an investigation to be successful.

The Art of Pivoting

Throughout the *Collection phase*, we will encounter data that leads us directly to other data, which may correlate findings and user accounts. This process of following breadcrumbs is called *pivoting*. Being able to spot and leverage potential connections within information is an invaluable skill as well as the basis for all OSINT collection. A high-level example of the pivoting process could begin with a piece of information like an email address. By entering the email address into tools or a search engine, we may correlate that email with additional data such as a username, password, phone number, address, name, or IP address. After we have collected all of these data points, each of them now become their own starting point that will lead to further expansion of our investigation. Effectively each piece of new information is built upon the last, and when compiled, it tells a story. However, finding pivot points takes practice. Figure 2.2 shows a few examples of how the previous email scenario might look.

Additional pivot points include the following:

- Name
- Alias
- Foreign name
- Date of birth
- Profile picture
- Emails
- Passwords
- Phone numbers
- Addresses
- Pictures of residence
- Usernames
- Businesses
- Associates
- IP addresses
- Spouse
- Relatives
- Children
- Vehicle information
- Wi-Fi/Bluetooth
- Social media accounts
- Digital currency wallets
- Travel details
- Technology used
- Domains
- Hobbies
- Pet names
- Community groups/ memberships

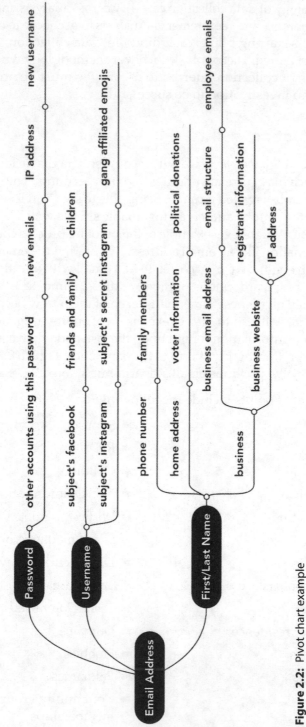

Figure 2.2: Pivot chart example

Learning to pivot quickly and efficiently can be an art form and requires training for our brains to better find and interpret what we see. In her book *Visual Intelligence*, Amy E. Herman writes that "Learning to see what matters can change your world." Using pieces of artwork as a tool, Herman trains the FBI, intelligence analysts, and Fortune 500 companies how to analyze and reconsider the way we have previously looked at the world. Suggesting we need to look at things twice to gain a full understanding of it, Herman believes that this can be directly applicable to the art of pivoting. Using her method can help us to first look at something with no outside influence and then again, informed by new data.[3]

1. Look first.

2. Consult other preexisting information or opinions.

3. Look again.

Herman believes that often important details are hidden in plain sight, and if we become overly focused on the larger details, we may miss what is right in front of us. To combat our nature to overlook the ordinary and help us uncover hidden details in our work, she developed the COBRA method.[4]

THE COBRA METHOD	
C	Concentrate on the camouflaged.
O	One thing at a time.
B	Take a break.
R	Realign your expectations.
A	Ask someone else to look with you.

Concentrate on the camouflaged. Our brains are hardwired to spot things that stand out as different or out of place as a survival mechanism. To notice things hiding in plain sight, we must force ourselves to slow down and look again, considering what we see without bias.

---

[3] Herman, A. E. (2017). In *Visual intelligence sharpen your perception, change your life* (pp. 55–56). essay, Mariner Books.
[4] Herman, A. E. (2017). In *Visual intelligence sharpen your perception, change your life* (pp. 97–102). essay, Mariner Books.

One thing at a time.   Avoid multitasking and focus on just this task to avoid cognitive overload. Multitasking makes us less efficient and effective, allowing information to slip past.

Take a break.   To retain long-term focus on the task, we must take breaks. Sensory overload can lead to stress, and often stepping away for a bit before refocusing leads to breakthroughs.

Realign your expectations.   By looking for something specific within our research, we run the risk of missing information our brain feels is irrelevant. Our personal bias plays a huge part in our expectations of a case, and it is healthy to recognize bias and seek to look past it.

Ask someone else to look with you.   Because we all see the world through a different lens, it can be helpful to solicit different opinions and perspectives on our work. Seek the insight of someone with a different background, opinions, and perspective from your own, and this just may lead to a breakthrough.

Continuous learning is necessary for OSINT analysts. We should train our minds to remain sharp and open to not only the small, intricate details in a situation but also the larger, more obvious details. As an example, if we look at a small section of one of Ukranian painter Oleg Shuplak's optical illusion paintings,[5] we see what appears to be a man sitting on a log playing an instrument while a woman sits nearby listening.

Though, zooming out to look at the whole painting reveals something exciting as all of the elements within the painting begin to visually connect. If we had looked at only one small part of the image, we would have missed that the man and woman are part of a larger optical illusion creating a face.

---

[5] www.tuttartpitturasculturapoesiamusica.com/2012/04/oleg-shuplyak-1967-mighty-optical.html.

Let's not move on just yet! This painting has one more hidden element to find. While we focused on the main two subjects in the painting as well as the wider optical illusion of a person's face hidden in the elements, there is still one more face to be found. Looking closer at the tree in the painting, you can see a hidden face within the tree bark.

The point of this exercise is to help you understand that during an investigation we don't always need to focus our attention on either the fine details or the broader picture but rather to weigh the two equally to prevent overlooking key details that may be right in front of our eyes. Learning to identify important data and move through it can be a lot of work. It's worth noting that the job of pivoting can be automated and outsourced to tools that can collect large amounts of data across many sources and correlate it through algorithms or artificial intelligence technology. Expensive automation tools can offer many new data points to investigate; however, without live analysts to make sense of the correlations and produce intelligence from the information, the collection is useless.

As an instructor for several professional OSINT courses and bootcamps, I have come to learn that the concept of pivoting through data is the hardest, yet most important skill, for new OSINT students to learn. Often, training a student how to use complex collection tools can be easier than teaching someone how to be inquisitive and to think critically. While technical skills are of course sought after, we often overlook the value of soft skills, creative thinking, and innovation. For some analysts, analytical thinking comes naturally, but it should be comforting to know that these skills can be learned through practice. The following are a few exercises to help you strengthen your analytical thinking and pivoting skills:

Develop a report on a subject (you).   Use your own information for this exercise to see how much of your personal data is available through open sources.

- Using just your personal email address and a search engine, how much information are you able to find on yourself?
- Did you find any of your personal usernames or social media accounts?
- Could you find any official records such as voting information or house purchases? What did these records reveal about you, and how could that information be used?

Develop a report on a business.   Pick any company for this exercise and try to answer the following questions that could help you write an OSINT report:

- Can you determine the company's email naming structure such as `firstname.lastname@email.com` or `firstinitial.lastname@email.com`?
- Using the naming structure from the last question, can you use a search engine to locate additional company emails?
- What other information can you find on social media sites like LinkedIn about this company and the employees?

Uncover information about a username.   Use one of your personal usernames for this exercise and attempt to answer the following questions:

- Run a search on a username enumeration web tool such as `whatsmyname.app`. How many accounts use that username?
- Do all the accounts listed in `whatsmyname.app` belong to you?
- Using your email address prefix as a username, can you find additional accounts that belong to you? For example, using `Email123@example.com`, **Email123** is the prefix you can search as a username.

- From each social media account you found, what other data is available? Could you find a date of birth? Were there any current photos? Did you see any pictures with your house number?

Overcoming OSINT Challenges

Even the best OSINT analysts can hit roadblocks in cases where they just can't seem to make headway or to find any useful pivot points. There often comes a point in an investigation where we feel we have chased down all possible leads or that our normal search strategy isn't working. In these instances, the best lesson I learned when starting in the field is that *the absence of information is still information*. The point of this concept is that sometimes there is just no data and no matter how hard we look we will never uncover any, which can be frustrating at times, but the lack of data might be an anomaly that must be reported when we look at the whole picture of the investigation.

If the absence of data is not a possibility and you know there is further information to be extracted from an investigation, the RESET technique and gap analysis are great methods for helping to lift brain fog and keep analysts moving forward.

RESET Technique

In a blog for the no-profit group The OSINT Curious Project, Nico Dekens outlines how to utilize the RESET technique to restart and clear your brain, which is meant to facilitate better analysis.[6] This technique is a fantastic way to take a mental "breath" and allow your overloaded mind to become open to new possibilities and avenues of exploration. The following are the five steps that can help our brains move past investigation roadblocks.

Routine	Instead of getting into a performance rut doing the same processes the same way for every investigation, keep a list and write down new ideas as they come to you. Maintaining a continuously evolving routine will help keep your ideas fresh.
Emotions	It is good practice to be present with our emotions, especially in traumatic and high-stakes investigations. Journaling our feelings and thoughts can help to prevent bias and tunnel vision that may affect a case.
Sever	Sever the mental ties you have to your work and step away. Time away from the investigation and your computer will leave your mind feeling refreshed and able to process data more efficiently.

---

[6] https://osintcurio.us/2021/02/09/using-reset-for-better-osint.

Explore	Take time to explore and learn outside of the current obligations. Check out a new tool and try something new!
Think	Try not to build walls around your mind, and allow it to dream big and run wild. Often the freedom to dream without boundaries can inspire new and refreshing ideas.

Analysts should run through the RESET technique steps whenever they are feeling stuck or looking for a new perspective on a situation. One way I have implemented RESET is by getting up from my desk and taking a 30-minute walk. The mental break from the work usually helps to provide a new perspective. RESET is a great method for resetting your mind, but there is another technique called *gap analysis* that we can use for analyzing a large amount of information and quickly making sense of it.

Gap Analysis

Gap analysis is a technique that can be applied to methodically break down an investigation through questions meant to help to evaluate the information in its entirety and then identify the gaps in knowledge.[7] The following are the four main questions used in gap analysis:

1. What do I already know?
2. What does this mean?
3. What do I still need to know?
4. How do I find out?

The benefit to employing the gap analysis method is that it enables us to quickly distill a large amount of information down into something more structured and manageable.

An Example of Gap Analysis   Using the four-question gap analysis methodology, let's solve a geolocation quiz posted by Lars Wienand[8] on the daily Verification Quiz Twitter account, Quiztime.[9] The quiz is an image of a vessel positioned on a body of water and Lars asks us to answer the question, "Where did I take this photo?" We can begin by breaking down what we already know about this photo.

---

[7] https://nixintel.info/osint/
using-gap-analysis-to-keep-osint-investigations-on-track.
[8] https://twitter.com/LarsWienand.
[9] https://twitter.com/quiztime.

What do I already know?   The provided image shows an elongated boat traveling from east to west across a calm body of water. The flag of Germany is being flown on the pier in the bottom right of the image as well as on the stern of the ship. The ship features the name *Temptation* on the bow along with an indistinguishable logo. There is a road situated on both sides of the waterway; one appears to lead through a town, and the other road has a bike lane alongside it. A structure with a glass ceiling sits in the bottom corner, and based on the umbrellas and outdoor seating, it may be a restaurant. Both areas of foliage in the image appear to be farmland; based on placement of the plants, it might be a vineyard.

What does this mean?   The data we have found means the photograph location is most likely in Germany positioned near a waterway used for both travel and pleasure. Roads and a vineyard lie on both sides of the water, with a restaurant in the bottom-right corner and what appears to be a dedicated cycling lane. All of this information leads to this photo location being a possible tourist destination.

What do I still need to know?   We still need to know what the name of the restaurant or town is.

How do I find out?   We can start by looking for the ship's name in free maritime tracking databases, like VesselFinder,[10] to find where it was headed or where it often goes. Using satellite imagery from Google Earth,[11] we can methodically search across Germany for waterways that also have a road and vineyard located on both sides. Using reverse image searching techniques on the original image can potentially lead to similar photos that reveal the town or identifiable features from another angle.

Using the technique of gap analysis, we can determine that the location of the original Quiztime photograph was taken at Beilstein and Metternich Castle along the Moselle River in Germany.[12] Taking the approach of systematically breaking down the challenge into small, digestible pieces so that we can focus only on relevant information is not only great to use on large overarching research questions but also can be used to answer any question that arises during our analysis.

---

[10] www.vesselfinder.com.

[11] https://earth.google.com/web.

[12] One Million Places.com / https://one-million-places.com/en/germany/beilstein-castle-metternich-sleeping-beauty-of-the-moselle/last accessed February 15, 2023.

Why We Have So Much Data

In 2009, amid the rise of the smartphone and social media sites, a coordinated citizen journalism network started focusing on protesting the Iranian regime.[13] Using social media and forums, citizens were able to effectively evade the government-mandated lockdown on communications and protest on the open Internet where the rest of the world could bear witness. This network of citizen journalists being able to manipulate communication perfectly illustrates how the apex between technology and connectivity has allowed for the rapid expansion of the Internet, with a whopping 64.2 zettabytes of data being created or replicated in the year 2020,[14] and an estimated 175 ZB by the year 2025.[15] Since much of the existing data is comprised of personal information being moved and stored, it has become a wellspring of open-source information that can be ingested, analyzed, and turned into intelligence.

The sheer amount of data available within open sources is exceptionally handy for OSINT research, but it is also the biggest hinderance to collection. Tasking humans to manually collect and parse through zettabytes of information not only would overload our collection but is also less likely to yield actionable leads. This collection barrier is a perfect example of a situation where the use of a tool can enhance an analyst's work. To ease the burden of manually harvesting usable data, we can use tools like data aggregators, APIs, and web crawlers.

Data Aggregator   A *data aggregator* collects, processes, and packages data from one or more sources and presents it in a useful way for human consumption. A few popular data aggregators often used for people searching are Lexis Nexis,[16] Tracers,[17] and Pacer.[18]

Application Programming Interface (API)   An *API* is a software interface connecting two pieces of software and providing developers with a set of rules for connecting to and modifying the software for their own use. The following are some examples of popular services APIs that are often integrated into other tools through their API:

- Shodan[19]
- VirusTotal[20]

---

[13] www.bellingcat.com/resources/articles/2016/07/14/
a-brief-history-of-open-source-intelligence.

[14] www.idc.com/getdoc.jsp?containerId=US46410421.

[15] www.seagate.com/files/www-content/our-story/trends/files/
idc-seagate-dataage-whitepaper.pdf.

[16] https://www.lexisnexis.com.

[17] https://www.tracers.com.

[18] https://pacer.uscourts.gov.

[19] www.shodan.io.

[20] www.virustotal.com.

- Dehashed[21]
- EmailRep[22]
- Greynoise[23]
- IntelligenceX[24]

Web Crawlers   In a process known as *crawling*, *web crawlers* go out on the Internet to look for open-source data such as links, names, and emails. Once a crawler identifies new sites or resources, it will pull the data down or "scrape" it from the Internet, enriching it with personal data harvested from indexing sites. Through crawling and scraping the Internet, indexing sites like the Real Estate website Zillow[25] and people search site That'sThem[26] are able to combine multiple sources to build their databases. Some popular paid web crawling tools used within OSINT are Pipl,[27] Spiderfoot,[28] and Skopenow.[29]

Web scraping is a controversial issue, and while much use is attributed to journalists, researchers, and archivists, artificial intelligence companies have admitted to scraping billions of social media photos for use in their facial recognition software.[30] Despite the obvious privacy implications, in April 2022, the U.S. Supreme Court upheld that scraping publicly accessible data is not an abuse of the Computer Fraud and Abuse Act (CFAA).[31]

Another limitation when using Big Data within our analysis is that with so much data at our fingertips we run the risk of seeing meaningful patterns where there are none.[32] This type of perception bias is defined by German neurologist Klaus Conrad as *apophenia*, or the *clustering illusion*. A 2018 study published in the *European Journal of Social Psychology* concluded that apophenia can accurately account for the development of conspiracy theories.[33] To avoid apophenia within our own work, we can remain conscious of our potential bias and seek out feedback from colleagues. Despite these potential challenges with

---

[21] www.dehashed.com.

[22] https://emailrep.io.

[23] www.greynoise.io.

[24] https://intelx.io.

[25] www.zillow.com.

[26] https://thatsthem.com.

[27] pipl.com.

[28] www.spiderfoot.net.

[29] www.skopenow.com.

[30] www.theguardian.com/technology/2022/may/25/techscape-clearview-ai-facial-recognition-fine.

[31] https://techcrunch.com/2022/04/18/web-scraping-legal-court.

[32] danah boyd & Kate Crawford (2012) CRITICAL QUESTIONS FOR BIG DATA, Information, Communication & Society, 15:5, 662-679, DOI: 10.1080/1369118X.2012.678878.

[33] Prooijen, J. v. (2018). *The Psychology of Conspiracy Theories*. United Kingdom: Taylor & Francis.

Big Data, one great advantage is that it can be sorted, queried, and fed quickly and consistently to the end user.

The streamlined process of Big Data ingestion significantly reduces collection time, allowing for faster development and analysis on the user side. Additionally, a level of threat intelligence risk scoring and anomalous findings alerts are often applied to collected data points within many off-the-shelf web crawling tools that will tip an analyst toward the most significant findings for immediate investigation. Being able to enrich and combine a multitude of datasets into one is just the icing on the cake. However, we do need to take into consideration the responsibility of possessing such a large dataset of personal information.

As analysts working with large amounts of personal data, we have an ethical responsibility, and in the case of GDPR, a legal responsibility, to narrow our collection to only the data required to answer the stakeholder requirements. The principle of limiting our data collection to only what is necessary and relevant to the initial request is known as *data minimization*. In practice, this means we must be very targeted in our collection and data storage strategies. For example, if the initial ask is for us to determine whether our subject traveled from point A to point B, we should have no real need to collect 10 years of personal breach data on the subject. In the case that we are unable to minimize data collection, we should strive to remove any unnecessary personal data from our documentation and our systems after we answer the request.

2.4   Documentation Methods

Documentation refers to the process in which we catalog and convey information. In simple terms, this is the way we will capture our notes throughout the investigation. Notes may be used purely for organizing our thoughts, or in the case of law enforcement or private investigation, they could be used as evidence. You should be beginning to see how proper preparation and organization are key to meeting our investigation requirements.

Effective documentation begins with capturing the needs and requirements of the stakeholder. Without knowing the questions that we need to answer or the data the stakeholder wants to see (and present as evidence), we have failed before we have even begun. Unorganized notes could end up being costly to the stakeholder if analysts must redo research because details were lost. Setting clear requirements for how we should compile and organize the data ahead of time can help with organization; there may also be collection laws by country or state that must be followed. Once the requirements are received and understood, we can move on to the best-practice techniques for notetaking.

Typical note-taking techniques tend to be uniquely personal to the individual that is capturing the information. For instance, a visual learner might prefer saving screenshots, while an auditory learner might use a digital voice recorder to collect their thoughts. However it is that we choose to document our findings, it is imperative we consider the following.

Notes need to be:

- Clear and easy for *us* to comprehend
- Clear and easy for *others* to comprehend

Because it is easy to get caught up in the exciting process of pivoting through OSINT findings, we are probably all guilty of dropping notes into the documentation with complete disregard for organization and structure. At the end of the investigation, we are bound to overlook something important and have to share our embarrassingly disheveled notes with our team or, worse, our boss. Imagine the following investigation scenario:

> *An analyst is tasked with finding a specific set of details on a predetermined subject over a month-long period. She works through all the steps of the intelligence cycle; she gathers the stakeholder requirements and properly plans the investigation. The well-executed Collection phase allows the team to process and analyze all the data and finalize it with a nicely written report that is disseminated to the FBI. However, during the Feedback phase the FBI expresses an interest in a person mentioned within the report and asks how the analyst found that piece of information.*

> *In a panic, the analyst returns to scour her notes only to realize that she never accurately documented the steps she took to find the person of interest. Now she must return to the FBI and either admit she doesn't have the notes or request additional hours to redo the research correctly. Unfortunately, because of the delay, the time window for a subpoena has now closed, and the FBI can no longer pursue the subject.*

This example may seem extreme for illustrating the importance of organization, but the fact is that this scenario can be a very real possibility when dealing with time-sensitive investigations. The accuracy of our notes is vital to running an efficient investigation, and this becomes more apparent when collaborating with other analysts.

Situations may also arise where our notes must be freely shared within a team either in real time using a note-taking platform like OneNote or by simply sharing a Word document. The benefit of this type of collaboration is that it can generate new leads due to the varying backgrounds and perspectives each analyst brings to the table. Every analyst looks at the same data and connections through a different lens based on their life experiences. Therefore, having a team that can collectively analyze data provides new opportunities for pivoting and can inspire the development of new collection approaches.

Unfortunately, with so many "hands in the pot," collaboration notes quickly grow unruly and disorganized, which may leave analysts struggling with data fatigue, having no clear spot to jump in to begin working. In this case, analysts might hoard their own set of notes and interact with the team notes only when necessary, negating the overall benefits of team collaboration. To prevent analysts from fleeing the disorganization, there should be an agreed-upon style ahead of time or the group can assign a lead who oversees the coordination of any notes taken. Additionally, if your investigation has no restrictions for automated collection tools, they may offer a solution to organization.

Automated Chromium-based browser tools like Hunchly and Vortimo can be used as both collection and documentation mechanisms; this allows the analyst more time to analyze and less time digging through hundreds of their open browser tabs to find what they need. Automated tools not only make it easy to collect images, snips, and text, but also help by tagging items and offering a place to take detailed notes all while we continue to browse. When finished, we can simply review our notes, tags, and links within these tools and generate a report based on the details we collected.

Depending on the complexity of our case, it may be necessary to include visualizations within our notes such as mind maps, charts, and graphs. Each type of visualization used should serve a specific purpose when we review our own documentation. Understanding entities, links, and attributes throughout an investigation is considerably easier when we can view these in a link analysis chart. On the other hand, mind maps can be used for deciphering connections and seeing pivots between data points.

While methods of documentation and capturing data are generally personal preference, it would be wise to test a few different approaches to see which can be applied most efficiently. You will want to bear in mind the specific use case while also considering any potential collaboration that may be necessary between team members or teams. The following are some important documentation tips and techniques used by the OSINT community:

- Always assume the notes will be shared.
- Include screenshots with captions.
- Record the URLs and sources you capture.
- Use defanged or disabled links to source pages.
- Include tables to organize selectors.
- Document processes and pivoting steps.
- Record the dates and times.
- Articulate what you did and how you did it.

Word Document   A word processing document refers to a text-based document that looks the same on the computer as it does in print. There are many different types of software used for word processing depending on whether you use a Mac, PC, or cloud-based system. Commonly used document programs include Microsoft Word, Google Docs, and LibreOffice.

> **Pros:** Easy to use and accessible.
> **Cons:** Cumbersome for large investigations, hard to keep organized when sharing across teams.

Spreadsheets   Spreadsheets allow analysts to perform data tabulation, calculation, organization, and analysis while also offering the ability to visualizations like charts, histograms, and graphs from the data. Spreadsheets are used within OSINT collaboration teams to efficiently capture and verify real-time data between analysts and other teams. The most common spreadsheet programs are LibreOffice Calc, Microsoft Excel, and Google Sheets.

> **Pros:** Easy to create visualization elements, analysts can run formulas for quickly counting and analyzing data, organized layout and transferrable files.
> **Con:** Formula learning curve.

Microsoft Teams   Teams is mainly used as a communications platform; however, it does have file sharing functionality to allow document collaboration between team members.

> **Pros:** Easy to use, often approved in corporate environments, cloud access from anywhere.
> **Cons:** Not meant for investigations and can be difficult to perform large analysis, can be buggy, interface leaves much to be desired.

Microsoft OneNote   OneNote is a digital notetaking app that allows you to create multiple notebooks, which include content tabs and separate pages while seamlessly integrating with the Microsoft suite of products.

> **Pros:** Easy to use, great for collaboration, easy to share full notebooks, utilizes Microsoft standards for word processing, you can import Microsoft documents, photos paste easily to share imagery among a team, often approved in corporate environments, cloud-based access from anywhere.
> **Cons:** Can be buggy, large investigations can get bulky if notetaking standards aren't agreed on beforehand.

Google Workspace   Workspace is a collection of cloud-based collaboration tools including Google Docs, Sheets, Slides, and Drive. Comparable to Microsoft Office products, these tools allow for seamless sharing between analysts and their teams with the expected usability of Google products.

Pros: Easy to use, collaboration is simple, access from anywhere.

Cons: Some issues with copy and pasting, less secure when dealing with sensitive material, hosted on Google servers versus personal hosting allowing potential access to your data.

Hunchly   Hunchly is a paid investigation tool developed by Canadian security consultant and author Justin Seitz. The software runs as an extension in your browser so that when an investigation is created, Hunchly captures URLs and screenshots allowing you to take notes and track your process seamlessly while you work.

Pros: Hunchly is a well-developed tool that is highly regarded within the OSINT community. Using the software minimizes the number of tabs open in your browser and collects and documents your process while keeping track of sources.

Cons: Paid tool, slight learning curve.

Vortimo   Vortimo was developed in 2019 by the founder of Paterva (the company that created Maltego), Roelof Temmingh. Vortimo is a free tool designed to run as an extension in your browser, much like Hunchly, capturing your processes and data in the background while you work and generally making analysis easier by maintaining a list of sources.

Pros: Free, captures dynamic content well and constantly analyzes for new pivot points, minimizes the number of tabs open in your browser.

Cons: Limited to only Chromium-based browsers, and the biggest con is that the floating overlay box often gets in the way while you work.

Obsidian   Obsidian is a note-taking, knowledge base software that uses directories and files of text along with media hosted on your local system for storing notes and generating slideshows, mind maps, and more; it allows for visualization of notes in various views like graph view, backlinks view, and outgoing links view.

Pros: Easy-to-use interface and free for personal use. Obsidian also uses local storage for better security and longevity. One cool feature is that you can manipulate your data to automatically generate slideshows and mind maps. Lots of tutorials for Obsidian are available to learn how to use the tool.

Cons: Presently has no self-hosted solution for collaboration and works best on a project that doesn't require sharing live notes with a team. Obsidian is also not free for companies or groups with two or more people.

Each documentation tool provides a unique way for an analyst to save time and minimize effort when documenting processes. Whether we choose to document our work manually or with the assistance of automatic tools, having a clear, well-formulated record of our findings will prove to be useful once we turn to the Processing and Evaluation phase of the intelligence cycle.

2.5   Processing and Evaluation Phase

According to the Office of the Director of National Intelligence in the United States (ODNI), "Intelligence is information gathered within or outside the U.S. that involves threats to our nation, its people, property, or interests; development, proliferation, or use of weapons of mass destruction; and any other matter bearing on the U.S. national or homeland security (index, 2022)." Possessing information does not automatically make that information into intelligence; in fact, all the data garnered throughout the *Collection phase* is just raw data. It is up to analysts to take this raw data, refine it, and turn it into actionable intelligence through the steps within the Processing and Evaluation phase.

During the process of data refinement, we can start to clean up data using tools like CyberChef,[34] a free web-based tool that can decrypt data strings. We can also begin to translate compiled foreign language text and, using the key stakeholder questions developed in the first phase, interpret any data linkages we noted within our documentation. At this point, we also need to consider whether the data we have collected is accurate and credible.

Because the need for information verification has grown exponentially in the last decade due to false news stories and imagery manipulation, I have dedicated an entire section to it later in the book; however, it is also integral to the Processing and Evaluation phase of the intelligence cycle, so we will touch on a few strategies for verification here as well. There are several professional rating systems in use for data verification within the intelligence community. Once such evaluation method is the NATO Admiralty Code meant to assess the reliability of the information gathered along with a level of confidence in the veracity of the data (see Figure 2.3).[35]

A data source is evaluated based on reliability and given the letter *A* through *F*. Then, the source is evaluated by credibility, based on the likelihood the information could be corroborated, and given a number of 1 through 6. Once the information is appropriately graded, it should provide the user with enough information to decide whether the data is verifiable, which is essential to providing intelligence based on truth. After we have processed and evaluated the collected data, we may need to ask further questions of the stakeholders to ensure they receive a successful product.

---

[34] https://gchq.github.io/CyberChef.
[35] FM 2-22 https://fas.org/irp/doddir/army/fm2-22-3.pdf.

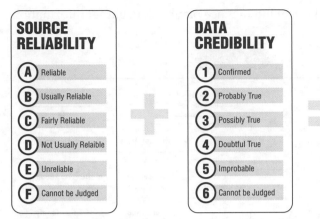

Figure 2.3: NATO Admiralty Code

Scoping

The act of refocusing, redefining, and narrowing efforts using stakeholder requirements in order to avoid lengthy misguided efforts is called *scoping*. Scoping can and will happen at any point in the intelligence cycle as deemed necessary by stakeholders. Often there is an initial scoping process even before the intelligence requirements are finalized and passed off to analysts. If the scoping process happens to change the intelligence questions and requirements, we will need to stop processing and restart the intelligence cycle focusing on the new requirements. You can imagine the scoping process as a funnel where data enters one end and through a series of clarifying questions and requirements it comes out the other end with only the most relevant data. During the process of scoping and refining our work, we may have the added opportunity to enrich our data with other closed data sources.

Data Enrichment

Of course, we are open-source intelligence analysts, but through the process of *data enrichment*, we can further enhance our own data by combining it with stakeholder-approved first-party internal and third-party external sources to fill gaps in missing or incomplete data. With the inclusion of internal sources, we can derive a deeper and more accurate picture from the data we collect.

Here are a few examples of how data enrichment can be used:

- Using an internal law enforcement database to look up vehicle information on a subject
- Querying a paid third-party database of marketing data to find subject information

■ Referencing an internal threat intelligence playbook to gather information on a threat actor

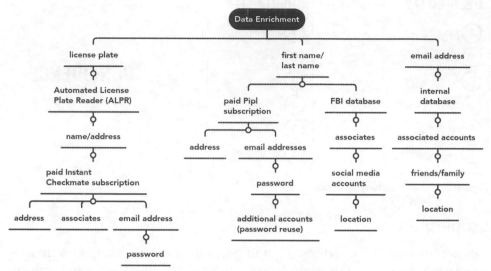

When properly implemented, data enrichment can assist with making correlations between data points. For example, let's suppose a financial fraud analyst is investigating a possible scammer and the only lead the analyst has is the email address that was used to commit the fraud. First, the analyst could run this email through internal fraud databases as well as external OSINT lookup modules to look for matches. One way to accomplish this is by using tools like Spiderfoot[36] that help to automate the discovery of connected accounts. The analyst's search reveals the following details about the target email account:

■ It is connected to active social media accounts.

■ It is presently active and in use.

■ It can be found in several credential breaches.

■ It was found connected to posts on a hacking forum.

Now, based on new information found through enriching our initial email address selector with first- and third-party data, we can determine that the email address is active and in use based on usage time stamps. Using social media accounts, breach data, and social media posts connected to the email address we can build a case against the individual behind the address.

---

[36] www.spiderfoot.net.

2.6   Analysis and Production Phase

In the *Analysis phase* of the intelligence cycle, we evaluate the processed data that has already been translated, decrypted, and interpreted to generate intelligence products. Conclusions are drawn based on our findings and then, depending on requirements, potentially fused with information identified within additional classified and unclassified sources. In other words, we should be asking ourselves "What does the data we collected tell us and why do we care?" Once the data is determined, we can begin to think about the ways in which we can disseminate this information to our stakeholders.

Depending on urgency, intelligence products may take the form of immediate action reports or longer-term evaluation with continuous products. It is important that within these reports we address the questions identified in the *Planning and Requirements phase* and create the reporting in a format that is based on the stakeholder's needs. Although probably the least exciting phase for many analysts, this phase is a crucial part of the overall investigation process. The entire intelligence cycle is nothing without intelligible reporting, and if we can't provide stakeholders with a cohesive and comprehensive assessment of our findings regardless of their technical savvy, we have failed as analysts. When constructing an intelligence report, it is essential that the information within is vetted and scrutinized for accuracy and follows the five main principles of intelligence.[37]

- It must be timely.
- There must be a clear sense of certainty versus uncertainty.
- Reports must be customized for the reader.
- Reports must be easy to digest.
- Reports must answer the intelligence questions.

Visualizations

There are many ways to arrange data so that we can interpret and understand it on a deeper level, not only during analysis but for collaboration and final reporting. How we visualize things for analysis depends on personal preference unless the graphics are being placed into a report being disseminated to stakeholders. In that case, we want to develop the graphics in the best format for the reader to understand our key points. The following are a few methods used for visualizing data:

---

[37] www.chds.us/coursefiles/NS4156/lectures/intel_7_step_intel_cycle/script.pdf.

Mind Maps: A mind map, used for organizing ideas, displays data visually to view the relationships between the pieces. This form of visualization is best kept internally for team members to collaborate and is often used to illustrate pivot points or connections between data points.

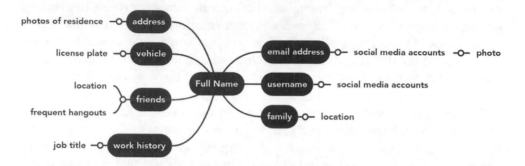

Tables: A table is a visualization meant to be an easy-to-read summary of information often used to visually sort data. An example is shown here:

SELECTOR TYPE	SELECTOR	ADDITIONAL DETAILS
Email Address	fakeemail@fake.com	Passwords: password123, bestengineer123, qwerty321
Date of Birth	01/28/1979	Found in the 'Birthdayapp' breach
Job Title	Chief Engineer, *Fake Corporation*	Previously employed as a ground surveyor for *Fake Company*

Graphs: Graphs such as bar graphs and histograms can be used to display quantifiable amounts of data. Graphs can be created using both free and paid software such as Microsoft Excel, Open Office Calc, and Google Sheets.

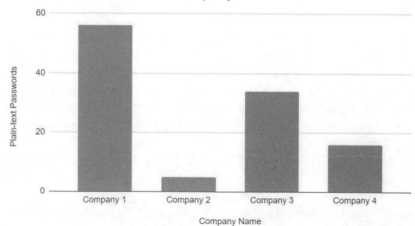

Plain-Text Passwords Found in Breach Data

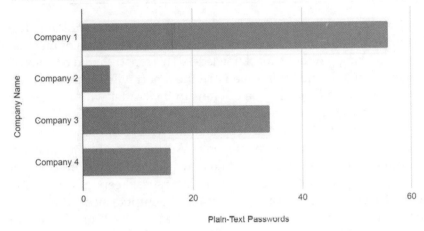

Link Analysis Charts: These types of charts are used as graphical representations of data and show the relationships between two or more data points. Many different charting software exists, and they range in cost depending on the capabilities provided; however, there are companies that provide free versions of their charting software with limitations. One such company is Maltego,[38] which offers a free community edition that can be used for information gathering and node-based link analysis charting to analyze connections (see Figure 2.4).

Figure 2.4: Maltego CE link analysis chart

---

[38] www.maltego.com.

2.7   Reporting

The OSINT report is where we get to convey all our findings to stakeholders. The purpose of a report is to inform the reader of our findings to provide recommendations for decision-making and contextual knowledge. This report should be tailored to the consumers, and it should be assumed that the report will be disseminated beyond them, so any details need to be obvious to the reader without further presentation by the analyst. Reporting styles will vary by company, analyst, and purpose, but there are some key tips to keep in mind when compiling a report.

First, consider who the consumer of your report is. Will the reader be a technology-focused individual, or will they be a CEO who may have no interest in technical details? Tailor your report for different personality types; keep in mind some people are data driven while others are more visual. Attempt to incorporate both of those concepts into one report. Always focus on the "so what?" and be sure to write in short and concise paragraphs. No matter who the reader is, they should understand the message, and all come away with the same key points. Use very deliberate and precise language to avoid any confusion. Carefully choose words that will convey your thoughts and the outcome of the analysis without jargon, redundancy, rhetoric, or vagueness. Attempt to remove any possibilities that the reader may misinterpret or misunderstand what they read.

You have probably heard the phrase "If it bleeds, it leads!" popularized by famous newsman William Randolph Hearst in the late 1890s. The phrase implies that the most shocking and gruesome news headlines get the most attention. The format of leading with the most important or shocking information can be seen in the writing guide for journalists known as the Inverted Pyramid.[39]

MOST IMPORTANT
Executive Summary:
Who? What? When? Where? Why? How?

IMPORTANT
Supporting details &
Remediation suggestions

OTHER
Appendix &
Index

---

[39] https://ohiostate.pressbooks.pub/stratcommwriting/chapter/inverted-pyramid-style.

The Inverted Pyramid begins at the widest point, leading with the most important information. In an OSINT report, this section would be our executive summary where we concisely summarize what we found. Next, the middle portion of the Inverted Pyramid is where we put all the important details that support our executive summary; this would be considered the body of the report and would consist of a breakdown on what we found and how we found it as well as any remediation suggestions. Finally, in the tip of the pyramid is our least important information such as an index or appendix.

Report Tone

When developing an OSINT report, the tone of the writing should be persuasive and have an analytic message. The way we formulate sentences within the report can drive how the reader interprets the message we are trying to convey. One way we can make our writing more impactful is by using an active, persuasive, and analytical tone.

Leading *without* an Analytic Message:

"We are researching the overall effectiveness of OSINT within the U.S. government."

Leading *with* an Analytic Message:

"The U.S. Government struggles to implement OSINT."

Report Design

The design and layout of our reports, if done correctly, should be clean, organized, and easy to read. If the stakeholder receives a disorganized report with different font sizes, colors, and spacing, we run the risk of key points we are trying to bring forward being missed, which may halt the investigation or reflect poorly on us as analysts.

First, consider who the audience is for the report; a CEO should receive a different report than the FBI or a private citizen. Be sure to tailor the format and terminology only with the end reader in mind. We should choose colors that are easy to read and cohesive (think shades of blue, green, and black) and font pairings that are legible in both type and size.

It is good practice to divide meaningful sections with bold headers or a divider like a horizontal line. The header should concisely define the information in the paragraph beneath it so that the reader can quickly scan the page for what is most relevant to them.

Imagery such as photos, graphs, and screenshots should include a figure number for reference, and all tables should include a table number. Website URLs and references should be cited appropriately using APA, MLA, or footnotes.

The sizing of imagery and tables should be consistent to avoid any confusion for the reader. Likewise, it is a good idea to standardize the naming of report files when possible.

Title and Date

Be sure to title the report something short but descriptive and include a report number if applicable. It may seem obvious, but we should always date the report to keep track of when it was disseminated.

Executive Summary

The executive summary is where we put our bottom-line-up-front (BLUF) statement. BLUF is a military term referring to a summary of the report that lays out all the important details up front to save the reader time. Readers who are chronically short on time like CEOs will appreciate not having to dig through the full report to get to the point.

Body or Analysis

This section is where the meat of the investigative work lies and where we answer any required intelligence questions asked by the stakeholder. The analysis section makes up the bulk of the report and should be divided into paragraphs that provide the reader with the necessary information to understand the process and findings of the investigation. Be sure to take time to define the "so what" of the report so the reader understands the value and takeaways. It is especially important to maintain an active and persuasive tone when developing the analysis section to inspire the reader to take appropriate action. We must also be careful not to speak in absolutes as this could be a liability issue. For example, we are not *certain* we found a subject's email address, but rather it is *highly likely* that this email can be attributed to our subject.

Summary

At the end of the report, it's important to restate the executive summary for the reader as well as a condensed version of our analysis and findings.

Recommendations

In addition to the summary, we must provide the reader with potential remediation and/or recommended action items based on our findings. The purpose of writing the report is to inform the reader of our findings, answer any intelligence questions, and provide our professional suggestions on how to proceed.

Appendix

If we referenced any large images, tables, or supporting details, they should be placed within the appendix and appropriately referenced within the report.

EXAMPLE CASE

Now that we have learned the skills necessary to perform an OSINT investigation and the key parts of an OSINT report, let's use an example case to walk through how we bring it all together.

The Case:
Our client, "Client X," believes one of his employees is leaking intellectual property on the Internet and wants John's Private Investigations to investigate.

Requirements:
Client X would like proof of the IP theft to use as evidence in a case against the employee, including any details we can find on how the employee may have exfiltrated the data. This investigation will last only 30 days, and then a one-page report is to be submitted to Client X.

Initial Selectors Given:
Email Address: employee02@clientxcompany.com
Full Name: Employee Willbfired

Collection and Pivoting:
For this project we can focus mainly on our subject and who they interact with online to determine their capabilities and motives. Pivot points might include the following:
Social Media Accounts
Usernames
Friends
Family
Email Addresses
Online presence
Dark Web presence

Data Enrichment:
Some examples of data enrichment in this scenario include the following:
Paid background check tools
Investigative databases
License Plate data
Downloaded databases (breach data)

Analyzing:
Analysis is performed using open source data enriched with paid database information. All collected information and process is documented within a One Note document hosted on the John's Private Investigations network.

Visualization:
Selectors are captured within a table on the One Note detailing where each was found along with the case relevance. The process of collection is documented using a mind map for internal analyst use only.

Reporting:
After 30 days, a single-page report is developed based on the stakeholder requirements and disseminated as requested.

Example Report

John's Private Investigations

Client X OSINT Report

Project Name: Client X, Intellectual Property Theft 004
Date: May 16, 2022
Time: 11:00am EST
Investigator: John Q. Investigator

Executive Summary:
Analysts at John's Private Investigations (JPI) observed through Open Source Analysis the sale of Client X intellectual Property by user "Ipthief" on the dark web forum "Money4IP" for $74,800 USD. The Paypal account within the post was associated to the email "employee02@clientxcompany.com" which was provided to JPI as an initial selector. Based on the association of the subject to the provided email, it is highly likely the employee stole IP from Client X by saving it to a USB drive to sell on the dark web for profit.

Analysis:
Observation 1: Email address "employee02@clientxcompany.com" was observed in breach data associated with the password "ipthief."

Observation 2: A post by user "Ipthief" on the dark web forum "Money4IP" mentions they work for ClientX and exfiltrated the data using a USB thumb drive.

Figure 1: Screenshot of post by user ipthief on dark web forum Money4IP

Observation 3: The same post by user "Ipthief" on the dark web forum "Money4IP" asks for payment of $74,800 USD via their paypal at "employee02@clientxcompany.com"

Summary:
It is highly likely based on observations made by JPI that Employee Willbfired knowingly exfiltrated ClientX's intellectual property on a thumb drive for the purpose of selling this information on the dark forum "Money4IP."

Recommendations:
JPI recommends installing a USB locker or lockdown software on all company systems as well as actively monitoring dark web forums for posts relating to ClientX.

Appendix:
Additional Selectors observed:

Email Address	Willbfired@email123.com
Username	Ipthief2

2.8   Dissemination and Consumption Phases

Lowenthal believes that the phases of Dissemination and Consumption should not be assumed in the normal five-step process but that they should be combined into one phase.[40] When a report is disseminated to a stakeholder, even if the material is compelling, it does not necessarily motivate them to act. Adding

---

[40] *Intelligence: from secrets to policy*/Mark M. Lowenthal.

Consumption as a step in the official process is more likely to bring about discussion and response. Additionally, the way a stakeholder consumes intelligence and understands their obligations as a stakeholder to the investigation is key, and we can do this through formal reporting and tippers.

Tippers

It may sometimes be necessary to immediately report critical information to the stakeholder to take immediate action. In the previous report example, we see what appears to be a Dark Web market sale of intellectual property. This is a good example of a scenario where the stakeholder will not want to wait for a finalized report but would rather receive an intelligence alert or "tipper" providing a quick BLUF statement of findings and possible remediations.

Feedback Phase

From the outset, the Planning and Requirements phase will have established active communication between stakeholders and analysts. It is essential that the communication is maintained throughout the entire process and even beyond the Dissemination phase. This ongoing communication allows the analysts to assess how well the initial requirement questions were answered and allow analysis adjustments to take place accordingly. Likewise, consistent feedback will help to determine whether more questions need to be answered and if further collection is required.

Challenges in the Intelligence Cycle

The intelligence cycle is meant to inform and guide procedure throughout the intelligence community and beyond, but it is certainly not without its challenges. In intelligence and national security, Arthur Hulnick outlines several challenges he sees within the intelligence cycle in its current format. He suggests that as analysts, we should not expect or rely on stakeholders to provide proper guidance within the Planning phase of the cycle.[41] This false idea that the intelligence system will automatically notify stakeholders of problems creates a reactive situation versus a proactive one. Ultimately, this lack of proactivity hinders the start of the Collection phase as analysts await guidance. A better approach according to Hulnick is to view the processes of Planning and Collection as equal and operating in parallel instead of sequentially.

Another major challenge as Hulnick sees it is that due to intelligence community fears, security concerns, and personal psychological barriers, the analytic and

---

[41] Arthur S. Hulnick (2006) What's wrong with the Intelligence Cycle, Intelligence and National Security, 21:6, 959–979, DOI: 10.1080/02684520601046291.

collection processes often work separate from each other. This process disengagement may lead stakeholders to construct requirements meant solely to confirm their views rather than remain open to the results. When the results are in the stakeholder's favor, they may see the analysis as confirming their own opinion and therefore useless because it was intelligence they already knew. When there is a conflict with the stakeholder's opinion, they may also be dismissive of the analysis and view it as potential interference.

The intelligence cycle is of course not perfect, and because OSINT stretches across such a wide variety of fields, we all perform our analysis uniquely with differing priorities or missions. Therefore, we should consistently reevaluate the intelligence cycle and apply it according to our specific sector of OSINT. Realistically, the intelligence cycle should remain fluid, and each analyst team would need to consider the obstacles both on a broader level and specific to their role.[42]

---

[42] www.asisonline.org/globalassets/security-management/current-issues/2018/01/white-paper_intelligence-cycle_11-29-17.pdf.

CHAPTER 3

The Adversarial Mindset

3.1 Getting to Know the Adversary

You may be wondering why we should bother getting to know and understand cyber adversaries when working in the OSINT field. In OSINT and more broadly cybersecurity, hacks, breaches, and ransomware are now becoming an everyday occurrence. As more systems come online, the attacks increase. Security professionals often focus on hardening our systems to keep the adversary out, but in addition we must also consider why these companies or individuals might have been targeted in the first place. From the perspective of OSINT, it is possible to determine the answer to that question by investigating an organization or individual from the outside looking in.

By changing the way in which we look at vulnerabilities, we may be able to determine if there is something interesting, revealing, or even inviting about an organization or individual's security and their digital footprint. Using the historical tactics of attackers, we can take a threat intelligence viewpoint to try to understand and even predict the behaviors of an attacker. Targeting assets, identifying vulnerabilities, pivoting, adapting and evolving tactics and procedures, and maturing tradecraft are all techniques used by an adversary in a cyber attack. This approach is used to gather information, gain entry, and pivot within a system. This way of thinking is referred to as the *adversarial mindset*. Using this technique should increase the likelihood of focusing our efforts on what they might go after, what data they can see, and what value that data might have to them. This knowledge allows us to develop more impactful reporting that can lead to stakeholder action.

Approaching a situation through an adversarial lens is a method that threat intelligence teams apply when developing cyber-attack countermeasures. Red teams also engage this type of mentality when performing an active vulnerability assessment on a stakeholder's system, and we can apply this mindset during an OSINT investigation. Become familiar with the techniques that attackers use to gain entry to a system or to surreptitiously collect information from users. By learning the methods and understanding the basics of how these processes are performed, we will be more useful in providing stakeholders with valuable intelligence that can illustrate the weak points in their organizational or individual infrastructure and digital footprint.

Common Hacking Terms[1]:

Brute-Force Attack

Commonly used against cryptography, this attack consists of trying all possible combinations methodically to find a match and obtain access to an account.

OSINT: By enumerating the weak passwords used by an individual or an organization, we can demonstrate how susceptible they are to a brute-force attack and offer suggestions for strong passwords or password requirements.

Credential Stuffing Attack

A subset of a brute-force attack, this involves using stolen credential pairs (username and password) that are automatically entered into web login forms to gain access to the account.

OSINT: Many users commonly reuse the same passwords in combination with their username and email, so when they end up in a breach, they can be used for credential stuffing. OSINT can be used to enumerate all the paired credentials used by an individual or company to present remediation suggestions.

Phishing, Spear Phishing, Whaling Attack

The attacker, masquerading as a legitimate person or business, tries to gather personal or sensitive data, often bank details, through a fraudulent email or website. Spear phishing targets a specific person, while whaling focuses on high-value subjects like CEOs.

OSINT: By using social media and other publicly available information, we can demonstrate how vulnerable an individual or an organization is to a coordinated phishing attack. By illustrating how effectively analysts can zero in on high-value subjects and craft-focused and enticing phishing emails, we can show that an attacker could as well.

---

[1] https://csrc.nist.gov.

Typosquatting[2]

A social engineering attack that targets users who mistype URLs into their browser taking them instead to a malicious website.

OSINT: By investigating network information such as DNS, IP addresses, and Whois data, we can locate and possibly identify typosquatting URLs associated with our subject. If we are lucky, we can see who registered the domains and what company hosts them to allow the stakeholder to take appropriate action.

URL Redirection

These attacks redirect users from the intended website to a new URL impersonating the original site but is malicious and used to steal user credentials.

OSINT: By investigating network information such as DNS, IP addresses, and Whois data, we can locate and possibly identify typosquatting URLs associated with our subject. We can also use the Wayback Machine[3] to see what the website looked like at various points in history. These details will prove valuable for a stakeholder if they intend to take action to have them removed.

Developing an idea of the types of attacks that hackers can perform along with what type of data that they may be interested in is only the first step. Next, we need to try to understand what motivates an attacker and what capabilities they may have access to. One way to analyze an attacker is to give them a persona based on what you already know. Create a "baseball card" for analyzing the attackers means, motives, and opportunities by asking the following questions.

- What tools could the attacker have access to?
- What times might they be active?
- What could be important to them? Why?
- What resources might they have?
- Could we detect any patterns in their attack?

Using this method of developing a persona "baseball card" for possible attackers will help you to analyze what their targets may be and what holes exist in the current security or infrastructure.

Former FBI special agent and head of Attack Surface Analysis at Palo Alto Networks and founder of DecodingCyber, Michael F.D. Anaya,[4] delivers a fantastic conference presentation called "Viewing a Situation from the Adversarial

---

[2] www.kaspersky.com/resource-center/definitions/
what-is-typosquatting.

[3] https://archive.org/web.

[4] www.linkedin.com/in/mfdanaya.

Perspective." He walks the audience through a scenario showing them four distinct houses, and then as a group, they discuss the advantages or disadvantages of each from the perspective of a burglar. Let's try this concept ourselves. Looking at the four houses shown here, let's develop our own pros and cons list from the perspective of a burglar (see Figures 3.1-3.4).

Figure 3.1: House1[5]

HOUSE 1	
Pros:	- Looks like it may have expensive items to steal
	- Low to the ground, not much climbing necessary
	- Bushes to hide behind
	- Remote, law enforcement might take a while to arrive
	- Large house, might not hear break in
Cons:	- May have a security system
	- Couldn't pretend we were just walking past

[5] todd kent / Unsplash / https://unsplash.com/photos/178j8tJrNlc?utm_source=unsplash&utm_medium=referral&utm_content=creditShareLink/last accessed February 15, 2023.

Figure 3.2:   House2[6]

HOUSE 2	
Pros:	- Looks like it may have expensive items to steal
Cons:	- Windows are not large enough to crawl through
	- May have security system

---

[6] Pixasquare / Unsplash.

Figure 3.3: House3[7]

HOUSE 3	
Pros:	- No real second floor, less to climb
	- In a development since there are so many houses.
	- In a development, so we could break into more than one house at a time
Cons:	- Might not be worth the effort
	- Neighbors could witness casing or break-in
	- Single floor makes it easier to hear break in

[7] Dillon Kydd / Unsplash / https://unsplash.com/photos/2keCPb73aQY?utm_source=unsplash&utm_medium=referral&utm_content=creditShareLink/last accessed February 15, 2023.

Figure 3.4: House[8]

HOUSE 4	
Pros:	- Lots of foliage cover to hide in
	- Probably have items worth stealing
Cons:	- Might not be worth the effort
	- Neighbors could witness casing or break in

As we can see, many things get factored into an adversarial attack, such as ingress/egress points, perimeter security, potential loot, and the existence of a neighborhood watch. Ultimately for the attacker, what it all boils down to is a cost-benefit analysis or the risk versus the reward. The burglar in this scenario has to make a choice on whether the benefit (profit) of the attack outweighs the cost (jail time). Similarly, cyber attackers weigh this exact cost-benefit analysis when determining what their next target will be: will the benefit of the profit, which might be in the form of a ransom or bragging rights, outweigh the cost, which is usually legal recourse?

---

[8] David Veksler / Unsplash / `https://unsplash.com/photos/VW5YwCYbPyk?utm_source=unsplash&utm_medium=referral&utm_content=creditShareLink`/last accessed February 15, 2023.

Imagine now that the thief has carefully weighed every option and decides that robbing House 1 will provide the best return for their efforts. However, upon approach, they notice the front door to the house next door has been left wide open. The burglar quickly abandons his original plan, enters the neighbor's house through the front door, and in 10 minutes is back out with a bag full of Grandma's silver without ever raising an alarm.

What this scenario illustrates is that if an individual user or an organization fails to properly secure their important data and it gets leaked on the Internet, an attacker is more likely to target that easily accessible information "through the open front door." As with any job, the motto is to "work smarter, not harder," which also applies to those who want to use our information for nefarious purposes. One way that we can provide value to our stakeholders is through identifying these organizational and infrastructure weaknesses through an exercise that involves shifting your perspective to "think like the adversary." What I mean by this is that we will put ourselves in the shoes of someone who is out to attack the weak points in an organization or individual's security. By assuming the role of an attacker, we can better identify and offer suggestions to remediate security issues and data leakages. An important distinction to make, however, is that although we are looking at things through the lens of an attacker, we are not permitted to actively access systems or accounts.

3.2   Passive vs. Active Recon

Looking at situations as though you are the attacker is a great way to improve your OSINT skills and add value to your reporting; however, it may also present scenarios where you feel the urge to dig into the information by actively accessing accounts or systems. These feelings to switch to active collection can be exceptionally notable when working on high-stress cases where the added access could potentially break the case. *It is imperative that as OSINT analysts we remain in a state of passive-only collection.* This means we collect information only from public sources and never through engaging with a system (network scanners), interacting with a user, or logging into an account. The ramifications of performing active reconnaissance without legal permission include harm to us, users, families, or others, as well as potentially damaging our case and experiencing legal consequences. Ultimately, the goal is to *think* like a hacker and not to *become* one.

When collecting large volumes of information, sometimes critical and sensitive in nature, we can run across user login data. Login credential pairs like a username and associated password for an individual can be useful to report on if we are investigating the user and need to illustrate their data spillage. What we absolutely cannot do is take those credentials and log into the user's accounts.

Because all the data we use while performing OSINT is publicly available, we would never gain access or "hack" into a system to find information. All our reconnaissance is done passively, and if an analyst were to cross over into "active" collection techniques, they would no longer be performing OSINT. That said, there are popular tools that do perform active scans for information from their systems and then present the data to the user. Because there is a layer of separation between the user and the tool, the active scan is unattributable to us. One example of an active scanning tool that OSINT analysts often use is Shodan.io.[9] Shodan is a search engine that actively scans the Internet for connected devices such as webcams, industrial control systems, and routers. By using Shodan, we can access the information without making active, detectable scans of the Internet ourselves. Being aware of the types of tools we use and what can be detected and traced back to us is an important part of maintaining our operational security and our personal safety.

---

[9] `www.shodan.io`.

Operational Security

4.1   What Is OPSEC?

Operational security (OPSEC) is defined by the national president of OPSEC Professionals Society (OPS), Patrick J. Geary, as the "Analytical process used to deny an adversary information."[1] Simply put, it is a process that identifies whether an adversary can exploit our critical information based on security gaps. This process determines if our actions are observable and useful to the adversary.

OPSEC is all of the following[2]:

- It is an analytic process.
- It focuses on adversary collection capability and intent.
- It emphasizes the value of sensitive and critical information.

---

[1] Davis, P. (2002). Analyze this: OPSEC is key in the war on terrorism. Journal of Counterterrorism & Homeland Security International, 8(2), 22—25. Retrieved from `https://ezaccess.libraries.psu.edu/login?url=https://www-proquest-com.ezaccess.libraries.psu.edu/scholarly-journals/analyze-this-opsec-is-key-war-on-terrorism/docview/59872415/se-2?accountid=13158.`
[2] `https://media.defense.gov/2020/Oct/28/2002524943/-1/-1/0/NTTP-3-13.3M-MCTP-3-32B-OPSEC-2017.PDF.`

The value of maintaining "good OPSEC" during our investigation is for the safety and security of all involved as well as the for the integrity of the case. The use of threat modeling methods can provide guidelines for the preparation and maintenance of our ongoing OPSEC.

Threat Modeling

If our actions can be observed, then we must then execute measures to reduce or eliminate these gaps in security by asking ourselves "What is our threat model?" OWASP[3] defines *threat modeling* as the process of "working to identify, communicate, and understand threats and mitigations within the context of protecting something of value." The following is a simple framework for developing a threat model and, when properly applied, it should provide the groundwork that our OPSEC strategy will be built on:

1. Assess the scope of the investigation.
2. Identify who the attackers could be.
3. Identify which individuals or systems might be targeted.
4. Identify OPSEC measures.
5. Assess your work.

Several systems and methods have already been developed for threat modeling within the IC and threat intelligence fields that we can effectively adapt to OSINT research.

Persona Non Grata Method

The *persona non grata (PnG) method* requires the analyst to develop specific personas for potential attackers identifying their possible goals, methods, and abilities. This approach helps us to view the situation from an adversarial perspective to realize and mitigate vulnerabilities in the OPSEC strategy. Building the personas involves giving the imaginary attacker a detailed name, history, and skillset (see Figure 4.1).

---

[3] https://owasp.org/www-community/Threat_Modeling.

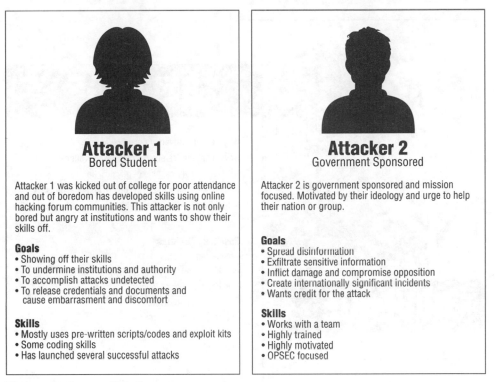

Attacker 1
Bored Student

Attacker 1 was kicked out of college for poor attendance and out of boredom has developed skills using online hacking forum communities. This attacker is not only bored but angry at institutions and wants to show their skills off.

Goals
- Showing off their skills
- To undermine institutions and authority
- To accomplish attacks undetected
- To release credentials and documents and cause embarrassment and discomfort

Skills
- Mostly uses pre-written scripts/codes and exploit kits
- Some coding skills
- Has launched several successful attacks

Attacker 2
Government Sponsored

Attacker 2 is government sponsored and mission focused. Motivated by their ideology and urge to help their nation or group.

Goals
- Spread disinformation
- Exfiltrate sensitive information
- Inflict damage and compromise opposition
- Create internationally significant incidents
- Wants credit for the attack

Skills
- Works with a team
- Highly trained
- Highly motivated
- OPSEC focused

Figure 4.1: Persona Non Grata

Security or "Baseball" Cards

Using *security cards* is much like the PnG method in that we are developing detailed archetypal personas for potential attackers. However, security cards are usually reserved for attacks that are sophisticated or out of the ordinary. A deck of 42 cards is created using the following 4 threat categories. Then the cards are randomized, and different combinations of threats are explored to inspire original perspectives when developing the OPSEC strategy (see Figure 4.2).[4]

- **Human Impact:** Impacts to human life
  - Relationships
  - Society
  - Ethics
  - Physical, emotional, financial well-being
  - Privacy violations
  - Victimization

---

[4] http://securitycards.cs.washington.edu/cards.html.

Figure 4.2: Security Card

- **Adversary Motivations:** Reasons for an attack
  - ○ Convenience
  - ○ Want/need
  - ○ Conflict
  - ○ Revenge/harm
  - ○ Politics
  - ○ Safety
  - ○ Money
  - ○ Religion
  - ○ Curiosity

- **Adversary Resources:** Assets the attackers have access to
  - ○ Tools
  - ○ Time
  - ○ Power
  - ○ Money
  - ○ Expertise
  - ○ Impunity
  - ○ Inside information

■ **Adversary Methods:** Possible approaches an attacker might use

- ○ Technological
- ○ Indirect
- ○ Cover-up
- ○ Manipulation

- ○ Coercion
- ○ Multiphase
- ○ Physical
- ○ Processes

Attack Trees

Attack tree diagrams are one of the oldest methods for determining threats and vulnerabilities and then developing countermeasures.[5] The diagrams are meant to illustrate a potential attack on a system by breaking down each step in the process within the "leaves" of the tree. Each attack goal is given its own tree diagram, and a set of diagrams can then be used to develop OPSEC measures and security decisions (see Figure 4.3).

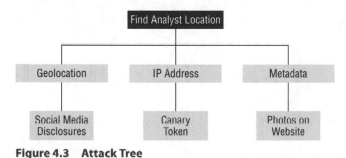

Figure 4.3   Attack Tree

These OPSEC modeling approaches and methods provide a great starting point for developing effective threat models and OPSEC countermeasures for ensuring safety and security during investigations. Next, we will learn the five steps for creating an effective OPSEC strategy.

---

[5] insights.sei.cmu.edu/blog/threat-modeling-12-available-methods.

4.2 Steps for OPSEC[6]

The following sections describe the steps (see Figure 4.4).

Figure 4.4: OPSEC Steps

Outlining the Five Steps of OPSEC

Step 1: Define Critical Information

Define what constitutes critical information while performing the investigation. Decide what needs to be protected and the level of protection and cost the stakeholder is willing to accept.

Step 2: Analyze the Threat

- Define the adversary: Who would have the means and the motive to cause a disruption?

- Define the adversary's goals: What is the reason for causing a disruption?

- Determine what the adversary's capabilities are.

- Define how the adversary might cause a disruption.

- Determine what information the adversary may already have.

---

[6] https://media.defense.gov/2020/Oct/28/2002524943/-1/-1/0/
NTTP-3-13.3M-MCTP-3-32B-OPSEC-2017.PDF.

Step 3: Determine Vulnerabilities

- Determine if the adversary may be able to detect our movements and collection points.

- Define the weak points in our OPSEC and what information the adversary can collect.

- Determine if the adversary can gather enough critical information to cause a disruption or develop a countermeasure.

Step 4: Risk Assessment

For this step, we should assess and apply our previous research findings. Then, we can perform a cost-benefit analysis using our defined OPSEC vulnerabilities, adversary motives and capabilities, and the anticipated disruptions. For example, here you will see two cases with two different OPSEC requirements and their cost-benefit analyses:

Case 1:

Four analysts are tasked with researching a state-sponsored advanced persistent threat (APT) group, and leadership has asked for a list of what technology is required to complete a 30-day investigation.

Technology Request:

- 4 research-only laptops
- 4 disposable or "burner" phones
- 4 VPN accounts
- 4 virtual private server accounts
- **Estimated Total Cost:** $5,360

Cost-Benefit: The cost for this solution is high; however, there is a high risk of retaliation and degradation of the task if caught. In this situation, the benefit appears to outweigh the cost.

Case 2:

Four analysts are tasked with researching several individuals at a large firm who are suspected of insurance fraud. Leadership has asked for a list of what technology is required to complete a 30-day investigation.

Technology Request:

- 4 research-only laptops
- 4 disposable or "burner" phones
- 4 VPN accounts
- 4 virtual private server accounts
- **Estimated Total Cost:** $5,360

Cost-Benefit: The cost for this solution is high; however, there is low risk to the analysts and mission if caught. Therefore, the cost outweighs the benefits.

This example shows how by effectively assessing the risk up front when tasked with performing analysis we can adequately prepare and develop necessary countermeasures that are only as costly as necessary.

Step 5: Apply Countermeasures

A *countermeasure* is simply an action we take to counteract a threat. In the case of operational security, that threat is usually being noticed or even targeted by the adversary. Many of the countermeasures we employ as analysts are meant to obscure our identities through deception. Research accounts along with location masking tools like VPNs are simple proactive countermeasures used to conceal details that might be valuable and possibly even used against us. Another useful countermeasure is controlling our identity exposure. This means limiting the amount of data available about us online or potentially curating it so the adversary sees only what we want them to. By reducing our online footprint, we can limit our attack surface or our total security risk exposure. The risks when dealing with OPSEC can be catastrophic to both the analyst and the investigation, as we will see in the following examples of OPSEC fails.

When OPSEC Fails:

The Silk Road Case[7]
Ross William Ulbricht, known in Dark Web forums as Dread Pirate Roberts, was arrested in 2013 as the kingpin behind the billion-dollar drug market Silk Road. Despite using Tor and Bitcoin to conceal the identities of buyers, sellers, and operators, Ulbricht made OPSEC mistakes that led to his downfall. In 2011, user altoid posted a message on a Bitcoin forum seeking an "IT Pro in the Bitcoin Community" to work on a startup, directing those interested to email "rossulbricht@gmail.com." Two of his previous posts under the same username also referred to a website "silkroad420.wordress.com." For years Ulbricht continued to leave breadcrumbs connecting his real identity with his Silk Road username. In 2012, he made a post on Stack Overflow using his real name to ask for help in connecting a Tor hidden service using curl in PHP, before quickly changing the username and account to "frosty." A 2013 analysis of the Silk Road hard drives revealed code that identically matched the code posted on Stack Overflow.

Operation Purple Dragon[8]
In the late 1960s during the Vietnam War, it became apparent that the North Vietnamese and Viet Cong were somehow receiving advanced warnings for

---

[7] https://arstechnica.com/information-technology/2013/10/
silk-road-mastermind-unmasked-by-rookie-goofs-complaint-alleges.
[8] https://media.defense.gov/2020/Oct/28/2002524943/-1/-1/0/
NTTP-3-13.3M-MCTP-3-32B-OPSEC-2017.PDF.

strike aircraft and Operation Rolling Thunder missions. They appeared to know near exact timing of events and planned attacks. To determine where the leaked information was coming from, a counterintelligence operation known as Purple Dragon was developed; however, they were unable to find a single source for the leak. Ultimately, it was the United States Pacific Command (USPACOM) OPSEC team that determined that during all aspects of the operation they were unknowingly providing the enemy with indicators of their plans. Through predictable patterns and by analyzing the Notices to Airmen (NOTAMs) that detailed information such as altitude clearances, times, and entry/exit points, the enemy was able to predict where and when these strikes would take place.

Mission "Op Ditroite" Revealed at Bus Stop[9]

In June 2021, a public citizen noticed a large pile of wet crumpled papers behind a bus stop in Kent, Southeast England. Quickly realizing the 50 pages contained sensitive information, the anonymous citizen contacted the media. The documents, seemingly lost by a senior Ministry of Defense official, focused mainly on the mission called Op Ditroite, where the Royal Navy's Type 45 destroyer HMS Defender made "innocent passage through Ukrainian territorial waters" expecting an aggressive response from Russia.[10] Many of the documents were classified as "official sensitive" except one that was marked as "Secret UK Eyes Only" and discussed "highly sensitive" recommendations for the UK in Afghanistan after the U.S.-run NATO operation comes to an end.

These are some great examples of how OPSEC fails led to the gathering of important information including plans, locations, crimes, and missions. Some OPSEC failures will have greater consequences and sometimes may lead to the loss of life. Analysts have to prepare their accounts, machines, and strategies prior to each investigation for both the safety of the case and the analyst.

Well-planned OPSEC should always be informed by our specific use case and adaptable as requirements change. When developing an OPSEC strategy, we must involve key stakeholders from the beginning, not only to keep them aware of the changing landscape but to build requirements while also considering budgetary restraints. This helps to determine what level of OPSEC is necessary.

It's good practice to periodically review our OPSEC strategies; we should base our level of OPSEC on our project requirements while consistently evaluating our activities and how they may inform the adversary. For instance, we would not employ the same OPSEC strategy while researching a corporate entity for fraud as we would for a suspected terrorist organization because for the latter the threat levels are vastly higher. We should also consider what the adversary may be capable and willing to do with public information. Just like analysts on the "right side" of the law, an adversary will pivot across publicly

---

[9] www.bbc.com/news/uk-57624942.
[10] www.bbc.com/news/world-europe-57583363.

available information and make similar data connections to answer their informational needs and intelligence gaps. Attackers don't need high-tech hacking tools to exploit systems; the reality is that they regularly exploit the easy to find information or "low-hanging fruit." Take, for instance, the recently leaked Conti ransomware chat messages between Conti members planning various ransomware events. As you can see, their password dictionaries are based on only a few leaked credentials with the addition of 123 or ! (see Figure 4.5). The members are not crafting complex exploits, but instead they are guessing the obvious password mistakes that users make to create a dictionary.

```
{
  "rid": "b3waFmEkyep694hCq",
  "ts": "2020-09-30T09:59:08.776Z",
  "msg": "what was the dictionary?",
  "username": "tl1",
  "name": "Team Lead 1"
},
{
  "rid": "b3waFmEkyep694hCq",
  "ts": "2020-09-30T09:59:26.883Z",
  "msg": "
M@tches2020!!
M@tches2020!
M@tches2020
Matches2014
matches123
matches123!
matches123!!
m@tches123
m@tches123!
m@tches123!!
Matches123
Matches123!
Matches123!!
M@tches123
M@tches123!
M@tches123!!
Dinham2323
Dinham2323!
Dinham2323!!
Dinh@m2323
Dinh@m2323!
Dinh@m2323!! ",
  "username": "user8",
  "name": "wewewe"
}
```

Figure 4.5: APT Conti image of chat showing discussion of leaked credentials

Developing a functional and effective OPSEC strategy means knowing our adversary, what they may be capable of, and preemptively protecting ourselves from it.

Additional OPSEC Tips

- Cover, remove, or install software to block the microphone and camera on your laptop or desktop computer.
- Block tracking cookies within the browser.
- Be aware of what data the user agents (software that helps the user communicate with the browser) within the browser are revealing.
- Keep machines patched and the software up-to-date.
- Adjust the time of day and location of social media posts to appear elsewhere.
- Keep browsers patched and up-to-date.
- Be aware that browser and IP fingerprinting are possible and may reveal uniquely identifiable information.
- Install all patches and updates to antivirus software.
- Use password managers to store and generate strong passwords.
- Use a VPN when accessing public Wi-Fi.
- Delete old unused accounts.
- Use multifactor authentication.
- Activate screen-lock on your device when idle.

As noted in the previous list, there are specific technologies that can assist in maintaining your operational security while performing investigations including VPNs, VMs, and Dark Web browsing tools.

4.3   OPSEC Technology

Operational Security is vitally important to protecting yourself and your work and preventing any connection between your online information and your true identity. There are several technology options to assist with these efforts such as VPNs, VMs, and privacy browsers.

Virtual Private Network

A *virtual private network (VPN)* offers users a layer of anonymity by creating a private connection between us and another device on the network (see Figure 4.6). Every computer connected to the Internet is given a unique IP address much like a home address. Just like we can look up a person's home address, we can trace an IP address because it is public. Using a private connection allows us to appear virtually anywhere in the world.

User Device   VPN Client   Internet Service   VPN Server   The Internet
                                       Provider

Figure 4.6: VPN

Why Use a VPN?

It may seem that only criminals would use a VPN, but they are often used by the public for things such as accessing private networks, unblocking streaming service content to watch media from another region, or bypassing government censorship. Being able to appear in another country within a matter of seconds has benefits beyond privacy for investigation, such as finding native content, which we will discuss in Chapter 5, "OSINT Touchpoints." Here are a few reasons for why you may want to consider using a VPN:

- Added security on public Wi-Fi
- Data privacy from ISP
- Data privacy from apps
- Data privacy from the government
- Access content from anywhere regardless of geofencing restrictions

Choosing a VPN

Consider the following when choosing a VPN:

- Cost (free versus paid)
- Payment methods accepted
- Multiple device support and whether there is a limit
- The number of simultaneous connections allowed
- How many servers they have and where they are located
- Whether there are service restrictions, connection throttling, or data caps
- Whether there are any third-party audit reports available
- Whether they offer dedicated IP addresses
- What their overall reputation is

VPN Concerns

A VPN provides a proxy IP address to facilitate private browsing; however, there are still a few things to be wary of while using one. For instance, if a user logs into an app that tracks behavior, someone may still be able to see what we are doing while using the app. Likewise, we can still be tracked across the Web through cookies that track our behavior. One additional area of concern many people voice when discussing VPNs is the retention of VPN logs.

There is an ongoing myth about VPN logs or records that all connections are being kept by providers and can be summoned by a warrant. If these logs were to exist, they would show when, where, and how we connected to the VPN as well as the destination we visited. Many VPN providers will advertise that they keep no logs, which is clever marketing because due to the nature of the Internet, there would be logs; rather, the service provider immediately deletes them. Furthermore, how would we prove the connection logs no longer exist? To cover our bases, it is a good habit to check the VPN company history for public breaches and to maintain as much anonymity during sign-up that we can. Although using a VPN can add a layer of privacy to browsing, the use of a VPN can be a telltale sign that someone is intentionally trying to obscure their public IP address.

All public IP addresses are owned by someone, usually a company, and it is relatively easy to look up the owner of an IP address. If an analyst browses to a subject's website, the subject could check their web logs for which public Ips visited their web server, and using IP lookup tools, they could determine if the analyst is using a VPN. This unwanted disclosure may be critical to our overall

OPSEC strategy and may draw unwanted attention. Using a VPN adds an extra layer of security and anonymity to our searching, but do keep in mind that if we are adding a VPN for security that an adversary can also be using a VPN to obfuscate their identity and Internet history. Consider how your subject may be actively covering their tracks when investigating their habits.

Privacy Browsers

These are some browsers you can use for accessing the Dark Web.

Tor[11]

Tor, short for *The Onion Router*, can be downloaded for free from the Tor Project allowing access to the Tor network. Tor is used for anonymizing Internet use by routing traffic through relay servers before reaching its destination. The random relay servers are part of a free volunteer network of more than 7,000 relays (see Figure 4.7). The use of Tor makes it more difficult, not impossible, for traffic to be analyzed, thus keeping the user's location and usage private and confidential.

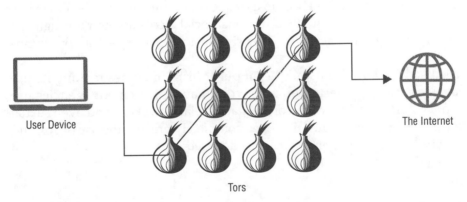

User Device

The Internet

Tors

Figure 4.7: Tor

Tor works by encrypting traffic multiple times and then randomly routing that traffic to a relay server. The relay server peels off the outer layer of encryption that tells the relay where to route to next, where the next relay pulls off another layer of the onion. Each relay knows only the last relay and the next relay and never knows the contents or the entire journey. Ultimately, the traffic

---

[11] www.torproject.org.

exits through an exit node where the inner contents are available for access. This process ensures that no one can easily determine your browsing habits or location. As an added layer of security, we can first connect to VPN and then connect to Tor. Since many ISPs assume Tor traffic to be nefarious and block it, using a VPN can prevent our ISP from detecting that we are using Tor.

Pros

The selling point for using Tor is the ability to browse and communicate anonymously. When used properly, the user's IP address, data, and browsing history through Tor should not be traceable back to them. This anonymity can be useful for bypassing censorship and practicing free speech in censored parts of the world or during crises or human rights violations.

Cons

Because of the way Tor relays work, it often runs much slower than a normal browser or VPN, making downloading content a difficult process. It is also important to note that Tor only *reduces* the chances that our browsing history, data, and actions can be traced back to us it does not completely prevent tracking. For example, if a user logs into their personal social media account through Tor, cookies might begin to track their browsing history, leaving a trail of crumbs back to the user.

Tor is used for both legal and illegal purposes, sometimes making its use appear suspicious if detected on a network. Law enforcement agencies use Tor to track criminals such as terrorists, gangs, black markets, and even sexual predators. Some governments, however, completely prevent the use of Tor, and some websites may not function if Tor is detected.

Freenet

Developed by Ian Clarke, a student at the University of Edinburgh, *Freenet* is a peer-to-peer platform using a decentralized distributed data store to provide anonymous communication. According to the Freenet Project, Freenet works by encrypting communications and routing them through other nodes to obscure the destination and the content (see Figure 4.8).[12] Freenet offers a way for users to create a trusted network with other users, visible only by those within that network, and all computers within the trusted network act as a router for sharing content.

---

[12] freenetproject.org/index.html.

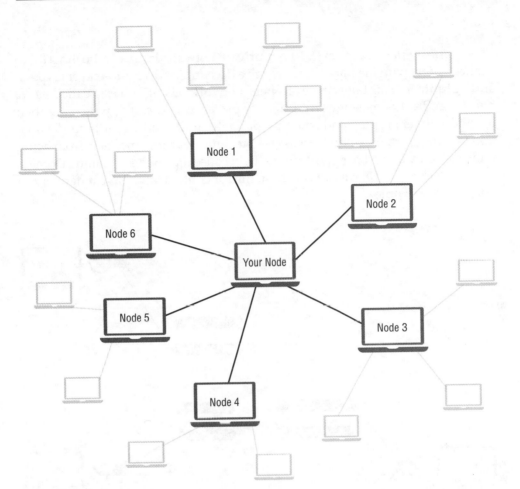

Figure 4.8: Freenet

Pros

Freenet will be less disrupted than Tor if a specific server or node is taken down. Lots of support across platforms like Windows, Linux, Android, and macOS.

Cons

By downloading content through Tor, we run the risk of the content reaching out to the Internet and exposing our uniquely identifiable information.

I2P[13]

The *Invisible Internet Project (I2P)* is a private network layer used primarily to connect safely with the Dark Web through a decentralized, end-to-end encrypted, and volunteer-maintained peer-to-peer network. Using what is called *garlic routing*, I2P splits messages into smaller pieces, called *cloves*, which are then individually encrypted and routed separately until reunited at their destination (see Figure 4.9). Splitting messages prevents the entire message from being intercepted by a third party. Additionally, because it provides a unique Domain Name System (DNS), we can self-host, mirror content, and have a network of only trusted people.

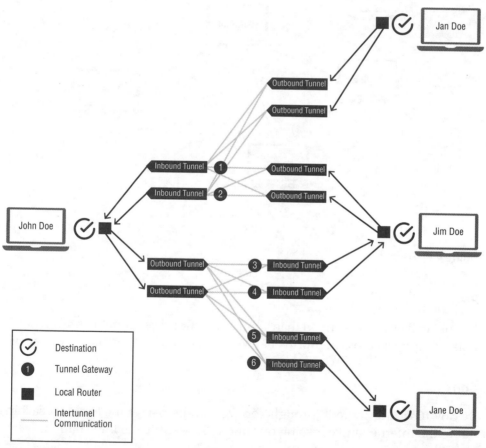

Figure 4.9: I2P

[13] https://geti2p.net/en.

Pros

It provides a very secure network that protects the user from message interception. Performance is efficient because of packet switching that breaks up a message into several parts and distributes the load across several peers to be reassembled at the destination.

Cons

I2P can be difficult to install and configure within the browser to work properly; however, online tutorials do exist to help with the process. There is also no guaranteed privacy when browsing indexed sites on the surface web, and with mandated login, users must be logged into the system to access their content, which reduces overall anonymity. There are also some vulnerability concerns with using I2P based on a previous exploitation of a zero-day vulnerability in 2014 where roughly 30,000 users were exposed.

Virtual Machine

Instead of using a physical computer system, a VM, short for *virtual machine*, allows us to set up and run multiple machines on the same physical host while digitally separating the machines to create a barrier between our host machine and the virtual machine. This setup allows us to do our collection work in a safe environment where we are free to click insecure links, open unsafe attachments, and otherwise explore data we wouldn't dare open on our private machines.

Virtual machines, managed through a local app, feature an interface where we can manage settings such as IP addresses, VPN setups, hardware preferences, and more. It is also possible to run several VMs at a time on one machine with the caveat that they can be incredibly memory intensive, which can cause them to become unstable. There are many uses for virtual machines; some people have dedicated machines running specific tools, while others divide their online identities between VMs to manage their research accounts. In other words, our OPSEC requirements and personal preferences all play a role in how and why we set up a virtual environment.

Practicing good OPSEC must be more than just monitoring your online identity and point of presence through a VPN or VM. Because there are endless ways for an adversary to monitor you across the Internet, we must remain alert and aware. For instance, one falsehood is that a VM can fully protect users from harm. However, there are situations like webcam hijacking and browser fingerprinting where a VM will do very little to protect the user's OPSEC. The process of hacking a person's webcam and activating it without the owner's permission is called *webcam hijacking*.

One of the most prolific examples of webcam hijacking is from a 2013 case where 19-year-old college student named Jared James Abrahams was arrested for threatening to distribute another person's private material, also known as *sextortion*.[14] Abrahams hijacked the webcams of several young women, including Miss Teen USA Cassidy Wolf, and took nude images with the intent to blackmail the victims for additional sensitive material under the threat of being exposed. Running his operation with 30–40 computers controlled by a main computer, he would change the passwords to user accounts and then change their avatar to a nude photo he had surreptitiously taken through the user's webcam. Soon after, Abrahams would send a message threatening to upload more nude photos if the victim refused to send additional photos, videos, or perform on a live Skype video. This case is a good example of a situation where running a virtual machine would have done very little to protect these women.

Another common way users are monitored online is *browser fingerprinting*, which involves the tracking of detailed information about a browser and settings using tracking scripts on websites. The purpose of these tracking scripts is to direct the browser actions; however, they also can uniquely identify a user and device to a high degree of accuracy based on attributes and behavioral patterns. The data collected with the scripts is sold off to data brokers who combine it with additional public data to be packaged and sold to advertisers for the purpose of more precisely targeting users with advertising.

Browser fingerprinting can collect data about the following:

- Font style
- Graphics card
- Drivers
- Web browser
- Operating system
- Hardware
- Audio hardware/software
- Media devices internal/external
- Online search history
- Time zone
- Screen resolution
- Language packs
- Ad blockers in use
- Browser extensions
- Advertising data

Unfortunately, not even a VPN or VM can circumvent the tactics of browser fingerprinting. While a VM can provide a virtual sandbox for browsing the Web, without intentionally randomizing our searching and behaviors or without tearing down and rebuilding our VMs regularly, we still stand the risk of being fingerprinted.

---

[14] www.cnn.com/2013/09/26/justice/miss-teen-usa-sextortion/index.html.

Mobile Emulator

A *mobile emulator* is a resource used for simulating a mobile device environment, such as a smartphone, from a computer. Using a mobile emulator, we are able to run mobile apps without having to install them on a phone. Mobile emulators are primarily used by web developers to tailor the look of a mobile website because they will often display and react differently between mobile platforms like Android and Apple iOS. OSINT analysts take advantage of mobile emulators because we sometimes need to gain access to social media platforms like Snapchat that are available only in mobile format. In these cases, an emulator provides a simple, free alternative to purchasing a disposable or "burner" phone or using a personal phone. In addition to running apps, mobile emulators can be used to send and receive SMS messages, calls, and chats, and serve as mobile verification for social media sites like Facebook and Instagram while retaining anonymity. Several mobile emulators are freely available for download; however, when choosing one, be sure to verify that it is reputable and does not host any malicious software that could interfere with your security and privacy; a few industry favorites are BlueStacks[15] and Genymotion.[16]

4.4   Research Accounts

Research accounts, often referred to as "sock puppet" accounts, are fictitious accounts created on the Internet for the purpose of masking the user's identity. Using research accounts helps us to not only blend in while we collect information but allows us to get around the fact that social media platforms will sometimes limit the amount of information that we can view without being a logged-in user. When performing an investigation, we wouldn't log in with our personal accounts because we don't want social media platforms to track our accounts and suggest us as friends to our subject. This type of suggestion algorithm will suggest people you may know based on who has visited your profile or who you are connected to. If we were to be suggested as a friend to a subject of investigation, it could bring unwanted attention, reveal the account as fake, or reveal our identity. Developing and maintaining a research account in an age where social media and account security is perpetually evolving is nothing short of an artform.

Creating a faux person can be a lot like writing a character for a novel or screenplay; we must consider many of the small details that make a person appear real. Before we start, it's a good idea to check our requirements, determine the reason(s) we need a research account, determine what the protocol is if

---

[15] www.bluestacks.com.
[16] www.genymotion.com.

the account gets burned, and ascertain what questions we are trying to answer with our analysis. For example, if an analyst is researching a specific subject, they should identify the personality traits that the specific subject would most be comfortable with. The same concept works for groups; by choosing personality traits that "fit in," we can ideally lurk in the shadows mostly unnoticed and continue to collect information. Begin to form your character around these requirements. A biker gang would most likely be more accepting of the persona of a fellow biker than they would be of the persona of a figure skater. With the goal being to blend in, this may require some research into profiles or groups matching your subject as well as their normal online behavior.

When writing out your persona's details, try to answer key questions about their lives and history. There are websites like `fakepersongenerator.com`[17] that allow you to generate fake persona information from email addresses to the vehicle they drive. Remember, we want our personas to blend in and to appear as real as possible. It's wise to mature accounts through repeated activity well before needing them because using a new account without friends or any posting history might set off alarm bells for the subject or community you are investigating. Be sure to keep a log of your persona's details in case you need to answer any security questions such as your "first pet's name" or your "mother's maiden name" when creating an account or resetting a password. To help you create a persona, I have included a list of details you may consider when making your accounts.

- First name
- Last name
- Nickname
- Username
- Pronouns
- Physical appearance (weight, height, tattoos)
- Date of birth/place of birth
- Astrological sign
- Location (country, state, city, borough, town)
- Phone numbers

- Education (high school, college/university)
- Employment
- Dependents (children, elderly)
- Résumé/work history
- Political affiliation
- Relationship status
- Pets
- Hobbies (gaming, running, sports)
- Relatives (mother/father, uncle/aunt, grandparents)

---

[17] `www.fakepersongenerator.com`.

Now that we have a developed a list of personal and professional details for our research persona, the next step is to pick out a profile image. Profile images are not only important for connecting with our audience and blending in, but the wrong profile photo can get your research account locked or removed. In recent years, social media platforms have begun to fight back against the creation of research and bot accounts by developing algorithms to detect certain behaviors and patterns used when creating these accounts. Profile photos used for research accounts have become a unique problem with the new algorithm detections. It is not recommended to use a profile image that can be associated with you in any way, so the next idea was to utilize other people's photos or stock photography. The use of a real person's image, while it *will* fool the algorithm, is not an ethically sound choice if you consider the innocent person's safety when we are researching bad people. The method of choice for many analysts has been the use of AI-generated images from sites such as `thispersondoesnotexist.com`[18] that can create a unique yet completely fake face to use as your profile picture. However, social media platforms are keeping up with our trends and have begun to detect these AI photos through the distinct placement of their eyes in the center of every generated photo. In a blog written by Senior Open Source Intelligence Specialist and former OSINT Curious Executive Board Member, Steven Harris, he discusses how humans can detect AI generated photographs by looking closely at the ears, hairline, and teeth for strange artifacts and by looking at the placement of the eyes, which will always be the same (see Figures 4.10-4.12).[19]

Figure 4.10: AI artifacts

---

[18] `https://thispersondoesnotexist.com`.
[19] NixIntel / `https://nixintel.info/osint/signs-youre-following-a-fake-twitter-account/`/last accessed February 15, 2023.

Figure 4.11: AI artifacts

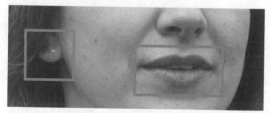

Figure 4.12: AI artifacts

Of course, the consistently changing goal posts do make research account creation more difficult, but with a bit of photo manipulation, we can often get around these detection algorithms. Through the manipulation of an AI-generated image—flipping it, cropping, changing the color, and adjusting it so the eyes are moved off center—we can often fool the platforms. Another option we have is to combine photos to change or morph their appearance, which helps with avoiding detection. If a platform doesn't require a photo of a person's face to create the account, I recommend picking out a photo that will appeal to your target audience. For instance, if you are researching a biker gang, a photo of a motorcycle would make sense, appeal to that specific crowd and be a good way to help add credence to your false identity.

Setting up research accounts often requires inputting one or more identity verification methods. Platforms are getting better at verifying that accounts belong to real users, and upon signup many will ask you to enter a phone number where a code will be sent as a second form of authentication. One issue with entering your own personal number into the account is that it will then be stored within that account and can potentially be associated with you. Another issue is that if your phone number is used to create multiple accounts, they may all be seen as exhibiting strange behavior and get locked down, including any personal accounts attached to that number. My suggestion for when a platform asks a user to enter phone numbers, use a prepaid sim card along with a cheap phone that has been factory reset to avoid cross-contamination. Sim cards are affordable and readily available, which makes it easy to purchase a different sim card for each research account we set up. Again, by having more than one phone number, we avoid triggering an account lockdown in the platform when the same number is reused across multiple accounts. It is also a good practice to avoid using Voice Over Internet Protocol (VOIP) numbers, which act like landline phone numbers but can be used to make calls over the Internet, because platforms have grown wise and can usually recognize them. Developing a convincing persona and getting a research account set up is just the first step; now we need to keep them active.

Once you have successfully created your research accounts, you should begin to consider how you will manage and maintain them. Try to think of your research account personas as babies that you are now responsible for keeping alive. The way we do this is by regularly signing into each account and performing normal human activities such as adding friends, commenting and liking posts, and talking about current events. When commenting and engaging as your persona account, try to embody that persona by liking, believing, and reacting in ways that they would. Embodying a persona can be especially challenging when we are investigating people and organizations we don't agree with or who are morally and legally wrong, but we still must speak and act as they would. Also, be aware of where your persona is located regionally and try to post at normal hours for that region. These everyday maintenance activities will help to prevent the platform algorithms from detecting odd behavior and locking or removing the account. Once an account is locked, many platforms now require an image of a governmental ID proving the user's identity to be uploaded before it can be reopened. Luckily, there are automation methods we can use to try to keep our personas alive.

To make the tracking, maintenance, and organization of our research accounts more manageable, there are ways that we can automate tasks that will maintain regular account activity and keep our personas active. One trick I learned from my friend and SANS Certified Instructor, Nico Dekens, is to implement an If-This-Then-That (IFTTT)[20] recipe to automatically submit posts to research accounts. IFTTT is a web and app-based platform that enables you to integrate apps, devices, and services and control them using triggers and actions known as *recipes*. In Nico's blog[21] he discusses his method for maintaining research accounts by developing several custom IFTTT recipes based on the individual details of each account persona. For instance, if the persona is a fan of soccer,

---

[20] https://ifttt.com.
[21] https://osintcurio.us/2018/12/27/the-puppeteer.

Nico builds a recipe that automatically posts the end score from a soccer match to the associated research account's timeline. These recipes maintain a real-life presence on the Internet, which not only makes them appear more human but, in many cases, will prevent the accounts from being shut down by the provider for exhibiting odd behaviors.

4.5 Congratulations!

We have reached the end of Part I, "Foundational OSINT," and you should be feeling more confident in your growing set of foundational knowledge. Together, we tackled the past, present, and future of OSINT to understand the historical challenges and wins in the field of OSINT. You should now have a solid understanding of what the intelligence cycle is and how each phase should be applied to an investigation. Along the way, you picked up critical knowledge on how to effectively pivot through data to find and collect new information, tricks for thinking critically, and instructions for how to expertly tailor an OSINT report. We discussed the reasons for remaining vigilant about your mental health as well as how to adapt an "adversarial mindset" to our analysis. Finally, we reviewed methods for protecting our personal information through OPSEC strategies, privacy tools, and research accounts. These Part I concepts are critical to becoming an ethical, safe, and exemplary OSINT analyst. Take a moment to congratulate yourself on how far you have come, and then let's refocus on the next section of skills.

This book was intentionally structured to provide you first with a solid base of understanding for OSINT investigation best practices and requirements. Now, we will shift to developing your tradecraft and techniques across specific OSINT focus areas and advancing your skills through robust, tool-agnostic examples of collection, pivoting, data enrichment, and reporting, enhanced by real-world case studies showing OSINT in action.

OSINT Touchpoints

In Part I, "Foundational OSINT," we talked extensively about how our brain is the best tool for OSINT analysis. If you focus on honing your basic OSINT knowledge, you will be able to continue working when tools are taken offline. However, some tools are so important to our analysis that we have no choice but to learn how to use them. One such tool that spans all planes of OSINT is the search engine.

A *search engine* is a software system for performing web searches. They systematically search the World Wide Web for the information specified in the text web search query. What makes search engines such as Google, Bing, Yandex, and Baidu especially interesting to an OSINT analyst is that they use crawlers to visit pages on the Web, analyze it for content, and store it in an index. These crawlers will grab all sorts of content including files such as PDFs, Word files, and Excel files. Sometimes the indexers capture things that the web host did not want us to have access to or metadata connections that otherwise we may have missed. A search algorithm is a process in which stored data is retrieved and ordered in a way that is meaningful.[1] These algorithms are meant to provide the most relevant content first in response to the user's query where it orders it by importance; this is known as *ranking*. Because of the algorithms and ranking

---

[1] https://moz.com/beginners-guide-to-seo/how-search-engines-operate

system, there are times when we may have to dig deep for content that may be less relevant to most users but highly relevant to an OSINT analyst. Not only are search engines incredibly versatile, but they are also completely free to use.

When using search engines, it is recommended to use different platforms based on your requirements. For instance, if I am looking into Chinese companies or individuals, I am sure to search the Chinese search engine Baidu for targeted results. Likewise, if I am looking for something Russian, I would use their search engine Yandex. Each search engine will serve up different results based on their specific algorithm and because they all index different parts of the Web, so be sure to use multiple search engines to get the most results. Another tip is to set your VPN to the location where your research is focused. If you are researching a Russian organization, you may get better results if you first set your VPN to appear as though you are within Russia. A tremendously skilled SANS instructor, intelligence analyst for the Royal Canadian Mounted Police (RCMP), and good friend Ritu Gill passed me a great tip about using the site `similarweb.com/top-websites`.

Despite search engines being so useful for targeted searching, there is an unfortunate stigma within the OSINT community that to be a great analyst we must use highly specialized tools. This way of thinking is unrealistic and counterproductive, and frankly it turns new analysts away at the door for not showing up with specialized skills. A similar situation happened to me when my team, The Federal Bureau of OHSHINT, played and won first place at the Missing Person's Capture the Flag event held during the DEFCON28 conference.

After our win, we were invited to do various interviews to discuss our in-game strategies and tips for competing. We faced backlash immediately from some members in the community because we mentioned mostly using search engines to find the information we submitted. To insinuate that we are not good analysts if we use simple tools is severely false; in fact, I will argue we are better analysts when we have the freedom to think and attack a problem from all angles with no judgment. If anyone new to OSINT is reading this book, please know that we all began somewhere, and you have nothing to prove. Analysts should use any tools they have access to that are within the scope of the project.

The method our team utilized for the competition was a process of structuring a search engine query to narrow down results called *Google dorking*.

Google dorking, Google hacking, or just dorking refers to crafting a search string that uses Google's advanced operators to refine the search and often to find information not viewable on a website. Dorks are powerful tools for extracting the data we want in a short amount of time by targeting our search strings in a way that will force the search engine to only look for what we want it to look for. Here are some of the more common Google dorks:

COMMON GOOGLE DORKS	EXAMPLES
Quotes (" ")	"Tricia Jones", "security"
▪ Plus sign (+) / AND / |	"Tricia" + "Jones"
	"Tricia" AND "Jones"
	"Tricia" | "Jones"
OR	"cybersecurity" OR "information security"
▪ Minus sign (-)	"front door" -wood
▪ inurl:	inurl: "osintcurio.us/admin"
▪ intitle:	intitle: "login"
▪ intext:	Intext: "camera monitoring system"
site:	"login" site: osintcurio.us
filetype:	"passwords" filetype: xls

Dorks work by applying one or multiple advanced operators to a search string to manipulate the output. For instance, when working on missing person's cases, one of the best ways to start is by Google dorking the missing person by name. Beginning with the person's first name and last name reduces the output to only those with results with both the first and last names.

```
"FirstName" and "LastName"
```

Next, we add the city of residence to narrow the search results to only those people with that first and last name who are associated with the city they live in. The point here is to reduce the results to a number we can comb through manually while being very targeted to exactly what we are looking for.

```
"FirstName" and "LastName" and "CityofResidence"
```

Sometimes we may want to remove things from the output that might muddy the waters of our search. A good example of this is if your subject has a name that matches a celebrity. When I search my own name, I get all the things that are linked to me but also all the things linked to Rae Baker, the British actress. To take care of this, we add a minus operator to exclude any mention of the words to exclude in the results.

```
"FirstName" and "LastName" and "CityofResidence"
              -"FamousActressName"
```

There are many ways to use Google dorks that will provide varying results. Using "OR" instead of "AND" will search for one thing or the other; using a pipe in place of "AND" will join two words.

Here is another example to show how using Google dorks can make our search more efficient. Let's use Nicolas Cage and figure out his favorite pasta shape. A search of *Nicolas Cage* with no dorks will search all data that mentions a Nicolas *or* cage and returns to us 36,800,000 results.

Google   Nicolas Cage   ✕   ⬤   ◉   Q

🔍 All   🖼 Images   📰 News   ▶ Videos   🏷 Shopping   ⋮ More   Tools

About 36,800,000 results (0.61 seconds)

Adding quotes around his name allows us to receive only the results that have both Nicolas *and* cage, which narrows our results down to 26,300,000.

Now because Nic did a Reddit Ask Me Anything (AMA) interview recently, we can refine the results even further to 35,100 by adding his full name in quotes, a plus sign, and *ask me anything* in quotes. This will find all places indexed where Nicolas Cage is mentioned along with *ask me anything*.

Google   "Nicolas cage" + "ask me anything"   ✕   ⬤   ◉   Q

🔍 All   🖼 Images   📰 News   ▶ Videos   🏷 Shopping   ⋮ More   Tools

About 35,100 results (0.40 seconds)

Finally, by adding another plus sign and the words *pasta shape*, we can refine the results to 315, which is vastly more manageable to search through. Running this query, we quickly see that square tube pasta is his favorite.

Google   "Nicolas Cage" + "ask me anything" + "pasta shape"   ✕   ⬤   ◉   Q

🔍 All   🖼 Images   ▶ Videos   📰 News   🏷 Shopping   ⋮ More   Tools

About 315 results (0.37 seconds)

We can see how Google dorking can be applied to subject intelligence and tracking down people, but let's do some quick examples of how it can be relevant for other types of OSINT.

Business and Organizational Intelligence Dorks

`"CompanyName" and "Misconduct"`
`"CompanyName" site: linkedin.com`
`intitle:"login" intext:"authorized users only"`

Industrial Intelligence Dorks

`"CompanyName" and "Siemens"`
`"Partners" site: companysite.com`
`intitle:index of "aws/credentials"`

IoT Intelligence Dorks

`"CompanyName" and "Misconduct"`
`"CompanyName" site: linkedin.com`
`intitle:"login" intext:"authorized users only"`

Financial Intelligence Dorks

`"CompanyName" and "Misconduct"`
`"CompanyName" site: linkedin.com`
`intitle:"login" intext:"authorized users only"`

Transportation Intelligence Dorks

`"CompanyName" and "Misconduct"`
`"CompanyName" site: linkedin.com`
`intitle:"login" intext:"authorized users only"`

TIP When searching foreign subjects or entities, try both English and native spelling.

If trying to remember the specific Google dork queries seems like an intimidating task, Google has provided an Advanced Operators page at `google.com/advanced` search that we can fill in with our search terms.

Now that you have learned how Google dorks can speed up and enhance our work, let's learn how to apply this concept across all the parts of OSINT analysis beginning with, Chapter 5, "Subject Intelligence."

Subject Intelligence

5.1   Overview

When tasked with performing OSINT analysis, conceivably this analysis could involve looking into a human being. There is an abundance of reasons that we would analyze a person; after all, there are roughly 7.75 billion people in the world. These billions of people own businesses, have families, and make connections, and, of course, some of them are criminals. In OSINT, we have a business need to understand the methods in which people interact, conduct business, maintain assets, and move around the globe. As the population continues to grow, almost every object will be outfitted with an IP address and be interconnected with our other devices, creating a record of use and transactions detailing everything about us from where we go to what speed setting our toothbrush is at. This invasion of privacy and continuous logging of events and minutiae from our lives is a veritable gold mine for analysts.

Take a moment to recall all the activities you enjoyed and the people you interacted with today.

- Did you go to the bank?
- Did you go to the gym?
- Did you go onto any social media accounts?
- Did you drive a car?

- Did you talk to your boss? Friends? Family?
- Where did you eat?

All these examples seem like innocuous events, but what if we could put all this gathered information together to develop a picture of your life? Imagine the value this kind of data could bring when analyzing a terrorist, following a scam artist, or tracking a hacking group. Furthermore, let's turn the tables for a moment and imagine what an adversary could do with a log of your activities and interactions. As we ponder the possibility of an adversary tracking our movements, Chapter 4 about OPSEC hits a bit harder, no?

Admittedly, performing analysis on a person does sound invasive, but as OSINT analysts, we know that our job is to only analyze data available through open sources. We use only open-source material and never analyze a person by logging into their accounts. Luckily for us, much of the open-source material about the individuals we look at comes from marketing databases through the legal sale of data through data brokers or social media. This act of tracking the behavior, interactions, and personal details of individuals through open-source means for the purpose of reporting is referred to as *subject intelligence*.

What Is Subject Intelligence?

Subject intelligence, also known as people searching, is the act of collecting information and producing intelligence about a specific person. Subject intelligence combines multiple intelligence disciplines to assist us in answering requests for information and producing intelligence reports. For example, an OSINT analyst would cover a subject's digital footprint passively, while a field agent would use their human sources for active information collection.

Much of what subject intelligence entails is the discovery of a person's digital footprint.

Digital Footprint

A digital footprint—sometimes called a *digital shadow* or an *electronic footprint*—refers to the trail of data you leave when using the Internet. In Chapter 4, we learned how to limit our own digital footprints using VPNs, virtual machines, and research accounts to avoid being the victim of an adversarial subject intelligence campaign. By collecting the tiny bits of personally identifiable information across the Internet and piecing them together, we can get a sense of a person's digital life, which may reveal important information that can help answer intelligence needs about them. The digital footprint may reveal past and future travel, digital friends and connections, interests, business networks, and vehicle usage.

Here are some typical digital footprint data points:

- Name
- Address
- Phone number
- Employment history
- Family/friends
- DOB
- Government identifiers (Social Security number)
- Hobbies
- Travel history
- Car/VIN/license plate
- Pattern of life (times/places they frequent)
- Memberships/groups

Frighteningly, these examples are just a small number of data sources available on the Internet about each of us. A user's digital footprint comes not only from data brokers selling our information, and our social media interactions but also through our communication with websites. Because of all this available data, we have a wide variety of options when performing subject intelligence. However, as with any tool, subject intelligence can be used for both good and bad reasons. The following are examples of good and bad subject intelligence:

The Good

Fortunately, many human-centric nonprofits are beginning to understand the value of open source intelligence for their mission. One such organization is Operation Safe Escape (OSE),[1] an organization that helps domestic violence victims escape and stay hidden from their abusers. As a lead volunteer on the OSINT team within the organization, one of my main tasks is assessing a victim's digital footprint.

When a person in an abusive relationship successfully escapes their situation, they often need to remain hidden for personal safety reasons. Unfortunately, an exceeding amount of our clients are in an abusive relationship with technologically savvy abusers *or* the abuser is good at manipulating the information they have so they appear they are tech savvy, which presents a challenge for victims. How do they stay hidden when their abuser can use publicly available

---

[1] https://safeescape.org.

sources, many times the same sources an OSINT analyst would use, to track down the victim?

At OSE, we employ adversarial thinking when looking at the victim's digital footprint. We ask ourselves key questions during our research such as the following:

- Can we determine the victim's location?
- Can we find the victim's social media accounts?
  - ○ What is the victim leaking on social media?
  - ○ Do the victim's photos or videos give away a location?
- Does the victim talk to anyone in a specific area?
- Is the victim's job public?
- Are the victim's children unknowingly leaking information?

One case that stands out in my mind is of a victim who needed to remain hidden to protect their children from an abusive ex-boyfriend, which sadly is a common occurrence. During the analysis of their digital footprint, I noticed that they routinely cropped their photos to protect their identity online. The victim needed to have photos posted online for their work, so removing them entirely was not an option. Overall, this is a great practice in OPSEC and a valiant effort. Unfortunately, I was able to perform a reverse image search on the cropped photo, which unveiled the original uncropped photo and their identity along with it. Moreover, the uncropped photo disclosed distinguishable location markers that may have enabled the abuser to find them. We immediately alerted the victim, and they were able to pull the photos down and check all their account photos.

In this case, thinking like the adversary, an abuser, helped us to prevent further abuse. Knowing that the adversary has access to many of the same tools and learning materials we do, we must stay one step ahead by understanding how they think.

The Bad

One of the most insidious ways that subject intelligence is commonly used for bad is through *doxxing*. The case that always pops into my head when thinking about how information on a subject could be used ethically wrong is GamerGate.[2] GamerGate is a 2014 case where a programmer, Eron Gjoni, wrote lengthy blog posts about the ending of his relationship. He accused his ex-girlfriend, indie game developer Zoe Quinn, of sleeping with a video game journalist to get

---

[2] https://time.com/3510381/gamergate-faq.

favorable reviews for her game *Depression Quest*. The Internet erupted with vitriol at her and her game. 4chan and IRC users posted personal information and nude photos and attempted to get her to commit suicide.[3] This gross attack using public information was just the beginning in the GamerGate saga.

In addition to Zoe Quinn, female game developer Brianna Wu was targeted in the same GamerGate campaign. Her personal information was published online including violent threats along with her home address. The abuse began online, eventually spilling over into the real world and forcing Wu to flee her home and go into hiding.

These cases of doxxing are horrendous and sadly too common. Maintaining awareness of the accessibility to our information is critical. Adversaries can and will purchase our data from online people search websites for less than $20.

The Ugly

Former CEO of security firm HBGary Federal, Aaron Barr, claimed in 2011 at the height of WikiLeaks that he had identified two key members of the Internet group, Anonymous, and supporters of WikiLeaks and would expose them.[4] Barr wrote in a private email to a colleague that his research project would ultimately expose members of Anonymous for publicity.

"They think I have nothing but a hierarchy based on IRC [Internet Relay Chat] aliases!" he wrote. "As 1337 as these guys are supposed to be they don't get it. I have pwned them! :)"[5] What Barr is implying is that although Anonymous claims to be made up of elite hackers, they are underestimating him by Assuming all he has is their organization mapped out based on usernames he found in an IRC chat.

In response, Anonymous took down the HBGary website replacing it with a message from the group, extracted more than 40,000 emails from the email server, and deleted huge amounts of HBGary backup data. At one point, the parent company president, Penny Leavy, was sent into the Anonymous IRC chat to beg them to drop the campaign against HBGary. According to the leaked emails, Barr used social media to scrape large lists of names and connections to draw conclusions about an individual's involvement in Anonymous. Barr also created sock accounts to infiltrate the Anonymous IRC chat and collect handles and communicate with who he felt were the key players, believing he had determined with near certainty who in the leadership was using publicly available information, correlating post times and dates.

---

[3] www.wehuntedthemammoth.com/2014/09/08/zoe-quinns-screenshots-of-4chans-dirty-tricks-were-just-the-appetizer-heres-the-first-course-of-the-dinner-directly-from-the-irc-log.

[4] www.ft.com/content/87dc140e-3099-11e0-9de3-00144feabdc0.

[5] www.wired.com/2011/02/anonymous.

Ultimately, Barr's Twitter account was compromised, the HBGary websites were taken down, and more than 40,000 emails were leaked on Pirate Bay at a time when HBGary was trying to sell the business, costing HBGary millions of dollars.

We can easily see from these stories how subject intelligence can be manipulated by the user for both good and bad. Because we work with so much data, it is imperative that as analysts we stay on the right side of the law, especially where privacy is concerned. It is best practice to stay up-to-date on local laws and to get stakeholder approval before beginning a subject intelligence analysis. European countries will have very different privacy laws than the United States regarding the collection and storage of personal data according to General Data Protection Regulation (GDPR), a component of EU privacy law regulating the use and retention of personal data.

Ethics aside, one thing that all these cases have in common is that they use a method of analyzing a person's day-to-day interactions and movements to discover details about the person. The technique used by OSINT analysts to develop and understand the habits and behaviors through observation is called *pattern of life analysis*.

Examining a Subject's Pattern of Life

Subject intelligence cases may present scenarios where it is necessary to understand how your subject habitually moves through their daily lives. This type of analysis is called *Pattern of Life analysis*. We can think of this method of reconnaissance as the online version of typical private investigator work. When envisioning a private investigator on the job, we might imagine them in an alley behind the wheel of a dingy car dutifully staking out a subject's home shrouded in darkness. I would say this mental image is fairly accurate, and the purpose of this mysterious stakeout is to log the subject's activities to see where they go, when they go, and whom they go with and then derive patterns and deviations from the data. Pattern of life analysis within an OSINT context works in much the same way, but instead of physical clues, we use digital footprint data to determine patterns, habits, and behaviors. In some cases, we may even be able to anticipate future actions or prove assumptions based on analyzing patterns in the subject's movements. Jeff Jonas, a United States Geospatial Intelligence Foundation (USGIF) board member once stated that to catch a criminal, "One must either collect observations the adversary doesn't know you have or be able to perform compute over your observations in a manner the adversary cannot fathom."[6] Although this statement was about geospatial collection, it can also be

---

[6] https://medium.com/the-state-and-future-of-geoint-2017-report/activity-based-intelligence-understanding-patterns-of-life-481c78b7d5ae.

applied to the collection of subject intelligence. Gathering observations about life patterns gives us insights into the adversary and what they might be able to do.

Pattern of life analysis works best when the information is pulled from multiple sources. The sources used may vary but typically include social media, people search sites, data brokers, public documentation, data leaks, and personal disclosures. Full pattern of life analysis should be detailed and incorporates visual tools such as network diagrams, timelines, and charts to best illustrate a subject's movements and patterns. Once a pattern or specific point of interest is identified, this information may be shared with stakeholders who can use our data and visualizations to initiate physical investigations by law enforcement agencies.

In subject analysis, we can apply the same gap analysis skills we learned in Part I, "Foundational OSINT," to clarify what we know and what we do not know.

These are key gap analysis questions to ask during a pattern of life analysis:

- What do I already know?
- What does this mean?
- What do I still need to know?
- How do I find out?

The following are considerations during a pattern of life analysis:

- Was there a time discrepancy between events?
- What caused the delay?
- What intelligence gaps exist?
- What outside influence is there on activities?

The following are example scenarios in which pattern of life analysis can be a useful tool for OSINT collection:

Scenario: An employee on a military base is not allowed to use their phone in secure areas; however, they have a fitness tracker watch. Each day at 7 a.m., 12 p.m., and 5 p.m. they make their security rounds on the perimeter of the secure facility.

Collection: Using a website like `strava.com`, we can see fitness tracker patterns and determine entrance and exit points or even see a building that has been hidden on satellite.

Scenario: A Dark Web marketplace owner suspected of peddling in child exploitation material makes regular posts on his website's social media accounts including Twitter.

Collection: By performing analysis on Twitter posts, we determine he is not posting anything on social media between the hours of roughly 5 p.m. EST and 1 a.m. EST. This could narrow down his location based on the time he might be asleep.

Next, let's analyze the user's tweet time to see what information can be collected from that information. There are many free marketing tools that analyze Twitter accounts. For this example, I am using `accountanalysis.app`[7] and looking at beloved *The Daily Show* comedian Jon Stewart's Twitter account. A graph of the 200 most recent tweets shows that Jon tweeted from his iPhone primarily Wednesday and Thursday from 9 a.m. to 12 p.m. EST (see Figures 5.1-5.2).

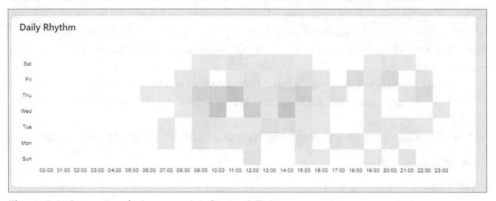

Figure 5.1: Accountanalysis.app on Jon Stewart's Twitter account

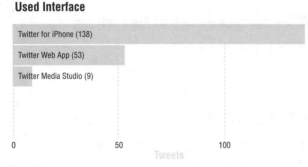

Figure 5.2: Accountanalysis.app

Meanwhile, an analysis of Stephen Colbert's[8] last 200 tweets shows that he posts primarily between Monday and Friday, with a focus of tweets between 7 p.m. and 10 p.m., posted from the Twitter app on his desktop (see Figures 5.3-5.4).

The posting time could be due to when *The Late Show* finishes filming. Based on a Google search, *The Late Show* films at 5:30 ET for roughly 75 to 120 minutes, which would be 19:00 on the chart, or 7 p.m. ET.

---

[7] `https://accountanalysis.app/twitter/account/jonstewart.`
[8] `https://twitter.com/StephenAtHome.`

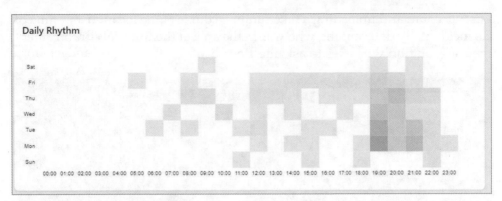

Figure 5.3: Accountanalysis.app on Stephen Colbert's Twitter account

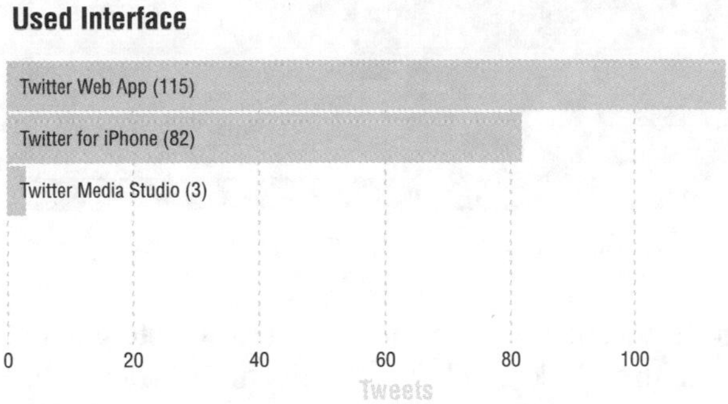

Figure 5.4: Accountanalysis.app

In these examples, we used Twitter to determine the pattern of life, but this process can be run on any platform that provides a timestamp. Posts and media are often timestamped, so social media is a great place to start collecting life patterns.

As shown in the first scenario, there are ways to track fitness trackers and other technologies that continuously broadcast signals such as Bluetooth. One of the purposes of this type of tracking is to reveal operational security vulnerabilities such as secret locations and roving patterns. Benjamin Strick outlined such a security breach at a natural gas storage facility in eastern Algeria (see Figure 5.5). Ben suddenly noticed many European-based workers at the Amenas Gas Camp.[9] The Strava[10] ranking shows profiles of the Europeans along with their hometown and walking patterns around buildings that pose an OPSEC risk.

In addition, fitness band tracking has been used by journalists to locate witnesses after major incidents such as riots and mass casualty events. In particular, the Strava Fitness app allows users to upload their running routes. We can take advantage of the activities of the athletes around us during the event by creating

[9] https://medium.com/@bendobrown/strava-segment-explorer-operational-security-risk-5f9879779e1b.
[10] www.strava.com.

a user account and uploading a fake running course at the location and time of the incident. By determining who was in the area at the time, law enforcement agencies can find witnesses to ask questions.[11]

Figure 5.5: Benjamin Strick's photo of an East Algeria natural gas camp

Understanding a person's habits and behaviors is an excellent way to garner information about a subject if you already know basic details about them. But what if you are in a position where you must start with just a single identifier like name, phone number, or username? Next, we will dive into the various OSINT techniques that we can utilize for each identifier.

5.2   Names

It is common within OSINT to be provided with a singular piece of information with the expectation that we can use it to derive meaningful connections and provide a full profile of a subject. Names are a typical starting place, and while researching them may appear straightforward, there are some tips and tricks that will help narrow the scope and identify the right person.

Subject Names

Imagine starting a job as an OSINT analyst and the manager hands us a sticky note with only a first and last name and a request to find the individual's email, address, and phone number. What is the plan of action for not only finding the

---

[11] https://keyfindings.blog/2018/08/31/
using-strava-in-law-enforcement-investigations.

person but verifying our findings? When looking for a person based on a name, we can start by understanding naming conventions.

Naming Conventions

Naming conventions are a set of rules agreed upon for naming that vary by region and culture. For example, in the United States typically we have a first name, middle name, and last name. Traditionally, in the West our surnames are inherited from our fathers. These naming conventions do not apply to everyone in the world, nor do they apply to everyone in the United States. Different cultures have distinct naming conventions that may inform the keywords we use to search for an individual.

For instance, I worked a case where I needed to identify a specific person from China connected to a network sending potentially nefarious traffic. When I searched his name in Google, I was met with hundreds of pages with the same name. I had difficulty pinning down exactly which result corresponded with the correct subject and spent days trying to unravel the web of names. Eventually, I worked backward through an email address I dug up and discovered he had emails and usernames for numerous variations on his name. Had I understood Chinese naming conventions at the time, I would have searched "last name, first name" instead of the westernized order. Moreover, I would have realized he went by a westernized name that was also connected to accounts. Without all the trial and error of figuring out the basic cultural naming conventions, I could have searched more efficiently and shaved hours off my analysis. This situation shows that having increased contextual knowledge about a subject can aid in the interpretation of data we find.

Because naming conventions differ across the world, I list only a few country's naming conventions here; however, there are additional resources available on my website at `raebaker.net/Resources`.

Arabic Naming Conventions[12]

Generally, Arabic names are made up of five parts that do not necessarily always follow the same order (see Figure 5.6).

1. First Name: Ism
2. The Laqab
3. The Nasab
4. The Nisba
5. The Kunya

---

[12] `https://medium.com/@bendobrown/`
`strava-segment-explorer-operational-security-risk-5f9879779e1b`.

Figure 5.6: Example of an typical Arabic naming order

1. **First Name: Ism**
   This is usually a traditional Arabic name from the Qur'an, a foreign name, or a compound word meaning "servant of," followed by one of Allah's 99 names.

2. **The Laqab**
   This is usually a religious, honorific, or descriptive title, defined as an epithet (see Figure 5.7).

> • physical qualities: الطّويلُ – *the tall*
> • virtues: الْفارُوقُ – *he who distinguishes truth from falsehood* or
>   الرّاشِدُ – *the rightly guided*.
> • compounds with الدّين (*religion*): *light of the religion* (نُورُ الدِّين)

Figure 5.7: Examples of The Laqab in Arabic

3. **The Nasab**
   The Nasab is basically a list of ancestors separated by "son of" or "daughter of" including the father's name (Abbas), grandfather's name (Hassan), and great grandfather's name (Kareem):
   "Abbas *son of* Hassan *son of* Kareem"

4. **The Nisba**
   This would be like what the West calls a surname, but it is derived from the place of birth, name of religious sect or family, and a profession (see Figure 5.8).

> • the place of birth, origin: الْبَغْدادِيُّ (*from Baghdad*);
> • the name of a religious sect or tribe or family: التَّميمِيُّ (*belonging to the Tamīm tribe*);
> • a profession: الْعَطّارِيُّ (*the perfume vendor*);

Figure 5.8: Examples of The Nisba in Arabic

5. **The Kunya**

   The Kunya is not part of an individual's formal name and not printed in documents. This is a name that someone would be called on the street usually named after their first child (father of, mother of). If the person has no children, symbolic qualities such as the father of health are used.

> **NOTE** Women do not take their husband's surname when married; they keep their birth name. However, children take their father's name (daughter of, son of).

Chinese Naming Conventions

Chinese names consist of two parts: surname and birth name. The name of a Chinese family is usually inherited from a person's father and is prepended to the name. Birth names are one or two syllables and can be hyphenated or written together in two words. A woman does not change her name when she gets married, but some choose to add her husband's name before her full name. For example, if CHEN Jiao marries YANG Kuo, she could be known as YANG CHEN Jiao.

There are many ways to express Chinese characters in English, so Romanizing Chinese names can be confusing. For example, GUO can also be spelled GWO, GUOO, and GUOH. Chinese people often adapt their names to the "Western" version to comply with Western naming conventions. For example, LIN Hong may be known as Tim LIN or Hong LIN.

Chinese names can also include references to family history and important dates/events including year of birth. For example, Jianguo represents the founding date of the People's Republic of China and is a popular name for people born in the 1950s and 1960s.[13]

Note that many Chinese individuals have multiple names that can be exchanged to identify themselves in different situations. For example, there are social names, married names, company names, school names, or westernized names.

Russian Naming Conventions

Russian names also have several parts: their given name, a middle name based on their father's first name, and a father's surname. In Russian, a daughter would be given a first name followed by her father's full name ending in an "a" to show gender. As an example, if Igor Mihajlovich Medvedev had a daughter Anya, her name would be Anya Mihajlovich Medvedeva. Igor's son Pavel, on the other hand, would be named Pavel Mihajlovich Medvedev.

---

[13] https://culturalatlas.sbs.com.au/chinese-culture/chinese-culture-naming.

Name Searching Techniques

Now that we have a firm grasp on how naming conventions work, we can focus our attention on how to find a person through a name. The secret to name searching is to find the right keywords to search for. That way, you can run the search on most platforms and get results.

Here are tips for name searching:

- Use Google dorks to focus the search on "Firstname Lastname."
- Test all variations of the person's name, using naming convention rules as a guide.
  - First, last
  - Last, first
  - Nickname, last
- Perform the name search in various locations.
  - Bing/Yandex/Google
  - Free People Search tools online
  - Paid people search tools like Pipl[14] that cross-reference and connect identity data from many sources across the Web
- Try the name as a username and email.
  - Example: `FirstnameLastname@gmail.com`

Identifying and verifying people by name can be a time-intensive task but does get easier with practice and a basic understanding of the different naming conventions around the world. Apart from searching for given names, there are other pseudonyms, such as usernames, that individuals use across the Internet that can be great identifiers.

5.3   Subject Usernames

Usernames, also known as user IDs, handles, screen names, login names, and account names, are used to identify an individual when logging on to a computer system. It used to be that usernames were simply a persona existing online in lieu of a person's real identity; with the rise of hacker culture, social media, and streamers, our usernames now follow us out of cyberspace and into the real world. For instance, I maintain an active Twitter account for the purpose of interacting with the OSINT community. Because of the nature of our work,

---

[14] `https://pipl.com`.

I only know many of my friends by their usernames and wouldn't be able to pick them out of a crowd. This may sound dystopian, but for those who work and spend most of their lives on the Internet, the boundaries are blurred.

For many, usernames are a great way to obscure their identity. As we discussed in Part I, there are many legitimate reasons to conceal who we are online: journalism, research, investigation, safety. But there are also some malicious reasons to hide who we are, such as illegal sales, trafficking, digital abuse, and exploitation to name a few. On forums like 4chan, 8chan, Reddit, and the Dark Web, users become known for their content. A prime example of the power of a username and the notoriety earned through an online persona is mysterious right-wing anonymous conspiracy theorist, Q.

A user known as Q first posted on the anonymous website 4chan in 2017.[15] He claimed to have a Q-level clearance within the government and access to the most classified information about the Trump administration and its opponents. Through Q's mysterious persona and thousands of cryptic conspiracy theories called *drops*, an entire QAnon movement began. QAnon followers have perpetuated several acts of violence based on the claims made by Q, a person or persons hiding behind the mask of a username. There are several theories about who is behind the Q identity, and after a three year long investigation by a documentary filmmaker, researchers seem to agree it is Ron Watkins, site administrator of 8kun (formerly 8chan). The user or users behind the Q username used the anonymity of 8kun to hide their true identities. Many people are not as technologically or operationally savvy and fail to realize that the reuse of a username across platforms provides pivots to additional information.

Because usernames replace a person's true name online, users tend to habitually reuse them across all the accounts they open. Think about how many accounts you have opened for shopping, emailing, and gaming that all use the same username or a close variation. The reuse of a username across user accounts makes it easier to collect and correlate all the websites, services, and apps that a subject has registered for.

Username Searching Techniques

Like with most OSINT touchpoints, there are countless ways to go about initiating a new workstream beginning with a username. Simply looking at what the username is telling us can be revealing. See if you can determine any useful assumptions from the following usernames:

1. Kellyf04231982
2. Gamer_Jim420

---

3. MI_Proud_Oathkeeper

4. Oorah89

Here are some details we can infer from these usernames:

1. Looking closely at the first username Kellyf04231982, we can see a first name (Kelly) and what we can assume is a middle or last initial (f) followed by an eight-digit number (04231982). The number could be random, but it is more likely that it signifies the date 04-23-1982, possibly a birthday or anniversary.

2. The second username, Gamer_Jim420, presumably tells us that Jim is a gamer who possibly uses drugs. While these details may seem unhelpful because the possible match in identities is too high, we may be able to confirm Jim's identity in photos and social media posts based on his drug use and gaming hobby.

3. The third username, MI_Proud_Oathkeeper, tells us a lot about the user behind the account. The first part of the name (MI) could be in reference to the state of Michigan. The second part of the name, Proud, could be nothing, but in the last few years words like Proud, Pride, and Patriot tend to refer to a connection to right-wing conservatism and often the alt-right movement. Considering the last part of the username Oathkeeper, we would want to confirm whether this user has a connection to any American far-right anti-government militias.

4. The final username, Oorah89, also provides some good information about the individual behind the name. The term *Oorah* is a common battle cry for the United States Marine Corps; therefore, our user could be a present or former Marine. The 89 in the name could be a birthdate or another significant day in the user's life.

From these few examples we can see how it is possible to extract useful personal and contextual information from the makeup of individual usernames. Let's now turn to methods for correlating individual user accounts by username.

Correlating Accounts and Subject Information by Username

The *correlation of accounts and information by username* simply means attempting to discover as many user accounts as we can that verifiably relate to one user. Any additional subject information we unearth along the way such as given names, email addresses, etc., we use to enhance the subject intelligence analysis. In Figure 5.9, we can see how one username led us on a path to identifying key details about our user including proprietary code, work email passwords, and political affiliations.

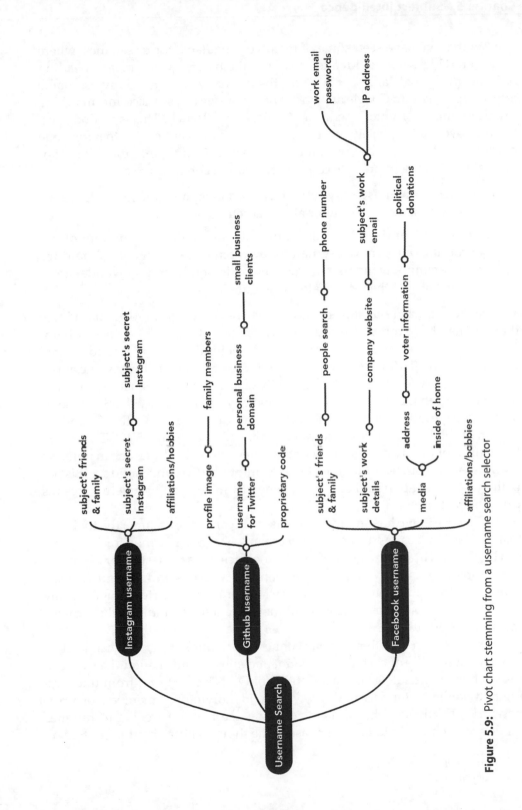

Figure 5.9: Pivot chart stemming from a username search selector

Now that we have seen some of the pivots available for usernames, where do we start? It is a great idea to start with the basics, which means heading back over to Google and searching for the username. I dropped my username *wondersmith_rae* into Google and on the first page we can see accounts matching my username on Twitter, Medium, YouTube, and Twitch. This is a good start, but if we were to rely solely on one source, we may never find out that for some platforms I also use variations on this username. Getting into the mindset of your subject can help provide context and lead to better results.

- **Ineffective Mindset:** My subject uses wondersmith_rae for 10 accounts, so she most likely uses it for all her accounts.

- **Effective Mindset:** My subject uses wondersmith_rae for a lot of her accounts, but I know usernames are often already taken. I should try wondersmith, wondersmithrae, raewondersmith, and thewondersmith to see if any of them correlate (see Figure 5.10).

Considering what our subject may or may not do can lead to great findings that we may have otherwise overlooked. Frequently, search engines will not provide comprehensive results, and it may be helpful to incorporate additional tools focused on finding usernames into our research like WhatsMyName.app.[16]

There are very few tools that I urge OSINT analysts to use regularly; however, the free tool WhatsMyName.app, developed by Australia-based OSINT Combine in collaboration with OSINT Curious President and My OSINT Training[17] owner, Micah Hoffman, is an exception to this rule (see Figure 5.11). The reason I use this tool for my analysis is that it was developed with privacy in mind by a very reliable source within the OSINT community, so I am confident it is not maintaining a log of user data. Plus, I generally have great luck getting results from the platform.

`WhatsMyName.app` has an input for a user to search a username; the tool then visits a list of websites to see if the username is registered there or if a name can be found within the user profile. The tool facilitates the testing of username variations very quickly across more than 400 websites and then provides a source link to validate our findings. WhatsMyName.app is certainly not the only OSINT tool for username research out there. For a list of additional username tools, check out `raebaker.net/resources`.

Usernames can be a tremendous connection to our subject that can lead us down a rabbit hole of correlated account and subject information. This type of research is invaluable across a spectrum of OSINT case types from uncovering petty online criminals all the way up to identifying key members of terror networks. I truly saw the value in adopting username searching techniques while working on child predator cases. The thing to note about predators on

---

[16] `https://whatsmyname.app`.
[17] `www.myosint.training`.

Figure 5.10: Google search for username *wondersmith_rae*

the Internet is that they are able to continue to operate only when shrouded under a veil of anonymity. Once the curtain is lifted and a predator is unmasked, they must face what their family, community, and the law think of their actions. Unfortunately, the same security and OPSEC principles that protect us as analysts also protect criminals. Prolific predators on the Dark Web, especially those who sell content to other predators, hide behind usernames. Just like Q from the QAnon movement, they gain notoriety within the predator communities for what they sell or provide, and their username effectively becomes a brand. When trained and legally backed, OSINT analysts can pivot from a predator's

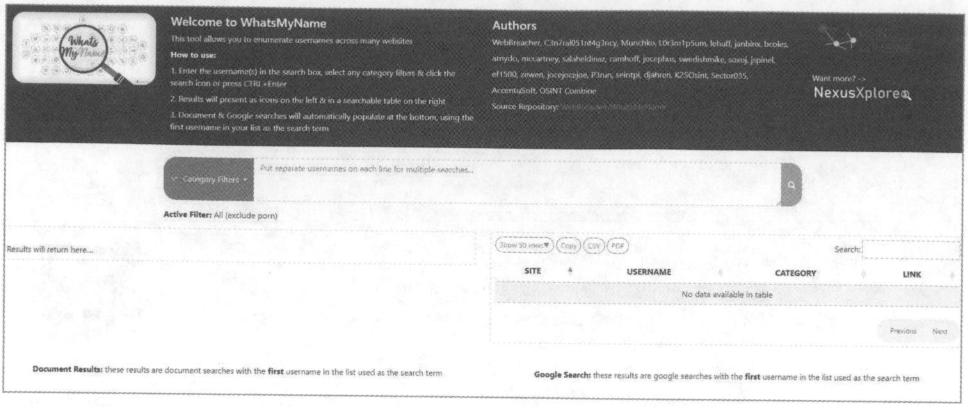

Figure 5.11: WhatsMyName.app

username, using the tools and techniques we just learned, to other accounts, an email, or even a name. This may lead to the takedown of an entire predator network. This is obviously an extreme example of how powerful username data can be in the right hands, but the purpose is to illustrate what is possible to find when pivoting from subject usernames.

The following is one of my personal favorite subject intelligence pivots. Interestingly, it shares a lot with the usernames: subject emails.

5.4   Subject Emails

"Emails are the window to our soul."

—Someone, probably

Emails are probably not a window into a person's soul, but they do tend to reveal a lot about our digital footprint. The very first email was developed in 1965 at the Massachusetts Institute of Technology (MIT) to allow users to share files and messages on a central computer. In 1971, a computer programmer named Tomlinson introduced the @ sign to target specific users on the Arpanet, a precursor to the Internet, at the U.S. Defense Advanced Research Projects Agency (DARPA).[18] Since 1971, email has grown tremendously, and in 2022 there are approximately 4.2 million email users worldwide.[19] What this means

---

[18] www.theguardian.com/technology/2016/mar/07/email-ray-tomlinson-history#:~:text=The%20very%20first%20version%20of,logging%20in%20from%20remote%20terminals.

[19] www.statista.com/statistics/255080/number-of-e-mail-users-worldwide.

is that a large number of people in the world have signed up for one or more email addresses.

We previously learned how a username becomes our online persona and follows us across the Internet as we register for accounts. Like usernames, emails are used to register for accounts online, following us wherever we go revealing details about our lives. The email username itself can tell us about the creator.

Here are a few examples:

DebbieNFrank02071974@email.com
This email hints that Debbie married Frank on February 7, 1974. Because they used two names, it is a safe assumption that the email is a shared account between the couple.

John.McCormick@companyname.com
Instantly we can see a first and last name for this user. The company domain indicates that this is a business account for where John works. If we were interested in finding more employee emails, we now have the naming convention of firstname(dot)lastname@companyname.com. If we know an employee name, we could easily guess their email address based on this naming convention.

deviantlinktrade@protonmail.com
The term *deviant* alone is not necessarily alarming, but this email appears to have a dark connotation to it. When we have the added context of how exploitative and illegal content is commonly shared through links, this email can become a potential lead for law enforcement. Furthermore, the use of Proton Mail, an email provider known for privacy, shows the user may be concerned with their privacy.

Not only can we learn a lot about the email user through the email username, but we can use the email as a pivot point to find more data. Figure 5.12 shows an example pivot chart from an OSINT project starting with only an email address.

As the pivot chart illustrates, there are a number of avenues that we can explore from an email address. Email addresses are essentially like the username of your email account, so it is possible to associate that username with other online accounts like websites and social media. Thankfully, many of the same techniques we employed for usernames are applicable to emails.

How to begin connecting accounts

Correlating Accounts and Subject Information by Email

Essentially, the first step in email analysis is running the email address we want to analyze through a search engine to see what results we get back. This process can immediately provide several pivot points to begin working from. Once all the results have been logged and verified, we can move to using specialized tools.

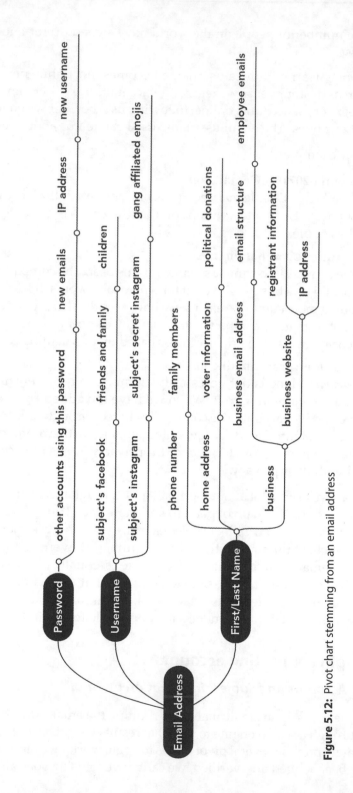

Figure 5.12: Pivot chart stemming from an email address

Steven Harris (@nixintel), a senior OSINT specialist, writes in his article on Resources for Email Addresses[20] that it is a good practice to use part of a subject's email address and run it through username tools such as the browser-based `WhatsMyName.app` and the Python-based Sherlock.[21] We touched previously on how WhatsMyName.app works by searching for a username across websites. Sherlock is a similar tool that asks the user for a username and then through a python script searches online for accounts with a matching username (see Figure 5.13). Sherlock comes pre-installed in the Kali Linux distribution.

```
[*] Checking username zewensec on:

[+] FortniteTracker: https://fortnitetracker.com/profile/all/zewensec
[+] G2G: https://www.g2g.com/zewensec
[+] GitHub: https://www.github.com/zewensec
[+] Gravatar: http://en.gravatar.com/zewensec
[+] Medium: https://medium.com/@zewensec
[+] NICommunityForum: https://www.native-instruments.com/forum/members?username=zewensec
[+] Reddit: https://www.reddit.com/user/zewensec
```

Figure 5.13: Username zewensec searched within Sherlock

Whether we use web-based tools or command-line tools, the concept remains the same. The tools typically scrape public data online and return results that match the user's query. Accounts are not the only data points an email can provide; depending on the email provider, we can find additional information like Google IDs.

Google Accounts

Gmail accounts, and more specifically Google accounts, have a Google ID associated with them that is a unique identifier for the account (see Figure 5.14). Because Google accounts use a Google ID to connect and integrate with various Google services such as maps, reviews, email, photos, and calendars if we have access to a person's Google ID, we have access to the user's publicly available data on these services.

The pivot chart offers a few examples of how we can expand our research based on Google ID results. When a Google user creates an account, they have the option to add a profile photo. This profile photo will show up in Google services when logged into that user account and can be reverse image searched to see if it appears anywhere else on the Web. For instance, if a subject uses the same profile image for both their Google account and social media accounts, we are now able to correlate those accounts. Users also have the option of uploading their photos to Google Photos, which, if made public, we would also be able to access.

---

[20] https://nixintel.info/osint/ 12-osint-resources-for-e-mail-addresses.
[21] https://github.com/sherlock-project/sherlock.

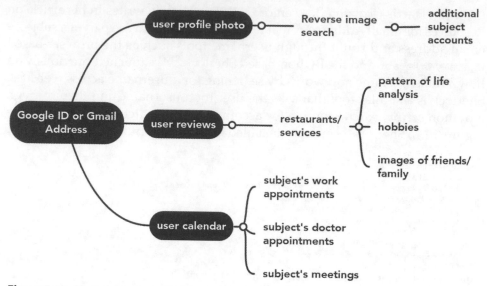

Figure 5.14: Pivot chart stemming from a Gmail or Google ID

Google has its own reviewing platform like Yelp called *Contributions* where people can leave reviews for services, events, and restaurants. If a Google user visits a restaurant, they can leave a star and/or written review about their experience. All the user reviews are then plotted on Google Maps giving us an idea of their pattern of life. I once worked on a case where I needed to pinpoint the potential area where a criminal lived based off a Gmail address found in the registration of a domain. Using Epieos,[22] a web-based tool that performs reverse email searches and social media lookups, I searched for the Gmail address and was provided a link to the subject's Contributions page. Luckily, the subject dined out frequently and reviewed many of his experiences with locations and photos. Using roughly 25 reviews pinpointed on the map, I was able to estimate where the subject lived based on his centrality to all the restaurants.

Correlating an Email with a Domain

An additional avenue of research for subject email addresses is tying them to the registration of websites to correlate the email with a domain. When starting a website, there are a few key things that need to be purchased for a website to work. The first is hosting space where the site will live; the second is the domain. When purchasing and registering a domain, what we are really doing is reserving the name for a specific period. Once the domain is registered, using personal information including name, address, phone number, and email address, that information becomes public.

To find out who owns a domain, we can search the *WHOIS database*, which is a database of information on who owns a domain and how to contact them (see Figure 5.15).

---
[22] https://epieos.com.

Raw Whois Data

```
Domain Name: kasescenarios.com
Registry Domain ID: 2721802822_DOMAIN_COM-VRSN
Registrar WHOIS Server: whois.one.com
Registrar URL: https://www.one.com
Updated Date: 2022-08-31T08:26:37Z
Creation Date: 2022-08-29T18:37:44Z
Registrar Registration Expiration Date: 2023-08-29T18:37:44Z
Registrar: One.com A/S
Registrar IANA ID: 1462
Registrar Abuse Contact Email: abuse@one.com
Registrar Abuse Contact Phone: +45.44451220
Domain Status: ok https://icann.org/epp#ok
Registry Registrant ID: REDACTED FOR PRIVACY
Registrant Name: REDACTED FOR PRIVACY
Registrant Organization: REDACTED FOR PRIVACY
Registrant Street: REDACTED FOR PRIVACY
Registrant City: REDACTED FOR PRIVACY
Registrant State/Province:
Registrant Postal Code: REDACTED FOR PRIVACY
Registrant Country: NO
Registrant Phone: REDACTED FOR PRIVACY
Registrant Phone Ext:
Registrant Fax:
Registrant Fax Ext:
Registrant Email: https://www.one.com/en/whois
Registry Admin ID: REDACTED FOR PRIVACY
Admin Name: REDACTED FOR PRIVACY
Admin Organization: REDACTED FOR PRIVACY
Admin Street: REDACTED FOR PRIVACY
Admin City: REDACTED FOR PRIVACY
Admin State/Province:
Admin Postal Code: REDACTED FOR PRIVACY
Admin Country: REDACTED FOR PRIVACY
Admin Phone: REDACTED FOR PRIVACY
Admin Phone Ext:
Admin Fax:
Admin Fax Ext:
Admin Email: https://www.one.com/en/whois
Registry Tech ID: ONECOMHM
Tech Name: Host Master
Tech Organization: One.com A/S
Tech Street: Kalvebod Brygge 24
Tech City: Koebenhavn V
Tech State/Province:
Tech Postal Code: 1560
Tech Country: DK
Tech Phone: +45.46907100
Tech Phone Ext:
Tech Fax:
Tech Fax Ext:
Tech Email: hostmaster@one.com
Name Server: ns02.one.com
Name Server: ns01.one.com
DNSSEC: signedDelegation
URL of the ICANN WHOIS Data Problem Reporting System: http://wdprs.internic.net/
>>> Last update of WHOIS database: 2022-08-31T08:26:37Z <<<
```

Figure 5.15: WHOIS record for kasescenarios.com

WHOIS records are managed by entities known as *registrars* that are accredited by the Internet Corporation for Assigned Names and Numbers (ICANN). WHOIS records can be accessed through many different free tools and services, but the two I prefer to use are `whoxy.com`[23] and `viewdns.info`.[24] Because the WHOIS records often contain the email of the person who registered the domain, we can use this email to pivot from the domain to additional information about the subject (see Figure 5.16).

NOTE   One caveat to a domain being public is that the domain owner can decide to not share any contact information.

Email Verification

Keep in mind that the associations we find are not always reliable when collecting public data that is not from a validated main source. *Email verification* is the process used to determine whether an email correctly correlates with our subject or entity. If the emails use the same username, even if they are unique, it does not necessarily mean that they are linked, and we should check all the results. One way to verify correlation between a subject and an email address is to collect it from more than one source. If we locate a subject's supposed email "`koalafanclub@email.com`" through an email address enumeration tool, that email is not verified or corroborated. If we then find an Instagram account "`@koalafanclub`" featuring our subject's name and profile photo matching the email account, it is fair to assume the email is a correlation.

Tools exist that are primarily used for marketing to help collect emails and to develop mailing lists for sales. We can use these email marketing tools to examine and collect emails for OSINT analysis. `EmailRep.io`[25] is a marketing tool that I frequently use when performing email research; I like this tool because from a single query of an email we can see the user accounts associated with it. As a test, I queried fakeemail@email.com on EmailRep.io. Figure 5.17 shows that the email has a "low" reputation, which means it's less likely to be a legitimate email. We can also see that the credentials for this email have not been leaked, so the passwords are probably not available publicly. If we scroll all the way to the bottom of the results, we see "twitter" listed as an associated account. We have learned from this email that it is a real email, the credentials have not been breached, and it was used to create a Twitter account. From here we could pivot to try to dig up the Twitter account, which may have more personal information on it.

---

[23] `www.whoxy.com`.
[24] `https://viewdns.info`.
[25] `https://emailrep.io`.

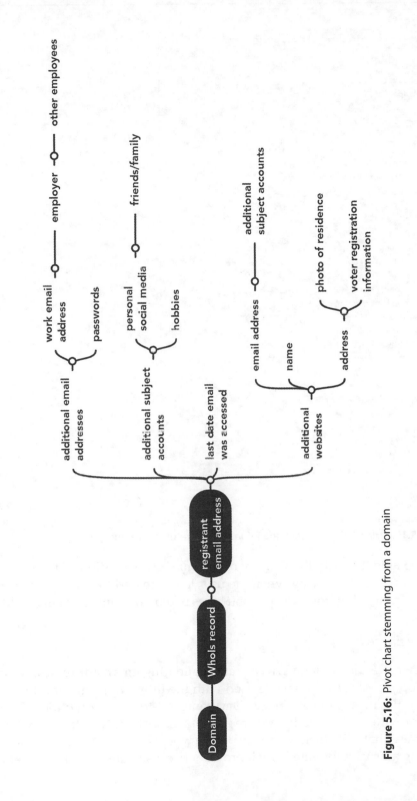

Figure 5.16: Pivot chart stemming from a domain

```
curl emailrep.io/fakeemail@email.com
{
    "email": "fakeemail@email.com",
    "reputation": "low",
    "suspicious": false,
    "references": 1,
    "details": {
        "blacklisted": false,
        "malicious_activity": false,
        "malicious_activity_recent": false,
        "credentials_leaked": false,
        "credentials_leaked_recent": false,
        "data_breach": false,
        "first_seen": "never",
        "last_seen": "never",
        "domain_exists": true,
        "domain_reputation": "n/a",
        "new_domain": false,
        "days_since_domain_creation": 9289,
        "suspicious_tld": false,
        "spam": false,
        "free_provider": true,
        "disposable": false,
        "deliverable": true,
        "accept_all": false,
        "valid_mx": true,
        "primary_mx": "mx00.mail.com",
        "spoofable": true,
        "spf_strict": true,
        "dmarc_enforced": false,
        "profiles": [
            "twitter"
        ]
    }
}
```

Figure 5.17: `Emailrep.io` showing information it returns on a query

Being able to verify the validity of an email gives credibility to everything related to it, and knowing when the user last accessed the email account can keep us from going down deep rabbit holes based on an inactive email address.

Privacy Emails

While we are discussing verifying and validating email addresses, we must touch on *privacy emails* that are used with the intent of protecting the user's identity. Because of the security, privacy, and end-to-end encryption offered by many providers, these addresses are great for OSINT analysts to use for OPSEC measures. That said, there are many people who try to protect their real identity by using a privacy-oriented email provider because many require no personal information on signup, making your account anonymous. These secure emails are much more difficult to verify and correlate with other accounts.

These are the top five privacy-oriented email services:

- Protonmail
- Startmail
- Tutanota
- Zoho mail
- Thexyz

Just because these emails are secure does not make them bulletproof. Many of these services, like Protonmail, are secure only when using Protonmail servers. If the user sends an email to a third-party platform or includes sensitive or revealing information in the subject line, it wouldn't be encrypted.

Data Breaches

We have touched on quite a few ways that an adversary could collect and leverage our personal information. We learned that an email address is not only a way to send mail but also a username that is part of our cyber identity. Email addresses, along with things like hobbies, IP addresses, and even plain-text user passwords are stored within databases on the websites we visit and applications we use. If an adversary were to exploit a vulnerability on these services and access the database, the data could be harvested and sold or leaked online in what is called a *data breach*.

Isn't That Illegal?

Data breaches are the result of a security incident that results in user data being exposed. Although data breaches are illegal access to user data, there are legitimate uses of the data that has already been leaked. However, research performed on data breaches can be an ethical gray area, and I highly recommend getting stakeholder approval to proceed with downloading and storing any breach data.

What Can I Do with Breach Data?

To illustrate some legitimate uses for breach data, here are some example client asks that we will walk through how to answer:

- **Client 1:** How many breaches has my subject's email been in?
- **Client 2:** Can you tell me if my employees are using work emails to sign up for personal accounts?
- **Client 3:** Can you tell me what an adversary can do with my breach data?

Determining "how many breaches a subject email has been in" is as easy as running a search. Using the free site HaveIBeenPwned (HIBP),[26] we can search to see how many and which breaches an email has been found in. The great part about HIBP is that it does not provide us with any credentials or PII, so analysts can use it without fear of crossing ethical lines. In Figure 5.18, I searched for "fakeemail@email.com," and HIBP found this email in 88 data breaches and 18 pastes (not including sensitive searches).

NOTE Breaches can contain data from as far back as 10 or more years, so be aware that not all of them will be active and in use. Checking HaveIBeenPwned can show the dates each breach happened.

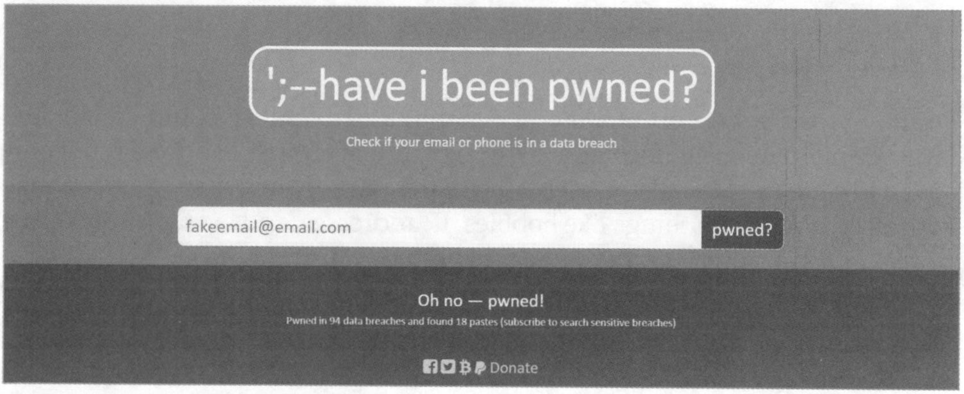

';--have i been pwned?

Check if your email or phone is in a data breach

fakeemail@email.com | pwned?

Oh no — pwned!

Pwned in 94 data breaches and found 18 pastes (subscribe to search sensitive breaches)

⬛ Donate

Figure 5.18: HaveIBeenPwned search

Additionally, HIBP provides the name and details about the breaches the email was found in along with a list of the specific compromised data (see Figure 5.19).

To answer our first client question, "How many breaches has my subject's email been in?" we could run a query on HIBP, get the number of breaches listed, and include it in my report.

Canva: In May 2019, the graphic design tool website Canva suffered a data breach that impacted 137 million subscribers. The exposed data included email addresses, usernames, names, cities of residence and passwords stored as bcrypt hashes for users not using social logins. The data was provided to HIBP by a source who requested it be attributed to "JimScott.Sec@protonmail.com".

Compromised data: Email addresses, Geographic locations, Names, Passwords, Usernames

Figure 5.19: HaveIBeenPwned showing specific breach details

The next set of questions assumes we have access to the breach data itself. A quick reminder here: OSINT is always passive, and analysts should never use a password to log into any account. One great tool for accessing breach data is

---

[26] https://haveibeenpwned.com.

IntelligenceX (IntelX),[27] a search engine based in the Czech Republic that is used for searching common selectors and pulls data from the Dark Web, document sharing platforms, WHOIS data, and public leaks.

To answer the client question "Can you tell me if my employees are using work emails to sign up for personal accounts?" we could perform a search for the company domain in IntelX to see how many company emails have been breached. Depending on the size of the client's company this could be a large task. Searching for "`email.com`" as the company domain, we get 1,000+ `.txt` files, and without a script to do the work for us, we would need to manually search them for company emails and passwords (see Figure 5.20). Many of the text files are obscured, and clicking "full data" in the bottom-right corner will open each file for deeper searching (see Figure 5.21).

NOTE IntelX has an educational discount offering limited free access to schools and universities.

Figure 5.20: Intelligence X search

Finally, to answer the question "Can you tell me what an adversary can do with my breach data?" we must understand the pivots that can be made from breach data. Breaches happen to many large companies and communities with billions of users including Adobe, AdultFriendFinder, Ashley Madsion, Ancestry, Dominos Pizza, and Facebook. Because so many users hold accounts on these sites, it is highly probable that your subject has one or more emails across several breaches. Since each breach leaks different compromising data, it is possible to collect information from several breaches to connect real names, IP addresses, passwords, and usernames all from one subject's email. Passwords can also be correlated across breach data; in the following example, by querying IntelX for the password "hij" found in Breach 3, we were able to match it with password "hij" found in Breach 5 using a different email address. Using this method of password correlation, especially with unique passwords, can help discover new subject email addresses.

---

[27] `https://intelx.io`.

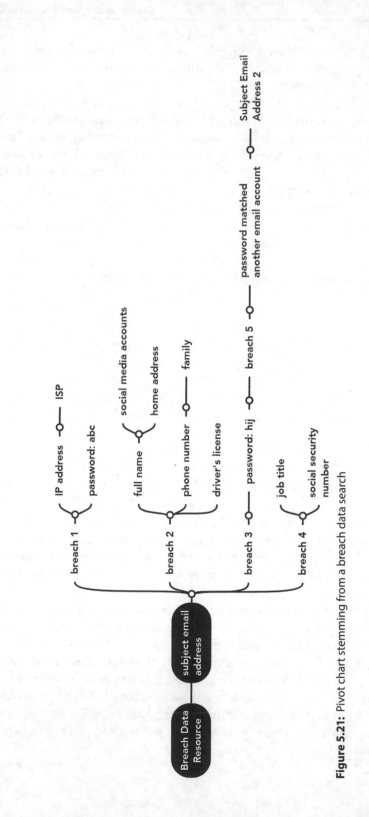

Figure 5.21: Pivot chart stemming from a breach data search

5.5   Subject Phone Numbers

So far, we've learned how to find usernames and email addresses and the pivot points that exist for both. Next, let's look at subject phone numbers. In the United States, marketing databases and searchable public records make far more PII accessible via phone numbers than many other countries. Because marketers buy, sell, and merge lists of our phone numbers with other marketing data, they become associated with additional identifying information within databases. These data connections are useful for learning more about a subject. Figure 5.22 shows some typical pivot points we can find when looking at subject phone numbers.

Typing Phone Numbers to additional selectors

Correlating a Phone Number with a Subject

Unlike emails and usernames, which people tend to reuse across accounts, we are constantly getting new numbers, and they can be shared (landline phone) or recycled (company-allocated numbers), so phone numbers don't always follow us throughout our lives in the same way. Although phone numbers can be tricky to validate, they still can provide us with new pivot points to explore, sometimes even using account sharing to our advantage.

In a recent case, I was tasked with uncovering information on a foreign national to find data indicating whether they may be covertly working for their government while living and working in the United States. I started this case the same way I begin most cases, by using a process of systematically querying each data point I find, first in a search engine and then in a personally curated set of tools for each data point. For instance, if I began with a subject's phone number, Figure 5.23 shows what my process may look like.

Phone numbers can be inaccurate, so we can better test our assumptions by querying multiple sources. If you are lucky enough to have access to paid tools, it is usually more effective to search through them before using the free tools.

While analyzing the foreign national from my story, I had a hard time determining if the subject I found was really who I was looking for. I had found a phone number for the subject but needed to verify its authenticity. Using the process of collection outlined in the pivot chart I started with a search engine query. From the query I was able to uncover a social media account appearing to belong to my subject's wife. Once I was confident I had unveiled the wife's first and last name, I methodically queried his phone number in all my usual free phone number tools. Eventually, the way I confirmed the subject's identity was by finding his wife and correlating their landline phone numbers in public data aggregators. Fortunately for me both of their names were associated to the same landline phone number. Pivoting from that phone number, I was able to locate

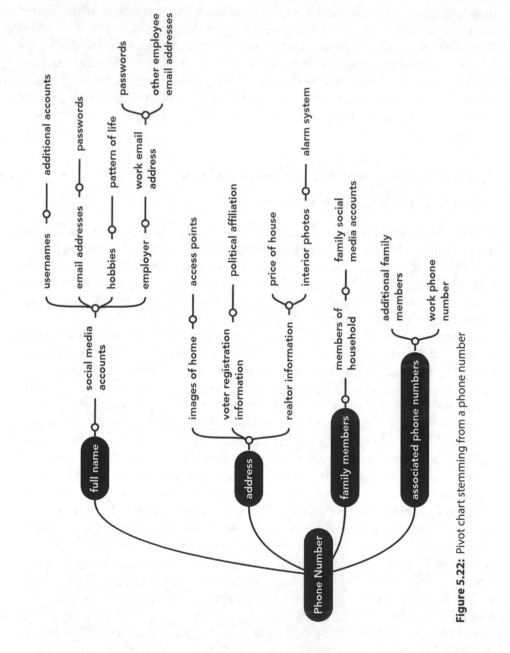

Figure 5.22: Pivot chart stemming from a phone number

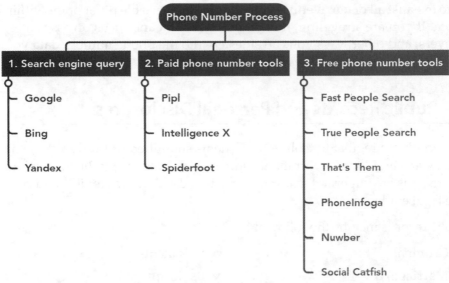

Figure 5.23: Process used to analyze phone numbers

his current address, email addresses, passwords, and IP addresses that could be further analyzed. I got lucky, it is not always easy to identify the owner of a phone number, and to add a level of complexity, it has become incredibly easy to spoof a phone number.

Phone Number Spoofing

The last thing we want is that the whole case depends on one phone number and it turns out to be fake. This scenario is possible if the number has been "spoofed." *Phone number spoofing* is the act of deliberately disguising the phone number to appear as a trusted number, falsified to cover the caller's identity.[28] Call spoofing is a common scam tactic where an incoming call appears to be coming from a trusted source to trick the person who answers into providing information or money. Commonly, scammers use free Voice over IP (VoIP) tools to substitute fraudulent numbers with their own.

Tracing spoofed numbers is difficult if not impossible in many cases, but by performing a search engine query for the phone number, we can do a quick look for any results that may mention the number being used for scams. I have had luck connecting data points by reading through the comments about the spoofed number on scam awareness forums. If the number has been used enough, it might reveal hints about who is using it.

In my experience phone number enumeration can be difficult and often inaccurate and frustrating. But sometimes a number is all we have to go on, so we

---

[28] www.fcc.gov/spoofing.

have to exhaust all of our avenues and hope to find a usable pivot point within the data. If you are struggling, think outside the box and focus on associates, employers, and other ways you can sidestep into the phone number data you are looking for.

5.6   Public Records and Personal Disclosures

Public records are regulatory source documents submitted or produced by the federal, state, and local governments and are available for public inspection. Public records are important to our research because they are credible and constitute legal evidence.

Public records include the following:

- Criminal
- Marriage/divorce
- Birth/death
- Property
- Census

- Judgments
- Bankruptcy
- Tax liens
- Voter information

Public records serve the analysis across many aspects of OSINT and are often a key source of verification for due diligence investigators, insurance investigators, lawyers, reporters, private investigators, and OSINT analysts. Public records are, by definition, publicly available unlike confidential records that are not accessible to the general public. However, there may be instances where confidential and trusted records may be unwittingly disclosed by the owner in a manner called *personal disclosure*. Examples of personal disclosure include someone scanning their Social Security card and posting it on a website, or a traveler posting a photo of their passport. As a result of these personal disclosures, sensitive documents are shared within the public domain. Analyzing public records can help us to discover information on an entity, business scams, and personal information on subjects such as location and assets.

Methods for incorporating public records searches

Collecting Public Records Associated with a Subject

In the past, to research public records we had to put on pants and go to the local courthouse or government office to request access, but fortunately now that we live in the future, public records are widely available and easily accessible online. There are numerous reasons we might need to look at public records, but in regard to subject intelligence, we are generally trying to gain a better understanding of an individual's life. Figure 5.24 shows an example of pivot

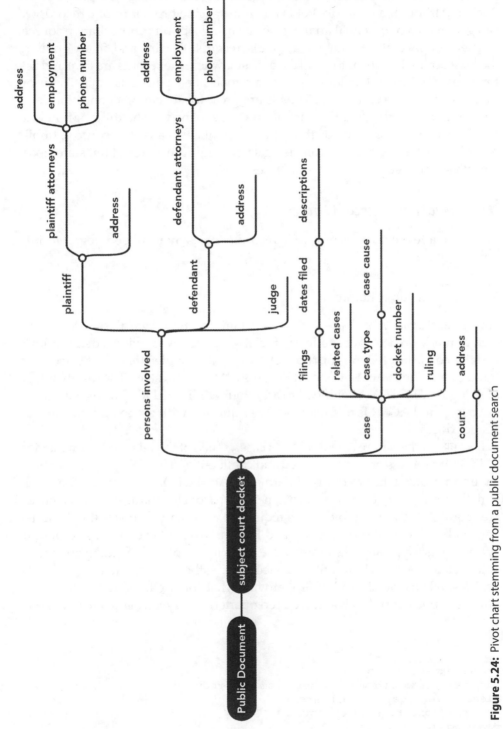

Figure 5.24: Pivot chart stemming from a public document search

points that may be possible through just a subject's record in a public court docket. Although a court docket is just one specific type of public record, we can get an idea of potential analysis points using a public authoritative source.

There are several ways to look up public records. The first and, in my opinion, the least optimal option is to go to the building where the records are kept and ask for access. The second option is to use paid tools like LexisNexis[29] and Thomson Reuters[30] to access records. Paid tools are great for revealing connections and speeding up analysis, but they are often very expensive. The third option is to find and access public records through free, publicly available resources. Public records may be analyzed for free using search engine queries, state/state/local websites, and free publication databases.

U.S. Official Public Record Sources

These are a few examples of public record sources that can be integrated into your analysis.

Federal-Level Public Records

Federal-level public records are any recorded information regardless of form, created or made on behalf of a federal official or agency. Accessible federal records usually consist of federal court documents and case files that can be accessed through the Public Access to Court Records (PACER)[31] system. The disadvantage of using PACER is that you need to add your credit card to your user account, but access to PACER is free up to $ 30 per quarter, with a maximum charge of $ 3 per document.

Because of the nature of federal-level cases, much of the related documentation is difficult to access or remains sealed and confidential. The U.S. government does have an act, called the Freedom of Information Act (FOIA), that provides the public with the right to request access to documentation from federal agencies.[32] Agencies are required by law to provide the requested information unless it falls under personal privacy, national security, and law enforcement exemptions. That said, FOIA requests typically take more than 20 days to complete depending on the size of the request and can be heavily redacted making them difficult to use for OSINT analysis. When federal records fail to provide what you need, check state-level documents to find court details and required quarterly and yearly entity submissions.

---

[29] www.lexisnexis.com.
[30] https://legal.thomsonreuters.com/en/products/clear-investigation-software.
[31] https://pacer.uscourts.gov.
[32] www.foia.gov.

State-Level Public Records

State-level public records are any recorded information regardless of form created or made on behalf of a state official or agency. State documents tend to be rich in state-level court records and required business documents for entities within the state that contain varying degrees of public disclosure. For example, as shown in Figure 5.25, the Pennsylvania Unified Judicial System (UJS) Portal offers court case searches if you know specific details about the case or subject under investigation to meet the requirements of the query (see `ujsportal.pacourts.us/CaseSearch`). Additionally, the online docket for each state can provide details and context for topics such as divorce, birth, death, marriage, and criminal cases.

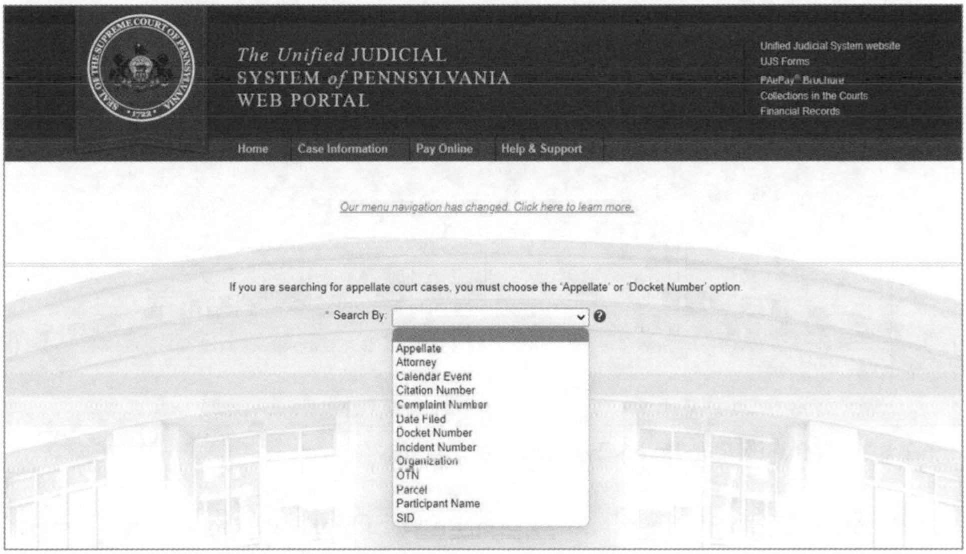

Figure 5.25: UJS Portal

The easiest way to find state resources is by using Google dorks to refine the search using the state plus the record source.

`"New Jersey" and "Criminal Records"`

`"California" and "Divorce Records"`

Note that many people try to profit from of selling public records online, be conscious to use only `.gov` sites versus unvetted secondary sources that resell documents.

Another great state-level official document source is each state's Secretary of State website. These sites provide free public access to many government records containing corporate entities and assets. Uncovering these documents may lead us to the names of shareholders, directors, and other subjects of interest that can be used to develop a full picture of an entity.

In Figure 5.26, I located the Pennsylvania Department of State website `corporations.pa.gov` and queried the Business Entity Search for "Nifty 50's," a greasy retro diner in Philadelphia and a staple of my youth.

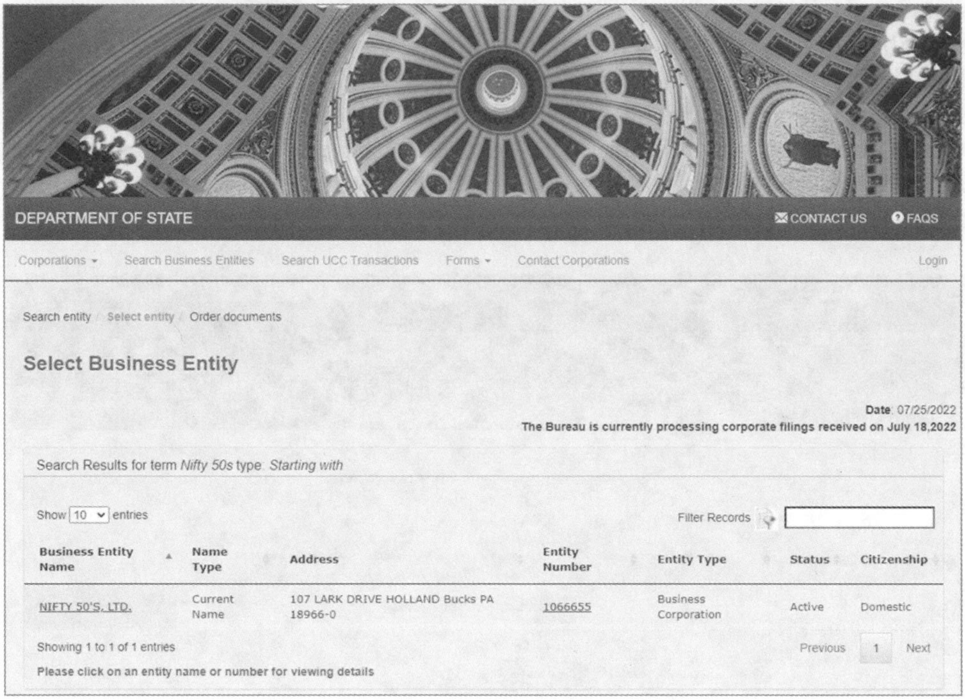

Figure 5.26: Nifty 50's found in `corporations.pa.gov`

In Figure 5.27, The Pennsylvania Department of State site requires a payment to view specific documents, however, we can still find the address, full business name, names of the entity's officers, and whether it is still active for free. Using entity documents like business filings can provide numerous points for us to pivot off of to find additional data. If I were performing analysis on this entity, my next steps would be to search the address to see if any other businesses were registered under it. Additionally, if we know the names of the officers, we can look into their connections with other entities, which could reveal any motivations they may have. One way to find verifiable information on an individual is through their registered voting records, which are often available publicly at the state level.

State Voting Records

Some states within the United States maintain publicly available and searchable online *state voting records* that provide information on the voter. The laws for the

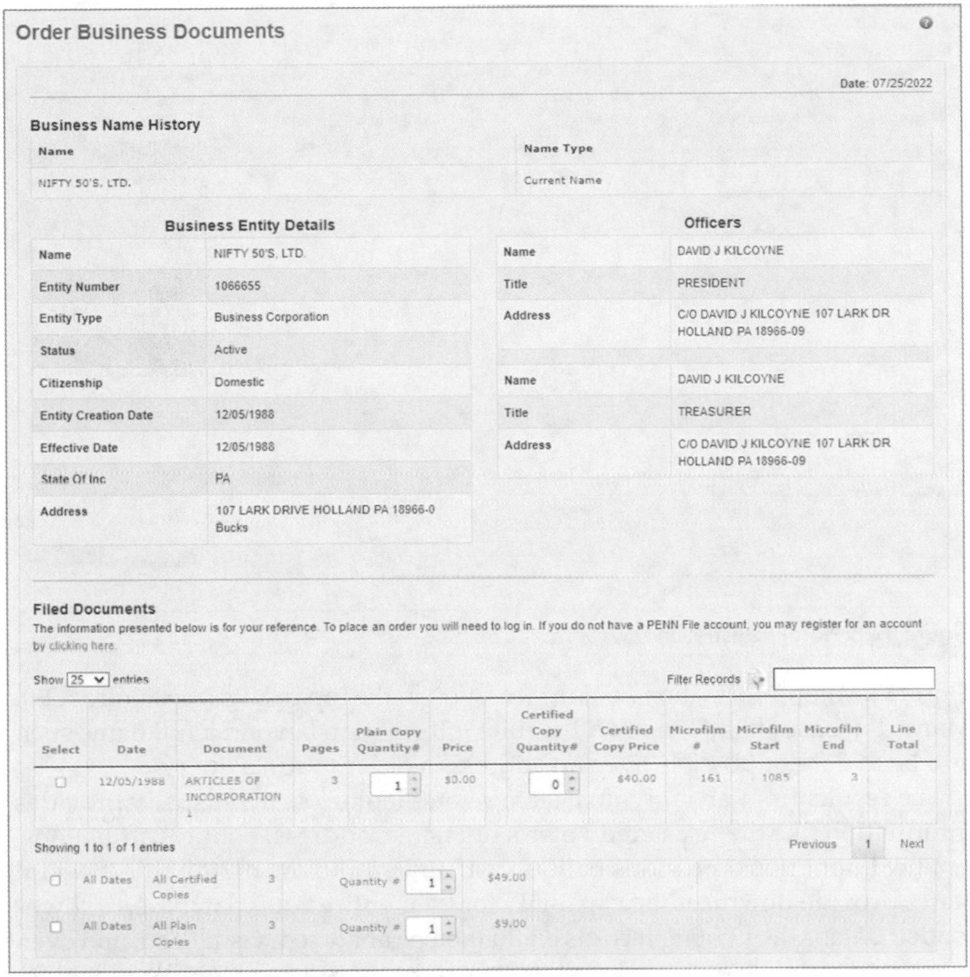

Order Business Documents

Date: 07/25/2022

Business Name History

Name	Name Type
NIFTY 50'S, LTD.	Current Name

Business Entity Details

Name	NIFTY 50'S, LTD.
Entity Number	1066655
Entity Type	Business Corporation
Status	Active
Citizenship	Domestic
Entity Creation Date	12/05/1988
Effective Date	12/05/1988
State Of Inc	PA
Address	107 LARK DRIVE HOLLAND PA 18966-0 Bucks

Officers

Name	DAVID J KILCOYNE
Title	PRESIDENT
Address	C/O DAVID J KILCOYNE 107 LARK DR HOLLAND PA 18966-09
Name	DAVID J KILCOYNE
Title	TREASURER
Address	C/O DAVID J KILCOYNE 107 LARK DR HOLLAND PA 18966-09

Filed Documents

The information presented below is for your reference. To place an order you will need to log in. If you do not have a PENN File account, you may register for an account by clicking here.

Show 25 entries Filter Records

Select	Date	Document	Pages	Plain Copy Quantity#	Price	Certified Copy Quantity#	Certified Copy Price	Microfilm #	Microfilm Start	Microfilm End	Line Total
☐	12/05/1988	ARTICLES OF INCORPORATION 1	3	1	$0.00	0	$40.00	161	1085	3	

Showing 1 to 1 of 1 entries Previous 1 Next

☐	All Dates	All Certified Copies	3	Quantity # 1	$49.00
☐	All Dates	All Plain Copies	3	Quantity # 1	$9.00

Figure 5.27: Nifty 50's documents found in `corporations.pa.gov`

access and use of public voter registration vary on a state-by-state basis; these laws can be found on the National Conference of State Legislatures (NCSL) website at `ncsl.org`.[33] In Figure 5.28, Voting records can be used in OSINT to find an individual's address by year, other people who may live at the address, employment, and political connections that might influence their actions.

Finding voter registration data for participating states can often be as simple as searching in a search engine for the state and *voter registration*. If we try this search method with the state of Florida using *Florida* and *voter registration*, we can find

[33] `www.ncsl.org/research/elections-and-campaigns/access-to-and-use-of-voter-registration-lists.aspx`.

State	Who can request the voter file?	What information does the file contain?	What is kept confidential?	What can the file be used for?	Programs to keep voter information confidential?
Alabama Ala. Code § 17-3-53, § 17-4-33	Political parties are provided with a state list, and counties may choose to make information available to others.	All voter registration information, except what is confidential.	SSN, month and day of birth.	Not specified.	All registration information except for the voter's name is kept confidential if a voter submits an affidavit affirming that they are a victim of domestic violence, a federal or state prosecutor, a federal, state, probate or municipal judge, a legislator, or a law enforcement officer.
Alaska AS §15.07.127, §15.07.195	Anyone can request a copy of the list or an electronic format.	Names, addresses, party affiliation.	Age or DOB, any part of SSN, DL number, voter ID number, place of birth, signature.	Not specified.	A voter may elect in writing to keep the voter's residential address confidential if the voter provides a separate mailing address.

State-by-State Table: State Laws on Access to and Use of Voter Registration Lists

Figure 5.28: Voter Registration Laws at `ncsl.org`

Florida's Voter Information Lookup website[34] in the top results (see Figure 5.29). Many databases like Florida will require information beyond a full name such as a birth date or possibly even an address in order to run a query.

The results from an individual state's voter lookup search usually provides information like the registered voter's full name, address, political affiliations, political donations, previous ballots cast, and employment/job title. Several states provide downloading capability for their entire voter database. A downloaded database of voting records could then be analyzed, visualized, and even integrated to enrich other tools. While state records are a great tool for providing a higher level of data on individuals and entities, sometimes we need to get a bit closer to home using local government records.

Local Government Records

Local government records contain information on counties, boroughs, municipalities, towns, and parishes within a state. The documents within the local government include misdemeanor crimes, traffic violations, and ordinance violations. Local records are available to the public at the behest of the municipality and their funding and capabilities to maintain a searchable database. A small, underfunded county may not have records available online while a

---

[34] https://registration.elections.myflorida.com/en/CheckVoterStatus/Index.

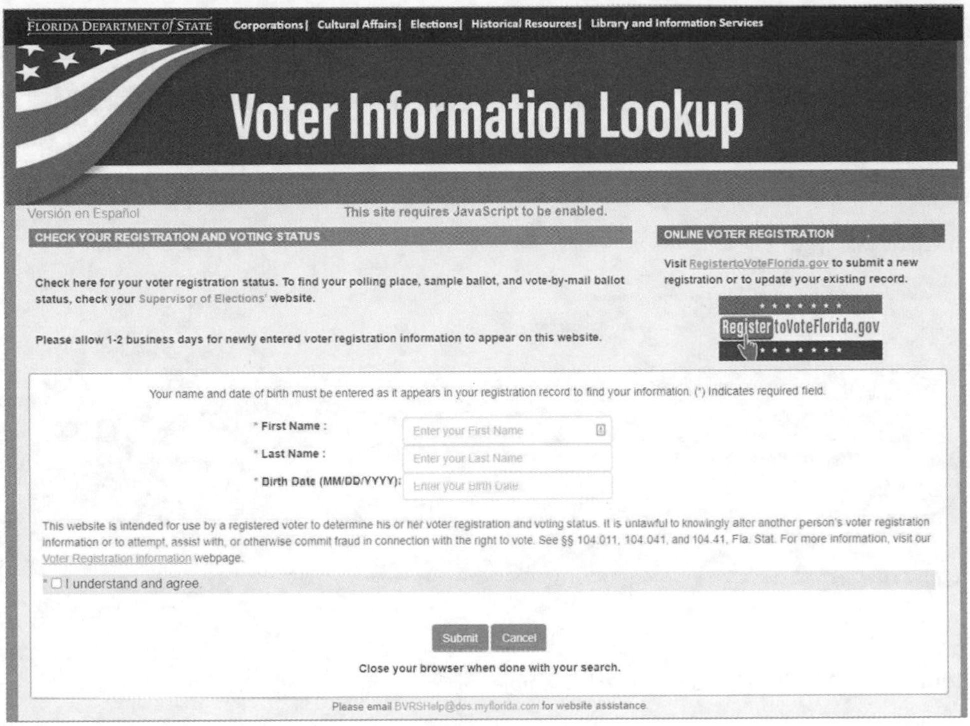

Figure 5.29: Voter Information Lookup Website

larger one would. The search criteria on the local sites may vary, for example, on the local Mobile Alabama site `cityofmobile.org`[35] by way of a third-party search on `municipalrecordssearch.com/mobileal` requires only a last name to return results (see Figure 5.30). The Pennsylvania state search, on the other hand, requires you to know your subject's first name, last name, and date of birth. One form of local record that can offer some insight into your subject's addresses, wealth, and family are property records.

Property Records

Legal documents that contain information about lands both private or commercial that landowners build or buy are called *property records*. Similar to the way that U.S. court records are publicly maintained, property records are available, aggregated, and stored in various databases across the Internet for public access. Property records are considered an authoritative primary source of information because they come directly from the government, making them usable and trustworthy data within the United States. The sources for property records

---

[35] `www.cityofmobile.org`.

SEARCH BY		LAST NAME			First Name		Date of Birth
Name ▾		smith ✱					
		Drivers License #		☐ Include similar sounding names		**🔍 SEARCH**	

✱ Indicates a required field.

202 results found for smith

Note: Names that do not match your search criteria are aliases.

Warrants are displayed in [RED]

SORT Citation Number ▾

Citation	Docket	Last Name	First Name	Offense	Violation Date	Status
12131004-01	200700922	SMITH	ALLEN	OLD MPD: NOISE ORDINANCE VIOLATION (VEHICLE) *****	4/17/2007	DOCKET CLOSED 5/23/2007
12141780-01	200700561	SMITH	ADELAIDE	OLD MPD: MINOR IN POSSESSION OF ALCOHOL*****	3/10/2007	DOCKET CLOSED 6/27/2007
12150001-01	200903842	SMITH	AARON	OLD MPD: NOISE ORDINANCE VIOLATION (RESIDENTIAL) *****	10/9/2009	DOCKET CLOSED 11/18/2009
208016-01	E020000033	SMITH	ALEXANDRIA	FAILURE TO CONFINE ANIMAL (FENCE)	10/31/2019	WARRANT ALIAS 8/5/2020 1:00pm
208017-01	E020000032	SMITH	ALEXANDRIA	FAILURE TO GET LICENSE	10/31/2019	WARRANT ALIAS 8/5/2020 1:00pm
208018-01	E020000031	SMITH	ALEXANDRIA	FAILURE TO VACCINATE	10/31/2019	WARRANT ALIAS 8/5/2020 1:00pm
208019-01	E020000030	SMITH	ALEXANDRIA	FAILURE TO CONFINE DANGEROUS ANIMAL	10/31/2019	WARRANT ALIAS 8/5/2020 1:00pm
C00409108-01	C00409108	SMITH	ALICIA	FORGERY FREE TEXT 3RD	12/9/2004	DOCKET CLOSED 9/8/2005

Figure 5.30: Municipal Records Search Example

are legal to access through the county tax assessor's websites and can provide us with information about the subject's property including value, sales, land, names of buyers, and more.

For most counties within the United States, a Google search of the county name + *tax assessor* in Google will take you to the county's official government website or database, and the built-in search capabilities allow you to search for records using an address located within the county (see Figure 5.31).

Q county name +"tax assessor"   ✕ | 🎤

Figure 5.31: Google.com

If property records are not publicly available through a state's county website, it may possible to pull this data from secondary sources. Real estate sites like Zillow[36] and Trulia[37] get their property information by scraping the public property data from county records and other public sources to use on their sites

---

[36] www.zillow.com.

[37] www.trulia.com.

to link property buyers with sellers. Because these sites aggregate information using multiple sources to provide property data and enriching it with additional data like photos, we can use them to learn relevant details about a home or business including building layout and placement of security systems. Real estate sites are not considered a primary source, and the listings could be out-of-date or incorrect, so always validate any findings. In the United States, so much personal information is public that we hardly stop to consider the laws in other countries. Personal data including property records can be highly protected depending on the country's laws.

> **TIP**   While websites like AirBNB and VBRO do not contain official property information, they can be great resources for pattern of life information, photos, building layouts, and the renter's personal details.

International Property Records

Property records for residential and business locations outside of your country of origin are *international property records*. The access to international property information outside of the United States will be regulated in different ways depending on the laws of the country. Internationally, public records can be far more protected, and privacy laws can restrict the use, disclosure, storage, and distribution of these records. In some countries, breaking privacy rules can lead to large fines and even jail time.

An unfortunate example of strict privacy laws is the 2013 arrest of a British investigator and his wife in China. Investigator Peter Humphrey's risk advisory business ChinaWhys was hired by the pharmaceutical giant GlaxoSmithKline (GSK) to investigate an alleged sex tape featuring the head of GSK China, Mark Reilly, that was used in a blackmail attempt.[38] The blackmailer accused Reilly of participating in corruption and the bribing of doctors with travel, money, and sex to boost sales and share prices. Humphrey and his wife, Yu Yingzeng, were arrested for allegedly illegally buying the personal data of Chinese citizens and selling it to GSK during their investigation. In the United States, gathering public information on a person is legal; however, in China, Humphrey and Yingzeng received 2 years in prison for similar research. To avoid breaking any privacy laws, it's important to research the laws in both the country you are located within while doing your work as well as the country of the residents you are performing analysis on.

A quick Google search can uncover the privacy laws for each country; for example CNIL (The Commission Nationale de L'informatique et des Libertés) at

---

[38] www.theguardian.com/business/2014/sep/19/
glaxosmithkline-china-mark-reilly-deported-uk-guilty-bribery-hunan.

cnil.fr[39] offers a data protection map with information on each country's privacy laws. Please don't rely simply on an online search; use it as a starting point and be sure to clear any analysis with your legal team. Once we have confirmation that our analysis will be legal, we can use Google dorks to develop a query to search for public records within a specific country. For example, the following query is a simple targeted search for public property records within Africa:

```
"Property Records" and "Africa"
```

Using targeted search queries should provide us with resources for countries that do not have strict privacy laws preventing this data from being public. Authoritative government source documents are the most reliable; however, sometimes the data we need just isn't available or it has been split up across sources with no search function. In these cases, it would be appropriate to supplement our data with unofficial (but vetted) sources like databases and publications.

U.S. Unofficial Sources

An *unofficial source* is an informal and unauthorized nongovernmental source of information. However, just because the source is unofficial does not make it off-limits for analysis; we simply need to be extra vigilant with verification of the data. There are plenty of great unofficial resources publications available for use like BRB Publications[40] that provides free access to a listing of datasets from government agencies and the Public Accountability Project[41] that provides the public with a curated public information dataset about people and organizations. Some digging might be required to find relevant sources for your use case, but I recommend performing some targeted search engine searching to narrow the focus down to something usable, for example, *court records* and *database*. For an extended list of both official and unofficial sources, check out my website at raebaker.net/resources.

Now that we have identified and collected both official and unofficial documents, they can be combined and enriched with supporting information like usernames, emails, and pattern of life analysis to aid in developing a complete and rounded picture of the subject. As you review the many data points collected from public records, take a moment to consider what harm an adversary might cause with the same data.

The pivot chart shown in Figure 5.32 begins with just the subject's name. From there we can pivot to find emails, passwords, court records, property records, and usernames, as well as the subject's friends and family. Taking the collection process one step deeper, we would begin to explore the subject's social media presence using the discovered usernames, emails, and other connections.

---

[39] www.cnil.fr/en/data-protection-around-the-world.
[40] www.brbpublications.com.
[41] https://publicaccountability.org.

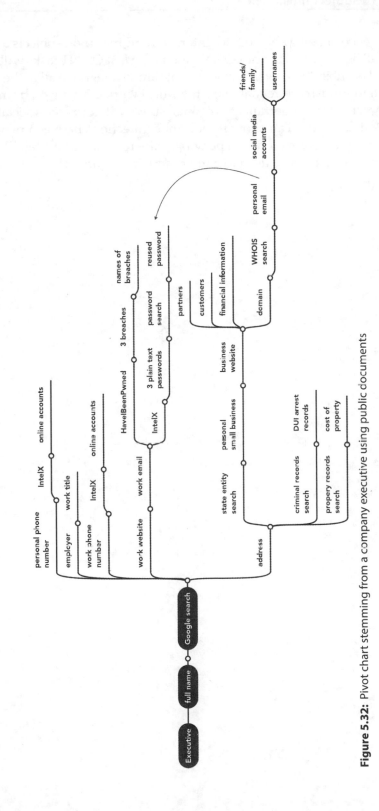

Figure 5.32: Pivot chart stemming from a company executive using public documents

The practice of being able to find, interpret, and report on subjects and their actions will be a key tool in your OSINT toolbox. Most OSINT tasks will require some level of subject intelligence since people are so integral to all of the entities, systems, and infrastructure that make the world work. Moving on from subject intelligence, the next important area of analysis we will focus on is social media. Social media accounts can show important connections between people and entities, provide information on a person's daily routines, and even illuminate other accounts that can be used to gather more information.

CHAPTER 6

Social Media Analysis

6.1 Social Media

Social media analysis, often referred to as *social media intelligence (SOCMINT)*, is personally identifiable information gathered from social media. In the context of subject intelligence, we are concerned with user accounts, what these users are posting, who they connect and interact with, the images, videos, and associated metadata they post, and any pattern of life we can determine. Social media analysis does not just use social networking sites like LinkedIn and Facebook but rather all forms of social media including media sharing sites, forums, gaming platforms, and blogging/microblogging sites.

Popular Social Media, Messaging Platforms, and Forums

■ Facebook	■ Twitter	■ Instagram	■ MeWe
■ Gab	■ WhatsApp	■ Telegram	■ QQ
■ WeChat	■ Tumblr	■ Skype	■ Viber
■ Snapchat	■ YY	■ VK	■ Pinterest
■ LinkedIn	■ Reddit	■ 4Chan	■ 8chan
■ YouTube	■ Flickr	■ TikTok	■ Discord

Today, social media analysis is often the crux of subject analysis because of free and easy access to personal information provided by users on many different platforms. The versatility and application of social media analysis can be spread across many use cases including the analysis of the following:

- Cybercrime
- Financial crime
- Fraud investigations
- Child exploitation
- Trafficking
- Community monitoring
- Terrorism
- Trends
- Organized crime
- Misinformation/disinformation
- Pattern of life analysis

To begin analyzing social media, we must talk about the various elements that make up a social media account. Knowing the key parts of social media accounts will help guide you in what to focus on during analysis.

Key Parts of Social Media

To understand what you can do with the data you find on social media, you first need to understand what points are of value. Social media is made up of several important parts, such as user data, user connections, user interactions, post content, media content, and metadata.

User data refers to the social media profile information provided by the user. This data could include birthday, hometown, full name, relationship status, and so on.

User connections are the people who follow and like the user profile as well as who the user follows back. On many social media accounts, the user has family and friend connections as well as online followers.

User interactions, on the other hand, are the likes, emojis, and comments between the subject and other users. If a subject likes every photo from another account, there is a good chance they may be associated in real life.

Post content is the text a user types into a post including user tags and hashtags. User posts can contain context surrounding a situation or viewpoint a user has.

Media content can be shared as post content, or in the case of certain platforms like TikTok, the media content is the post. Media, especially video, can provide additional context, location, or pattern of life data points.

Metadata in the context of social media is the hidden data within the post or media file that provides details about the time and location the media was developed.

Figure 6.1 shows an example of how each of these elements represents a potential pivot point for subject intelligence research. It's easy to see the volume of data we can get from just a single social media account.

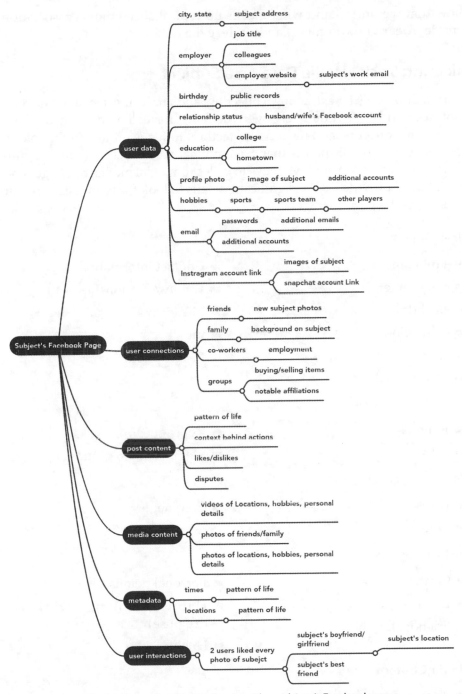

Figure 6.1: Pivot chart showing how to begin with a subject's Facebook page

Now that we understand what makes up typical social media association points, let's learn how to collect and analyze the data.

Collecting Social Media Data on a Subject

The number of tools for extracting, collecting, and analyzing social media data is enormous and often completely overwhelming. Instead of focusing on what tools exist to collect what data, a better tactic is to focus on the methodology of the collection and the pivots that exist in what we collect. Eventually, with practice, we all develop our own ways to collect on social media, but to get you started, I have provided a few significant details to look for within each of our key social media parts.

User Data

- Full name
- Username
- Birthday
- Education
- Employment/job title
- Places lived
- Contact information
- Family/relationships
- Life events
- Bio
- Profile photo

User Connections

- Friends
- Family
- Colleagues
- Memberships/groups

User Interactions

- Likes
- Emojis
- Comments

Post Content

- Context
- Locations
- Friends/family
- Personal details
- Habits (smoking, drinking, drug use)
- Hobbies

Media Content

- Photos of subject
- Identifying features (hair color, tattoos)
- Habits (smoking, drinking, drug use)
- Location
- Friend/family
- Hobbies

Metadata

- Locations
- Times
- Dates

I find it helpful when developing a social media analysis case to keep copious notes and create a link analysis chart to maintain a record of links and connections. These cases can quickly become unruly, and it is easy to forget where and how we found pieces of information. My preferred method of keeping track of data points is a OneNote and an i2 link analysis chart, but you could use any method that works for you if it keeps everything organized.

While collecting information, we can begin to note any accounts that appear to belong to the same person. Finding a subject's other social media accounts can reveal additional information about the subject.

Correlating Subject Social Media Accounts

Before diving deep into subject user account details, we must recognize the complexity of user accounts themselves. It is common for users to have more than one account on a platform, and many even have multiple accounts. If a user is the owner of 10 separate Instagram accounts, it is not necessarily for nefarious reasons; perhaps they own several businesses and maintain a social media account for each one.

I also find that the Instagram generation tends to maintain several accounts as a rule. The ability to change privacy settings providing access to certain people allows for a sanitized "fake" account to present for family (Finstas) and less family-friendly "real" accounts (Rinstas) for documenting teenage discretions with their friends.

The concept of the Finsta and Rinsta is always incredibly apparent when I take part in missing persons cases. A recent case I worked hinged on my team's ability to effectively correlate social media accounts to locate a missing child. Beginning only with the teenager's name and photo, I used Google and username search methods to locate two Instagram accounts and a Facebook account with matching profile images. Luckily, no profile was set to private, so I was able to view their entire friends' list, post history, and any media associated with the accounts. After gathering the information from these apparently unused accounts, I turned to the user's friends' list. Scrolling through the list of friends on the subject's Instagram profiles, I noticed an account that seemed unrelated, but upon closer inspection, the profile picture matched the other three accounts. This fourth account appeared to be kept up-to-date and had selfies not found on the other accounts.

Because the subject was of school age, much of the media that was being posted featured the school in the background, so it was easy to geolocate the exact school based on the building. However, one photo taken was a selfie

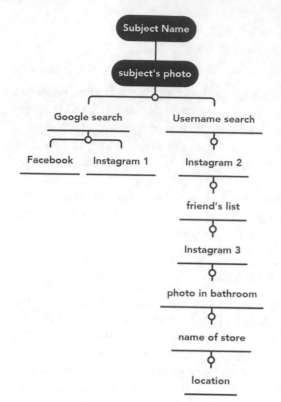

Figure 6.2: Pivot chart stemming from a subject's name into social media

of the subject standing in front of a public bathroom mirror, and reflected in the mirror behind them was a towel dispenser. Zooming in, the towel dispenser had words on it that appeared to be a brand name or store name. Digging deeper, we determined the words were in fact the name of a store, which ended up being a block from the subject's school. Since this bathroom photo was the last one posted to the account, it was the last evidence of the subject's location (see Figure 6.2).

When correlating user social media accounts, I typically focus my efforts on three main things.

- Profiles on the user's friends or follows that share the same username
- Profiles on the user's friends or follows that share the same profile photo
- Profiles that consistently react to the user's images or posts

The reason these three concepts are a good place to start is that they're all indicators that users are following and interacting with themselves. One trick when searching the friends and followers list on Instagram is to scroll to the bottom of the list and then run the browser extension Instant Data Scraper[1] to pull all the friends and followers into a `.csv` file. Not only will this allow us to search through the list more efficiently, but then we also retain documentation of our findings.

A 2020 case where the FBI in Philadelphia was able to track down a suspect accused of setting a police car on fire during the George Floyd[2] protests stands as another example of how social media account associations can uncover a subject and why OPSEC is important.[3]

---

[1] https://chrome.google.com/webstore/detail/instant-data-scraper/ofaokhiedipichpaobibbnahnkdoiiah?hl=en-US.
[2] www.nytimes.com/2020/05/31/us/george-floyd-investigation.html.
[3] www.businessinsider.com/fbi-uses-instagram-etsy-linkedin-to-find-george-floyd-protester-2020-6.

Footage from helicopter news cameras filming the protests caught video of a woman setting a police car on fire. To track down the subject, the FBI poured through Instagram and Vimeo and finally came across a peace sign tattoo on her right forearm. Other photos of the subject revealed the front of her T-shirt, which read "Keep the immigrants. Deport the racists." Using this specific saying, investigators were able to determine this shirt was sold only in a single Etsy shop.

The FBI browsed the Etsy store page until they found a review by the subject that was left for the shop, and the reviewer's profile indicated she was in Philadelphia. Using Google, they were able to correlate the subject's username to her Poshmark[4] account, which unearthed yet another username, lore-elizabeth. Googling the lore-elizabeth username ultimately led them to the subject's LinkedIn profile, which revealed she owned a massage studio. The Massage Studio website had video of the subject, which exposed her peace sign tattoo and confirmed her identity (see Figure 6.3).

This case is a great example of how important it is for analysts to understand the associations between accounts in their cases and the interactions, however small, that they have with other users.

Subject Associations and Interactions on Social Media

Who users interact with and *how* they interact is a huge part of social media analysis and can be an effective way to develop a profile on a subject. We can gain valuable knowledge by digging deeper into how subjects communicate with others through posts, comments, likes, and reactions.

Who Is Your Subject Associated and Interacting With?

The "who" in the case of social media is what friends, family, and followers the user interacts with. An interaction might be in the form of a comment, like, reaction, followback, GIF, etc. Determining who is connected to our subjects often means a deep dive and manual analysis of social media sites. Typically, when I am developing associations, I make a list of all social media accounts belonging to the subject and systematically make the connections to decipher who is a friend, family, best friend, or possibly enemy. To understand and visualize the connections between individuals, we can use an association matrix or a link analysis chart.

An association matrix is a method used by U.S. intelligence to show the connections between people.[5] In the following matrix we can see the black dots represent known associates, and white dots represent suspected associates. When the matrix is filled out with the connections we make while analyzing

---

[4] https://poshmark.com.
[5] https://publicintelligence.net/us-army-intelligence-analysis.

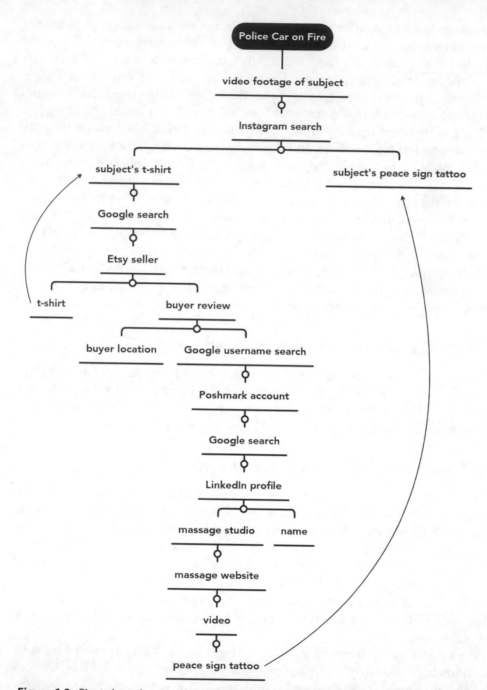

Figure 6.3: Pivot chart showing how information identified the subject in the police car case

social media accounts, we should be able to ascertain who the key people are in the group based on the number of associations (see Figure 6.4).

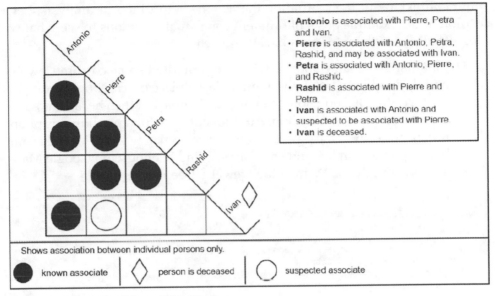

- **Antonio** is associated with Pierre, Petra and Ivan.
- **Pierre** is associated with Antonio, Petra, Rashid, and may be associated with Ivan.
- **Petra** is associated with Antonio, Pierre, and Rashid.
- **Rashid** is associated with Pierre and Petra.
- **Ivan** is associated with Antonio and suspected to be associated with Pierre.
- **Ivan** is deceased.

Shows association between individual persons only.

known associate   person is deceased   suspected associate

Figure 6.4: Example of Association Matrix

Another way to visualize this matrix is through a link analysis chart. Link analysis charts are typically made using i2, Maltego, mind maps, or any platform that allows the linking of ideas. Figure 6.5 shows an example of the data from the association matrix visualized within a mind map. It becomes much easier to analyze based on the strength of the connections between individuals when we can see it visually. Again, this is a manual process of making connections. However, there are advanced methods for generating social media associations, which we will touch on later in the chapter.

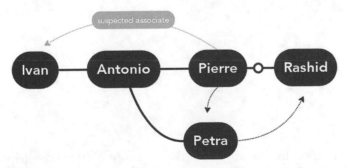

Figure 6.5: Chart visualizing the data from the association matrix

How Is Your Subject Interacting?

A subject's posts can reveal a lot about their lives, and sometimes we can even infer context about their situation that can be helpful to our analysis. Let's explore three example posts of different contextual situations to see what we could pull out of them for our OSINT research.

1. Jonathan Fakename and his wife have inherited some costume jewelry and decided to sell it on the Tampa Marketplace on Facebook. From this post we already know Jonathan lives in Tampa, but then he also provides cross streets for meeting him. Additionally, Jonathan provides his phone number directly in the post. If I were a thief, I can now locate Mr. Fakename by his phone number and cross streets, find his house on Google Maps, and potentially rob them of their jewelry (see Figure 6.6).

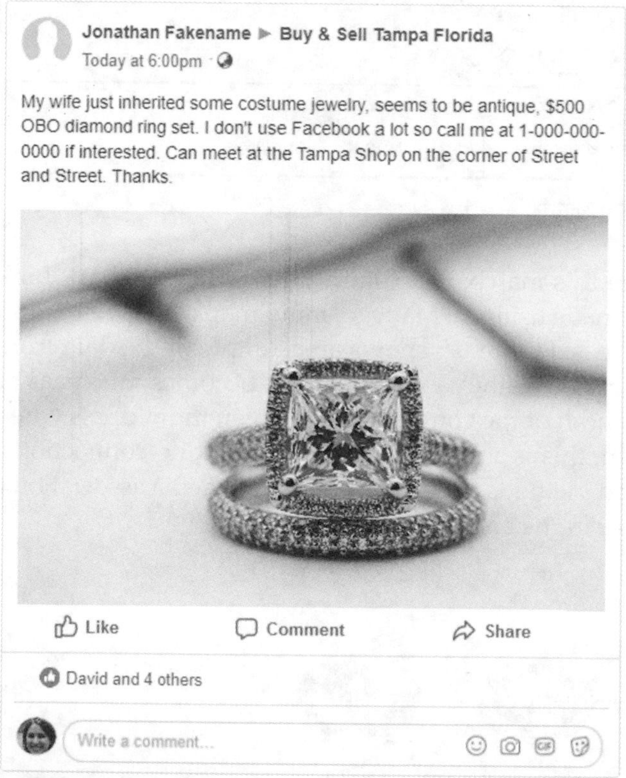

Figure 6.6: Fake scenario 1

2. Sarah Fakename posts on Instagram about the first day of her work trip going great. She has her location data hidden, but a reverse image search

shows she is in DC right outside of FBI headquarters. The clock in the photo also shows it is 3:15, so with the added context of knowing her day just ended, we can deduce that she may have just gotten out of work and came out of headquarters to snap a picture (see Figure 6.7).

Figure 6.7: Fake scenario 2

3. Chris Fakename posts frequently on a Facebook group for 3D printing. In this post he has uploaded an image of what appears to be a 3D-printed gun with some questions about the print failing. Within the comments section, Chris tells another user he has already printed 20 3D guns. To add context to this group interaction, looking at Chris's personal Facebook page shows that he is not sleeping well and obviously having trouble at work. Taking all of these factors into account, Chris may be a risk to himself or others (see Figures 6.8 and 6.9).

Figure 6.8: Fake scenario 3

Figure 6.9: Fake scenario (continued)

User Media and Metadata

Metadata is a small bit of data that gets attached to a social media post along with any shared images and video. Metadata itself can be described very plainly as data that provides information about other data. What this means is that every time a user makes a post, depending on their personal privacy settings, the platform receives metadata providing information about the user's location, date, time of posting, and device used. Anyone who frequently uses social media has probably come across metadata, possibly without even realizing it. In this Twitter post, the metadata is displayed at the bottom and shows the time, date, and device used to upload the content (see Figure 6.10).

Figure 6.10: Metadata included in the post

It used to be that analysts could analyze the images and videos that were posted with free forensic tools to get specific information about the user and their device. Fortunately, many platforms now strip out this data to protect the user's privacy. To gain an understanding of what basic metadata, such as device type, can tell us, let's look at this tweet on the following page from then President Donald Trump refuting his personal iPhone usage for Twitter (see Figure 6.11).

The reasoning behind the uproar over his personal iPhone usage, reported by Politico,[6] the New York Times,[7] and CNN[8] that year, is the very real possibility that using an unsecured personal phone is a national security issue. Imagine the panic the Secret Service would have endured if the metadata had captured and displayed his location.

Users oversharing on social media is obviously great for analysis but not great for users. Some users are beginning to understand the ramifications of oversharing and have made efforts to set their accounts to private, turn off sharing of data, or completely delete their accounts. Other users have taken to developing manipulation and obfuscation techniques.

---

[6] www.politico.com/story/2018/05/21/
trump-phone-security-risk-hackers-601903.
[7] www.nytimes.com/2018/10/24/us/politics/trump-phone-security.html.
[8] www.cnn.com/2018/04/23/politics/donald-trump-cell-phone/index
.html.

Figure 6.11: Twitter, Inc./`https://twitter.com/ByKellyCohen/`last accessed Feb 16, 2022.

The Shmoocon[9] conference in Washington D.C. in 2020 had an interesting talk on manipulating social media data called "Teen Hacks for Obfuscating Identity on Social Media."[10] Samantha Mosely, A Girls Who Code instructor, and her father, Russell, talked about how a group of teenagers devised methods to confuse social media algorithms to obfuscate their locations and identities.

The process involved each teenager in the group, based in different locations, owning multiple Instagram accounts. The accounts were then shared among the group when the owner resets the password and sends the password reset link to the next teenager to rotate accounts. By using reset links, the owner of the account maintains control and can log everyone else out of the account and retake ownership if locations and identities are compromised or if content is inappropriate. The intent behind rotating accounts across, and even outside, the country is to confuse the algorithms that track user location.

If User 1 wants to post a selfie while at the beach, she would send the photo to User 2 in the group using an outside source such as email or chat message. A posting time and caption would be agreed upon by Users 1 and 2, and then User 2 posts the photo as decided. Through this sophisticated cooperative obfuscation method of posting photos and liking content from various locations, the Instagram algorithm becomes disoriented. The group verified the algorithm's confusion by looking at the targeted ads each user account was receiving, which matched the supposed location versus the legitimate one.

This talk serves as a great example of why we must vet all the information we gather, especially on social media. Adversaries may use similar tactics to hide their true identities or develop misleading profiles and content to throw us off their trail.

---

[9] `https://shmoocon.org`.
[10] `www.youtube.com/watch?v=WTCBEimhXMM`.

Social Media Pivots at a Glance

Below are some examples of pivots that can be made from social media data.

User

- Alias
- Name
- Username
- Birthdate
- Employer
- Email
- Address
- Hometown
- Education

Posts

- Mentions of frequented locations
- Mentions of life changes, relationship, pregnancy, rehab, etc.
- Tagged people that my subject could be hanging out with
- Indications of stress, family problems, addiction, etc.
- Links to other SM accounts, TikTok, Snapchat, YT, cashapp
- People who liked/commented the most (they could be good friends and know where the subject is located)
- Check-ins/tagged locations
- Emojis indicating code (gangs, trafficking, exploitation)
- Code words (gangs, trafficking, exploitation)
- Medical issues
- Device

Media

- Notable things in appearance, moles, freckles, piercings, tattoos
- Changes in appearance, hair color change, new tattoo, new piercing, weight change
- Who is appearing in photos/videos with the subject
- Whether the photos/videos indicate a location
- Is there anything notable like gang signs, outfit color choice, drug use, etc.
- Car make/model

Once we have identified social media accounts of interest, how can we effectively keep an eye on the content they post and interact with? Through continuously monitoring communities of social media accounts, we can gain a deeper understanding of their behaviors, patterns, and risk.

6.2   Continuous Community Monitoring

In situations where our case involves researching a group of individuals or a community online, we can use *continuous community monitoring techniques*. Through consistently and continuously observing the interactions within communities, we can potentially gather real-time insight into a group's thoughts, movements, organization, and plans.

The following are recent examples of online communities that have been the focus of ongoing monitoring by analysts, journalists, and the authorities:

- Alt-right and militia groups
- Pro-Russian groups
- Hacker/ransomware groups
- Q-Anon groups
- Terrorists/extremist groups
- Child exploitation groups

When we talk about continuously monitoring communities, what we are referring to is the act of observing, either manually or with tools, the interactions and communication within a public or private group space. The point of monitoring them is to passively gain an understanding of the group's modus operandi and to be aware of potential new information or threats. For instance, a journalist may create a sock account and get invited to a known violent hate group's telegram channel to gather information and write an article on how the group functions internally. On the other hand, an OSINT analyst might get invited to the same group based on a law enforcement tip to determine where the group plans to start a riot.

Methods for the Continuous Monitoring of a Group

The first step to monitoring a community is to locate where they communicate. Some of the most used platforms for communities are Facebook, Telegram, Reddit, 4chan, 8kun, and Discord. Communities decide how to let new members join, whether through invitation or answering challenge questions, or be completely open to the public. For privacy reasons, many community groups are abandoning public forums in lieu of more privacy-conscious platforms like Telegram and in some cases even developing their own "alt-tech" platforms like Gab and Parler. Finding these communities is sometimes as easy as Googling their name and finding a direct link, but other times the search requires some trial and error.

NOTE   How far we can go to infiltrate a private social media group is a decision for your stakeholders. Make sure to also get approval ahead of creating and using any sock puppet accounts to join groups and communities. Also, as a reminder, an OSINT analyst within these communities does not interact with other members. That said, some communities have interaction requirements to maintain membership that would need to be approved for legality before attempting.

One example of continuous community monitoring in action is the analysis immediately after the January 6 Capitol riot. When the Capitol was stormed, many rioters filmed the event or took photos of their actions inside the Capitol. The FBI then released images of individuals they had not yet identified from inside the building. Immediately amateur web sleuths and OSINT analysts took up the cause, with Netherlands-based investigative journalism group Bellingcat starting to link images through OSINT and image analysis techniques.

Analysts were infiltrating and analyzing alt-right and U.S. militia social media groups for mentions of involvement or connections to the event. Intelligence X rapidly archived social media materials by scraping the Web, and Bellingcat developed an Excel spreadsheet to begin linking and tracking items they saw in photographs and videos from that day like zip-ties.[11] Within days the group had detailed Air Force Veteran and capitol rioter Ashli Babbit's transition from Obama supporter to Trump before ultimately attending and participating in the violent insurrection where she was killed.

Bertram Hill,[12] an OSINT analyst with BBC Africa Eye, told GIJN that an effective monitoring plan is necessary to know what accounts are important during an event, who will be at the event, and who is a bad actor. He also takes a similar approach to analysis as I do and uses TweetDeck to maintain columns specifically for the event to track key words, users, hashtags, etc. Figure 6.12 shows an example of the kind of pivots we could expect from a social community like Telegram.

Facebook Groups

Facebook groups are communities within Facebook that can be public or private. If a group is set to private, the user needs to request access from the group owner to see any member names or shared content within the group. If your stakeholder has approved the use of sock accounts, we can tailor a sock account to match

---

[11] https://gijn.org/2021/01/15/
how-open-source-experts-identified-the-us-capitol-rioters.
[12] https://twitter.com/bertram_hill1?lang=en.

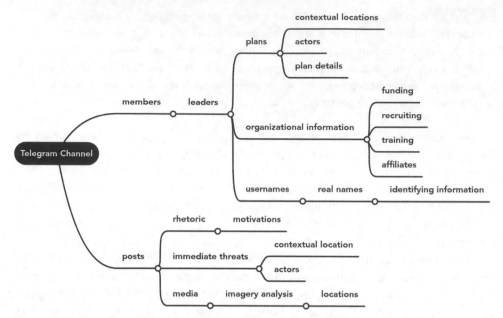

Figure 6.12: Pivot chart illustrating pivots starting from a telegram channel

the expected user who would join the group and request access answering any questions as though we were the target audience. Once the owner approves, we will be granted access to the group's membership and content including media and posts.

Finding Facebook groups can be done through searching Facebook for a specific topic or by querying Google with the topic or keywords followed by "site:

"site:facebook.com/groups."

Telegram Channels

Telegram is a privacy-focused, end-to-end, encrypted cloud-based messaging service. This means that when you send messages in secret mode, they are encrypted through the journey from you to another user. Because of the added security, it has become a meeting place for illicit actors and hate groups. Telegram channels are groups where admins can broadcast one-way messaging to their subscribers. Channels are automatically private on creation, but admins can set their channels to private in the settings. The content of public Telegram channels is indexed by search engines and viewable without an account. Telegram channels allow the sending of all large file types including photos, audio, and video including live streaming.

Finding Telegram channels can be done through a keyword search directly within Telegram, through various online repositories of channels, or by locating a direct link. Here are some examples of Telegram channels we might look into as an analyst:

- Hacker communities used to discuss cyber-attacks, share leaks, and plan future attacks
- White supremacist communities for "online activism"
- Pro-Kremlin communities for spreading Russian propaganda on the Ukraine invasion
- Cyber financial crime communities used for selling stolen financial accounts

The two methods I commonly use for finding the Telegram channels for specific groups of interest are first finding the admin's social media accounts and searching group catalogs. Many of the problematic groups that develop Telegram channels like hacker groups and alt-right communities want their message and actions to be noticed, which means the admins and members will share links to their channels on their social media bios and posts (see Figure 6.13).

Figure 6.13: Telegram / `https://t.me/lemonfortea` / last accessed 15, Februaury 2023, an investment telegram channel

Second, we can search using the site `TGStat.com`,[13] which offers a groups catalog for several foreign countries (see Figure 6.14). Each catalog page lists top Telegram channels by category, and TGStat provides stats and a posts feed for viewing open channels.

---

[13] `https://tgstat.com`.

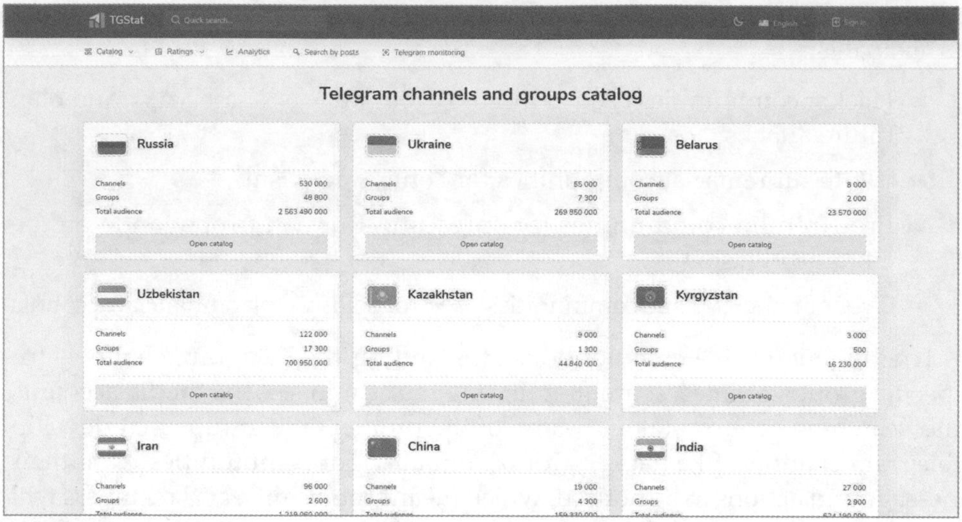

Figure 6.14: TGStat

Just as with Facebook groups, to gain entry to private Telegram channels, it may be necessary to develop a sock account with no connection to yourself. The odds of being accepted into a private group are more in our favor if we tailor our sock Telegram accounts for the specific group of interest. Joining channels can be done either on a PC or on an app, so this allows freedom to utilize VMs or mobile emulators to further reduce attribution.

Reddit

Reddit is a collection of forums, on every topic imaginable, called *subreddits*. Users can create threads to share content, links, images, videos, or comment. Threads on Reddit are promoted or demoted based on users voting on individual threads. Reddit features many wholesome subreddits like r/baking, r/aww, and r/stickerexhangeclub, but like any large forum, it has had its fair share of controversies. Some of the more toxic banned subreddits include the following:

- r/beatingwomen
- r/braincels (involuntary celibate or incel)
- r/jailbait
- r/fatpeoplehate
- r/greatawakening (QAnon)
- r/thefappening (stolen celebrity nudes)

Reddit is free to use but does require registration to the site; it is common for users to create additional anonymous accounts when posting personal or embarrassing information. Reddit threads remain available if the subreddit and original poster remain active. There are tools that can aid in the analysis of Reddit like OSINT Combine's Reddit Post Analyzer,[14] which analyzes based on a subreddit thread URL and returns post responses, sentiment of the responses, and an analysis of the replies to each response that can all be downloaded in several document formats (see Figure 6.15).

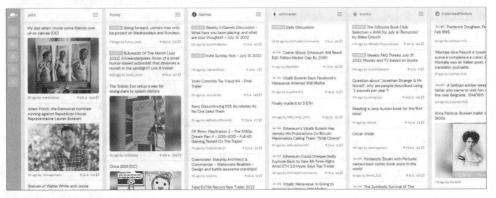

Figure 6.15: OSINT Combine's Reddit Post Analyzer

For ongoing monitoring, a good tool to use is Reditr,[15] which works like a TweetDeck and makes it easy for us to curate a feed based on our analysis needs (see Figure 6.16).

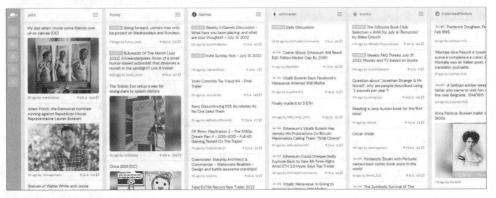

Figure 6.16: Reditr

---

[14] www.osintcombine.com/reddit-post-analyser.
[15] http://reditr.com.

4chan and 8kun

4chan is an anonymous image-based bulletin board "fringe community" site that features a wide variety of topics but has become synonymous with misogyny and the alt-right (see Figure 6.17). Because the site does not allow any post to have more than 10 pages at a time, threads are often available for only a few hours or days before expiring or being removed.

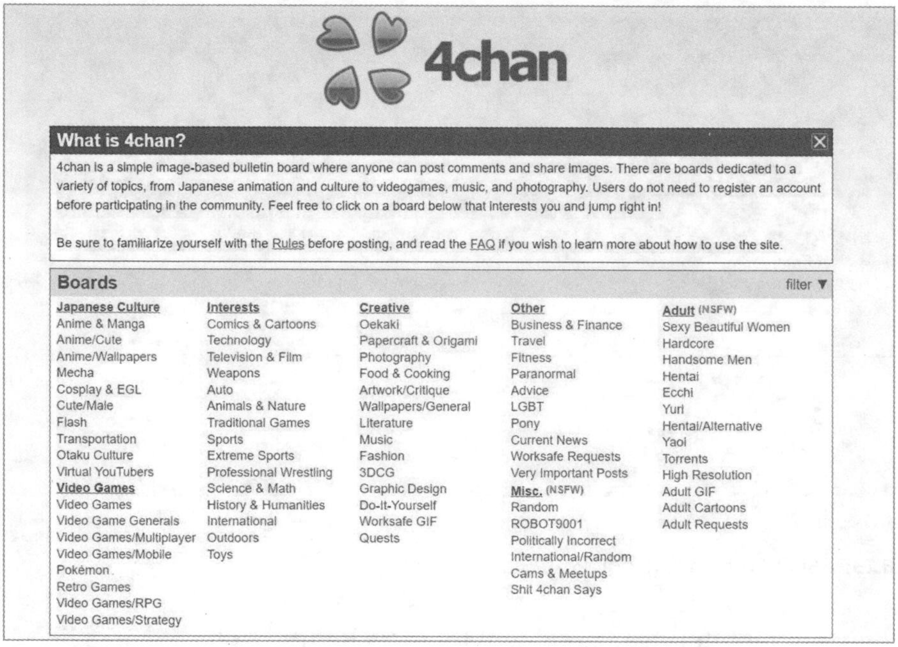

Figure 6.17: 4chan

The anonymity offered by 4chan not requiring an account to post and the lack of a content filter means a range of toxic material gets posted. Interestingly, a University of Alabama study showed that fringe communities like Reddit and 4chan have a large influence on the flow of information to more mainstream sites like Twitter, meaning misinformation and disinformation is often traced back to the users on fringe platforms (see Figure 6.18).[16]

8kun, formerly 8chan, is like 4chan but is somehow even less moderated. The former site was shut down in 2019 when a gunman in El Paso shot and killed 22 people after uploading his manifesto to 8chan. 8kun, a relaunch of 8chan, carries the torch and remains a platform for troubling violent extremism and illegal material.

---

[16] www.uab.edu/news/research/item/8840-study-says-fringe-communities-on-reddit-4chan-influence-flow-of-alternative-news-to-twitter.

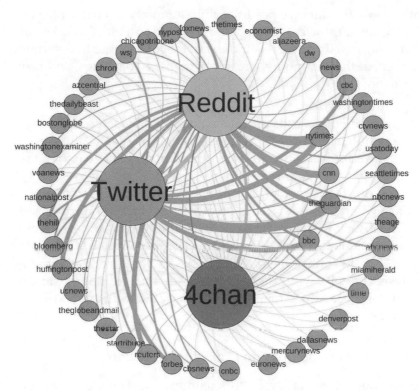

Figure 6.18: UAB photo showing how main media sources connect to the three social media sources

Because the chans are anonymous, any user can make a nonattributable sock account to browse threads. However, the threads disappear quickly, so it is imperative to track and log our findings as soon as we come across something.

I Joined a Community, Now What?

When an analyst joins a community with the intent of monitoring them over time, there are some important things to consider:

OPSEC
It is important to maintain the OPSEC standards we developed for our analysis back in the Planning and Requirements phase of the intelligence life cycle. Depending on the technical savvy of the community being analyzed, poor OPSEC could result in doxxing and personal safety concerns.

Focus on the Goal
The purpose for monitoring an online community should be hashed out in the Planning and Requirements phase. When observing a community, we

should collect only the data we need to fulfill our analysis goal. Collecting "everything" is not an efficient method and will lead to a lot of unnecessary information being saved and stored. If the goal for collection is to determine who the leaders of the community are, focus on posts, hashtags, and users that lead to an answer.

The Strategy for Collection

Again, the strategy and methods for collection should be determined in the Planning and Requirements phase prior to ingesting any data. At that point, we would decide what platforms to focus our efforts on, the length of time we will collect, and the tools and note-taking methods we will use.

For example, if our focus is to observe pro-Kremlin communications on social media, we may choose to focus on Telegram channels, forums, and Facebook. The observation will last 3 months with the goal of determining any main accounts distributing pro-Kremlin content regularly. The plan is to use OneNote to collect information with the final product being an i2 link analysis chart showing the connections to and from the users. Be sure to outline a process for archiving evidence and securing text-based communications.

I Am Unable to Join a Community, Can I Still Monitor Them?

There will be situations where analysts work within a social networking group that is limited due to legal privacy reasons. Don't give up just yet; there are still free ways to collect information about groups from the outside. Sometimes it is possible to capture data through links posted by members of the community to other sites by using a search engine to run a targeted query on the community or its members. Another possibility for finding information outside of a closed group is to use the Internet Archive's Wayback Machine.[17]

The *Internet Archive* is a nonprofit creating an archive of the Internet and offering free access to historical snapshots of public content including web pages and social media posts that are then accessed through what they call the Wayback Machine. Figure 6.19 shows the dates that my Twitter page was archived by the Wayback Machine; if I had deleted any tweets after the site had been archived, they would still appear here.

---

[17] Internet Archive / `https://archive.org/` last accessed February 15, 2023.

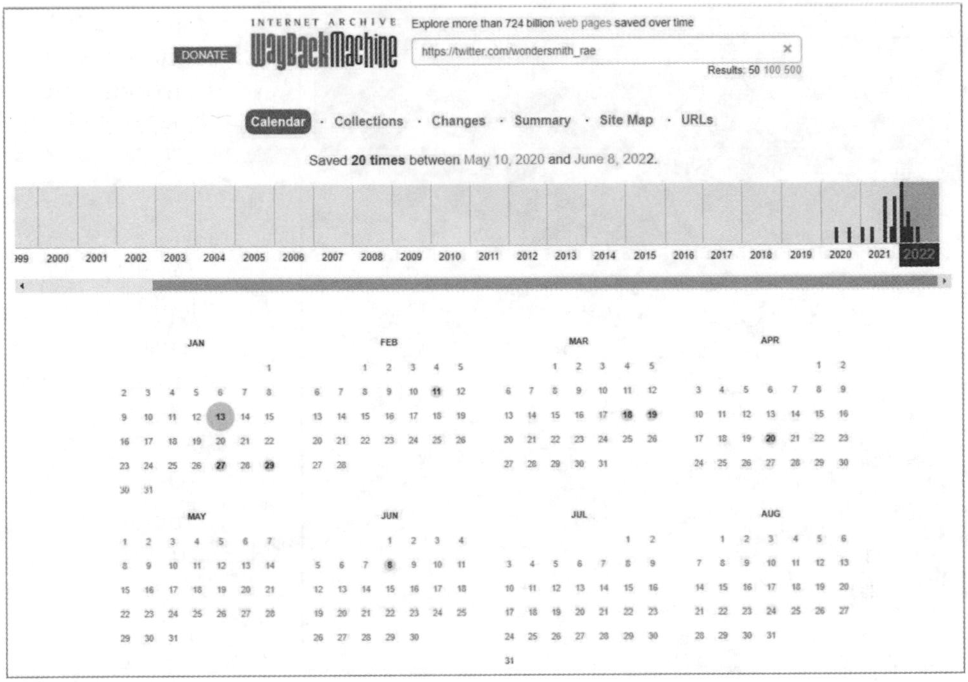

Figure 6.19: Wayback Machine

6.3   Image and Video Analysis

Imagery analysis is the process of thoroughly examining an image and extracting important information and then interpreting that information in relation to the objects, terrain, structures, and situations within. The analysis of imagery in the form of photos and video can provide a great deal of beneficial information to an OSINT analysis. Using imagery analysis techniques, it may be possible to determine the location where the image was taken and provide information about the subject's actions or possessions. We can use imagery to broaden the pivoting possibilities within our analysis to create a clearer picture of our subject. We will learn various techniques for attributing a photo to an owner and other accounts, geolocation, and how to decipher metadata. First, we must learn how to properly analyze an image or video.

How to Look at an Image/Video

A friend of mine and excellent OSINT and geolocation analyst, Benjamin Strick,[18] taught me some invaluable techniques for how to properly look at an image and gather information (see Figures 6.20-6.23). He says to focus on five main areas.

---

[18] https://benjaminstrick.com.

Figure 6.20: Imagery Analysis Example 1[19]

- Context
- Foreground
- Background
- Map markings
- Trial and error

Figure 6.22: Imagery Analysis Example 3

Figure 6.21: Imagery Analysis Example 2

Figure 6.23: Imagery Analysis Example 4

[19] Tilman / https://twitter.com/twone2/status/1526899966035247104/ photo/1 / last accessed 15 February 2023.

Context
Do we know the meaning behind the photo? Does anything in the image provide obvious context for where it might have been taken?

Foreground
This is what falls in the front of an image closest to the viewer.

Background
This is what falls in the back of an image farthest from the viewer.

Map Markings
These are things in an image that will directly tell you where you are or could be used to orient yourself in satellite images taken from above.

- Billboards
- Street signs
- Unique roof structures
- Waterways

Using the technique of "seeing" an image versus just looking at it allows us to remain open to what we might find and prevent bias or expectations from tarnishing our analysis. Image analysis like this can be used in many different ways in OSINT.

One way image analysis techniques can be employed for the greater good is through Europol's Trace an Object program. The objects posted are from the background of an image of sexually explicit material involving minors where the case hasn't been solved, and they are hoping someone recognizes a piece of clothing or item in each photo. For all the images shown in Figure 6.24, every other analysis avenue has already been examined, and now they are asking the public for help in determining where these objects come from. This type of analysis can prove to be difficult because to protect the identities of the exploited, they remove any identifying parts of the image and leave the item in question. According to their site, more than 27,000 tips have been sent in, and 23 children have been removed from harm.[20] Because of the success of this program, Australia has also implemented a trace-an-object website.[21]

Being able to spot context clues and properly analyze imagery are the foundational techniques to all forms of image analysis. The process of analyzing imagery can be painstaking, but sometimes it can be as easy as searching the image in a search engine and letting it do the work to find the source.

---

[20] `www.europol.europa.eu/stopchildabuse`.
[21] Commonwealth of Australia / `www.accce.gov.au/what-we-do/trace-an-object/` last accessed Feb 16, 2022.

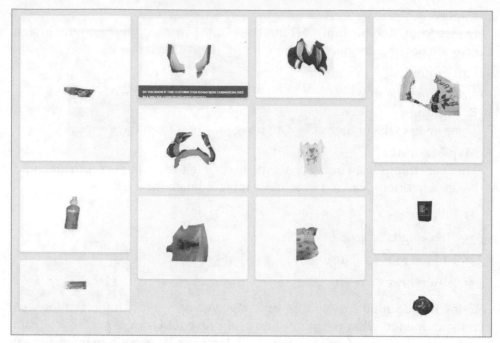

Figure 6.24: Australia's trace-an-object website

Reverse Image Searching

Reverse image searching or using an image as a search query within a search engine to return all similar photos is one of those tricks that almost always comes in handy during analysis. The process is simple enough. We go to our search engine of choice (the top picks are Google, Bing, and Yandex) and click their images page. The images page should have a box that allows you to copy/paste a URL or upload a photo directly from your device to search. What returns are all the images that the search engine feels are like your queried image. This is the basic concept of reverse image searching, and it can be applied in various scenarios to gain a deeper understanding of the subject and additional accounts they hold.

> **Scenario 1:** You find a partial logo with a distinctive flourish on it but can't make out the full business name. Reverse image search the logo and see if it appears in full anywhere else online.

> **Scenario 2:** You have a social media profile photo of your subject showing a partial tattoo. Reverse image search the picture to find other social media images that have not been cropped.

I worked a case like Scenario 1 in which I was seeking to confirm the location of a known criminal but the only information that I had to go on was a rather generic and blurry sports team logo in the background of an image and a vague idea of what state they were located in. Using a combination of Google dorking the sport/state and reverse image searches, I systematically waded through page after page of sports logos until finally hitting on the exact logo in the background of a fundraiser photo. I was able to pass the new information onto the team lead who was in contact with law enforcement.

There are some inherent issues with reverse image searching to be aware of, however. *Reverse searching* can be an exercise of patience as it is sometimes necessary to scroll through hundreds of images before finding one that matches. Additionally, it does not work efficiently on all social media sites and can require a bit of trial and error with Twitter, Instagram, and Facebook imagery.

If an image that looks like our subject is found but no further context exists, we might be left asking ourselves "Is this really the same person?" We may have some luck visually comparing imagery and attempting to find facial characteristics that match such as hairlines, moles, and face shape. Another option is to double-check with a facial recognition tool. Facial recognition can also be spotty at best, but it might provide enough confidence to your image to attribute it appropriately.

Another technique we can use on images and video to uncover details and often geographically locate the origin is imaged-based geolocation.

Image-Based Geolocation

It is possible in many instances to determine the location a photo or video was taken using learned analysis techniques and critical thinking. This practice of identifying the geographical location from details within media is called *geolocation*. Geolocation relies on the image analysis techniques we learned, looking at landmarks, skylines, shadows, foliage, signs, and buildings, to figure out where in the world the photo was taken. This kind of geolocation is often used to determine the location of an event such as a crime. Let's use our image analysis skills to solve some imagery puzzles (see Figure 6.25).

Image Analysis

What is the context?
We have no context for this image and no obvious location cues.

What is in the foreground?

- A small bridge that looks to be next to a road.
- A sidewalk.
- A metal railing.
- Slow moving small body of water, possibly river.

Figure 6.25: `https://twitter.com/bayer_julia/status/`
`1513612215143837700?s=20`

- Brick buildings with tile roofing.
- A cathedral on the left.
- Vehicles on either side of the water.
- Antique-looking lamps along the road.

What is in the background?

- Another small bridge connecting the sides of the waterway.
- The water curves to the right beyond the bridge.
- Tents sent up beyond the bridge.
- A clock tower and cathedral right of center.

Are there any map markings?

- A flag on the first building in the left foreground.
- Blurry road signs.
- What appears to be an Italian flag on a Light-colored building in the right foreground.
- Graffiti along the waterway walls that looks backward.

Geolocation Steps

There are many different methods for geolocating an image, these are my steps based on the information I gleaned in my image analysis research (see Figure 6.26).

Step 1: Reverse image search the entire image. This step showed me several images that looked remarkably similar located in the Province of Pisa, Italy (see Figure 6.26). We still need to know exactly where in Pisa the photo was taken.

Figure 6.26: Krzysztof K / www.tripadvisor.com/LocationPhotoDirectLink-g187899-i418773593-Pisa_Province_of_Pisa_Tuscany.html/Feb 16, 2022.

Step 2: Reverse image search just the background bridge, clock tower, and cathedral. Using the Bing Visual Search I cropped the image and searched just these landmarks. The query returned the right clock tower but on the opposite side of the bridge (see Figure 6.27). One of the links says the bridge is called "Ponte di Mezzo" or middle bridge.

Step 3: Use Google Maps and Street View to find the location. When we search Ponti di Mezzo in Google Maps, we see two bridges on either side (see Figure 6.28). One of those bridges is the correct location of this photo.

Step 4: Dropping the pegman onto the far right bridge on Google Street View shows us the correct location, but as you can see, the original image was reversed (see Figure 6.29)! That explains the backward-looking graffiti.

Solution: Ponte della Fortezza Pisa, Tuscany

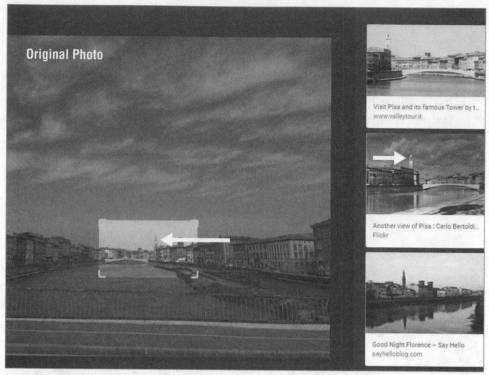

Figure 6.27: Bing visual search

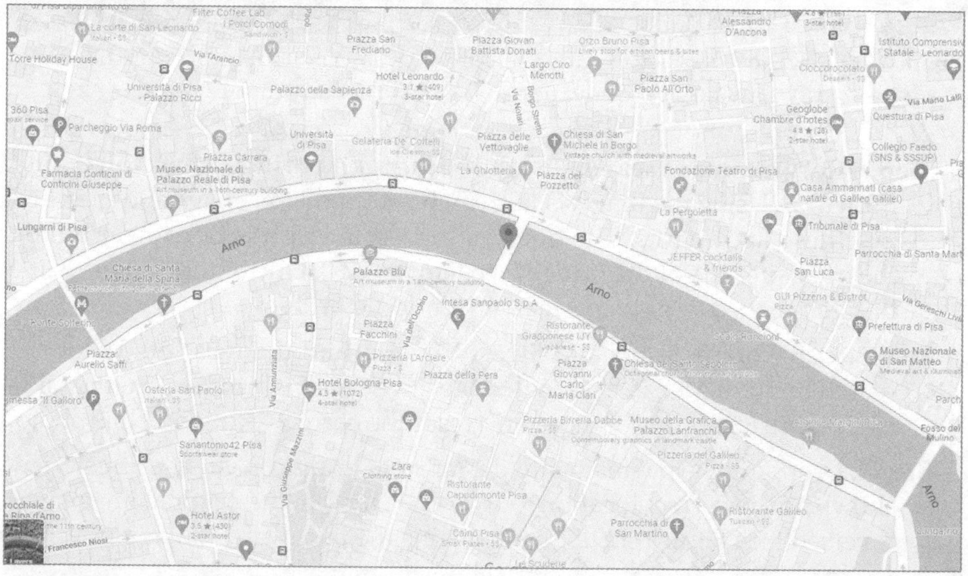

Figure 6.28: Google Maps

Figure 6.29: Google Street View

Image Analysis

What is the context?

A child exploitation photo was posted to a forum. This intersection was in the background of the photo, and we were requested to find the exact location (see Figure 6.30).

Figure 6.30: Google Street View

What is in the foreground?

- A paved road.
- A dirt or mixed material sidewalk.
- Concrete blocks lining the sidewalk.

- Words on the road in front of the stop sign possibly say "stop" in English.
- Words past the stop sign appear to be in English and possibly say "Start EWL."
- Palm trees.
- A metal fence with boulders inside and in the back there is some kind of animal, maybe a goat.
- Buildings/houses.
- Colored dirt.

What is in the background?

- Desert with a road sign on the right.
- Residential on the left side and continues on with white housing.

Are there any map markings?

- Telephone pole with green sign reading "Staan op! Registreer en stem, vf plus."
- Beside the stop sign a road sign that says "Plein st" or "Plan st."

Geolocation Steps

There are many different methods for geolocating an image; these are my steps based on the information I gleaned in my image analysis research.

Step 1: Search text from large sign on telephone pole. The text on this sign looks Dutch to me, and since the environment looks hot and desert-like, I can deduce this may be South Africa. South Africans speak Afrikaans, which is based on the Dutch language. I want to confirm my assumptions, so I run the text from the signs in Google (see Figure 6.31).

The query resulted in a Facebook page for VF Plus written in Afrikaans. The logo on the sign matches the logo on this advertisement about the prevention of an education law called the Bela Bill. A quick Google search of "Bella Bill" says it is a bill to propose changes to the South Africa Schools Act.

Step 2: Search street name plus South Africa. I didn't even finish the query before Google told me Plein Street was in Cape Town, South Africa (see Figure 6.32).

Step 3: Verify the location in Google Maps. Remember, Plein Street was the cross street in our image, so we need to find the corner. Lucky for us, Plein Street is not that long, so we can drop the little map guy on and move up the street until we find the exact location. After digging around this road, I realize there is more than one Plein Street (see Figure 6.33).

Figure 6.31: `www.facebook.com/search/top/`
`?q=Staan%20op!%20Registreer%20en%20stem%2C%20vf%20plus`

Figure 6.32: Google

Figure 6.33: Google Maps

There is also a Plein Street in Northern Cape Town (see Figure 6.34).

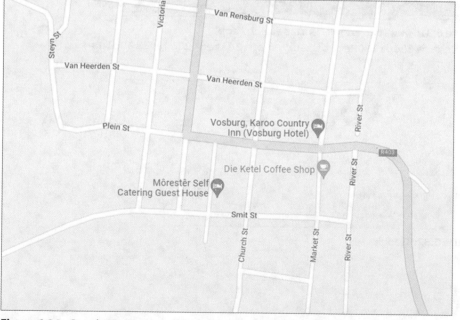

Figure 6.34: Google Maps

And right at the cross streets of Plein and R403 is our location (see Figure 6.35).

Figure 6.35: Google Maps

Solution: Plein Street and R403 Vosberg, Northern Cape Town South Africa

You can see that it is possible to find very precise locations around the globe with even the smallest of details. This tradecraft can be integral to processing imagery from high-stress real-time events that require fast analysis to be relayed to another team on the ground or to a stakeholder to take immediate action.

Image Analysis and Geolocation for Real-Time Events

There may be instances in our work where we must figure out the exact location an event took place. These situations could range from the location of an assault or crime to war crimes or military movements. The difference between typical imagery analysis and geolocation and real-time analysis is the element of time. Situations where real-time analysis and geolocation might be providing ongoing support to someone at the site of the event means that we have to be able to recognize and interpret things very quickly. One such situation where geolocation and image analysis have been integral has been the monitoring of the Russian invasion of Ukraine. The Centre for Information Resilience (CIR) Eyes on Russia[22] team have been monitoring the military movements prior to

---

[22] www.info-res.org.

and during the invasion in February 2022. They often use image analysis techniques to help geolocate specific events happening.[23]

One event they tracked that stands out is when they monitored the Russians building an outpost in Chernobyl's exclusion zone. Investigators noticed in early March that a camp had been set up near the #4 Chernobyl Reactor (see Figure 6.36).

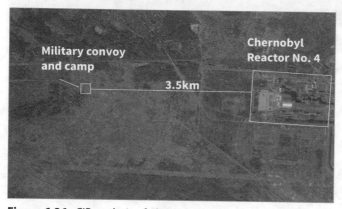

Figure 6.36: CIR analysis of Chernobyl's exclusion zone

Using satellite imagery and drone footage of the camp, CIR could see a large amount of digging and temporary shelters being put in place. Comparing the February 26 imagery to the March 13 imagery shows a distinct difference with structures being built (see Figure 6.37).

Figure 6.37: www.info-res.org/post/digging-in-danger-how-russian-forces-built-an-outpost-in-chernobyl-s-exclusion-zone

---

[23] Centre for Information Resilience / www.info-res.org/post/digging-in-danger-how-russian-forces-built-an-outpost-in-chernobyl-s-exclusion-zone last accessed February 15, 2023.

We now know there was a large fire at the camp near the reactor, and CIR confirmed it using satellite imagery on March 28 (see Figure 6.38).

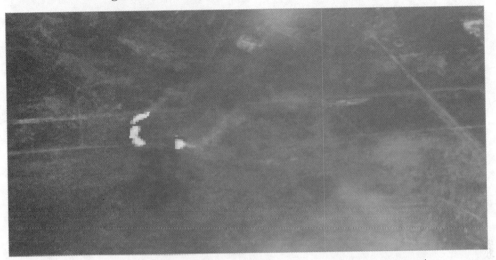

Figure 6.38: `www.info-res.org/post/digging-in-danger-how-russian-forces-built-an-outpost-in-chernobyl-s-exclusion-zone`

CIR points out that due to the camp being so close to reactor #4, there may have been a risk of radiation poisoning. A report from the director of the Institute for Nuclear Power Plant Safety of the National Academy of Sciences of Ukraine claimed that they treated 73 critical injured people.

CIR also noted that Chernobyl was a regular route from Belarus into Northern Ukraine, which they verified through video footage showing a road close to the Russian Camp near reactor #4 (see Figure 6.39).

Figure 6.39: `www.info-res.org/post/digging-in-danger-how-russian-forces-built-an-outpost-in-chernobyl-s-exclusion-zone`

In April, experts in radiation visited the site and reported excess radiation in the areas near the campsite, and a video confirmed that there had been a fire in the area (see Figure 6.40).

They lived right here in this forest and they burned a lot of it

Figure 6.40: `www.info-res.org/post/digging-in-danger-how-russian-forces-built-an-outpost-in-chernobyl-s-exclusion-zone`

Image analysis techniques are not only helpful for geolocation but serve an important purpose in fact-checking information. As false information campaigns gain traction on social media and spread to traditional media outlets, analysts will require the skills to perform verification on all forms of data including photography, digital imagery, video, audio, and text.

6.4   Verification

We all have that relative on social media who is always resharing unbelievable stories like "Elvis Presley's Backup Singers Walk Out on a Concert After He Said They 'Smelled Like Catfish.'"[24] or "Never Pick Up Folded Fentanyl Dollars from the Ground."[25] If you are anything like me, you immediately send them a `Snopes.com`[26] article proving them wrong in hopes that next time they will verify the information before resharing, which they rarely do. The term for the process of fact-checking information to verify the accuracy, credibility, and reliability is *verification*. Content verification is typically used in a research journalism context, but because the spread of false and inaccurate information on the Internet has become so prevalent it often crosses over with our OSINT analysis.

---

[24] `www.snopes.com/fact-check/catfish`.
[25] `www.snopes.com/fact-check/folded-fentanyl-laced-dollar-bills`.
[26] `www.snopes.com`.

As we learned over the last few chapters, there is a lot of public data available across social media platforms that shows us interactions, connections, and personal data about a subject. Unfortunately, not all subjects verify the data they share, which leads to an echo chamber of incorrect information that is taken as fact. If there are enough users parroting the same incorrect information, it can become harmful as we saw happen with COVID information. Many people on the Internet believe the false information they share and are not intending to cause harm; however, some users purposefully spread incorrect and inaccurate information even though it could cause harm.

Misinformation, Disinformation, and Malinformation

Social media can spread and propagate so easily that it is a major source of media manipulation, and we commonly refer to this type of media as being misinformation, disinformation, or malinformation (mis/dis/mal). The following are the descriptions of each type of information and why it is so important in verification (see Figure 6.41).

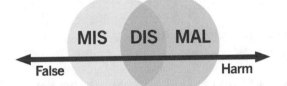

Figure 6.41: Illustration showing the range of mis/dis/mal

Misinformation: Misleading or incorrect information that is not knowingly deceptive
  Example: Your grandmother posting an article about vitamins curing cancer

Disinformation: Misleading or incorrect information that is deliberate
  Example: The mascot for the New Jersey Devils hockey team 'NJ Devil' posting false information about the Philadelphia Flyers mascot 'Gritty' being arrested for lewd acts to start a feud

Malinformation: Information based in reality but is purposefully harmful
  Example: A political party posting a fake story of a Black man assaulting a white woman to ignite hatred

Intentionally misleading people is not a particularly new concept, especially in politics. I always follow the advice of 1990s television hit series *X-Files* lead Fox Mulder: "Trust No One." However, back in the 90s information didn't travel at breakneck speeds across the globe. Now, misinformation can cause damage and real-world panic incredibly quickly. What makes verification so difficult is that much of the misinformation circulating online is actually based on partial truths or previously debunked but recirculating information.

These are some examples of debunked but returning narratives:

- The Pizzagate scandal[27]
- Celebrity deaths
- Vaccine related posts (COVID, autism, etc.)
- 5G-related posts and 5G related to COVID[28]

How Do We Verify If Content Is Mis/Dis/Mal?

The verification of content that might be mis/dis/mal requires a methodical approach to break down the who, what, why, and how. The following are the first questions we should ask ourselves when analyzing information that appears to be incorrect or false:

- Who posted the narrative?
- What is the motive behind the narrative?
- Who benefits from this narrative?
- Can we determine where the narrative originated?
- What behavior are they exhibiting?

Many of the same concepts used for traditional OSINT analysis are relevant and usable for verification. Verification analysis often begin with a single post, narrative, or user that is posting questionable content and the desire or requirement to prove whether it is legitimate.

Is the Content Legit?

Tracking down and verifying the content to determine whether it has any truth can be incredibly difficult and time intensive. The practice often involves scouring the Web to find the very first iteration of a post, news story, or detail within the narrative. As you go, be sure to take a screenshot of all the important data you discover along the way in case you need to go back and look again. Many times, the disinformation is based in some element of truth and is just the illusion of perspective being presented in a damaging way (see Figure 6.42).

---

[27] `www.nytimes.com/2020/06/27/technology/`
`pizzagate-justin-bieber-qanon-tiktok.html`.
[28] `www.snopes.com/fact-check/cov-19-inscribed-on-5g-board`.

Figure 6.42: Reuters/Hannah Mckay

The *Verification Handbook* by Craig Silverman[29] recommends using a site like `archive.org` to digitally archive the content you find and record the URLs in a spreadsheet. As with most OSINT analysis, we are trying to find patterns and links in information, and a spreadsheet will help us make those associations through visualizations. Reverse image searching is another great tactic for tracing back shared memes to find the origin. Once the post is verified as being mis/dis/mal, it's time to figure out why it was shared in the first place.

To determine motive behind a specific narrative, it is necessary to develop the broader context around the post and who posted it. Does the original poster have something to gain by misleading their followers? This gain could be financial, status, political, or even for recognition. Does the poster immediately benefit, or are they part of a bigger organization or movement driving the narrative? Often, we see disseminators of misinformation are just a cog in a larger disinformation campaign and sometimes the posters are not even human.

Spotting a Bot Account or Bot Network

Social media bots are accounts created and automated using AI and Big Data analytics to impersonate real users, and because bots are designed to mimic human behavior, they can be hard to spot. While there are some legitimate uses for bots such as customer service and sales interactions, these automated accounts are often used to spread narratives and influence people's opinions on a large scale. Bots can be developed to perform actions such as liking and reviewing social media posts for clout or monetary gain and spreading misinformation and disinformation as we have seen with the 2016 election and COVID.

---

[29] http://verificationhandbook.com.

In social media research, bots can make attribution even more difficult than normal. Trying to connect, track, and monitor bot networks can quickly get out of hand, and it is essential to organize our data through network analysis charts, spreadsheets, or your note-taking method of choice. One way to quickly spot bot-like behavior on Twitter is through the tool Bot Sentinel,[30] a community project to help fight disinformation and targeted harassment. The Chrome extension uses machine learning to give users a score from 0–100 percent. The higher the number, the more problematic the account. The site `botsentinel .com` has additional tools and trackers for further Twitter analysis. Figure 6.43 shows how the Bot Sentinel extension has added an 89 percent problematic score to this account based on its exhibited behavior.

Figure 6.43: Twitter, Inc. / `https://twitter.com/SoCalTrumpMAGA/` last accessed February 15, 2023.

Inexpensive to buy and easy to create, content amplification and dissemination bots are used to sway public opinion or falsely increase a user's follower count. These types of bots exist to distribute content, hijack hashtags, and harass users. *Hashtag hijacking* occurs when bots are used to push topics to trending lists by repeatedly spamming the platform with hashtags.

When searching for bot accounts, there are common patterns of fraudulent and automated behavior that bot accounts show. *Bot networks (botnets)*, or a collection of bots programmed to perform certain actions or behaviors, can be incredibly large, and creators cut corners because it takes effort and time to create realistic individual profiles for each account (see Figure 6.44).

Many bot accounts are created with cartoon images to avoid inconsistencies when uploading a random collection of photos to each profile. The usernames are created automatically and usually have the same number of characters and the same creation dates as all the bots created at the same time. The number of tweets can also be an indicator because bots usually have a few followers and

---

[30] `https://botsentinel.com`.

Figure 6.44: Bot account analyzed with Twitonomy shows 243 tweets per day average.

make many tweets in a short period of time. In addition, bots follow each other and amplify each other's messages, making it easier to identify the bot network by analyzing tweet patterns and user retweets.

Bots are used frequently in larger manipulation campaigns to sway public opinion or spread disinformation quickly and broadly across communities. These targeted disinformation campaigns are preplanned and seeded across many social media platforms and the greater Internet being constantly adapted and adjusted to influence within new environments. It is possible to trace these campaigns and visualize them through social media network and link analysis.

During the 2016 U.S. Presidential election, the Russian-based Internet Research Agency (IRA)[31] pretended to be U.S. citizens on social media, creating and operating fake accounts, pages, and groups to appeal to U.S. citizens. According to the DHS, on Twitter alone, the IRA created approximately 3,000 fake accounts

---

[31] www.intelligence.senate.gov/press/new-reports-shed-light-internet-research-agency%E2%80%99s-social-media-tactics.

that posted more than 10 million tweets. These accounts had more than 6.4 million followers and followed 3.4 million other Twitter accounts.[32]

Russia used the U.S. political divide to target vulnerable U.S. audiences, which then spread quickly to mainstream news outlets, proving just how fast modern disinformation campaigns can spread and why it is important to track the connections and spread surrounding these campaigns using visualizations to analyze social networks.

Visualizing and Analyzing Social Networks

Finding patterns quickly within data can be time-consuming. That is where visualizations can fill an analysis gap and aid in making connections that otherwise our brains might miss. In Part I, "Foundational OSINT," we talked about different types of visualizations to capture data, and we touched on link analysis charts. Social media is an area where *link analysis charts* and *social network analysis (SNA)* can be valuable and help humans to see patterns surrounding specific accounts and networks paired with content communication such as hashtags. This type of network analysis relies on graph theory, which is system of nodes and edges and the relationships that exist between them.

A *node* is an element in a graph, and in the case of Figure 6.45, each node represents a Twitter account.

An *edge* in graph theory refers to the connection between the nodes. Our Twitter account nodes shown previously are connected because they all mutually follow each other (see Figure 6.46).

The *weight* between these node relationships increases the more they interact individually with each other. If one account retweets another account, their relationship weight increases (see Figure 6.47).

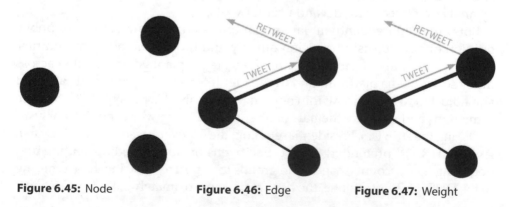

Figure 6.45: Node   **Figure 6.46:** Edge   **Figure 6.47:** Weight

---

[32] www.dhs.gov/sites/default/files/publications/ia/ia_combatting-targeted-disinformation-campaigns.pdf.

The *degree* is the number of connections a node has to other nodes, and *direction* shows the flow of information and where edges are directed from one node to the other (see Figures 6.48-6.49).

Centrality measures the importance of each node in the network and is a common way we see social network graphs displayed (see Figure 6.50).

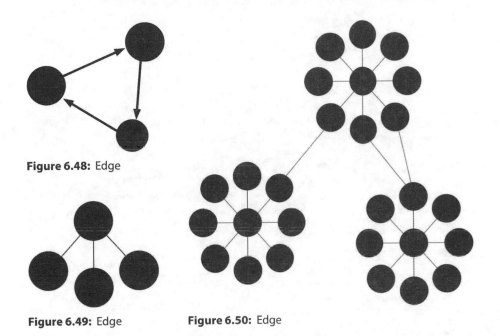

Figure 6.48: Edge

Figure 6.49: Edge   **Figure 6.50:** Edge

Viewing social networks by using network analysis allows analysts to get a 30,000 foot view of the entire network rather than trying to make connections in pieces. There are many social network analysis tools available to do the complex graph calculations necessary to develop these revealing graphics, but three of the more commonly used options are Neo4j Community Edition,[33] Gephi,[34] and Maltego Community Edition. *Gephi* is a free open source visualization software used to analyze networks for centrality, density, paths, modularity, clustering, and more. The following image is an example analysis of the viral *Plandemic*[35] video by Judy Mikovits, a controversial virologist insisting the novel coronavirus was a "manipulated flu vaccine" and that wearing a mask will activate it

---

[33] https://neo4j.com.
[34] https://gephi.org.
[35] www.npr.org/2020/05/08/852451652/seen-plandemic-we-take-a-close-look-at-the-viral-conspiracy-video-s-claims.

within your system (see Figure 6.51). Through Gephi, we can quickly visualize the key nodes spreading the misinformation and how they are connected. These types of visualizations can be helpful for your stakeholders to see in order to understand the full scope of your analysis.

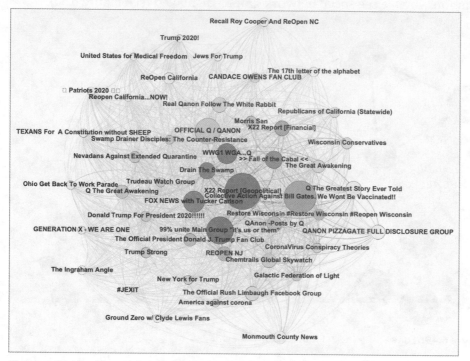

Figure 6.51: Gephi model on the spread of the debunked *Plandemic* video[36]

As an example of how Gephi (and other social network analysis tools) can make connections during analysis, we can look back at more of Benjamin Strick's fantastic work analyzing Twitter accounts connected to a pro-Indonesian bot network. Strick analyzed the hashtags #FreeWestPapua and #WestPapua for 5 days back in 2019 when he noticed odd behavior among spreading the hashtags. He noticed that as the conflict in Indonesia grew, the posts were increasing, indicating a coordinated effort to spread pro-government messaging. Building a dataset of usernames tweeting the tags, retweeting, liking, timestamps, and URLs, Strick used Gephi to analyze the network. One of the networks stood out in comparison to the others providing a set of Twitter accounts that were responsible (see Figure 6.52).[37]

---

[36] https://dfrlab.github.io/Plandemic (Zarine Kharazian, DFRLab).
[37] www.bellingcat.com/news/2019/09/03/
twitter-analysis-identifying-a-pro-indonesian-propaganda-bot-network.

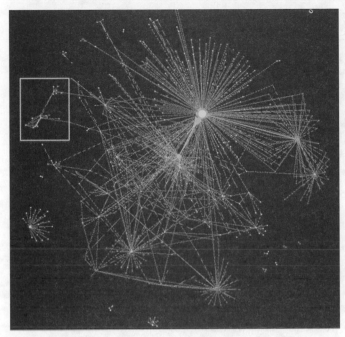

Figure 6.52: Bellingcat

Spotting Digitally Altered Content

With the advent and widespread access to new image, audio, and video manipulation software, we can no longer trust the naked eye when performing OSINT analysis. While traditional OSINT methods like reverse image search are always a useful practice, they can't always detect what's manipulated.

None of us is a stranger to digital manipulation techniques that are used to appear thinner, prettier, or stronger than our true selves, but politics is rife with digital manipulation for vanity and propaganda purposes. The media has also begun to incorporate more crowdsourced and community-generated content in their reporting, which requires an increase in verification knowledge to combat publishing edited imagery.

A major problem with image manipulation is that many images begin as legitimate content before being edited; this lends inherent credibility to the content. For instance, during Hillary Clinton's 2015 campaign for the White House, the Clintons were photographed walking in Manhattan with their daughter and grandchildren (see Figures 6.53-6.54). The photo on the left is the original image (albeit unflattering), while the photo on the right is a tweet by an account flagged as being problematic by the Chrome extension Bot Sentinel. The most notable difference between the photos is the way Bill's mouth has been edited and the contrast has been adjusted to give the appearance of frailty and stress. The post itself was pushing the conspiracy narrative that the Clinton's are tied to Epstein.

Figure 6.53: Original photo of Bill and Hillary Clinton

Figure 6.54: Twitter, Inc. / `https:// twitter.com/NavyFlyBoyUSA/ status/1263254999129186304/` last accessed 15 February 2023

For fun I searched Google with this exact text, and it returned another Twitter account for John K. Stahl sharing the same message. What was interesting to me is that this tweet was not a retweet; Mr. Stahl posted it from his own account with the same messaging (see Figure 6.55).

Figure 6.55: Account suspended `https://twitter.com/JohnKStahlUSA/` last accessed 15 February 2023

Since curiosity is a key trait of an OSINT analyst, you will understand why I had to dig little bit deeper into John Stahl. Reverse image searching Stahl's photo on Bing Image Search (see Figure 6.56),[38] I was able to find a John Stahl who ran for Congress in California in 2012 (and lost) with a profile image that matched (see Figure 6.57).

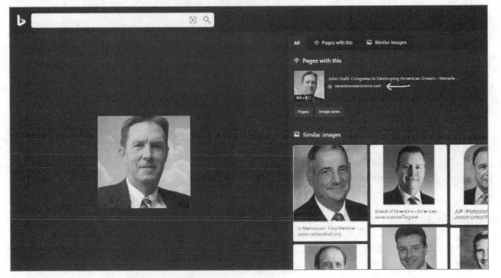

Figure 6.56: Bing image search on photograph of man

2012

See also: California's 52nd Congressional District elections, 2012

Stahl ran in the 2012 election for the U.S. House to represent California's 52nd District. He was defeated in the open primary on June 5, 2012 [1][2]

U.S. House, California District 52 Open Primary, 2012		
Candidate	Vote %	Votes
✓Brian Bilbray (R) *Incumbent*	43.1%	61,930
✓Scott Peters (D)	23.7%	34,106
Lori Saldana (D)	23.2%	33,387
John Stahl (R)	3.8%	5,502
Wayne Iverson (R)	3.1%	4,476
Shirley Decourt-Park (D)	1.6%	2,368
John Subka (R)	0.8%	1,091
Gene Hamilton Carswell (R)	0.6%	828
Total Votes		**143,688**

Figure 6.57: Ballotpedia, `ballotpedia.org/John_Stahl`

---

[38] `www.bing.com/images`.

Perhaps the most damning piece of evidence for how disinformation and manipulation is spread is that I was able to find articles stating then President Trump shared tweets promoting the pedophile conspiracy and calling Hillary a "skank" (see Figure 6.58).

Trump shares tweets calling Hillary Clinton a 'skank,' promoting Joe Scarborough conspiracy

Updated May 24, 2020; Posted May 24, 2020

Figure 6.58: `www.pennlive.com/daily-buzz/2020/05/trump-shares-tweest-calling-hillary-clinton-a-skank-insulting-stacy-abrams-nancy-pelosi-and-promoting-joe-scarborough-conspiracy-after-wrapping-up-golf-trip-reports.html`

Manipulation can take many forms, but there are some common types we can touch on along with methods for detection.

Photo Manipulation

Photo manipulation or "Photoshopping" an image by digitally manipulating the pixels is often used to hide something, deceive someone, or change someone's opinion. Much like the Bill Clinton image, we often see photo manipulation used in disinformation campaigns. One pervasive type of photo manipulation is done for governmental propaganda. North Korea is well-known for its horrendous attempts at Photoshopping propaganda and Kim Jong Un vanity photos. More recently, the Russian invasion has brought a slew of deliberately manipulated or falsely attributable photos that are being increasingly shared by trusted media sources. `BBC.com` reported on several debunked images that came from old footage, different conflicts, or even video games[39] (see Figure 6.59) leaving analysts with the immense job of verifying imagery sometimes in real time. One way to detect digitally altered imagery is through the use of error level analysis (ELA).

Error-Level Analysis

Error-level analysis identifies regions of an image at different levels of compression. The more a JPEG image is saved, the more it compresses, so when it is analyzed, the edited sections of the image become less uniform and thus more

---

[39] Twitter, Inc. / `www.bbc.com/news/60528276/` last accessed February 15, 2023.

Figure 6.59: Footage from a video game

apparent. Error-level analysis is often considered subjective by many, but it may help you to identify otherwise unseen edits within an image. With ELA all high-contrast and low-contrast edges should look similar. If there are huge differences, then you can suspect an image was altered.

For ELA there are many options, but I tend to use two main tools: Forensically[40] and FotoForensics.[41]

Forensically is a free web-based digital forensic tool that can be used to detect cloning, error-level analysis, image metadata, and more. Error-level analysis is used to identify the different levels of compression artifacts in a JPG image. In Figure 6.60, which shows a turtle-headed man, it should be obvious to you what part was edited.

If we click the Error Level Analysis button on the right and adjust the sliders, we can quickly see the turtle head stands out as brighter and less uniform than the rest of the body and the background (see Figure 6.61). With ELA, all high-contrast and low-contrast edges should look similar. If there are huge differences, then you can suspect an image was altered.

---

[40] https://29a.ch/photo-forensics/#forensic-magnifier.
[41] https://fotoforensics.com.

Figure 6.60: Forensically image showing ELA before

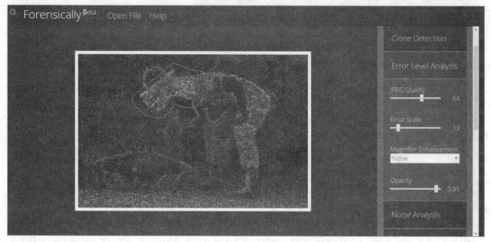

Figure 6.61: Error level analysis

Clone Detection

Another tool available in Forensically is the Clone Detection tool, which makes it possible to see all the locations where an image has been cloned or copied from one spot to another. The accuracy of this tool depends a lot on the position of the sliders and the quality of the original image. For example, most likely not all the spots highlighted in Figure 6.62 are cloned, but if you play around with the slider positions, you can better target and identify the cloned edits. However, as with any imagery manipulation tool, the results are subjective, and we have to use it as a tip to cue further analysis rather than take it as 100 percent fact.

Figure 6.62: Image from the website Forensically showing Image manipulations

Typical photography manipulation is similar to video as they can both be edited and changed to look or act like something they are not. Just like images have "tells" that they have been manipulated so do video files.

Video Manipulation

Here are some video manipulation techniques.

Deep Fakes

Deep fakes are a form of synthetic media that uses deep learning technology to simulate the faces and actions of real people, making it appear that they are saying or doing things they would never actually do. The AI learns what a person's face looks like at different angles and then applies it to the real person like a digital mask. Because new technology has made deep fake technology cheaper and more accessible, it has become easier to implement, but at the same time, they have become harder to detect. Deep fakes are often used for amusement, like the infamous parody account deep fake Tom Cruise on TikTok,[42] but other times they can be used for more sinister purposes like spreading false information.

Unfortunately, nonconsensual pornography is one of the leading uses for deep fakes. Black market sites exist to buy and sell AI-generated nonconsensual revenge and celebrity porn. Many women have become victims of these nonconsensual deep fakes that have used images of their face on other women's bodies performing often grotesque sexual acts.[43] As if this use case wasn't bad

---

[42] www.tiktok.com/@deeptomcruise.
[43] www.vice.com/en/article/qjb7b7/
ethical-deepfakes-deep-tom-cruise-ai-generated-porn.

enough, we have also begun seeing deep fakes used in government disinformation campaigns.

Government propaganda and political parties actively embrace the use of deep fake technology. Using pre-existing images of political opponents in targeted deep fake campaigns, including world leaders like Biden, Obama, Putin, Trump, and Zelensky, increases the chance of causing panic and inciting hatred throughout the world. If deep fakes are becoming hard to detect, how can we possibly detect and verify the information? There are some tools that exist for deep fake detection, but in some cases we can use information within images to determine if a video is real or fake.

Spotting Deep Fakes

Spotting deep fakes requires using verification and image analysis skills to decipher the common signs of false imagery.[44]

- Much like `Thispersondoesnotexist` has glitches, so do deep fakes. Watch for facial distortions like smooth skin and strange shadowing.

- Lighting on glasses is often not well represented in deep fakes and may be too bright, too dark, or at a strange angle.

- Look for strange edges around facial hair and moles as deep fake technology has a hard time making these natural when removed or added.

- Does the coloring of the face and lips match?

- Watch for abnormal blinking.

- Lack of detail within the teeth.

- Glitching when turning from side to front.

An important skill for OSINT analysts is being able to take all of the disparate tools and concepts and put them together to use in your day-to-day- analysis. The following chapter was developed to show how we can combine multiple techniques and tradecraft to develop a real-life case.

6.5   Putting It All Together

Let's put it all together.

Chasing a Puppy Scam

Over the last few years, I have worked on a wide variety of cases ranging from minor cases to national security level, but one case stands out as my personal

---

[44] www.media.mit.edu/projects/detect-fakes/overview.

"white whale." She is the Joker to my Batman, the Dr. Eggman to my Sonic, the Nicolas Cage to my John Travolta. . .or the John Travolta to my Nicolas Cage? Regardless, she is the thing that keeps me up at night, gears spinning, trying to spot new angles. She is "Jane Doe," the puppy scammer.

The case itself, although altruistic, does not seem at all like it would be a Sherlock Holmes experience, but I assure you there are some wild turns. The entire case presented itself on a day where I was trying to find an example scenario for a blog I intended to write on puppy mills that resell their cast-offs as rescue dogs for a profit. I had pitched this idea to another OSINT blogger who wanted to work with me to develop a co-written blog. While doing research for our blog, my associate stumbled upon several negative reviews across numerous consumer websites accusing a company SmallTeacupDogs of running a dog scam. Looking closer, we both realized there were an exceptional number of negative reviews stating the buyers were scammed out of tens of thousands of dollars. The whole scenario sounded wild to me as we began piecing together story remnants from the consumer posts.

The way we determined the puppy scam works is that the seller often referred to as "Jane Doe," but also several other names, offers specially bred teacup-sized puppies for sale on her website for several thousands of dollars. The buyer fills out an interest form online, and "Jane" returns the call promising the delivery of a puppy via air delivery as soon as the buyer sends a SWIFT transfer to the seller. When the day of delivery comes, the buyer goes to the airport to meet their new puppy, and it never arrives. Sometimes the buyers receive excuses about the airport regulations causing delays or the crate being too big, so they need more money to get the puppy to its home. Because the money is sent through a SWIFT transaction, there is no real recourse for the buyer to claim their money was stolen. This is a classic example of one of the most common types of confidence scam, the advance fee scam.

Luckily, "Jane" had given the buyers many pieces of identifying information while running her scams including a full name, several phone numbers, and a domain. My associate and I began by Google dorking her full name to see what other information was connected to her on the Internet.

`"Jane Doe" and "puppy" or "scam"`

To our surprise we got a ton of results on "Jane Doe" that hinted at a long career in scam artistry that went well beyond puppies. Continuing our deep dive into "Jane" we began to capture these associations into a pivot chart including a possible personal website "`JaneDoe.com`." Using a VM, I visited the website listed in many of the consumer complaints "smallteacupdogs," which was set up as a marketplace for designer teacup dogs. As a graphic designer, I immediately noticed many of the images looked digitally altered or manipulated to make the puppies appear tiny. A Google reverse image search on the photos revealed that most had been stolen from other websites. Browsing the website, it became apparent that most of the text had been poorly translated, which led me to believe someone possibly outside the United States had used a translator to write it. The contract page not only requests more than $8,000 for a puppy but asks the buyer to input personal information such as physical address, email, and family details to determine the "right fit" for the puppy. The website footer confirms that two of the phone numbers pulled from consumer complaints were attributable to the site and had links to social media sites Twitter, Facebook, and YouTube (see Figure 6.63).

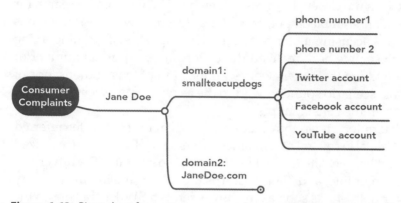

Figure 6.63: Pivot chart for puppy scam case showing social media connections

So far, the only connections we have between Jane Doe and SmallTeacupDogs are the anonymous reports on consumer websites. At this point, I realized we needed to verify that she was in fact connected with the site at all. Turning to the company Twitter account, I used an ethically gray technique called password knocking to confirm she was the owner. Password knocking involves requesting a new password, which will, on certain occasions, provide the user with a partial email address to send the new password. I do not use this technique often as it is very risky and can notify the owner that someone is attempting to reset their password. In this case it worked, and I was presented with the partial email "J***D**@g****.***." This email is certainly no smoking gun, but a fair assumption would be that it is JaneDoe@gmail.com.

Scanning the Twitter account for more information led me to the account bio, which showed that although the name of the page was Small Teacup Dogs, the actual account username was @puppysale012. The page also provided a location of Toronto, Canada, which seemed to me like it didn't add up with the poor translation on the website; perhaps she hired someone to develop it or maybe she has partners.

I decided since I partially confirmed her association with the email address found in the Twitter account, I would pivot to the domain registration information to see if any more connections exist. I researched both "JaneDoe.com" and

"SmallTeacupDogs" by using WHOIS data to check for registration data. Lo and behold, although both websites had registration protection enabled, I went back in history far enough and found the email address "JaneDoe@gmail.com" had registered both sites. Using that email address I looked through domain data to see which other sites she had registered. The list of domains I found read like a rapsheet of scams across time and included the following:

- JaneLane
- Richtinydogs
- VIPpuppies
- PureBeautymakeup
- Handicappedlife

Now that I had several domains tied directly to my subject, I began visiting each one to pull as much information as I could from each. What I learned from this process was that each domain was created using the same template, most likely WordPress, with the same style and writing. The other thing that was similar across all of the domains was the use of the same social media platforms; each site had links to Twitter, Facebook, and YouTube. The JaneLane site served as a pseudo résumé or promotional site for Jane, and she used it to talk about her beauty line Pure Beauty Makeup, the book she wrote on how to be a marketing genius, and how she overcame tragedy when she was paralyzed in a fall. Each résumé point aligned with another domain I had found, indicating she had stood up websites for all of her endeavors. I also noticed that none of her other "legitimate" websites mentioned her puppy scams.

Again, I visited each Twitter account for the domains, gathered the usernames, and used the same password knocking technique to determine several more partial email addresses and with context I then turned into real email accounts. You can see all of these data points on the pivot chart in Figure 6.64.

I was able to pull the username, emails, and any other identifiable information from the bio and posts to create a link chart. Each domain provided additional information as she had registered many of them with her personal email accounts.

By now I had collected her name, emails, usernames, domains, and social media. After spending a large amount of effort pulling information from her Twitter accounts, I switched over to YouTube. I was curious what a scammer would post if she had no real product to sell. The SmallTeacupDogs YouTube page was filled with a lot of videos featuring small puppies and people just off camera. The videos seemed to be filmed in very different locations with different people. However, what caught my eye were two videos: an instructional video called "Purchase process for buying a puppy from us" and a testimonial video from a happy customer. The process video was a younger woman in her late 20s in front of a blank wall, going through the process of filling out the contract form to buy a puppy. The second video also featured a woman but older, probably early 40s, seated on a couch in a suit jacket. During the entire video the woman talks about how much she loves her puppy and how great the

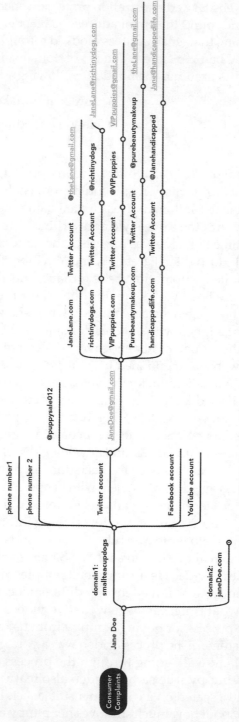

Figure 6.64: Pivot chart for puppy scam case showing Twitter accounts connected to email addresses

purchase process was, but the dog never once makes an appearance. I paused each video in a spot where their faces were neutral and clear and grabbed a screenshot using the snipping tool. Using Yandex, I uploaded the images and performed a reverse image search on the still images. Both queries returned similar results: many other videos where the women are giving testimonials or discussing a product. They were hired actors who had read a script and not legitimate customers or employees of the company!

Because this case has lots of parts and we had collected a ton of information already, we needed to perform a gap analysis to determine what data was still missing from our case to know what to work on next.

Gap Analysis:

What do I already know?

- Full name
- Possible location
- What the scam is
- Jane's biography
- She hires actors
- Key emails
- Phone numbers
- Domains
- Usernames
- Social media accounts
  - Twitter
  - YouTube
  - Facebook

What does this mean?

Although Jane is running scams, she is not very careful about leaking information about herself and her businesses. She is making several thousand dollars from each puppy sale, and from the looks of the reviews she makes pretty good money.

What do I still need to know?

- What the usernames lead to.
- What the phone numbers lead to.
- Does she have accomplices?
- Can I locate her?
- Is Jane Doe a real name or alias?
- What does she do with the money?

How do I find out?

- What the usernames lead to.
  - I can check the usernames in `WhatsMyName.app`.
- What the phone numbers lead to.
  - I can check the phone numbers in Google and people search sites.

- Does she have accomplices?
  - I can check her social media to see her followers.
  - I can look for documents with other names.
  - I can look for significant others or family members.
- Can I locate her?
  - I can look at the backgrounds in her social media photos to attempt to geolocate her.
  - I can look for context clues in her posts.
  - I can look for metadata in her posts/images.
- Is Jane Doe a real name or alias?
  - I can use public records to find out.
- What does she do with the money?
  - I can look for transactional information.
  - I can analyze her SWIFT accounts.

Ultimately, by using these gap analysis questions my associate and I were able to determine quite a lot about Jane Doe, enough to fill a book on its own. By the end of the analysis, we had more than 100 pages of data and context on this woman, her boyfriend "John," and her service dog. We were able to geolocate several of her locations and developed a pattern of life analysis showing consistent travel between Canada and the UAE with a primary residence in Toronto. Because I knew her boyfriend's name, we used his social media and digital footprint to link their location to several blocks from the vape shop he worked at. Using her dog and his personal social media account I determined the pet daycare she used in the UAE. This might seem like a lot of research on a woman who runs puppy scams, but we uncovered countless other scams and failed businesses that left customers and business partners angry.

Soon after I ran the initial blog story, I had several people reach out to me anonymously about Jane—so many that I had to set up an email just to gather their stories. Normally, as an OSINT analyst I would not be engaging with anyone during an analysis, but this one sparked a huge conversation. One day I received an anonymous direct message on Twitter from one of her associates. Throughout our conversation, I posed questions in a way that wouldn't give away the information I knew in order to prove their relationship to Jane. This person independently verified many of the findings I had not published in my blog and seemed to be close with Jane, enough to know her personal details. They told me she said my blog post was "just OK."

After that I received a message from a distraught victim of Jane's. Jane had been staying at the victim's mother's house and destroyed the inside leaving thousands of dollars in damages. Jane and a few accomplices then fled the scene in a U-Haul leaving some of things behind including pill bottles and cameras all over the house. The victim sent me photos of the pill bottles with Jane and her boyfriend's name on them.

The next message I got a few months later ended up being a former nurse who was hired to help Jane with getting dressed and taking care of herself but was ultimately not paid. The live-in nurse told me she had grown suspicious of Jane's businesses and once found her credit card in Jane's possession. After Googling Jane, she found my blog and reached out. Remember, I did not publish or speak publicly about the house Jane ruined before fleeing the scene. This nurse offered up a wild story about being told to come with Jane in a U-Haul to pick up her things from her old apartment. The nurse went along to help, but it quickly turned bad when the police showed up. The nurse soon realized that Jane was trying to run out without paying rent. She had also completely independently verified the story that I received a few months earlier. I analyzed all of the accounts that sent me messages, and they all appeared completely legitimate.

The final contact I received was from a detective in the Toronto Police Department who had also been tracking her scams and movements. Seems Jane is someone else's "white whale" too (see Figure 6.65).

This case study serves as an example of all of the techniques you have learned within the previous chapters. You have learned how to locate information about a subject through the selectors and associated social media accounts. You then learned how to identify and verify whether information is false and how to monitor and visualize large networks of individuals. Now, let's move on to the assets a person may own and where they may spend much of their day by learning tactics and tradecraft for the effective analysis of businesses and organizations.

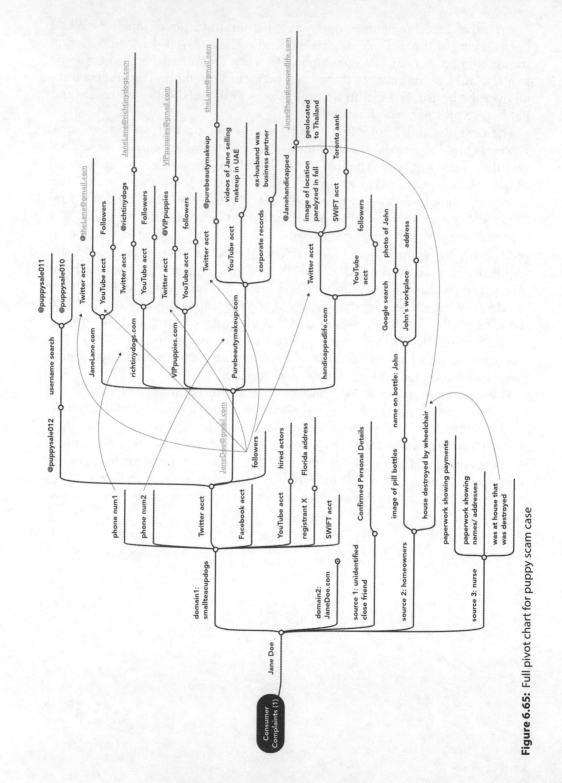

Figure 6.65: Full pivot chart for puppy scam case

Business and Organizational Intelligence

7.1 Overview

What Is Organizational Intelligence?

In 2019, Wirecard, an electronic payment provider and one of the 30 most valuable companies on the Frankfurt Stock Exchange, was accused of fraud involving shell companies, fake acquisitions, faux customers, and forgery, in what turned out to be one of the largest fraud scandals in German history.[1] Following investigative reporting by the *Financial Times*[2] along with whistleblower complaints, Wirecard ultimately filed for insolvency revealing the termination and subsequent arrest of its CEO, Markus Braun, as well as reporting they were "missing €1.9 billion."

Dan McCrum was the investigative reporter who dug into Wirecard for more than 6 years and ultimately exposed their fraud in his *Financial Times* series "House of Wirecard." According to an interview with the Global Investigative Journalism Network, he employed many of the same OSINT techniques in his analysis and research that we are going to learn in this section.

---

[1] www.reuters.com/article/us-germany-wirecard-inquiry-timeline/
timeline-the-rise-and-fall-of-wirecard-a-german-tech-champion-
idUSKBN2B811J.
[2] www.ft.com/content/19c6be2a-ee67-11e9-bfa4-b25f11f42901.

The basis for the type of investigations journalists like McCrum work on is a foundational knowledge of how organizations are supposed to work and how to examine them for abnormalities. This exploration into companies, nonprofits, partnerships, cooperative structures, affiliations, competitors, employees, and their products is what I like to call *organizational intelligence*.

Like the inter-disciplinary OSINT techniques that we learned in the previous chapters, organizational intelligence can stand alone as its own specialty, or it can be seamlessly integrated with other OSINT disciplines like subject intelligence, social media analysis, and network analytics. If your present career goals don't require any sort of business reconnaissance work, I assure you that by adding these skills to your repertoire it can make you a more versatile and therefore more desirable analyst.

Nonetheless, there are still quite a few jobs that do require organizational intelligence experience within the OSINT industry. Some titles frequently found on job sites include due diligence analyst, anti-money laundering analyst, counterproliferation analysis, competitive intelligence analyst, investigative journalist, fraud investigator, and business intelligence analyst. Many of the job opportunities appear to focus solely on businesses and corporations, but it is important to note that organizational intelligence includes any group of organized people who come together for a purpose like charities and political groups. Traditionally, the term *organization* includes the following categories:

- Corporations/businesses
- Nonprofits
- Charities
- Political groups
- Governments
- Partnerships
- Cooperatives
- Educational institutions

Considering these categories, some examples of OSINT work that could be performed include due diligence analysis for a corporate acquisition, embezzlement analysis on a nonprofit, analysis of a political Super PAC and their funds, and the connections of educational institutions to other nations. Regardless of the direction your analysis may take, it is valuable to have a base-level knowledge in the types of data and the sources that are useful when performing organizational OSINT. Here is a list of a few top data points used for organization intelligence research:

- Corporate/business structure disclosures
  - Parent
  - Subsidiary
  - Holding companies
- Contract disclosures
- Financial records/annual reports
- Affiliations and relationship disclosures
- Procurement/supply chain disclosures
- Innovative/proprietary technology disclosures
- Business discretions and lawsuits
- Sanctions/illegal activity
- Public disclosures
- Published material disclosures

The pivot chart shown below in figure 7.1 illustrates a few of the key pivots we can make starting with a Corporate Entity.

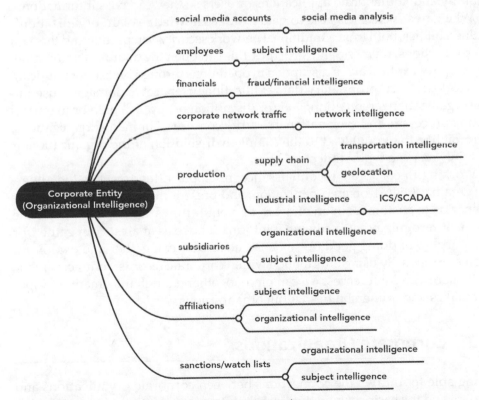

Figure 7.1: Pivot chart stemming from a corporate entity

The significance of organizational intelligence from an analysis standpoint is clear, but let's now turn the tables and view the situation from an adversarial perspective. Many of the largest reported data breaches begin with the adversary performing some level of information gathering on the target company.

In 2013, an external actor broke into the network of retail chain Target after using organizational intelligence tactics to figure out the company's third-party vendors, including an HVAC company, which they then stole network credentials from to gain access to Target's systems.[3] Unfortunately, the Target payment system was not segregated from the externally accessed network, and the attackers were able to push malware to most of the point-of-sale devices within the retail stores and collect customer card information for nearly 40 million accounts. In yet another example of how adversaries are using the same intelligence techniques, a data breach was reported in April 2022 for email marketing service Mailchimp.[4] An external actor used organizational intelligence techniques to determine Mailchimp employees. From there, the actor employed social engineering attacks to gather information from the targeted employees that compromised their accounts. The actor then used the compromised employee accounts to access the customer support tool and more than 300 Mailchimp accounts exporting customer mailing lists and API keys, which identify and authenticate applications or users so they can pass information.

When an adversary is able to gain insider knowledge of an organization's vulnerabilities, both from a traditional network security perspective and through its connections, finances, and structure, this can open the door for exploitation. This type of exploit causes disruption in operations through breaching physical/network security, proprietary data exfiltration, irreparable damage caused to the organization's reputation, and/or disruption of supply chain or manufacturing processes, and even national security concerns. For many organizations, turmoil like this could lead to the complete dissolution of the organization or possibly an even worse outcome.

Working in corporate reconnaissance, my job is often to act as the adversary, gather OSINT on an organization, and present these types of doomsday scenarios to customers in an effort to prevent future attacks. Therein lies the value of recognizing not only what information we as analysts can gather for the purpose of doing good but what an adversary can gather and exploit for their own ends. By using information within corporate records, contracts, public disclosures, and inferences, we can piece together enough information to spot anomalies and vulnerabilities within organizations.

7.2   Corporate Organizations

Being able to unravel the connections between corporate organizations and understand the basics of how they work is integral to identifying and analyzing businesses.

---

[3] https://krebsonsecurity.com/2014/02/target-hackers-broke-in-via-hvac-company.
[4] www.bleepingcomputer.com/news/security/hackers-breach-mailchimps-internal-tools-to-target-crypto-customers.

Understanding the Basics of Corporate Structure

Within every legal corporation, there are requirements for organizations that help the company work toward meeting its goals and objectives. This organization is called the *corporate structure*. The corporate governance, or rules and structure, generally break the corporation into a board of directors elected by shareholders that supervise the company's activities, corporate officers that run the daily operations of the company, and shareholders who own a portion of the company through stocks or "shares." There are various types of shareholders, but with equity shareholders they typically hold veto power over the decisions that management make within the company. As a corporation grows, the need to move into new locations and markets increases. One solution to this is to find new entities and subsidiaries. Recognizing the way that corporations are typically structured and the terminology that they use will help us as we dig through documentation to uncover irregularities.

Commonly, because of the nature of varying markets across many locations, large legitimately run corporate entities will have a confusing network of holding companies, subsidiaries, shareholders, and intermediaries supporting the business. Now imagine these corporations attempting to hide illegal activity by deliberately confounding the structure making an already arduous task into a near impossible one. One place we can start to unravel the ball of yarn is through defining some key entities within corporate structure.

Entity Types

The following are entity types:

- **Holding Company:** A financial entity used to hold the controlling stock in other companies and often oversees management decisions
- **Parent Company:** A company that controls interest in one or more companies known as a subsidiaries
- **Subsidiary:** A separate legal company that belongs to another company that controls more than half of its stock
- **Wholly Owned Subsidiary:** A company that belongs to another company that controls 100 percent of its stock
- **Limited Liability Company (LLC):** An organization that is created to protect the owner's personal assets during litigation
- **Beneficial Owner:** The person who gains or benefits from assets that belong to someone else
- **Intermediary Company:** Entities that connect buyers and sellers, often referred to as a *middleman*

- **Foreign-Registered Entities:** Entities that have been incorporated in a country, state, or jurisdiction while operating in another
- **Nonprofit Organization:** A nonbusiness entity operated for social benefit versus profit generation

To demonstrate how an ordinary corporate entity is structured, let's look at the layout of the McDonald's Corporation (see Figure 7.2). The McDonald's Corporation is in the position to control the interest of the other companies within its corporate umbrella, making it the parent company. Because McDonald's is a global company and must have representation in each location, it holds many country-based private subsidiaries such as McDonald's USA LLC, McDonald's Korea, and McDonald's Deutschland LLC. Furthermore, within each of the private subsidiaries sits a second layer of private subsidiaries. In the United States, this second layer of subsidiaries is positioned within each state e.g., "McDonald's Restaurants of California Inc." Finally, to make it even more confusing, within each state subsidiary exist branches for each city location within the state.

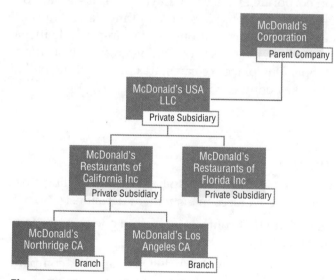

Figure 7.2: Example of organizational structure using the McDonalds Corporation

All said, including their real estate company, McDonald's Real Estate Company, and a nonprofit named Opnad Fund, they have a total of 6,070 corporate entities linked across the world. Now, imagine the level of effort it would take one individual to analyze each one of these entities for an ongoing case. This is precisely why using OSINT techniques to quickly uncover public documents and disclosures has the potential to speed up the analysis process and provide actionable information.

Knowing how an organization is structured is only the first piece of the puzzle. Now we will go through the various ways we can uncover deeper information from their documents and what kinds of crimes are prevalent in organizations.

7.3   Methods for Analyzing Organizations

The analysis of organizations should begin in the same way that all OSINT must, with a research question. A question is posed either from stakeholders prior to the start of work or within the Feedback loop of the intelligence cycle in ongoing analysis that we must attempt to answer through open source research (see Figure 7.3).

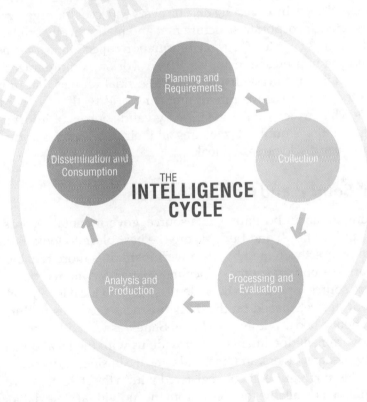

Figure 7.3: The Intelligence cycle

Research questions for organizations will vary depending on the needs of the stakeholder but may look like the following:

"Is there anything we should be concerned about before merging with X company?

"Can you identify any information data leaks from our company?"

"Are you able to uncover evidence of fraud or illegal activity within X company?"

Once the initial Planning and Requirements are done and a research question(s) is solidified, we can begin the Collection process. Information collection on organizations can be wide and all-encompassing, and therefore my suggestion is to attempt to reign in the focus of collection as close as possible to answer the research question and gradually expand the data. For example, if the research question is "Are you able to uncover evidence of fraud or illegal activity within X company?" we could begin by collecting data on every aspect of the organization, or we can focus on their corporate structure first and methodically branch out as needed. By keeping a targeted focus on information collection, we can avoid wasted time chasing unproductive angles. When working on organizational intelligence cases, I like to start with a few quintessential sources that provide credible data either through government reporting or directly from contract databases. Somewhat less credible but still very valid sources of information include the organization's public disclosures on their public pages and social media, and employee disclosures and leaks.

Government Sources and Official Registers

If you are looking for an authoritative data source, governmental records like reports, filings, publications, and budgets are the best place to look. Because the information is directly created by the government, it is more reliable and trustworthy than a secondary source, which may have been altered before we see it. Since these sources operate on the federal, state, and local level, each can provide different datasets based on the daily business activities within that specific governmental body. Within the United States, as with other countries, using official government documents can provide us with the legal details on company structure, shareholders, and financial data. If a business is incorporated in the United States, it is required to be registered within the state of incorporation; this information is available for access from the individual state databases. It is not very practical to search every state database within the United States, so thankfully free aggregated databases exist that combine all the data into one searchable directory through a simple user interface. One of my favorite databases of aggregate company information sourced from official primary source government data is *OpenCorporates*,[5] the largest free database of companies in the world (see Figure 7.4).

Figure 7.4: Screenshot of `OpenCorporates.com`

Examples of the types of data that can be found on Open Corporates include the following:

- Incorporation date
- Alternative names
- Jurisdiction
- Branches/subsidiaries
- Agent name
- Addresses
- Directors and officers
- Latest events
- Similarly named companies
- Trademark/patent registrations

An investigation into the exploitation of U.S. Paycheck Protection Program (PPP) loans by the Miami Herald and the Anti-Corruption Data Collective used

---

[5] `https://opencorporates.com/info/about`.

Open Corporates data to show misuse of funds.[6] Investigators were able to combine data from state registries[7] and a publicly available dataset of loan receivers to identify recipients of PPP loans and determine fraudulent activity. What they found was that loans were being provided to companies that failed to meet eligibility criteria, even some with previous fraud convictions. They also found that one man was loaned roughly $3.5 million to five separate businesses registered in his name. Having free access to such a large amount of searchable primary source data is invaluable to these types of corporate analyses. Further mastering the ability to quickly find and understand the corporate documents based on what's "normal" regarding structure, funding, and operation offers opportunities to identify misconduct and illegality. In your quest for information, you might require more than free resources have to offer. There may be a situation where the stakeholder within the case has a specific request that can be fulfilled only through a paid service like D&B Hoovers,[8] Dow Jones Risk and Compliance, or World Compliance Lexis Nexis. The advantage to using a paid source is that it may have access to more comprehensive data than a public source. I have found paid sources like D&B Hoovers to make uncovering subsidiaries and other corporate structure linkages vastly easier. Paid sources often include privately held firm details and sanctions designation information that could be harder to collate from public sources.

EDGAR

The Securities and Exchange Commission (SEC) was established by Franklin D. Roosevelt after the Wall Street Crash of 1929 for the purpose of maintaining fair markets and protecting investors.[9] All publicly traded companies within the United States are regulated by the SEC and required to disclose company information, such as financial records, to the public under the 1933 Securities Act. The data disclosed by U.S. companies to the SEC, both quarterly and annual statements, are gathered, analyzed, and maintained by *EDGAR, the Electronic Data Gathering, Analysis, and Retrieval system*. Since 1993, the EDGAR system has been a publicly searchable online database of millions of collected company filings (see Figure 7.5). The downside to the EDGAR system is that sometimes it can be clunky to search and hard to separate data from companies with similar names.

---

[6] https://blog.opencorporates.com/2020/10/29/covid-relief-funds-how-opencorporates-data-helped-expose-exploitation-of-the-us-paycheck-protection-program.

[7] https://opencorporates.com/registers.

[8] www.dnb.com.

[9] www.sec.gov/about/what-we-do.

Figure 7.5: EDGAR

Annual Reports and Filings

Government required documents are an excellent primary resource and starting point for organizational analysis. As we saw with Open Corporates and EDGAR, publicly traded entities are required to submit quarterly and annual documentation to their state of registration. These officially filed reports provide comprehensive data on the organization, and peripherally they also provide opportunities for pivoting to other data collection actions like integrating subject intelligence.

Companies cannot function without a semblance of coordination in the form of board members, directors, shareholders, and employees. From a subject intelligence perspective, all these individuals are within the scope of the analysis and can be looked at for their links to other entities, people, and foreign interests. If a company is structured to have shareholders, it is beholden to keep those shareholders happy to get changes approved. If an individual or entity owns the majority shares in a company, they have a lot of say over what the company can do and who they answer to. Using annual reports, it's possible to determine who owns the majority shares of a company; then by pivoting to Open Corporates we could see if they have direct connections to a sanctioned entity or a foreign government of note. Taking it one step further, we could dive into the social media of individuals involved at the shareholder level to provide additional context on their potential motives. There is a document that large organizations present annually to their shareholders that outlines a substantial amount of company information from that year called an *annual report*.

Annual Report to Shareholders

Most large organizations in the United States that have shareholders are required by state to distribute an annual report document to their investors. This report must be completed so the company can retain tax benefits and corporate designations within the state of registration. Generally, annual reports are artfully designed and detail the activities, finances, and operations from the previous year. The main purpose of the document is to preserve confidence from current shareholders and to attract new investors. The value this report brings to the table for an analyst is an extensive recounting of the company's:

- Officers, directors, and other integral employees
- Office locations
- Financial status and breakdown
- Teaming, subsidiaries, partnerships
- Key competitors
- Operational insights and future organizational plans

Forms 10-K, 10-Q, and 8-K

Like many documents in the United States, the form 10-K is a report completed by publicly traded companies and sent to the SEC. This report is a watered-down version of the annual report without all the artful flair. We can find the 10-K within the company search in the EDGAR database. Like an annual report, the 10-K provides detailed information about the company's prior reporting year allowing investors to make informed decisions about buying, selling, or investing in the company.

In addition, these companies are required to file a quarterly 10-Q report. This report allows the company to adjust their 10-K on a quarterly basis and to add an 8-K report, which is used to note significant events including mergers, acquisitions, change in management, and/or legal actions.

All the various forms and reports required by the government serve as primary and authoritative sources of data for our research. Many of these reports may duplicate information as they cross over for differing governmental requirements; however, this can serve as a useful verification as we cross-check data.

Digital Disclosures and Leaks

Hands down, the most reliable source we can pull from is an authoritative governmental resource, but another extremely useful source can be the company itself through digital disclosures and public leaks. While certainly less reliable, a company can still disclose information publicly that can help us develop our case. Repeatedly, we find in OSINT that information is disclosed because it appears harmless while standing on its own, but the advantage of the analysis process in the intelligence cycle is that by combining and enriching this "harmless" data it becomes intelligence.

Think of a large corporate manufacturing company like Samsung or Siemens; these companies would have websites, social media accounts, vendor portals, customer portals, and so on. The company needs to market new products, sell products, purchase parts, support sales, impress shareholders and future investors, and support shipping/receiving of their products. Social media posts might divulge new partnerships or conferences they plan to attend, while the corporate website lists all the company's vendors, the portal login pages might reveal vulnerable technologies within their network, and poor configurations within their website could leak proprietary manufacturing specs. Each one of these examples is where we OSINT analysts gather information to piece together information and pivots within our analysis.

Organizational Websites

It doesn't matter the type of organization we are digging into, most, if not all, will have a website. The organization's website is the easiest place to start when trying to figure out what they deem is important and relevant to display to the world.

NOTE: If you are tasked with researching entities outside of your country, you may find your IP address has been geoblocked. To sidestep geoblocking, you can use a VPN and set the location to the country or area of interest or a friendly neighboring country.

Because much of the public information is the same across organizations, we can rely on their websites to follow comparable formats and provide similar data. Keep an eye out for company history, key partnerships and contract awards, current products, important people, and financial information. The following are a few possibilities and common pivots for each:

ABOUT US PAGE

Content	Pivot
Organization History	■ Notable things the dates correspond with.
-Key Dates	■ Ownership affiliation.
-Current/Former Ownership	■ Former partner/name business history.
-Former Company Names/Partners	■ Former partner/name news reports.

ABOUT US PAGE

Current Products
- Customers for the products.
- Uses for the products.
- Manufacturing or development process?
- Locations the products are made?
- Can we find the contracts associated with the products?
- Are these products an integral piece within a larger contract?

Location(s)
- Which location is the HQ?
- Which locations manufacture?
- Are any locations used for R&D?
- Are any locations in foreign countries?

CONTACT PAGE

Content	Pivot
Names/Titles	<ul><li>Do they own shares in the company?</li><li>Ownership affiliation</li><li>Former partner/name business history.</li><li>Power within company.</li></ul>
Email Addresses	<ul><li>Do they have social media connected to the emails?</li><li>Are the emails in breach data?</li><li>Do the emails reveal other associations?</li></ul>

NEWS PAGE

Content	Pivot
Mergers/Acquisitions	<ul><li>Explore financials for entities.</li><li>Explore new entity owners/directors.</li></ul>
New Projects	<ul><li>Customers for the products.</li><li>Uses for the products.</li><li>Manufacturing or development process.</li><li>Locations the products are made.</li><li>Can we find the contracts associated with the products?</li><li>Are these products an integral piece within a larger contract?</li></ul>

NEWS PAGE	
Funding/Investments	▪ Names and history of investors.
	▪ Are they a foreign investor?
	▪ Are they a designated entity?
	▪ How many shares do they own?
Ownership Changes	▪ Are there any lawsuits pending?
	▪ Is there any news about the company?
	▪ Who is the new ownership?
	▪ Are the new owners/directors shareholders?
Acquired or Lost Assets/Locations	▪ What are the addresses of the new locations?
	▪ Is the location significant?
	▪ Is the location in a foreign country?
	▪ Is the location performing critical tasks?

PARTNERSHIPS AND CONTRACTS	
Content	**Pivot**
University Partnerships	▪ What universities are partnering with the company?
	▪ Where are the universities located?
	▪ Is there significance to these affiliations?
Winning Contracts	▪ Which companies are teaming or subcontracting with the company?
	▪ What is the contract for?
	▪ Can you find the contract for more details?
	▪ What dates will the contract be started/ended?

Collecting information from an organization's website and then combining, analyzing, and enriching this data can help to develop a more complete picture of the history, status, and key players within. Sometimes, there are also legal requirements for certain industries that compel these organizations to report certain data on their public-facing website.

In my work, I frequently use corporate websites to gather information on key university partnerships, and likewise I use university partnerships to discover companies that assist in their research. University and school networks are often a target of attack for collecting PII and confidential research and for holding university resources hostage with ransomware.

Because universities across the world work closely with their governments on defense-related research, they can be a significant target. In 2019, more than 26 universities in the United States reported being the target of Chinese hackers in an attempt to steal U.S. military maritime research.[10] Understanding the universities that an organization partners with can provide insight into possible defense research projects and nation-states that fund them.

To help identify the risk of partnering with these universities, many informational databases have sprung up. The Australian Strategic Policy Institute (ASPI) hosts the Unitracker,[11] a Chinese Defense University Tracker that provides risk details about research and defense labs affiliated with the People's Republic of China. We can keep tabs on the research projects of universities in the United States through their small business loan and seed fund applications at SBIR.gov.[12] It is good to bear in mind that as an adversary, the ability to identify information about governments or entities that hold power or have inside access within an organization helps to develop a targeted attack like the phishing attacks used in the effort to steal maritime research. Another possible scenario based on information gleaned from an organizational website could be the focused targeting of a system administrator to gain access to a corporate network.

Of course, generally system administrators are not listed on an organization's website because that space is reserved for C-suite level employees. However, we can gather details about products used, technology partnerships, and possibly even contracts listing specific product versions. Pivoting to a search engine, we can use the methods we learned for subject intelligence to query using the following text to locate any listed System Administrators for the company on LinkedIn:

"System Administrator" and "company name" site:`linkedin.com`

Once we have identified the System Administrators at the company, we can crawl through their job duties to see if they list specific hardware and software used at the organization. Cross-referencing this software with the contracts and tech partnerships from the website, an adversary could look each up on the NIST Vulnerability Database to find specific CVEs for the identified technology.

Often, these types of public disclosures are found on social media pages for organizations where they announce partnerships, new technology, and expansion projects. All of this can be used to gather insight for further pivot points into the organization.

---

[10] `www.collegian.psu.edu/news/`
`penn-state-among-other-universities-targeted-in-international-hack/`
`article_645aaca6-41b7-11e9-af89-ffe0930611fa.html`.
[11] `https://unitracker.aspi.org.au`.
[12] `www.sbir.gov`.

Social Media for Organizations

Individuals are not the only ones to use social media pages to post content to the public; organizations use it to market products, convey ideas, promote the work environment, and celebrate events, contracts, and partnerships. For organizations, especially larger ones, social media is an extension of their marketing strategy. For an OSINT analyst, we can extract details from an organization's social media the same way we would an individual person. Using subject intelligence tactics, we can enumerate the organization's usernames to discover their various social media accounts across the Web. Additionally, we can find their accounts on the header and footer of their official website. Once we have the accounts, we can look through them for indicators that may answer our analysis question or provide pivots to additional information. Using the Tesla Twitter account as an example, let's see what information they present that would create pivoting opportunities for us (see Figures 7.6-7.8).

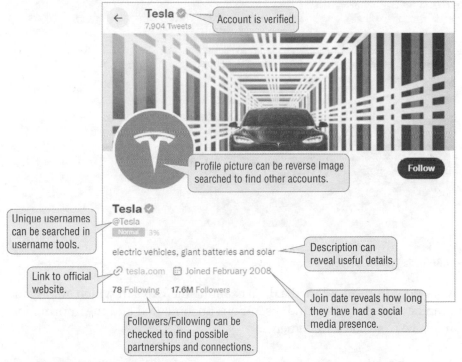

Figure 7.6: Tesla Twitter account

In just a few posts we can see the possibilities for utilizing social media to deepen our understanding in an organization and to broaden our collection through unique pivot points.

Figure 7.7: Tesla Twitter account

Figure 7.8: Tesla Twitter account

Moving now from social media, let's examine the ways in which an organization can have their actions and discretions documented and the information we can derive from these documents.

Business Indiscretions and Lawsuits

One of the more fun things to scrutinize regarding organizations is their publicly documented recklessness. Examining the seedier sides of a business adds a rich layer of context to their overall actions and company posture. A good method for this form of research is to integrate the publicly accessible court documents and filings we learned how to find earlier with free database tools like the Project on Government Oversight's (POGO) Federal Misconduct Database (FCMD).[13]

POGO is a nonpartisan independent watchdog organization investigating and exposing abuse of power, corruption, waste, and wrongdoing within the federal government and their contractors. Not only is this database incredibly fun to look through, but the FCMD sources data from several different data sources including state agency press releases and reports, federal agency press releases and reports (including SEC, DOJ, GAO), federal and state court documents, law firm press releases, Freedom of Information (FOIA) requests, and other media reports.

> **NOTE**   As of November 2022 the database is no longer maintained, however the underlying data is still made available upon request to `contractor .misconduct@pogo.org`.

Some of the misconduct presented within FCMD includes the following:

- Discrimination
- Improper billing
- Drug switching
- Deceptive claims
- Kickbacks
- Contamination

- Theft
- Wrongful termination
- Arms control violations
- Class action lawsuits
- Anti-trust violations
- Toxic contamination

Obviously, the value in collecting this data would be to illustrate impropriety; however, thinking further, we could use it to show a pattern of illegal activity, context for covering misdeeds, and potential kickbacks or even hush money. Sometimes the wrongdoing is a willful violation of federal or state regulations, and when that is recognized, it becomes public record.

A good resource for finding and analyzing regulation violations is the Good Jobs First Violation Tracker (see Figure 7.9).[14] The tracker uses similar sources as FCMD including official federal, state, and local resources including civil and criminal cases to reveal where regulatory violations and misconduct have taken place.

Famously in 2015, Duke Energy pleaded guilty in North Carolina to federal environmental violations. After a leak in 2014 spread coal ash from Duke Energy across 70 miles of the Dan River bordering Virginia, Duke agreed to pay $102 million in compliance fines and restitution as well as excavate 80 million

---

[13] `www.contractormisconduct.org`.
[14] `https://violationtracker.goodjobsfirst.org`.

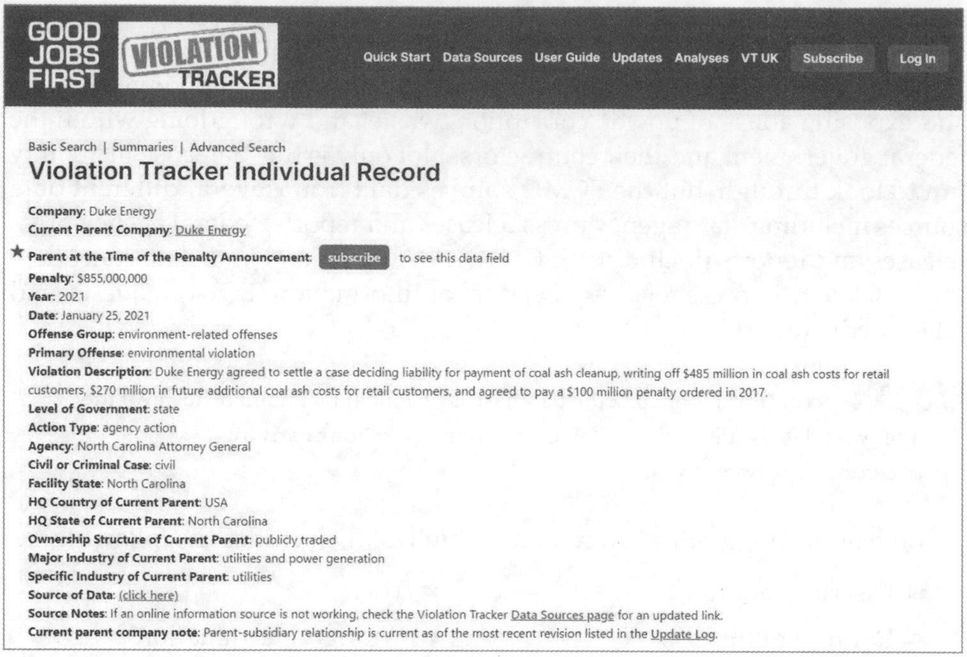

Figure 7.9: Good Jobs First

tons of coal ash.[15] This environment violation and subsequent penalty can be found on the Violation Tracker.[16]

Legal actions and penalties found within violations databases and primary source documents are invaluable to OSINT, especially in due diligence investigations. I am reminded of the Theranos case[17] where many of the investors gave millions of dollars to the company, and Elizabeth Homes, without independently auditing their financial statements or reviewing their history of legal actions and fraud indicators.

Many times we can find a lot of information that reveals the history between entities in government contracts.

---

[15] www.nytimes.com/2015/02/21/us/
duke-energy-is-charged-in-huge-coal-ash-leak.html.
[16] https://violationtracker.goodjobsfirst.org/violation-tracker/
nc-duke-energy-corporation.
[17] www.businessinsider.com/theranos-founder-ceo-elizabeth-holmes-life-
story-bio-2018-4#as-a-sophomore-holmes-went-to-one-of-her-professors-
channing-robertson-and-said-lets-start-a-company-with-his-blessing-
she-founded-real-time-cures-later-changing-the-companys-name-to-
theranos-thanks-to-a-typo-early-employees-paychecks-actually-said-
real-time-curses-10.

Contracts

Formal and legally binding agreements between parties defining the rights and obligations of each party are called *contracts*. There are different types of contracts for different uses such as general business contracts, bill of sale contracts, employment contracts, licensing agreements, and promissory notes. Contracts are a primary source of information, and they contain a tremendous amount of material that can provide insight on an organization's future/past projects, which projects they spend a lot on, if they are building or expanding property, and so much more! Let's dive into the different types of contracts and what they have to offer.

Government Contracts

As we learned, contracts are primary source and legally binding documents. For transparency, in many countries, the details held within government contracts are required by law to be made publicly available. In the United States, government contracts are available in searchable databases at the federal, state, and local levels. Here are examples of a few research questions that would send me down the path of doing contract exploration:

- What is the organization spending its money on?
- What third-party vendors does the organization use?
- Can you find information on a specific construction project the organization paid for in 2019?
- Can you find evidence of specific technology the organization has implemented?

Realizing the need to analyze government contracts for your research is only the first step; understanding what they say is the next. Contracts are legal documents, and between legalese and corporate terminology they can be arduous to comprehend. The following terms and definitions are commonly used within contracting and procurement and should be enough to get you going with your research:

- **Contractor:** A person or group that provides services or materials based on a contract
- **Subcontractor:** A person or group that is hired by the contractor to do specific tasks within the contract based on their skills
- **Purchase Order:** Document issued from the buyer to the contractor authorizing the purchase and outlining terms and conditions
- **Request for Proposal (RFP):** Used to solicit proposals from potential contractors and provides the ability to negotiate all terms

- **Request for Quote (RFQ):** An invitation for vendors to submit quotes for work
- **Bid:** A submission in response to an RFP
- **Scope of Work:** A written description of the materials and services within the RFP
- **Statement of Work (SOW):** A written description of the deliverables, timelines, and other requirements
- **Proposal:** An offer and response to a request for services that offers a solution to the requirements
- **TAS Code:** An ID code assigned by the Treasury Fiscal Services to the financial transactions for reporting to the Department of Treasury
- **Task Order:** Ordering services within an already established contract
- **Teaming:** A form of subcontracting where a smaller business teams up through an agreement with a larger company to fulfil a contract
- **NAICS Code:** A classification within the North American Industry Classification System for use by the Federal Statistical Agencies
- **PSC Code:** Product and service codes are four-digit codes used by the federal government to describe a product, service, or R&D activity
- **IDIQ:** Abbreviation for Indefinite Delivery/Indefinite Quantity meaning they provide an indefinite number of services in the contracted period

Some of you are surely cringing at the thought of pouring over contract details for hours, and believe me I get it. I implore you to avoid overlooking this tremendous resource. I will let you in on a little secret about government contracts: they often hide unbelievably juicy OSINT content within the attached documents and notes. While the documents and data vary by contract request and fulfillment, I have found things like entire building blueprints and technology schematics that were complete enough to allow you to rebuild it from the ground up. Now that I have your attention, let's take a look at some of the other things we can find within government contracts:

- Details about teaming and partnerships
  - Contractors
  - Subcontractors
- Dates of services
- Detailed descriptions of products or services
  - Specific technologies used
- Attached documents
  - Blueprints
  - Building specs
  - Processes and procedures
- Contacts
  - Names
  - Emails
  - Addresses

Now that we know what can be found and the terminology used within to describe these things, let's dive into how to read, find, and interpret a contract.

Contract Reading 101

So, you have come to terms with the fact that you need to analyze government contracts, and you know the key terms and what is possible to find within them. Now where do you find them? In the United States, the official source for federal government spending data based on the Federal Funding and Accountability Act of 2006 (FFATA) is USASpending.gov.[18] The data is sourced directly from government systems like the Federal Procurement Data System,[19] making USASpending.gov an aggregate of official primary sources searchable to the public. By walking through an example contract search, let's see how the site returns results (see Figure 7.10).

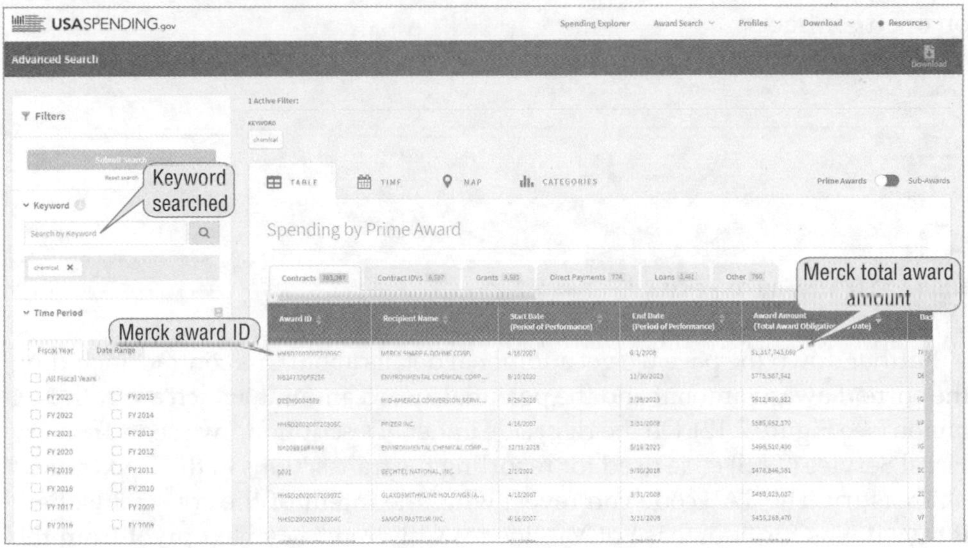

Figure 7.10: Viewing contracts

In this example, I searched USASpending.gov for the keyword *chemical*, which returns 763,387 contracts. The contract with the top total award amount, meaning the most money was given to them for services, is Merck Sharp & Dohme Corp. at the top of the list. There are other tabs to narrow down the search by loans and grants depending on the research question you are attempting to answer.

---

[18] www.usaspending.gov/search/USAspending.gov / last accessed 15 February 2023.
[19] www.fpds.gov/fpdsng_cms/index.php/en.

Each contract is given an ID code when created. The Merck award ID is HHSD200200720306C. You will find these codes are searchable in search engine queries that might lead to other details about the award.

Clicking the Award ID takes us to a contract summary for this specific award (see Figure 7.11). Looking at this contract, there are a few data points and potential pivots of note. First, the awarding agency is listed as the "Department of Health and Human Services (HHS)," and the recipient is Merck and Company Incorporated. This tells me that HHS paid Merck for a service, and based on the award amount, it was a significant one. The recipient address is listed on the contract, which could allow us to determine the location of a subsidiary or a satellite office or even dive deeper into the headquarters. The start and end dates of this award are also outlined in this summary, and it shows this contract was completed on June 1, 2008. The dates tell me this is not an ongoing contract that is presently open; it has been completed and would be substantially less important to the company and an adversary if the research question was focused on open contracts.

Figure 7.11: Viewing contracts

Further down the page we get additional details about this contract including the current award amount and the potential award amount, which are both $2.4 billion (see Figure 7.12). On the right side under "Description," we see a Treasury Fiscal Service (TAS) code used for reporting the transactions to the Department of Treasury. The TAS code can reveal what the intent of the contract is; here it says it was for "Purchase of Vaccine for Children." My next pivot from the TAS code would be to figure out which vaccine this award was for. The North American Industry Classification (NAIC) system code also declares a bit of information about the award as it lists the contract under "Biological Product Manufacturing," which fits with what we know about the purchase of vaccines. Finally, the Product and Service Code (PSC) lists the award under "Chemicals."

Underneath "Potential Award Amount" there is a link to view "Transaction History" for the entire award (see Figure 7.13). The Award History/Transaction History tab shows the transaction history for the entire length of the contract including dates, amounts, actions, and descriptions. Each modification to the award is given a number, which appears on the left of this chart, and if documents are present with the contract, this modification number can be used to connect them to the history. Additionally, if this contract had subawards or had

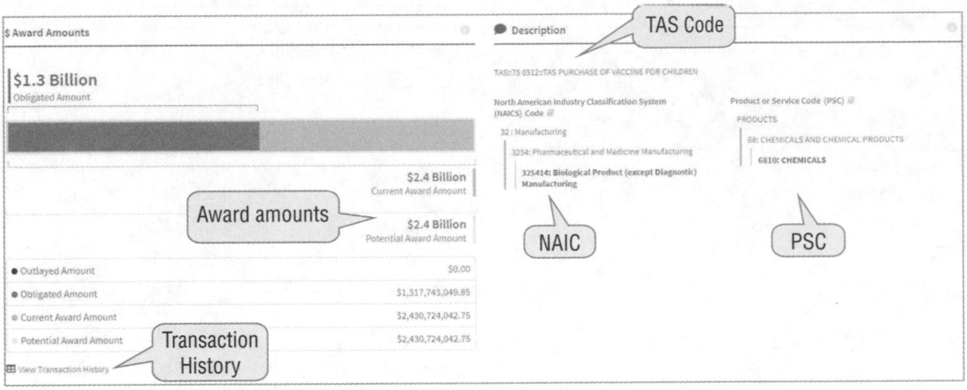

Figure 7.12: Viewing contracts

received federal funding, they would show up here under their respective tabs; this contract did not have either.

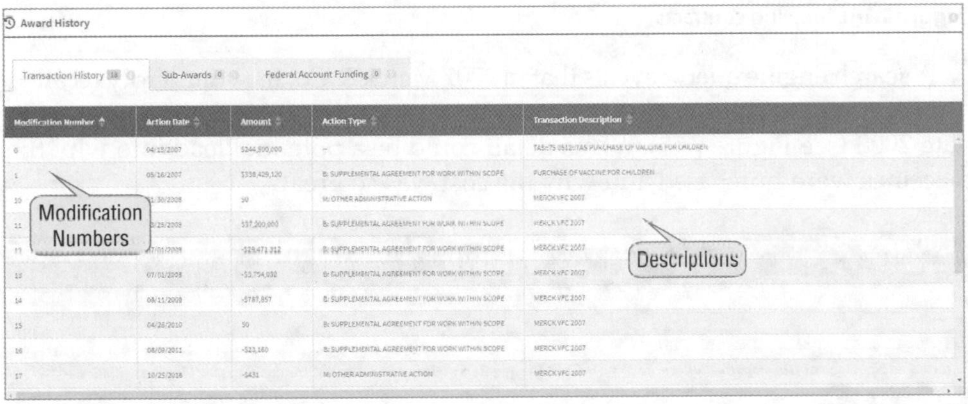

Figure 7.13: USASpending.gov

At the bottom of the page on usaspending.gov under "Additional Information" is where we can find supplementary data about the award, including a breakdown of agencies and offices providing the award, addresses and identifiers for the recipient of the award, place of performance, and even corresponding executive compensation details (see Figure 7.14).

At this point, we have collected quite a bit of data on the vaccine award between HHS and Merck; here we could pivot through any of the selectors we found to further analyze other contracts awarded for these entities. I would ask the following questions:

■ What other things are performed at these addresses?

■ Can I determine what vaccine was purchased?

■ What other organizations does HHS contract with?"

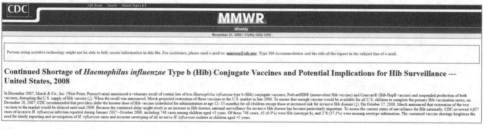

Figure 7.14: Viewing contracts

A search engine query reveals that in 2007 Merck & Co. Inc voluntarily recalled flu vaccines for children and expected the restoration to hit the U.S. market in late 2008 (see Figure 7.15).[20] This detail could be a potential lead into why the vaccines were purchased and why the cost was so great.

Figure 7.15: CDC

USASpending.gov is not the only free resource available for searching government contracts. The United States also offers the System for Award Management or SAM.gov,[21] which is an official U.S. government site allowing access and search of publicly available award data. This time, instead of looking at an award, let's look at an opportunity. An opportunity is simply a procurement notice posted by an organization so that anyone interested in the project can submit a proposal.

---

[20] www.cdc.gov/mmwr/preview/mmwrhtml/mm5746a2.htm.
[21] https://sam.gov.

The following is a contract opportunity for "Soil Hauling for Yosemite Park" that was posted to SAM.gov (see Figure 7.16). The opportunity is being offered by the PWR SF/SEA MABO Office, within the National Park Service, which falls under the Department of the Interior. A quick Google search tells me PWR SF/SEA MABO means Pacific West Region San Francisco Major Acquisition Buying Offices. It seems obvious that Yosemite National Park wants some soil moved, but why?

Figure 7.16: Contract opportunity

At the very top of the listing on the website there is a green dot that indicated at the time I pulled this image the listing was still active. The "General Information" section of the opportunity offers further details about the contract such as the date the original opportunity was posted, when it was updated, when offers are due, and when it will become inactive. Again, sometimes inactive contracts can be out of scope in a case, so these dates are helpful indicators whether it is worth it to dig deeper. Moving through the links on the left side of the page, next is "Classification."

The "Classification" section is most often used to illustrate where the award funding is originating from (see Figure 7.17). In the case of large contracts, there can be many subcontractors working across various parts of the whole contract. For instance, if I am building a satellite, I may need to contract out the work on the dish, the technology pieces inside, the installation, etc. All this work can be performed separately by subcontractors or teaming contracts but awarded under one large government fund that has been set aside as an umbrella fund for many large projects categorized in the same way.

Looking closer at the classification of our soil removal opportunity, the funding appears to be coming from a Small Business Set Aside. According to Google,

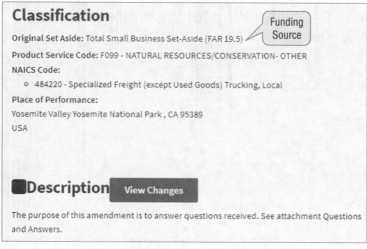

Figure 7.17: Contract opportunity

the Small Business Set Aside is for awarding acquisitions to only small business concerns.[22] Just as we saw from USASpending.gov, each award can have PSC and NAICS codes, which are government procurement details and classifications for business establishments that we can pull contextual details from to use within our analysis. Although the description section for this particular listing is sparse, this is a great place to answer questions about the expected work to be performed. If we imagine for a minute that the opportunity is for constructing a new secure building at a data center, by using opportunity listings and contract award details, we can potentially determine where it will be located, what technology they use to secure the building, and any vulnerable points in the structure.

I teased them earlier in this chapter, but I am always most curious about the documents and files that are sometimes attached to the RFIs, RFPs, and final contract awards. I have run across full construction blueprints of a protected

---

[22] www.acquisition.gov/far/subpart-19.5.

government facility, detailed security guard shift schedules, and schematics of RFID badge and door access technology. Fair warning, finding these nuggets of gold can be hit or miss, and I will admit to personally succumbing to many hours of manual digging through hundreds of pages of contract details to find what I need. To locate these files in SAM, just click the attachment link on the left side of the site (see Figure 7.18).

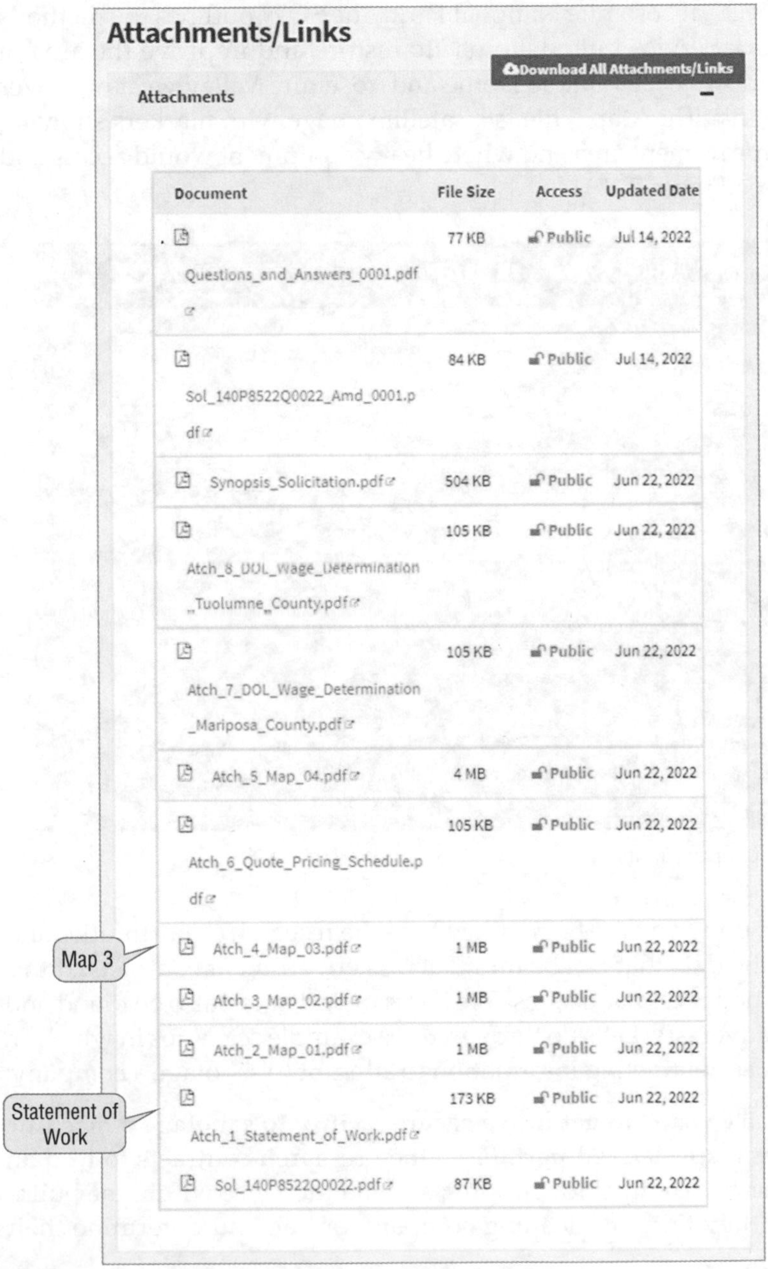

Attachments/Links

⬇Download All Attachments/Links

Attachments   —

Document	File Size	Access	Updated Date
Questions_and_Answers_0001.pdf	77 KB	🔓 Public	Jul 14, 2022
Sol_140P8522Q0022_Amd_0001.pdf	84 KB	🔓 Public	Jul 14, 2022
Synopsis_Solicitation.pdf	504 KB	🔓 Public	Jun 22, 2022
Atch_8_DOL_Wage_Determination_Tuolumne_County.pdf	105 KB	🔓 Public	Jun 22, 2022
Atch_7_DOL_Wage_Determination_Mariposa_County.pdf	105 KB	🔓 Public	Jun 22, 2022
Atch_5_Map_04.pdf	4 MB	🔓 Public	Jun 22, 2022
Atch_6_Quote_Pricing_Schedule.pdf	105 KB	🔓 Public	Jun 22, 2022
Atch_4_Map_03.pdf	1 MB	🔓 Public	Jun 22, 2022
Atch_3_Map_02.pdf	1 MB	🔓 Public	Jun 22, 2022
Atch_2_Map_01.pdf	1 MB	🔓 Public	Jun 22, 2022
Atch_1_Statement_of_Work.pdf	173 KB	🔓 Public	Jun 22, 2022
Sol_140P8522Q0022.pdf	87 KB	🔓 Public	Jun 22, 2022

Map 3 → Atch_4_Map_03.pdf

Statement of Work → Atch_1_Statement_of_Work.pdf

Figure 7.18 Contract opportunity

SAM shows a list of documents provided throughout the course of procurement and awarding of contracts. In the list for the Soil Hauling opportunity, I was immediately intrigued by the map files, but to be thorough I downloaded all of the document files to my computer. Upon inspecting the files, the Statement of Work (SOW) (`Atch_1_Statement_of_Work.pdf`) and Map 3 (`Atch_4_Map_03.pdf`) immediately provided me with detailed information on what exactly the proposed project is. The opportunity being offered is for the "Pothole Thumb Restoration Project" at Yosemite National Park. The SOW outlines the methods the National Park Service intends to use to restore and improve the area of Tuolumme Meadows near Pothole Dome and Yosemite Valley west of Lower Pines Campground. The Map 3 file is a satellite image with markers showing the intended improvement area and where heavy equipment would access and move the soil (see Figure 7.19).

Figure 7.19: Contract opportunity

Ideally by this point you are beginning to see the research opportunities and implications of the data that can be found across government contracts. If this contract information is easy and accessible for us to find, it can also be found and exploited by an adversary. Let's go through three example scenarios in which an adversary may use contracting information to attempt to sabotage a company:

1. **An adversary wants to get into a secure facility to sabotage a machine that makes a specialized part.** First, they research contracts to find an ongoing service contract for cleaning and maintenance within the building. Next, they find the cleaning company online and determine their

uniforms. Faking the uniform, the adversary walks freely into the building past security.

2. **An adversary wants to get into a secure facility to steal proprietary information.** First, they research contracts and find a detailed blueprint of the facility attached to a construction contract for adding a new wing onto the company building. Next, they find the contracts for the security company, and within the details it shows what times armed guards will be at the door. The adversary notices a gap in time when shifts change and using the blueprints sneaks into the building directly to the area with proprietary information.

3. **An adversarial group wants to intercept a shipment from the company and alter the product.** First, the adversary performs contract research to determine what company provides transportation services. Using that information, the group determines a stopping point along the shipping route to intercept the product. The adversary pays the transporter to switch the product with the altered version and continue to the destination.

These scenarios may seem far-fetched, but in February 2022 the Department of Defense released a report[23] that addressed the vulnerabilities in the supply chains critical to the defense industrial base. The report outlines their strategy for mitigating foreign ownership, control, and influence through assessing our acquisition strategies and mitigating influence before awards are granted. The report goes on to detail a robust cybersecurity strategy for the supply chain and specifically mentions the need to ". . . ensure investments are not lost through insertion of counterfeit/compromised materials, IP theft, the embedding of malicious logic into microelectronics, or malicious programming impacting DoD networks."

Organizations are governed by power, whether it is the power of the executive team, power of the market, or power of shareholders they are beholden to. Being able to map who within a community holds power can help us form hypotheses about their behavior.

Power Mapping

All organizations function with roles of power, whether the power comes from investors, C-level job titles, or high-ranking board positions. Understanding who holds the power in an organization and even within a community as well as what motivates them is called *power mapping*.

The technique of power mapping is used as a tool to identify who holds power and then influence those people who make decisions to do what you want them to do. Power mapping is often used for political campaigns to determine potential

---

[23] https://media.defense.gov/2022/Feb/24/2002944158/-1/-1/1/
DOD-EO-14017-REPORT-SECURING-DEFENSE-CRITICAL-SUPPLY-CHAINS.PDF.

community allies and identify those who may oppose campaign positions and how to influence them to switch sides (see Figure 7.20).

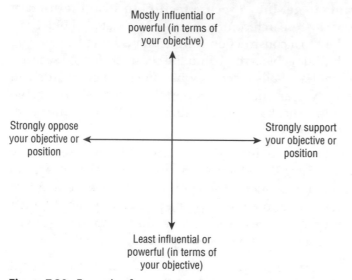

Figure 7.20: Example of power mapping

For OSINT, power mapping can provide leads about who may be influenced through investments and donations. Power mapping can reveal political affiliations, donations, and links to organizations like Super PACs, a type of independent political action committee that is legally allowed to raise unlimited funds unlike a political campaign. Further, we can identify associations to think tanks, councils, and other organizations that may compel a leader to make decisions that benefit the associations. One of my favorite sites for analyzing power mapping is the grassroots watchdog site LittleSis (see Figure 7.21).[24]

The LittleSis free open-source dataset details the way in which money and power dictate policies, contributions, and contracts. On the website, a user can enter the name of an organization or individual in the search field to query the dataset and return relationships, interlocks, giving, and more. For the following example I searched the U.S. Department of Labor. The Relationships tab lists leadership and staff for the organization along with the dates they served, while the Interlocks tab shows the connections people within the Department of Labor have to other organizations. On the Giving tab it shows the individual employees within the Department of Labor that made political donations. We can see the names of the individual donors, which party or candidate received the donation, and the total amount to each. On each search page, LittleSis also offers the source links for all of the data so each item can be individually researched (see Figure 7.22).

---

[24] LittleSis / `https://littlesis.org/`/last accessed February 15, 2023.

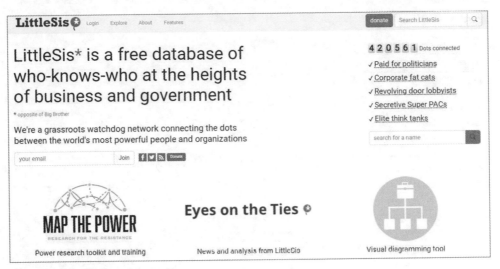

Figure 7.21: Contract opportunity

U.S. Department of Labor

Relationships | Interlocks | Giving | Data

People Have Given To
People with positions in U.S. Department of Labor have made donations to

Recipient	Total	Donors
Republican National Committee	$118,031	Kenneth M Duberstein, Roderick A Dearment, Patrick Pizzella, Mark D Cowan, John T O'Rourke, Elaine Chao, David M Walker, William Emerson Brock III, Diana Furchtgott-Roth, Randel K Johnson, Peter J Gunas III, Steven J Law, Michael H Moskow, Dennis M Kass
Barack Obama	$76,927	Alexis M Herman, Hilda Solis, Weldon J Rougeau, Edward Montgomery, Alan B Krueger, Robert Reich, Katherine Archuleta, Alex Mas, Phyllis C Borzi, Oscar Ramirez, Lawrence Katz, Cheryl Dorsey, Jennifer Duck
Mitt Romney	$64,800	Kenneth M Duberstein, Roderick A Dearment, Patrick Pizzella, Mark D Cowan, John T O'Rourke, Elaine Chao, William Emerson Brock III, Randel K Johnson, T Timothy Ryan Jr, Peter J Gunas III, Eugene Scalia, Steven J Law, Richard F Schubert, Richard Manning, Alex Acosta
Republican Party of Kentucky	$60,000	Elaine Chao
George W Bush	$46,800	Kenneth M Duberstein, Jon William Breyfogle, Patrick Pizzella, Mark D Cowan, Elaine Chao, William Emerson Brock III, T Timothy Ryan Jr, Peter J Gunas III, Eugene Scalia, Steven J Law, Michael H Moskow, Dennis M Kass

Updated 7 months ago

Basic Info

Types Organization, Government Body
Website https://www.dol.gov/
Aliases Dept. of Labor, Labor, Dept of (DOL), Department of Labor

External Links

Wikipedia: United_States_Department_of_Labor

Tags

tracking

Figure 7.22: LittleSis

If you visit LittleSis without a definitive research question in mind, you can peruse their user-created lists outlining power structures ranging from January 6 to Trump Rally speakers to the billionaires in Florida and in between. Perhaps some of these lists can provide a jumping-off point for your research. If you are a visual person, there is also a section to explore user-created power maps (see Figures 7.23-7.24).

Lists

Your Lists   Create

Name ▽	Entities ▽	Created At ⬇
Jan. 6 2021 "Stop the Steal" Trump rally speakers	13	February 10, 2021
Biden Agency Review Teams	512	November 12, 2020
Climate Mandate campaign Biden cabinet suggestions	36	November 12, 2020
Biden-Harris Transition COVID-19 Advisory Board	12	November 09, 2020
Biden-Harris Transition Team's Advisory Board	21	November 08, 2020
Trump administration Hatch Act violations/accusations as of Nov. 2020	45	October 26, 2020
Steve Mnuchin & Louise Linton wedding attendees	48	September 29, 2020
Florida billionaires Sept 2020	56	September 28, 2020
Top 10 Fortune 1000 Food and Drug Stores (2018)	10	September 23, 2020
Raleigh City Council	16	September 23, 2020
FinCEN Files investigation: suspicious international money transfers - suspected money laundering	32	September 20, 2020
Trump Supreme Court potential nominees - full running list Sep. 2020	46	September 20, 2020
Acid Dreams	190	September 05, 2020
News Corporation Board of Directors mid-2020	10	August 19, 2020

Figure 7.23: LittleSis screenshot

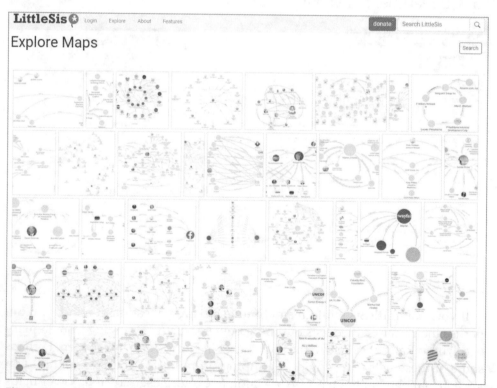

Figure 7.24: LittleSis Power maps

Recognizing a power structure within communities can help to illuminate situations of "dark money" spending and fraud. A recent example of power and money influence is the 2019 college admission scandal involving actresses Lori Loughlin and Felicity Huffman.[25] The two wealthy actresses along with 32 other parents paid enormous sums of money in a scheme to circumvent college admissions requirements. A man in California, William Rick Singer, provided false records, test scores, and staged photos falsifying the student's athleticism while raking in somewhere between $200,000 and $6.5 million from parents. In addition to the parents and Singer, athletic coaches from Yale, USC, Stanford, Georgetown, and Wake Forest were among those implicated.[26] In this case, wealthy parents used their power to bribe their way into some of the top universities in the United States.

Tips for Analyzing Organizations Outside the United States

While I am based in the United States, I would be remiss not to discuss some of the top resources for analyzing organizations outside of the United States. While many of the OSINT techniques are the same, it can be helpful to have a list of resources for other areas of the world.

Canada

In Canada, the public business filing program is called System for Electronic Data Analysis and Retrieval (SEDAR).[27] Like EDGAR in the United States, the site maintains a database of all Canadian companies that have been issued securities. The documents found in SEDAR are primary source authoritative documents.

United Kingdom

The following resources are for the United Kingdom:

Companies House

All incorporated companies in the UK are made available to the public through the official registrar Companies House.[28] Accessing the free primary source database lets you search for a name to see an overview of the company, filing history with downloadable files, officers and people in power, and legal charges (see Figure 7.25).

---

[25] www.npr.org/2019/03/12/702539140/u-s-accuses-actresses-others-of-fraud-in-wide-college-admissions-scandal.

[26] www.justice.gov/usao-ma/investigations-college-admissions-and-testing-bribery-scheme.

[27] www.sedar.com/homepage_en.htm.

[28] www.gov.uk/government/organisations/companies-house.

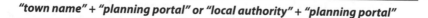

Figure 7.25: LittleSis Power maps

UK Planning System

Another place to find information on UK businesses and subjects is the UK Planning System.[29] When a person or entity wants to construct, alter, or demolish on UK land, they are required to submit a planning application to the local authority. Using a technique, I learned from a great OSINT analyst and friend, Steven Harris (@Nixintel), we can use some simple Google dorks to find the specific local authority:

> *"town name" + "planning portal" or "local authority" + "planning portal"*

Planning portals contain planning applications featuring details such as name, address, building plans/changes, and other documents. Let's look at a case study using Steven's techniques to see what kind of information we can glean from the UK Planning System.

---

[29] https://nixintel.info/osint-tools/
using-the-uk-planning-system-for-osint.

Case Study:

The West Bridgford Wire posted a news story about officially objecting to a very expensive building plan for Linby council.[30] Let's try to find the building plan objection and see if it has any more details. A Google search for Linby UK told me that Linby is located in Nottinghamshire, so I searched for "Nottinghamshire" + "planning portal," which leads me to their local planning page[31] (see Figure 7.26).

Councillors officially object to £15.7 million Linby council building plans

By Wire

🕒 12:12 pm 27 Jun 2022   UPDATED: 7:52 pm 27 Jun 2022

Hucknall's Ashfield Independent Councillors Dave Shaw, Lee Waters and John Wilmott have officially objected to the planning objection for a new £15.7million office block at Top Wighay Farm, Linby near Hucknall.

The Councillors, in their joint objection claim that the application is "...clouded in uncertainty" and that "It's impossible to assess the impact on highways...due to the

Figure 7.26 `Westbridgfordwire.com`

By using the search feature on the planning page, we can narrow down the criteria. Because I know this was an objection to a planning objection, I am going to start with pending applications (see Figure 7.27).[32]

---

[30] `https://westbridgfordwire.com/councillors-officially-object-to-15-7-million-linby-council-building-plans`.

[31] `www.nottinghamshire.gov.uk/planning-and-environment`.

[32] Nottinghamshire County Council / `www.nottinghamshire.gov.uk/`/ last accessed February 15, 2023.

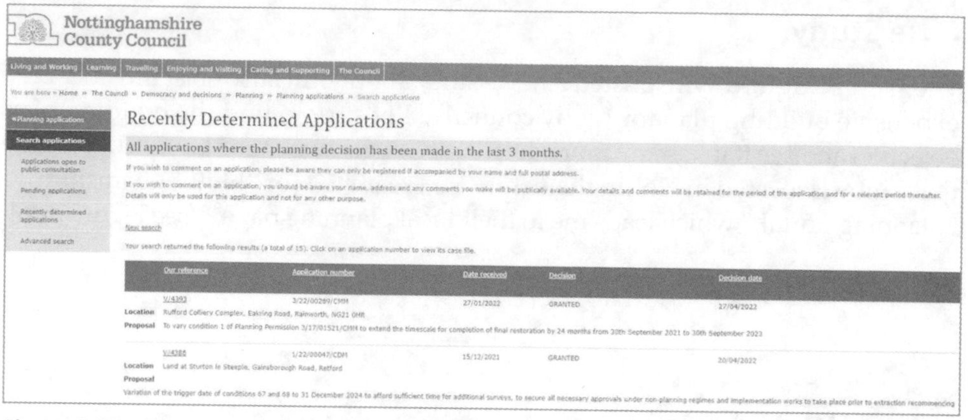

Figure 7.27: County council page

That gives us a list of pending applications, and one of them has the address and site details provided in the article. The actual planning application has case officer details including name, phone, and email address. This information is followed by a long list of PDF documents ranging from agent comments to schematics and blueprints of the proposed building (see Figures 7.28-7.29).

China

Much like the United States and UK, Chinese companies are required to disclose details about their business. In China, they register this information through the State Administration of Market Regulation's National Enterprise Credit Information Publicity System (NECIPS). This database contains all legally registered entities in China, people in key positions, and often identifiable information relating to the people mentioned. Using a translator like Google Translate, we can view the pages on the site and pull unique information like the company's Unified Social Credit Code (USCC), which is an 18-digit business registration number given to all entities in China (see Figure 7.30-7.31).

Russia

In Russia, businesses are required to register to the Russian Federal Tax Registry (ERGUL). This is a state-sponsored database for legal entities and their statuses. Russian companies have a shortened name and a full name; for this reason, it is often easier to search by the entity's tax ID number. Again, using Google Translate we can translate the database site at `egrul.nalog.ru`. As always, it is a good practice to use a VPN when connecting to foreign government websites.

Documents

Name

☑ **Group: Application Form & Location Plans**

3a. Location Plan

Application form_Redacted

☑ **Group: Supporting Statements**

Agent Comments on NCC Highways Concerns_Redacted

Reasons for not installing a formal pedestrian crossing point

Applicant response to Highways Consultation Comments_Redacted

Framework Travel Plan

Ecology Addendum Letter_Redacted

Ecological Impact Assessment_Redacted

Noise Assessment_Redacted

SUPERSEDED Surface Water Model Calculations

Security Needs Assessment_Redacted

Surface Water Drainage Strategy Plan_Redacted

Detailed Unexploded Ordnance (UXO) Risk Assessment_Redacted

Express Preliminary UXO Risk Assessment_Redacted

Flood Risk Assessment & Drainage Strategy_Redacted

Noise Mitigation Plan

Heritage Desk Based Assessment

Air Quality Statement_Redacted

Covering Letter_Redacted

Geo-Environmental Assessment_Redacted

TRANSPORT & INFRASTRUCTURE PLANNING

Construction and Ecological Management Plan_Redacted

Design and Access Statement

Validation amendments Covering letter_Redacted

Planning Statement

Preliminary Geo-Environmental Risk Assessment_Redacted

Trial Pit Log_Redacted

Figure 7.28: PDF documents

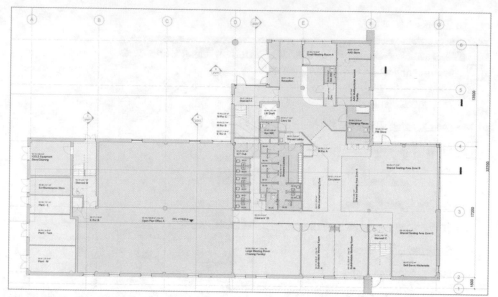

Figure 7.29: Nottinghamshire screenshots

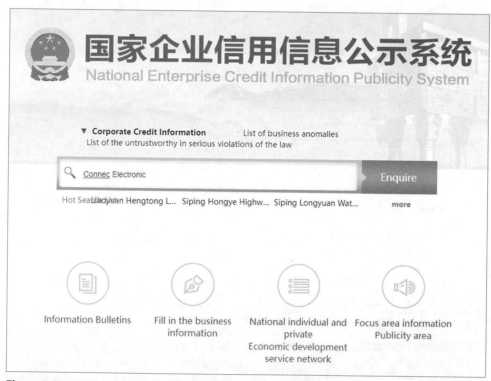

Figure 7.30: National enterprise credit information publicity system

Figure 7.31: National enterprise credit information publicity system

Middle East

In Iran the most difficult task with public company records is translation and understanding how the records are presented. If searching in English does not yield results, it may be necessary to translate the business into Persian. To avoid any ambiguity, we can use common numbers. The common ID numbers for legal entities within Iran are the National ID and the entity Registration number. The National ID number is a unique 11-digit number given to legal entities within Iran.

Iran's Official Gazette (Rooznameh Rasmi)

Iran has an official publication for self-reported business entity announcements called the Official Gazette or the Rooznameh Rasmi. In the Gazette, business activities including changes are reported. Many times, entities within Iran are legally required to post announcements for financial statements and filings. Within these announcements it is possible to find the National ID Number of an entity. Because this information is self-reported, it is important to be aware that there could be errors like transposed numbers.

Tehran Chamber of Commerce

The Chamber of Commerce publishes a list of companies. The information within the details is self-reported much like the Gazette; however, the main selling point of this publication is that it provides both the Farsi and English translations of business names. Because trying to translate an English name into Farsi can cause errors and possibly provide the wrong company, it is great that this is offered.

Once we are able to find the information necessary to understand the way an organization works, how their employee structure is determined, and what their financials look like, we can begin to start looking for anomalies that might indicate impropriety.

7.4   Recognizing Organizational Crime

OSINT analysts seem to be drawn to certain types of cases that affect them personally; for me, I love researching fraud and illegal activity. There is something exciting about digging deep and uncovering something that was supposed to be a secret and then revealing it to the world. I am not sure what that says about me as a person, but I know I am not alone in my interests. Being able to recognize abnormalities that can lead to organizational crime including illegal business practices, misconduct, and fraud is a worthwhile skill to have.

Organizational crime is a form of crime that is carried out by a people on behalf of their organization.[33] White-collar organizational crimes can be difficult to spot because they are intentionally masked through complex systems of control, ownership, and individuals across many entities, financial institutions, and jurisdictions. Think of crimes that are committed in plain sight like embezzlement, money laundering, securities violations, and racketeering; by hiding the criminal activity out in the open, it makes it hard to tie owners to assets.[34] Sometimes, we get a glimpse into the shady inner workings of corporate and organizational greed when their data is surreptitiously leaked to the public.

In 2016, the German Newspaper Süddeutsche Zeitung (SZ) revealed the anonymously leaked 11.5 million encrypted and confidential documents called the "Panama Papers" from the Panamanian-based, fourth largest law firm in the world, Mossack Fonseca. These documents exposed 214,000 tax havens and a network of rich people, entities, and public officials across the world. Most of the contained documents did not indicate illegal activity; however, several of the shell companies created by Mossack Fonseca were used to evade taxes and sanctions, and fraud.

In 2017, another 13.4 million confidential digital documents were leaked to Süddeutsche Zeitung (SZ) revealing the offshore activity of the wealthy, national leaders, and companies. This time the leak originated from a law firm in Bermuda called Appleby and included emails, statements, and agreements. While holding an entity offshore is not illegal and neither are shell companies, some organizations do use them as a method of concealing acts of fraud and the identities behind them. If we can spot potential shell corporations using a set of outlined criteria, we may be able to get faster and more efficient at uncovering

---

[33] www.britannica.com/topic/corporate-crime.
[34] www.fatf-gafi.org/media/fatf/documents/reports/
FATF-Egmont-Concealment-beneficial-ownership.pdf.

this type of organizational deceit. The following are some important terms that will help you make sense of the potential for criminal activity schemes:

- **Shell Corporation:** A business with no active operations or assets often used to disguise ownership from law enforcement or to create a tax haven offshore

- **Front Company:** A fully functioning entity meant to appear legitimate but is ultimately used to obscure the illegal financial activity being conducted

- **Blackhole Jurisdictions:** Beneficial ownership obfuscated behind intermediary companies in jurisdictions where the legal owners are not disclosed

- **Straw Men:** Informally nominated shareholders such as children, spouses, family, and business associates

- **Boiler Room Operation:** A call center where high-pressure sales tactics are employed to sell stocks to potential investors

Shell Corporations

A *shell corporation* is a company that solely exists on paper with no real employees or office locations. These corporations can hold bank accounts and be a registered owner of assets. While some shell companies exist for legal purposes like acting as a trustee or establishing business in other countries, they are also used as an anonymous vehicle for money laundering, tax evasion, and fraud. A shell company can be registered and owned from a different country, often "tax haven" countries with relaxed tax regulations like Bermuda, the British Virgin Islands, the Cayman Islands, Bahamas, the Channel Islands, Switzerland, and Luxembourg, which is legal if the money was earned in the host country. Furthermore, if a law firm sets up the shell company within the host country, like Mossack Fonseca did in the Panama Papers, it adds a layer of anonymity protecting the true owner. In the United States, states like Delaware, Wyoming, and Nevada are often used for registering shell companies due to the ease of incorporating and privacy laws protecting anonymity.

A case I am reminded of that used shell companies to commit investment fraud and money laundering is the arrest and ultimately the conviction of Robert Lenard Booth in 2022. Booth was sentenced to 10 years for running an international boiler room scheme to pressure people into investing in securities they never received. Booth along with several co-conspirators targeted victims by pretending to be licensed brokers and used high-pressure sales tactics to sell discount stocks to victims over the phone. Victims were told to wire hundreds of thousands of dollars to shell companies in New York, Hong Kong, and

Singapore, leaving some without their life savings. According to the U.S. Justice Department, Booth defrauded "at least 17 victims of $2,003,993."[35] Booth was able to mask a lot of their illegal activities and money laundering through illicit shell companies because of how difficult they are to detect.

Here are some of the reasons criminals may use a shell company:

- Masks the origins and flow of money
- Conceals the identity of the owner
- Obscures possible motives
- Hides profits/losses

The "Tells"

Because illegal shell companies are hard to detect and unravel, I put together some criteria to help you with identifying them throughout your research.[36,37] The tells in this list are of course analysis tips and certainly not a foolproof guide for detecting illegal shell company activity, but finding several of these "tells" may assist in distinguishing the real from the fake. Taking the time to understand and recognize the following tells will help you in future analysis:

- Does the incorporation assist with maintaining anonymity?
  - The company is registered in a tax haven offshore: Cyprus, Panama, Hong Kong, etc.
- Does the company have a meaningless or uninspired name?
  - A vague name can mean it was batch created with other companies.
- Do the owners exist on the Internet?
  - No website or mention of owners on the website.
  - No social media presence.
- Is there no real way to contact the company?
  - Generic or fake email addresses.
    - Address is a personal home or apartment.
  - Partial or no physical addresses.
  - Registered agent address is shared with other companies.

---

[35] www.justice.gov/usao-sdny/pr/robert-lenard-booth-sentenced-ten-years-defrauding-investors-over-2-million.
[36] https://aml-toolbox.medium.com/finding-shell-companies-an-investigators-guide-258c3f244bfd.
[37] www.fraudconferencenews.com/home/2018/6/17/breaking-the-shell.

There are many ways in which an organization and its employees and stakeholders can manipulate records and use their work to hide crimes. One way that nations try to handle issues on a global scale relating to financial crimes, human rights abuses, and wars is through the implementation of sanctions.

7.5   Sanctions, Blacklists, and Designations

A *sanction* is a penalty imposed to force someone to obey a rule. In the political sense, a sanction is used prevent things like escalation of conflict, terrorism, human-rights violations, and narcotics sales, and to stop nuclear proliferation. For analysts who work in areas like supply chain investigations, due diligence, counterproliferation, counter terrorism, and geopolitics, monitoring sanctions activity can be crucial to providing answers to the critical and often national security-level questions that are no doubt being asked by your stakeholders.

There are several categories of political sanctions:

- **Economic Sanctions:** Financial and trade penalties imposed on a country to stop or deter specific policies and actions
- **Diplomatic Sanctions:** Reduces or entirely removes the diplomatic ties between nations
- **Individual Sanctions:** Demonstrates displeasure with an individual's actions by freezing assets or banning travel

The value that observing and monitoring ongoing sanctions offers to an OSINT analyst is a historical pattern of activity and an easy tipoff to illicit actions. As a maritime OSINT enthusiast, I find myself deeply invested in the surveillance of sanctioned companies and their vessels sailing around the world.

For my work, it is highly important to understand the context behind a specific sanction designation, the entities involved, and the historical patterns of activity so that I may compare it to what I can presently see. A good example of how OSINT research can be enhanced through sanctions monitoring is through the lens of illicit oil transfers. The facilitation of illegal oil sales to sanctioned countries can be tracked through business intelligence research that unravels the corporate structure masking the origins. We can also use transportation intelligence techniques to track the vessels that carry, transfer, and deliver the oil. Social media monitoring can offer insights into movements and imagery, and official sanctions reporting can alert us to organizations, individuals, and vessels to keep an eye on.

Organizations that designate sanctions

There are two main organizations that hand down sanctions and offer official reports: the United Nations Security Council (USNC) and the Office of Foreign Asset Control (OFAC).

The United Nations Security Council

The primary role of the USNC is maintaining peace and security internationally and often that means using sanctions. The measure of sanctions varies but includes economic and trade, arms embargoes, travel bans, and financial restrictions for designated countries. Each sanctioned regime is overseen and monitored by a specific sanctions committee, and they are available to view on the USNC website.[38] Each committee maintains detailed documentation on the measures taken by USNC, background information, listing criteria, press releases, documents, annual reports, and more.

The Office of Foreign Assets Control

OFAC[39] is a department positioned within the U.S. Treasury Department that is charged with enforcing trade and economic sanctions that have been imposed by the United States on foreign regimes, terrorists, and traffickers. OFAC is made up of lawyers and intelligence analysts and most of the cases are brought forth through investigations by the Office of Global Targeting (OGT).

OFAC has the authority to block specific assets and restrict trade and has been integral in handing down sanctions to Cuba, Iraq, Iran, and Russia to further foreign policy interests and protect human rights. Additionally, OFAC publishes a Specially Designated Nationals (SDN) list that outlines the specific people, organizations, and vessels that are prohibited from doing business. Active OFAC Sanctions programs can be found on their website[40] along with a form to sign up to receive sanctions alerts by email for their three lists: Specially Designated Sanctions, Consolidated Sanctions, and Additional OFAC Sanctions.

Other Blacklists

Outside of the USNC and OFAC sanctions lists there are other blacklists that can affect an organization and their ability to do business around the world.

---

[38] www.un.org/securitycouncil/sanctions/information.
[39] https://home.treasury.gov/policy-issues/office-of-foreign-assets-control-sanctions-programs-and-information.
[40] https://home.treasury.gov/policy-issues/financial-sanctions/sanctions-programs-and-country-information.

The Paris MOU on Port State Control is an organization consisting of 27 maritime administrators across Europe and North America assembled to maintain international safety, security, environmental, and human rights standards across vessels.[41] The Paris MOU maintains White, Gray, and Black lists that demonstrate vessels with poor performance and that are deemed high risk. The ranking is based on inspections and detentions across a 3-year period, and the lists are available for download at `parismou.org/detentions-banning/white-grey-and-black-list`.

The Financial Action Task Force (FATF),[42] whose main goal is to combat money laundering and the financing of terrorism, maintains a FATF Black list and Gray list. These lists are meant to encourage the improvement of regulations and anti-money laundering (AML) standards from listed countries while drawing attention to the high risk that doing business in these countries presents to organizations and individuals. The two lists are updated regularly on `fatf-gafi.org`.

We have looked extensively at for-profit organizations, how they are structured, and how we can glean information from their disclosures and documents. Nonprofit organizations work in a very similar way; let's take a look at how to find information using primary and secondary sources.

7.6   501(c)(3) Nonprofits

An organization that meets the U.S. Internal Revenue requirements for 501(c)(3) status is exempt from federal income tax, and all donations made to the org are tax deductible, making them a *not-for-profit organization*. The nonprofit organizations typically eligible for 501(c)(3) status are private foundations, churches, religious organizations, and charitable organizations. Analyzing nonprofits is much like researching any other organization where we employ techniques for illuminating structure, key players, data leaks, and discrepancies. The largest difference between a nonprofit and a typical for-profit organization is that to maintain 501(c)(3) status, the organization must not serve any private interests including the creator or any shareholders. Additionally, a nonprofit is legally forbidden from participating in political campaigns, lobbying, and influencing legislation. That said, corruption of nonprofits is a widespread issue that we can use OSINT analysis to research and expose.

During the COVID pandemic in 2021, the FBI reported massive amounts of fraud in programs using pandemic aid for needy children. A nonprofit organization called Advance Youth Athletic Development claimed to be able to prepare

---

[41] `www.parismou.org/about-us/organisation`.
[42] `www.fatf-gafi.org/publications/high-risk-and-other-monitored-jurisdictions/documents/call-for-action-october-2022.html`.

5,000 dinners per night for children in the northeast Minneapolis region. The state of Minnesota funneled $3.2 million dollars of federal aid into the food program to assist with feeding the children. In January 2021, 200 FBI investigators carried out raids of 15 homes and offices, revealing a massive investigation into the large nonprofit Feeding Our Future, which was responsible for proper spending of funds provided to the smaller nonprofit groups like Advance Youth Athletic Development. The FBI said that these groups had received more than $65 million, and filings say almost none of it was used for feeding children; instead, it was used to purchase other items including real estate and cars. Ultimately, Feeding Our Future was prevented from receiving state aid and formally dissolved in late February 2021.[43]

The type of financial fraud seen in the Feeding Our Future case is not unique. The 2022 Report to the Nations fraud study by the Association of Certified Fraud Examiners (ACFE) states that nonprofits suffer an annual median loss of $60,000.[44] Illegal schemes within nonprofits can include vendor kickbacks, misappropriation of funds, check fraud, embezzlement, and theft of money or property. Because nonprofits typically operate under less oversight and internal controls and regulations, they are especially vulnerable to fraud. As depressing as these facts are, we can use OSINT techniques along with primary source documents, consumer reporting, and public disclosures to analyze and possibly spot nonprofit misuse.

Primary Source Documents

These are primary source documents.

IRS Form 990

Form 990 is a tax form used to gather information annually about tax-exempt organizations that can be searched on public sites like ProPublica[45] and Candid.[46] Every tax exempt organization that makes less than $200,000 in revenue and has less than $500,000 in assets is required to file Form 990. If the organization makes less than $50,000 annually, they do not have to file but do have to update the IRS as to their status.

The nonprofit explorer on ProPublica shows valuable information pulled from 990 forms including incorporation date, employee identification number, classification, and annual tax filings by year (see Figure 7.32).

---

[43] www.nytimes.com/2022/03/08/us/politics/
food-aid-nonprofits-fraud-investigation.html.
[44] https://legacy.acfe.com/report-to-the-nations/2022.
[45] https://projects.propublica.org/nonprofits.
[46] https://candid.org/research-and-verify-nonprofits/990-finder.

FISCAL YEAR
ENDING DEC.

2020

PDF

Audit

The IRS has provided extracted financial data for this filing, but has not yet released the source documents.

Total Revenue $8,806,000,909

Total Functional Expenses $8,708,873,824
Net income $97,127,085

Notable sources of revenue		Percent of total revenue	
Contributions	$0		
Program services	$8,774,084,732		99.6%
Investment income	$28,049,375	0.3%	
Bond proceeds	$0		
Royalties	$0		
Rental property income	$0		
Net fundraising	$0		
Sales of assets	$3,866,802	0.0%	
Net inventory sales	$0		
Other revenue	$0		

Notable expenses		Percent of total expenses
Executive compensation	$0	
Professional fundraising fees	$0	
Other salaries and wages	$0	

Other	
Total Assets	$2,870,766,607
Total Liabilities	$1,819,084,041
Net Assets	$1,051,682,566

Figure 7.32: Pro Publica Inc. / `https://projects.propublica.org/nonprofits/organizations/133783732` / last accessed February 15, 2023.

IRS Tax Exempt Organization Search

The IRS offers a public database search for tax-exempt organizations on their website at `apps.irs.gov/app/eos`. The search filters information from Publication 78 data, the auto-revocation list, determination letters, copies of returns (990, 990-EZ, 990-PF, 990-T), and Form 990-N Postcards (see Figure 7.33).

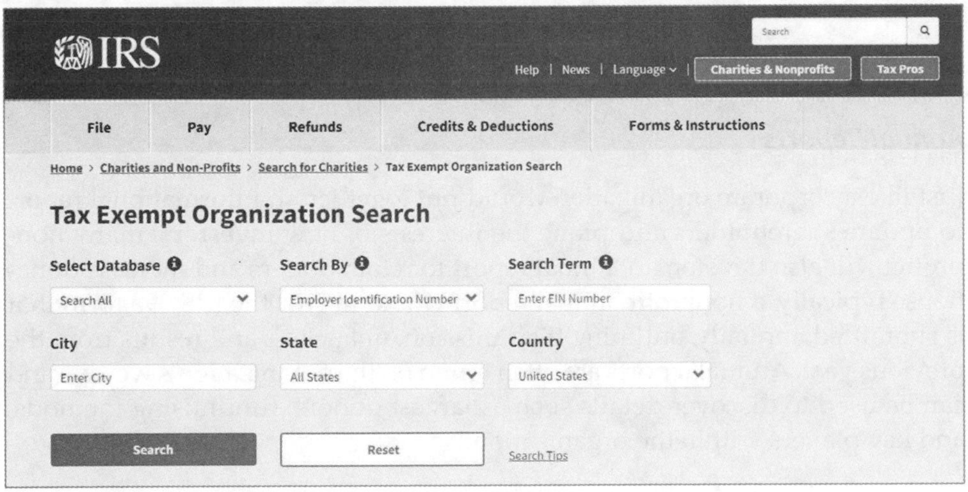

≋IRS

Search

Help | News | Language ∨ | **Charities & Nonprofits** | **Tax Pros**

| File | Pay | Refunds | Credits & Deductions | Forms & Instructions |

Home > Charities and Non-Profits > Search for Charities > Tax Exempt Organization Search

Tax Exempt Organization Search

Select Database ❶

Search All ∨

Search By ❶

Employer Identification Number ∨

Search Term ❶

Enter EIN Number

City

Enter City

State

All States ∨

Country

United States ∨

Search   Reset   Search Tips

Figure 7.33: IRS tax exempt organization search

The Federal Audit Clearinghouse

The federal government provides billions of dollars annually to many types of recipients including nonprofit organizations. A single audit was developed by the government to oversee the proper use of these funds. When the audit is complete, it is sent into the Federal Audit Clearinghouse (FAC), which stores the data in a publicly accessible database (see Figures 7.34-7.36). As an example, I searched the EID of the nonprofit Feeding Our Future whose status was revoked by the IRS. The search returned two audits from 2021 that can be downloaded in PDF form for review. The report contains an audit of the organization including auditor notes, statement of financial position, statement of activities, statement of functional expenses, and statement of cash flow.

Figure 7.34: Federal audit clearinghouse

You have selected 2 items for download. If an electronic audit does not exist then no audit download link is available

Selected Audit Reports ✔   Download Audits

Auditee EIN	Auditee Name	City	State	Fiscal Year End Date	MDL Start Date[1]	Date Received[2]	File Name	Form	Audit ⓘ	Download
814343304	FEEDING OUR FUTURE	ANTHONY	MN	09/30/2020	07/14/2021	07/12/2021	25050920201	Form	Audit	☑
814343304	FEEDING OUR FUTURE	ANTHONY	MN	09/30/2019	05/14/2021	05/11/2021	25050920191	Form	Audit	☑

Figure 7.35: Federal audit clearinghouse

Annual Reports

Just like a corporate organization would put together an informational report to update shareholders and pique the interests of new investors, many nonprofits will also develop an annual report to retain doners and increase donations. Typically, a nonprofit annual report would mirror the IRS 990 form that is submitted annually, outlining their mission, financials, and results from the previous year. Annual reports are often found on the organization's website and can be used to discover details such as largest donors, fundraising methods, and key players within the organization.

FEEDING OUR FUTURE
STATEMENT OF ACTIVITIES
SEPTEMBER 30, 2020 AND 2019

	Without Donor Restrictions	With Donor Restrictions	2020 Total	2019 total
Support and Revenue				
Support				
Contributions	$ 13	$ -	$ 13	$ 2,000
Afterschool CACFP	7,809	-	7,809	-
Adult Day Care CACFP	656,832	-	656,832	205,232
Emergency Shelta CACFP	38,764	-	38,764	-
Child Care Center CACFP Grant	-	8,238,351	8,238,351	2,105,227
Total Support	**703,418**	**8,238,351**	**8,941,769**	**2,312,459**
Revenue				
Child Care Consulting Revenue	$ 206,530		$ 206,530	125,315
Professional Development Revenue	11,790		11,790	400
Non- Program Revenue	1,056		1,056	3,124
Other Revenue	76,419		76,419	
Total Revenue	**295,795**	**-**	**295,795**	**128,839**
Total Support and Revenue	**$ 999,213**	**$ 8,238,351**	**$ 9,237,564**	**$ 2,441,298**
Expenses				
CACFP Program Expenses	$ -	$ 4,449,829	$ 4,449,829	2,094,491
Contract Servies	127,714	-	127,714	7,500
Operating Expenses	125,789		125,789	21,399
Other Expenses	28,292		28,292	19,014
Payroll Expenses	596,787		596,787	299,395
Bank Charges	20		20	
Legal Fees			-	
Occupancy and Insurance	36,334		36,334	15,683
Miscellaneous Expenses	106,604		106,604	474
SFSP Expenses	-	3,767,436	3,767,436	
Computer and Software	29,333		29,333	
Travel Expenses	5,227		5,227	644
Travel Expenses	**1,056,100**	**8,217,265**	**9,273,365**	**2,458,600**
Increase (Decrease) in Net Assets				
Without Donnor Restrictions	$ (56,887)			$ (17,302)
Without Donnor Restrictions		21,086	(35,801)	
Opening Net Assets	(13,217)		(13,217)	4,085
Total Ending Net Assets	**$ (70,104)**	**$ 21,086**	**$ (49,018)**	**$ (13,217)**

Figure 7.36: Example statement

Consumer Reports and Reviews

Consumer reports and reviews are independently researched, reviewed, and provided to consumers to protect them from predatory organizations. This could include reviewing websites, reporting on specific fields, and reporting on charities.

Charity Navigator

The Charity Navigator search at charitynavigator.org rates 501(c)(3) organizations on a 0–4 star scale based on the weighted sum of scores from a proprietary scoring methodology evaluating the performance of the organization in impact and results, accountability and finance, leadership and adaptability, and culture and community (see Figure 7.37). Having searched this system for Feeding Our Future, the nonprofit accused of fraud, Charity Navigator gives the nonprofit a High Advisory rating. The advisory outlines by date a detailed list of news articles and court filings illustrating the impropriety and why they received a High Advisory score.

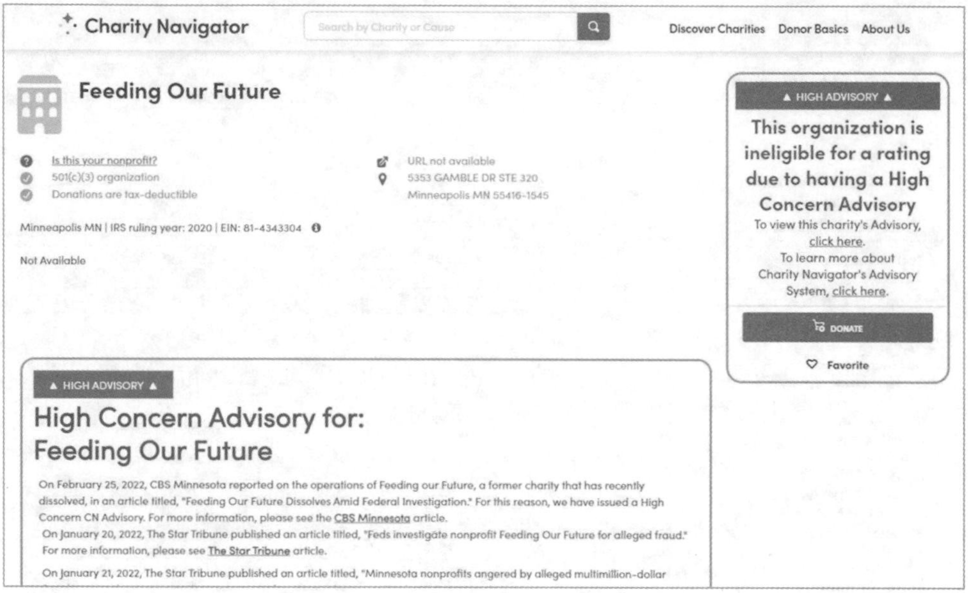

Figure 7.37: Charity Navigator

We should now have a good grasp on the ins and outs of effectively performing analysis on organizations using documentation, disclosures, and reporting. Now let's turn to what can be revealed by the internal infrastructure of an organization.

7.7 Domain Registration and IP Analysis

We have already learned the difference between primary and secondary sources, studied how to recognize organizational fraud, and dug into some cool ways to get information through power mapping, sanctions research, foreign sources, and nonprofits. Now, let's go behind the scenes and delve into websites, domains, and IP addresses and how to use them to answer research questions and further your research. However, before we go into the how, let's talk about the what and the why.

An Organization's IPs, Domain Names and Websites

What Is an IP address?

Internet Protocol (IP) is a set of rules that dictate the format in which data is transmitted across the Internet or to local area networks (LANs). An *IP address* is a unique identifier that allows the Internet to discriminate between various routers, websites, and computers. An IP address is a set of four numbers separated by periods that are allocated by the Internet Assigned Authority (IANA). Each number within each 4 sets can range from 0 to 255, so the entire range would be 0.0.0.0 to 255.255.255.255.[47] The term *IP space* is sometimes used to describe the group of IP ranges that make up an individual network.

What Is a Domain Name?

A *domain name* is the text that a user types into a browser that points to an IP address. Imagine trying to remember an IP address for every web page you visit; it would be impossible. Instead, we use domain names like "google.com" that directs you to the right place. Domains must be registered by users for a specified period of time to retain the domain name and can be reserved with different extensions that vary by country (.com, .org, .fr, .edu, .gov) (see Figure 7.38).

Figure 7.38: URLs

What Is a Website, and Why Does All of This Matter?

A *website* is a group of pages and their resources that are linked together and have a unique domain name. As an organization, to run a website where the public can find you, you must first purchase a domain name. When purchasing and reserving the domain name, you are required to provide specific details about the organization such as registrant name, address, phone number, organization name, and organization address.

---

[47] https://usa.kaspersky.com/resource-center/definitions/what-is-an-ip-address.

This act of purchasing a domain is called *domain name registration* because an ICANN-accredited registrar verifies availability of the domain and creates a WHOIS record with the provided registrant information. If the registrant does not pay extra to mask their information, it is made public and searchable through `whois.icann.org`. By combining the bits of data revealed through analyzing IP space, WHOIS records, and the front end of the user website, we can deduce a substantial amount of information about the organization.

Analyzing Organization Websites

The front end of a website is the part that users can interact with like fonts, colors, and imagery; the back end of a website is where servers, databases, APIs, and operating systems all come together to ensure the site works properly. By looking at the front end and parts of the back end of a website critically, we can extract information about the organization and its employees.

```
# Directories
Disallow: /includes/
Disallow: /misc/
Disallow: /modules/
Disallow: /profiles/
Disallow: /scripts/
Disallow: /themes/
# Files
Disallow: /CHANGELOG.txt
Disallow: /cron.php
Disallow: /INSTALL.mysql.txt
Disallow: /INSTALL.pgsql.txt
Disallow: /INSTALL.sqlite.txt
Disallow: /install.php
Disallow: /INSTALL.txt
Disallow: /LICENSE.txt
Disallow: /MAINTAINERS.txt
Disallow: /update.php
Disallow: /UPGRADE.txt
Disallow: /xmlrpc.php
# Paths (clean URLs)
Disallow: /admin/
Disallow: /comment/reply/
Disallow: /filter/tips/
Disallow: /node/add/
Disallow: /search/
Disallow: /user/register/
Disallow: /user/password/
Disallow: /user/login/
Disallow: /user/logout/
# Paths (no clean URLs)
Disallow: /?q=admin/
Disallow: /?q=comment/reply/
Disallow: /?q=filter/tips/
Disallow: /?q=node/add/
Disallow: /?q=search/
Disallow: /?q=user/password/
Disallow: /?q=user/register/
Disallow: /?q=user/login/
Disallow: /?q=user/logout/
Disallow: /?q=user/q=node/
```

Figure 7.39: `Robots.txt` file for `tesla.com`

Robots.txt

Starting at the top of a website index page we have the URL; this is where the domain is located. If we click another page within the site, we see the URL change to show that specific page within the domain; for example, `tesla.com` would change to `shop.tesla.com`. Each of these pages on a website gets crawled repeatedly by search engines like Google, Bing, and Yandex, which makes them searchable on the Internet. If you were to go to Google and query `shop.tesla.com`, it would show results because that page has been indexed. There is a way to prevent a web page from being indexed by specific or all search engines, and that is with the `robots.txt` file.

The `robots.txt` file tells search engine crawlers which URLs on a website the crawlers are allowed to access (see Figure 7.39). When you add `robots.txt` to the end of the domain, it will display text listing which directories, paths, user agents, and files are allowed to be crawled by search engines. The value of viewing `robots.txt` files is that they may sometimes reveal hidden pages on a website that the organization doesn't intend for anyone to find that may add context to our analysis.

Next, we can copy the domain and query search engines directly to see where else on the Internet that domain is mentioned. In this case, searching `tesla.com` might reveal partnership organizations who are backlinking directly to the Tesla website.

Sometimes it is useful to dig deep into a website, but there are times where the information could be right at the surface level within the design, content, and layout of a website.

Website Design and Content

While the design of a website might seem trivial in an OSINT analysis, sometimes it can be rather telling. For instance, if an organization's website appears hastily made, like the same template is used across a group of websites, text was never changed from the template, and links do not lead anywhere, this could be an indication that the organization might be fraudulent. One trick to verify that the text on the site is original is to copy some of the text and paste it into Google and see where else on the Web it shows up.

The images used on the site can also provide us with information if they contain people, places, or assets of interest. It's a good idea to also perform reverse image searches on the images to see where else on the Internet they appear as well as check them for metadata using a site like fotoforensics[48] to see if they offer additional data we can use.

The actual content on the site, meaning links, text, and pages can all hold background details on our organization. Be sure to jot down any names, titles, and linkages you note while looking through the website pages. Try to answer a few key questions while you peruse the organization's website:

Does the website reveal the C-level employees? Employees can be a great pivot into LinkedIn research and other subject intelligence techniques. Determining what other organizations, the individuals are affiliated with can make useful connections.

Does the website provide details about possible subsidiaries, parent companies, affiliates/partners, contracts? This information can be taken over into corporate records searches and contracts to find additional details.

Do you see social media links in the header or footer of a page? These links provide the accounts for social media as well as usernames that can be searched in username tools to enumerate additional accounts.

---

[48] `https://fotoforensics.com`.

Does the organization have contact info listed, and is it legitimate? Search the contact information in corporate records to see what other organizations are connected to that address and check on maps for the location of the building.

Is any media available in the form of photos and video? Media can provide context and new selectors and pivot points to analyze.

Website Metadata

In addition to the content that we can see across an organization's website, there is a great deal of content we can't see in the form of metadata and hidden documents, which can range from financial spreadsheets to printer names within the organization. There are two methods that I use regularly to uncover this data:

- Google dorks
- FOCA

In Part I, "Foundational OSINT," we learned about using Google dorks to develop advanced search engine queries that return specific data. Using Google dorks, we can target the filetypes within a domain to return publicly exposed documents. For instance, using the Tesla example again, if we craft a Google dork to find files on the Tesla site based on their file extension, it would look like this:

site:`tesla.com` ext:doc | ext:docx | ext:odt | ext:rtf | ext:sxw | ext:psw | ext:ppt | ext:pptx | ext:pps | ext:csv

This dork queries the site and returns all publicly available files with those extensions whether they are viewable from the front end of the website or not.

Another method of discovering hidden files and data within a website is by using the tool FOCA. *FOCA*[49] stands for fingerprinting organizations with collected archives and can be found here: `github.com/ElevenPaths/FOCA`.

FOCA runs searches on a user inputted domain using Google, Bing, and DuckDuckGo, looking for various filetypes including DOC, PDF, XLS, PowerPoint, and even Adobe (see Figure 7.40). The metadata extracted from these files can contain names, dates, systems, and the technologies used to create the files, which may provide additional pivot points within your analysis.

FOCA is a great tool for analyzing the hidden information within files pulled from a website, another way to find information on a selected domain is by looking at the records, called WHOIS records, that are created when a user first registers the domain.

---

[49] `github.com/ElevenPaths/FOCA`.

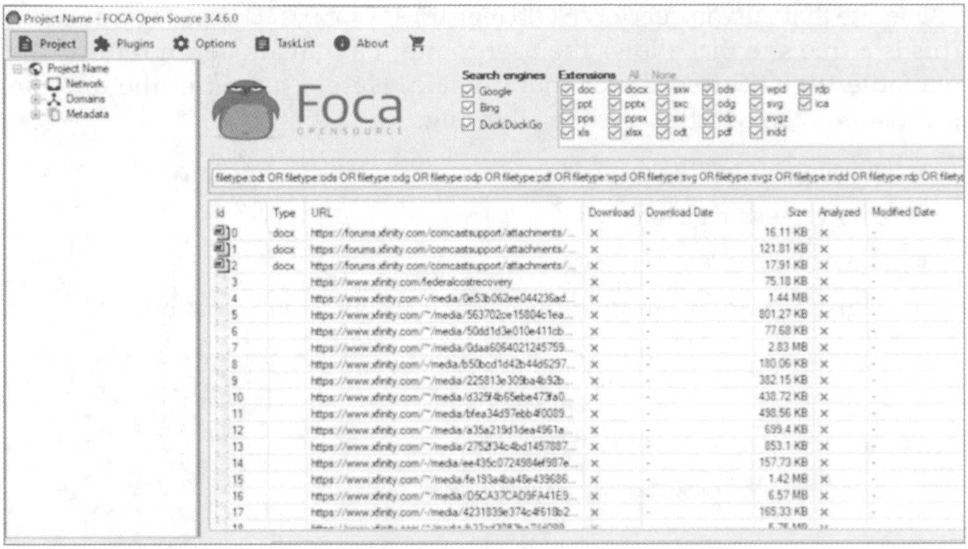

Figure 7.40: FOCA

Analyzing WHOIS Record Data

Previously, we learned that every domain name must be registered and maintained within a central database at ICANN. The domain name registration contains information about the person or entity that paid a fee to register the domain, and this *WHOIS record* includes names, addresses, and phone numbers.

To illustrate the importance of WHOIS data to an OSINT analyst, imagine for a moment that you are a criminal with a plan to set up a fraudulent nonprofit to accept donations. The first thing you do is purchase and register a domain name and then develop a website for your nonprofit that receives donations. Now you have been raking in thousands of dollars a month through your fraudulent nonprofit website until the FBI comes knocking on your door. "How did they know it was me?" you think to yourself. When you registered your domain name, you filled out the form stating your real name and address, which then becomes public record in the WHOIS database. FBI agents simply needed to run a search on your domain to see exactly who had paid to register it.

WHOIS records are available to access through many free tools, and it is a personal preference which one you choose. Some tools provide historical WHOIS data records that can show up who owned a domain over time, which can be handy when someone privacy protects their WHOIS data. It is inexpensive when registering a domain to add on the additional service of privacy protection, which is usually listed in WHOIS records as "Perfect Privacy LLC" or "WHOIS Guard." However, having access to historical WHOIS records can sometimes circumvent this privacy addition by being able to look back in history to before it was added onto the account.

One site that I use to query WHOIS registries is Whoxy.com (see Figure 7.41).[50] This is a free site that allows the user to input a domain and it returns the available WHOIS records for that domain. Here, I have run the domain oscarmayer.com which shows the following:

- Who registered the domain
- When it was registered
- The name servers
- Registrant, administrative, and technical contact information

| 🔲 WHOIS | 🔲 RAW | ⟨⟩ JSON | ⟨⟩ XML |

A Registrar handles the reservation of domain names.

Domain: OSCARMAYER.COM (59 similar domains)
Registrar: CSC CORPORATE DOMAINS, INC. (1.49 million domains)
Query Time: 5 Nov 2022 - 5:54 PM UTC [LIVE WHOIS]

Registered: 20th November 1998 [23 years, 11 months, 16 days back]
Updated: 16th November 2021 [11 months, 20 days back]
Expiry: 19th November 2022 [13 days left]

Registration dates can tell us how long the domain has been active.

DOMAIN STATUS

clientTransferProhibited

Name servers translate a domain into an IP.

NAME SERVERS

udns1.cscdns.net
udns2.cscdns.uk

REGISTRANT CONTACT

Name: Domain Admin (15.7 million domains)
Company: Kraft Foods Group Brands LLC (4,934 domains)
Address: 200 E Randolph St.
City: Northfield
State: IL
ZIP Code: 60601
Country: United States (177 million domains from **United States** for $4,750)
Email: domainnames@kraftheinzcompany.com (3,669 domains)
Phone: +1.8476462000
Fax: +1.8476468591

ADMINISTRATIVE CONTACT

Name: Domain Admin (15.7 million domains)
Company: Kraft Foods Group Brands LLC (4,934 domains)
Address: 200 E Randolph St.
City: Northfield
State: IL
ZIP Code: 60601
Country: United States (177 million domains from **United States** for $4,750)
Email: domainnames@kraftheinzcompany.com (3,669 domains)
Phone: +1.8476462000
Fax: +1.8476468591

Contact info can provide details about ownership or third-party vendors.

(Continues)

[50] www.whoxy.com.

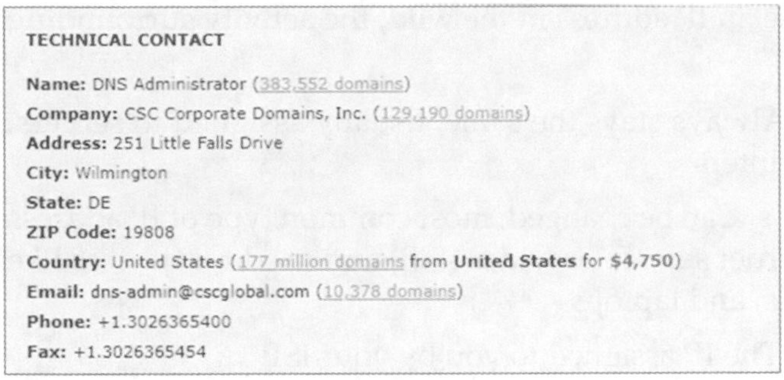

TECHNICAL CONTACT

Name: DNS Administrator (383,552 domains)

Company: CSC Corporate Domains, Inc. (129,190 domains)

Address: 251 Little Falls Drive

City: Wilmington

State: DE

ZIP Code: 19808

Country: United States (177 million domains from **United States** for $4,750)

Email: dns-admin@cscglobal.com (10,378 domains)

Phone: +1.3026365400

Fax: +1.3026365454

Figure 7.41: Whoxy

Analyzing IP Addresses

As we learned, an IP address is a unique identifier that allows the Internet to discriminate between various routers, websites, and computers. Because IP addresses are unique, it is possible to use them to trace an IP address back to a specific device and owner. One thing I hear often from individuals who are interested in OSINT is that they are afraid they won't be a good fit for a career in OSINT because they don't consider themselves to be highly technical. However, I staunchly believe if an analyst can grasp a few simple concepts about how the Internet works, they can recognize potential pivot points and use a search engine to query the answers to most technical questions they have. So put your fears of technical OSINT aside, and let's dive into some light education on IP addresses.

IP Addresses 101

IP addresses exist in two types:

- **IPV4:** IPV4 consists of four groups of numbers separated by a decimal ranging from 0–255. For example: 123.1.23.123.
  Because there are a limited number of IPV4 addresses available (4.3 billion), all of which have been taken now, IPV6 addresses were created. There are about 340 trillion, trillion, trillion IPV6 addresses available, which means we probably will never run out.

- **IPV6:** IPV6 addresses are much longer at eight groups of four numbers separated by colons. For example: 2001:0db8:85a3:0000:0000:8a2e:0370:7334.

The Different Categories of IP Addresses

There are a few different categories of IP addresses that are used for different purposes, and it can be helpful when analyzing to understand just a bit about them so that when you see an IP address in the wild, the activity surrounding it has more context.

- **Static IP Address:** Always stays the same, usually assigned to servers, large equipment, printers
- **Dynamic IP Address:** Can be changed, most common type of IP address provided by an Internet service provider (ISP) and used for devices like phones, desktop PCs, and laptops
- **Public IP Address:** The IP assigned to you by your ISP
- **Private IP Address:** An IP assigned automatically to your device by a router

Determining an IP Address

There are many free online tools available to help you determine a subject or entity's IP address based on a known domain. For this example, I am using nslookup.io,[51] which is a tool used to query the DNS records for a domain name. I queried the `oscarmayer.com` site using their domain name, which I was able to find through a search engine query. The results from `nslookup.io` show that `oscarmayer.com` has the IP address 75.2.4.93 and their autonomous system number (ASN) used to exchange routing information with other systems is AS16509. Both of these numbers are selectors that can be pivoted from to find further information about the technical infrastructure of `oscarmayer.com` like the registrant's contact details (see Figure 7.42).

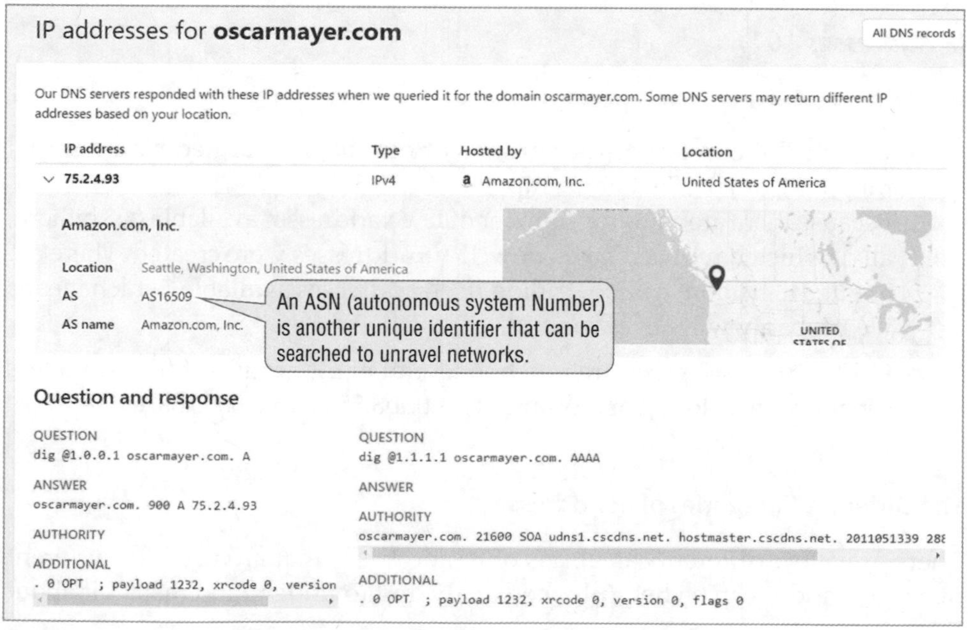

Figure 7.42: `Nslookup.io` showing Oscar Mayer's site information

---
[51] `www.nslookup.io`.

Finding the Owner of an IP Address

We can find the owner of an IP address by using the registry search for the country of origin (see Figure 7.43). A *regional Internet registry* is responsible for managing the registration and allocation of Internet number resources by region. There are five IP regional Internet registries across the world: ARIN, APNIC, RIPE NCC, LACNIC, and AFRINIC.

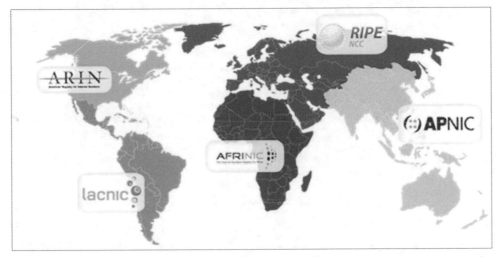

Figure 7.43: www.apnic.net/about-apnic/organization/history-of-apnic/history-of-the-regional-internet-registries

Using the American Registry for Internet Numbers (ARIN) as an example, I searched the IPV4 address 8.8.8.8, which returns data revealing the IP address belongs to Google. Using this method, you can search any IP address and get the associated registered information including WHOIS records for that IP address that may reveal registration names, addresses, phone numbers, and email addresses (see Figure 7.44).

What Can I Do with an IP Address?

Knowing the IP address and the full IP space of an organization is incredibly useful for understanding the full technical landscape of the organization, determining things they might be hiding, or seeing ways in which the organization may be unknowingly vulnerable through their technology. Sometimes examining IP space can show connections between organizations where they share internal infrastructure. If these connections are with a third-party vendor, there may be vulnerabilities in that connection such as misconfigured technology and open ports that an adversary could use to infiltrate the system. For instance, if a university has a partnership with a large technology company,

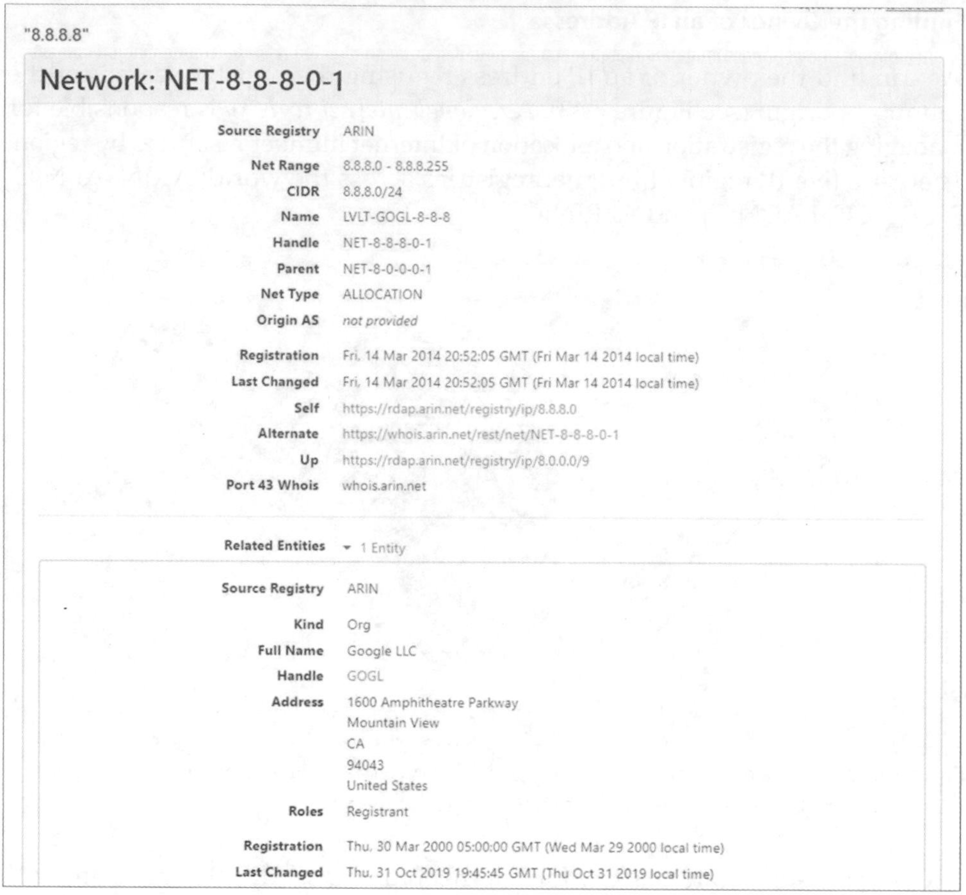

"8.8.8.8"

Network: NET-8-8-8-0-1

Source Registry	ARIN
Net Range	8.8.8.0 - 8.8.8.255
CIDR	8.8.8.0/24
Name	LVLT-GOGL-8-8-8
Handle	NET-8-8-8-0-1
Parent	NET-8-0-0-0-1
Net Type	ALLOCATION
Origin AS	*not provided*
Registration	Fri, 14 Mar 2014 20:52:05 GMT (Fri Mar 14 2014 local time)
Last Changed	Fri, 14 Mar 2014 20:52:05 GMT (Fri Mar 14 2014 local time)
Self	https://rdap.arin.net/registry/ip/8.8.8.0
Alternate	https://whois.arin.net/rest/net/NET-8-8-8-0-1
Up	https://rdap.arin.net/registry/ip/8.0.0.0/9
Port 43 Whois	whois.arin.net

Related Entities   ▾ 1 Entity

Source Registry	ARIN
Kind	Org
Full Name	Google LLC
Handle	GOGL
Address	1600 Amphitheatre Parkway Mountain View CA 94043 United States
Roles	Registrant
Registration	Thu, 30 Mar 2000 05:00:00 GMT (Wed Mar 29 2000 local time)
Last Changed	Thu, 31 Oct 2019 19:45:45 GMT (Thu Oct 31 2019 local time)

Figure 7.44: Search in `https://seach.arin.net`

they may have shared digital spaces. Using a technical discovery tool like `dnslytics.com`,[52] we are able to visualize and understand information about domains, IPs, providers, and the relationships between them. Free technical discovery tools can quickly help even the least technically savvy of us to begin to pull basic information about our entity of interest. When looking at infrastructure, there are a few things to be aware of that will save you hours of time and help prevent you from straying too far from your goal.

Words of Caution

When analyzing technical OSINT data points such as IP addresses, it can be incredibly easy to fall down a rabbit hole making connections between websites

---

[52] `https://dnslytics.com`.

and drawing conclusions founded on incorrect assumptions. If a hosting company hosts many different websites on a single server, this could lead to the assumption that the organizations are connected when in fact they just share a hosting provider.

If you note hundreds of websites on the same server or an organization like Cloudflare[53] or CloudFront[54] are listed on the WHOIS registration, this is a red flag that the website has been placed behind a content delivery network (CDN), which distributes content throughout the world by caching it near to each user. The CDN IP address will not directly correspond to the domain IP address because they will change often. A good rule of thumb when analyzing IP addresses is to take note of the number of websites hosted on the same server. Generally, the lower the number of websites on the server, the larger the possibility of connection through ownership. Additionally, we can rely on WHOIS record data including contact information to help determine commonality between domains.

Throughout this book each chapter is meant to build upon the skills of the previous one to develop your tradecraft in a well-rounded and implementable way. This chapter has provided the base-level information on organizational analysis and technical infrastructure to help move into more advanced-level OSINT analysis including transportation intelligence, Wi-Fi enumeration, and financial intelligence including cryptocurrency and NFT exploration.

---

[53] www.cloudflare.com.
[54] www.amazonaws.cn/en/cloudfront.

CHAPTER

8

Transportation Intelligence

8.1 Overview

What Is Transportation Intelligence?

Since the pre-modern world, trade has been an international motivator of advancements in transportation. Beginning with horses and carts in the 4th millennium BC, boats in the stone age, rail and highways during the industrial revolution, and finally modern-day air and space exploration, humans have found methods to travel from one place to another. As humans utilize modernized technology for travel and trade, bits of information become available to the public. We can no longer ride a train without the schedule being posted on the railroad website or travel in an automobile without an Internet-connected GPS system guiding the way. When an analyst collects these bits of transportation-related information and enriches it with other data, that is called *transportation intelligence*.

Collecting information on transportation requires research into how people and things travel from one place to another, what those people disclose on the Internet about their travels, and what the vehicles of travel either knowingly or unknowingly disclose through technology. Before we get too in the weeds, let's look at the five main methods of transportation.

- **Road:** The transportation of goods or people by road using an automobile, truck, bus, bicycle, or motorcycle.

- **Rail:** The transportation of passengers or goods by vehicles powered by steam diesel, or electricity on tracks called a *railway*. High-speed rail requires specially built tracks.

- **Water:** The transportation of passengers or goods on a watercraft over a body of water.

- **Air:** The transportation of passengers or goods in a vehicle specially designed to generate lift and fly.

- **Intermodal (Multiple Modes Together):** The transportation of goods through multiple modes of transportation.

The Criticality of Transportation Intelligence

Take a moment to think about all the items you may have purchased online in the last month, how many groceries you bought that came from overseas, the trips you have taken to and from work or for vacation. Now, because it is estimated that roughly 80 percent of goods globally are transported by sea,[1] imagine a scenario where all transportation grinds to a halt. We got a glimpse of what this could be like in 2021 when the ultra-large container vessel (ULCV) *The Ever Given* got lodged in the Suez Canal backing up vessel traffic for 6 days causing supply chain delays for months. Bottlenecks at ports have been wreaking havoc on intermodal operations across the U.S. The delays trickle down to freight rail and trucking causing supplies to sit for 20 percent longer than average.[2] A disruption to the supply chain could be catastrophic on a global scale leading to food and electronics shortages and overall higher costs for labor.

There are also geopolitical concerns when we talk about not only the supply chain but the transportation modes themselves. As of 2022, nearly all countries have armed forces that include warships, amphibious assault vessels, submarines, aircraft carriers, helicopters, drones (both air and underwater), bombers, fighters, attack planes, military railways, tanks, missile transport and launch vehicles, and so on. Because the political climate is ever changing and often unstable and unpredictable, we may be tasked as analysts to research conflict areas amid war or social unrest, and this often involves the analysis of the transportation of weapons, supplies, troops, and refugees.

I can hear you saying "Rae, but I don't work within supply chain, and geopolitics is outside of the scope of my daily work; I still don't know why I should

---

[1] www.statista.com/topics/1728/ocean-shipping/?#:~:text=It%20is%20 estimated%20that%20an,to%20nearly%2010.7%20billion%20tons.
[2] www.wsj.com/articles/u-s-port-backups-are-extending-into-freight-rail-supply-chains-11656094494.

care about transportation!" Most people use transportation for their daily commute, when they go on vacation by cruise, airplane, automobile, or train. If you are tasked with tracking the movement of a subject, you will no doubt run into a situation where transportation becomes important. If you are a criminal, you use the same transportation methods to get to and from the scene of the crime. Coupling transportation intelligence with subject intelligence can allow us to track a person more efficiently and effectively, providing enhanced information.

As you can see, each of these forms of transportation present their own challenges and vulnerabilities. Being able to track, predict, or gather information on any of them could provide valuable data on the supply chain, government, or just humanity.

Some example questions we might get during analysis could include the following:

- "Can you track the subject's movements across the border checkpoint?"
- "Can you anticipate future movements based on past movements?"
- "Can you determine if there is illegal activity taking place?"
- "Can you track a shipment from point A to point B?"
- "Do any vulnerabilities exist within this specific transportation line?

This section will break down the five transportation methods and demonstrate what can be found, why it's important, and how to find it. Then we will go through some case study examples for each.

Transportation movements can be tracked several ways. First, we can track visually. What this means is that we can gather information on an automobile, train, plane, or ship by physically seeing it in person, by seeing a photo or video, or by viewing on satellite imagery.

Visual Intelligence

Here are several types of visual intelligence that can be integrated into your OSINT analysis.

Spotters

Believe it or not, there are groups of people around the world called *spotters* who observe things as a hobby. These enthusiasts track movements, photograph, video, and record detailed information for their transportation of choice and publish it on spotting websites. Maritime, rail, and aviation all have rabid spotter communities. Thousands of plane spotters worldwide spend their free time staking out airports to get the best photos possible of an aircraft. The value in this data for an analyst is that the photos and video uploaded and logged by date helps us not only to track places the vehicle has been but to verify the identity.

When I am looking for a maritime vessel that is actively obfuscating its identity, I will check out sites like `shipspotting.com`,[3] a central site for hobbyists to post timestamped photos and information about vessels they spot. Looking through those posts, I can sometimes verify the vessel has been in a specific location on a specific date as well as verify the color and identification on the side of the vessel.

Social Media Disclosures

As we have learned so far throughout this book, social media is a great place to gather information especially when users disclose more than they need to. When looking at transportation, there are generally three sets of individuals who could leak visual information about transportation.

- Employees (captain, driver, pilot, workers)
- Passengers
- Coordinators (shore services, ground stations, hub)

Employees tend to catalog their journey with photos, videos, in-depth internal videos, and photos of the inner workings of their job. For instance, employees working vessels sometimes do video walkthroughs of the entire lower deck of the vessel outlining all the industrial control systems on board and showing the names and versions of the software before continuing onto the captain's deck to unwittingly disclose details about the global navigation system on board. There has been an uptick in "A Day in My Life" posts across TikTok and YouTube where users disclose an overwhelming number of details from their daily work and routines. Even if the individual doesn't work directly on the vehicle, they may have a position where they coordinate schedules and traffic giving them access to detailed information about the routes and technologies creating a security issue if posted online. Likewise, passengers on transportation love to document their travel often posting timestamped photos and videos of locations along the way that could be used to develop a timeline of their movements and pattern of life.

Webcam

A web *camera* is a video camera used to record or stream video to a computer or through a network. You have no doubt grown accustomed to using a webcam in or attached to your computer since the COVID pandemic to access live meetings and talk to family and friends. Beyond your typical computer webcam, it's hard

---

[3] `shipspotting.com`.

not to notice the growing number of cameras everywhere in public. Most of the surveillance cameras are closed circuit TV (CCTV) and located on telephone poles, traffic lights, and buildings. There are also cameras that are not closed circuit, and they stream video live and available around the world for reasons such as watching traffic conditions, and weather. Additionally, webcams can be set up to show border crossings, docks, ports, rail stations and tracks, airports, and highways that would be of interest to an analyst.

Web cameras are a fantastic way to determine visually if a train, ship, truck, or car is where it claims to be or to verify what it looks like and possibly who is traveling on it. We can access these webcams free through several webcam websites or through Google dorks targeting a specific mode of transportation or company. One site that I use for accessing web cameras is `Windy.com`,[4] a privately owned weather-focused site with satellite overlay, route planners, and loads of web cameras across the world.

As an example of how web cameras can be used for OSINT, we can look at the case of two NATO vessels, the U.K. *Royal Navy HMS Defender* and the Royal Netherlands Navy's *HNLMS Evertson*, performing exercises in the Black Sea. According to the ship's signal that transmits their location, they both left Odessa and sailed to Sevastopol near the harbor where the Russian Black Sea Fleet is homed. Social media and news outlets exploded with news of a Russian vessel firing warning shots at the vessels after the provocative move. OSINT researchers quickly determined using a port camera that the ships never actually left Odessa, and they were still in port during this supposed event. This means that the ships were likely a result of falsified signal positions.[5]

We have also seen the value of live webcams during the Russian invasion of Ukraine. Prior to the invasion, a camera was set up outside a tourist information center at a checkpoint near the Chernobyl nuclear power plant. The Chernobyl Tour was a guided trek into the exclusion zone around the plant and facilities. Unwittingly, on February 24, 2022, this tourism camera captured a large number of Russian tanks and equipment at the plant. The Russians shut down the larger surveillance cameras but failed to see the small webcam streaming their troops along the gray road. A few days later, Russian troops had seized the power plant, but the video had already been passed to the Ukrainian government (see Figure 8.1).[6]

---

[4] `www.windy.com`.
[5] `https://news.usni.org/2021/06/21/positions-of-two-nato-ships-were-falsified-near-russian-black-sea-naval-base`.
[6] `https://apnews.com/article/russia-ukraine-kyiv-technology-e11322452c4d41970e992257db01dbcd`.

Figure 8.1: Video still from AP story

Access to webcams that are filming in the right place at the right time can be tricky. When visuals are not available from the ground, another great method used for tracking and verifying is satellite imagery.

Satellite Imagery

Orbital satellite imagery dates all the way back to 1959 when the first satellite images were taken over the North Pacific Ocean by the *U.S. Explorer 6*.[7] In 1972 the Landsat program was developed by NASA and USGS in the United States to capture images of Earth to create a historical archive of the Earth's surface.[8] This was the largest program developed for acquiring Earth imagery from space. All the images collected by NASA are published and available to the public at `earthobservatory.nasa.gov`.[9] Satellite images are images collected of Earth through imaging satellites that are within the Earth's orbit.

Satellite imagery is used for many different applications including cartography, meteorology, oceanography, regional planning, education, and intelligence. Two main types of satellites exist for imaging. First is the Geostationary Satellite, which orbits in line with Earth's rotation in the same spot with high temporal resolution but limited spatial resolution. Second is the Polar-Orbiting satellite,

---

[7] `https://nssdc.gsfc.nasa.gov/nmc/spacecraft/displayaction?id=1959-004A`.
[8] `https://landsat.gsfc.nasa.gov`.
[9] `https://earthobservatory.nasa.gov`.

which circles over the North and South Poles at a low altitude passing the same point only two times per day. By knowing which type of satellite imagery you are looking at, you can determine how many passes, what resolution, and what other options will be available to you. As satellite imagery grows in popularity, many countries have developed their own imaging programs. The following are a few of the more popular public domain programs:

- **MODIS:** On board the NASA Terra and Aqua Satellites
- **Sentinel:** ESA
- **Meteostat:** Geostationary weather satellites
- **ASTER:** An imaging instrument on board the Terra and is a joint project between U.S. NASA and Japan's METI
- **CORONA:** CIA reconnaissance satellites

Sentinel Hub's EO Browser[10] is an excellent web tool that combines the imagery of Sentinel, Landsat, Meris, MODIS, and many other satellites in one database.

Beyond the public domain satellites, many satellites are owned and operated by private companies like Planet, Maxar, and GeoEye who then sell or license the imagery. Several platforms exist that aggregate both public and private domain satellite imagery for consumer use like soar.earth[11] and Google Earth.[12]

For analysis, satellite imagery is incredibly important for providing a top-down view, often in areas across the world that would otherwise be impossible for the average analyst to see. Imagery has been used in cases of identifying human rights abuse, illegal fishing, changes in military buildup, and construction over time. Additionally, satellite imagery is an effective way to spot, track, and identify the following:

- Vessels on the water
- Vessels in port
- Changes at port or sea
- Railroad lines
- Railroad stations
- Highways
- Vehicles at a location

Landsat and remote sensing satellites like it are considered passive optical imagery; there is another type of active collection called Synthetic Aperture Radar (SAR). SAR imagery relies on the sensor producing energy and then recording the amount that gets reflected from Earth, making the imagery more reactive to structures.[13] Unlike its optical counterparts, SAR sensors can function both day

---

[10] https://apps.sentinel-hub.com/eo-browser.
[11] https://soar.earth/satellites.
[12] https://earth.google.com/web.
[13] www.earthdata.nasa.gov/learn/backgrounders/what-is-sar.

and night because they don't rely on the sun's energy to work. Because SAR sensors use microwaves, they are extremely good at seeing through extreme weather, clouds, ash, and other conditions where an optical satellite would be useless. Figure 8.2 is a comparison between optical sensors and SAR that shows how the SAR sensors return imagery regardless of the clouds.

Figure 8.2: Comparison between SAR and Satellite imagery

Satellite Imagery Analysis Techniques

Once you have decided which type of imagery will work best for your analysis, there are a few things to consider when examining the pictures. We can use knowledge we already have about a location or an entity to help us determine whether we are looking at what we think we are looking at. It is easy to make assumptions during analysis, so it is best to go in with the facts you know before making a determination. When I analyze maritime vessels by satellite, especially around busy ports, it becomes incredibly difficult to tell which ship is my target ship. First, I am only seeing the ship from above, which removes features like the identification and color on the side and makes it hard to count the number of stacks or cranes on the deck. What I can rely on, however, are the known facts about the vessel, how long and wide it is, what color the deck is, and what shape it is (see Figure 8.3). Using cues like this can help prevent us from making assumptions and to better focus our analysis. These are a few key things to bear in mind when looking at satellite imagery:

- Size/scale
- Location
- Patterns, shapes, textures
- Time of year

- Depth and height
- Colors
- Shadows/light
- Any additional knowledge about the entity/location

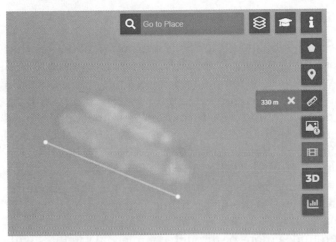

Figure 8.3: EO browser in the Singapore strait, a ship-to-ship transfer. The ship measures 300m.

The biggest thorn in my side while using satellite imagery for my analysis is that my success is so dependent on the weather and satellite coverage in the area on the date and time I need it. For instance, imagine that you know a military convoy arrived at a specific location at 9 a.m. on January 1, 2022, and you want to catch them on satellite imagery. You must now hope that across all the orbiting satellites one of them passed that location on that date at that specific time. Further, you must hope that there was no inclement weather creating impenetrable cloud cover preventing you from seeing anything in the image. The process of satellite imagery analysis can be incredibly rewarding for our cases, but it can also be challenging.

Signal Detection

Signal intelligence (SIGINT), or the interception and interpretation of electronic signals, has been an important part of intelligence collection since the early 1900s, which involved intercepting electronic signal communication between people and electronics. Since then, with the invention of modern technology and travel, SIGINT has expanded to the collection of data from worldwide navigational systems such as GPS, GNSS, ADS-B, MLAT, and AIS that have become commonplace in public and private transportation. Freight services and supply chain have a growing need for tracking their shipments, and because of this, the public now has increased access to low-cost or free signals' tracking platforms. Analysts can use these platforms to track transportation like ships, trains, and planes, and understand the movements of the people on board. Before learning some of the methods used to track transportation, we should first understand what signals they emit, how they work, and what we can do with it.

Understanding Navigational Systems

The Global Navigation Satellite System (GNSS) is a group of satellites that receive and transmit geospatial position data. The difference between GNSS and GPS is that GNSS is worldwide terminology, while GPS is a type of GNSS system.[14] Both the Automatic Identification System for vessels and ADS-B for aircraft rely on GNSS for positioning. GNSS information gets embedded within each AIS and ADS-B transmission for accuracy.

The Automatic Identification System (AIS) was developed in the 1990s to help prevent maritime vessels from colliding in dense areas and works as a transponder on the VHF maritime band transmitting real-time data about the vessel.[15] AIS is required by the International Maritime Organization (IMO) on all international vessels exceeding 300 tons and all passenger vessels. AIS can be detected by on shore ground stations or through commercial satellites with AIS receivers (see Figure 8.4).

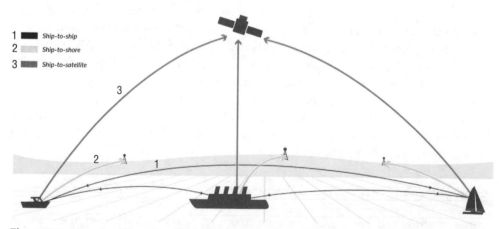

Figure 8.4: How the AIS on a vessel transmits signals

---

[14] www.symmetryelectronics.com/blog/
what-is-the-difference-between-gnss-and-gps.
[15] https://gssc.esa.int/navipedia/index.php/AIS-VTS.

Commercial products in the maritime domain offer free tier tracking of vessels using AIS and GNSS signals. Two such products are `marinetraffic.com` and `vesselfinder.com`. Both allow for nonhistorical tracking based on "pings" from the vessel's AIS system on board that provides information like the following:

- Identity
- Destination
- Weight
- Position

We can utilize all this information in our OSINT analysis because each detail indicates what the ship could be doing. The critical downside to AIS is that because it resides on board, it can be easily manipulated and thus not fully trustworthy. If a crew wanted to obscure the vessel's identity, they could manipulate the signal to display a different name, weight, destination, position, etc. In the previous *HMS Defender* example, the motivation for manipulating or faking AIS signals could have been to create justification for an attack, to distract from another event happening, or to just cause chaos in the media. As we will learn, there are several forms of AIS and GNSS manipulation that can have an impact on our analysis.

Much like AIS for vessels, the Automatic Dependent Surveillance-Broadcast (ADS-B) is a technology used for aircraft combined with GNSS, flight technology, and the ground station. ADS-B is split into two services: ADS-B In, which provides the crew with weather and traffic information, and ADS-B Out, which broadcasts the aircraft's precise position, altitude, speed, and more (see Figure 8.5).

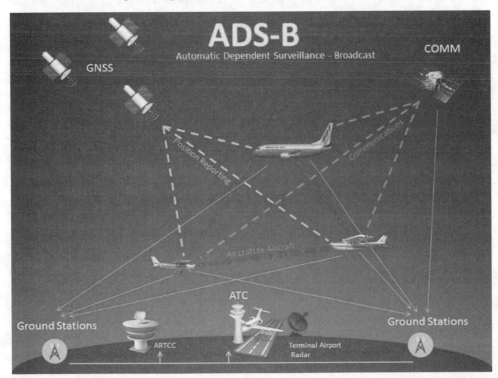

Figure 8.5: How ADS-B transmits signals

Mode-S are selective mode transmissions from aircraft that do not contain location information. Using radar, air traffic control can determine the aircraft's location, but without access to radar, the public can use Multilateration (MLAT) calculations to determine an aircraft's position by combining data from at least four different receivers to estimate the position of an aircraft's Mode-S transmissions. Because at least four geographically diverse receivers are needed, MLAT works better in urban or built-up areas where there are more likely to be multiple receivers (see Figure 8.6).

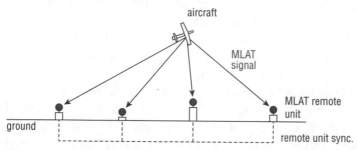

Figure 8.6: How Mode-S transmits signals

Dark Signals

Let's explore the meaning and purpose of transmission signals going "dark."

"*Going dark* is a phrase used when a vessel's AIS signal suddenly stops transmitting. This is not necessarily indicative of a crime or illegal activity, it could be a malfunction of the AIS on board or have gone out of range of local AIS receivers; however, it can be a sign to look further. Here are a few examples of reasons a ship may "go dark":

- The vessel is transporting illegal goods to a sanctioned country. When the vessel gets near the port of unloading, it shuts off the AIS so the public cannot track which port it goes to. After offloading the illegal cargo, the vessel sails back out to sea and turns the AIS back on, leaving no transmission record of its journey to the port.

- A fishing vessel is heading out to illegally fish in regulated waters; they turn the AIS off during fishing so they cannot be tracked through AIS signals and then turn it back on upon returning to the port.

- A tanker carrying oil plans to transfer the oil to another vessel who will then deliver it to a sanctioned country. Upon reaching a midway point between countries, both tankers shut off their AIS while performing a ship-to-ship transfer of oil. When both vessels are far enough away from each other, they turn the AIS signal back on.

- The owner of a yacht is wanted for fraud; he secretly flees at night in his yacht with his AIS off to evade capture.

- Navy vessels are performing an exercise including live fire testing, so all the vessels turn off their AIS during the entirety of the exercise until they return to port.

While the ability to track dark activity typically relies on access to paid historical AIS data, if you do have access to these paths, there are telltale signs that can be used to spot this activity. When viewing a vessel path from point A to point B there will be a break in the path when the transponder is turned off. It's as if the vessel did not exist for the period of darkness, and then suddenly the transponder will show up again (see Figure 8.7).

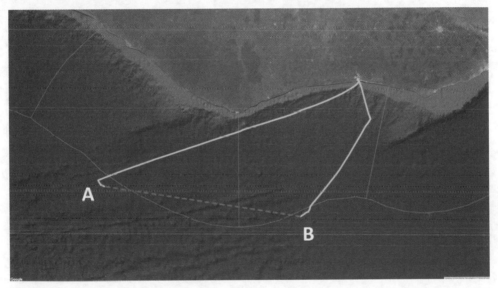

Figure 8.7: Showing a "dark" vessel path

Signal Spoofing

Below are some ways that signals may be spoofed and some possible explanations.

AIS Spoofing

Ship AIS spoofing involves using AIS signals to create a nonexistent vessel or to obscure a vessel's identity, resulting in hiding or transmitting false positional data so that a vessel appears to behave legitimately. Spoofing is far more deceptive than dark AIS because it is an intentional obfuscation of vessel position. Spoofing is a likely explanation for the *HMS Defender* example and would explain how a vessel was seemingly showing in one location while being spotted on a webcam in an entirely different location.

AIS spoofing has a distinct pattern when we look at historical vessel paths. The paths will be hard straight lines that jump across land or water in a time frame that is not humanly possible. A normal vessel path must follow the shipping lanes in the ocean and will look jagged and slow (see Figures 8.8-8.9).

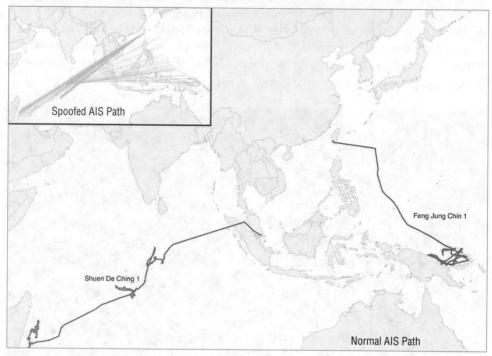

Figure 8.8: Example of a spoofed signal path

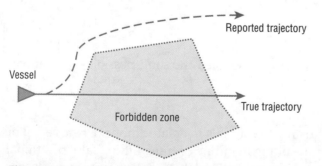

Figure 8.9: Example of a spoofed signal path

Here are some examples of when AIS spoofing might be used:

- A Navy vessel is carrying out a top-secret mission and manipulates the AIS data to appear across the ocean in another port.

- A vessel is engaging in illegal activity and uses spoofing to appear in another location while it performs these activities.

- Shore transceivers broadcast a fake vessel in the area of a sabotaged pipeline to manipulate the public into believing a different vessel was responsible.

GNSS can be spoofed in the same way that AIS can be spoofed.

Identity Manipulation

AIS Manipulation

Sometimes the best obfuscation for a vessel is simple identity manipulation using AIS. It is possible within the AIS onboard to manipulate the details that the AIS broadcasts including weight, destination, name, IMO, and MMSI. There is no need to spoof a vessel path if we can just change the name of the vessel to a different vessel. Because the IMO is a legal number given to a vessel, manipulation of a vessel's identity is illegal.

Here are some examples of how this may be used:

- Vessel 1 is performing illegal activity, so it manipulates the identity of the ship to be Vessel 2 during the activity and then switches back.

- Navy vessels will share IMO numbers and often switch back and forth between them giving the appearance of spoofing on vessel paths, but it's just identity manipulation.

- A cargo vessel carrying illegal grain changes its vessel type to appear as a fishing vessel so that no one knows it is in the vicinity.

- A country is performing a missile launch and wants to obscure the platform and tugs moving the missile out to sea for the launch. The vessel changes the IMO and name to something else.

GNSS Jamming

One way that GNSS can be compromised is through GNSS signal jamming.[16] Jamming is a form of degrading or masking of a satellite signal by flooding or

---

[16] www.maritimeglobalsecurity.org/media/1043/
2019-jamming-spoofing-of-gnss.pdf.

overpowering the receiver, transmitter, or ground station either intentionally or unintentionally. Jamming is a real issue for all transportation that broadcasts and receives data through GNSS. If a navigation system is interrupted on a vessel, it could cause collisions, running aground, and even geopolitical problems if the vessel sailed into the wrong exclusive economic zone (EEZ). If GPS is jammed on an aircraft's guidance system, it could cause the aircraft to go off course, cause an accident, or cause panic and appear as though it is an equipment failure (see Figure 8.10).[17]

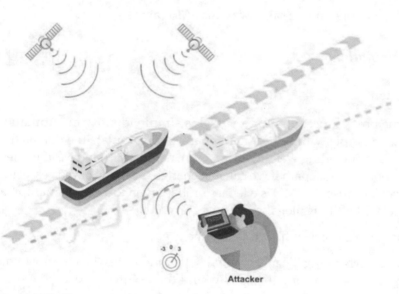

Attacker

Figure 8.10: How an attacker can spoof AIS signals

GNSS Meaconing

Meaconing is the interception and rebroadcast of navigation signals. These signals are rebroadcast on the received frequency, typically, with power higher than the original signal, to confuse navigation (see Figure 8.11). Meaconing can be confused for spoofing as they would both transmit a false location, but meaconing is considerably easier for an adversary to accomplish.

For instructions on how to make your own AIS and ADS-B receivers using a Raspberry Pi, you can go to my website at `raebaker.net`.

---

[17] `www.bizavadvisor.com/gps-signal-jamming`.

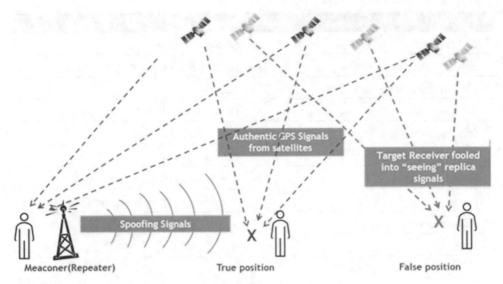

Figure 8.11: How an attacker can meacon a signal

8.2   Vessels

Now we will focus on the information available on vessels themselves.

Introduction to Maritime Intelligence

Maritime trade is an integral segment within the overall global supply chain; it also contributes to the daily commutes of people around the world and holds a wealth of significance geopolitically. From the perspective of an OSINT analyst, I am sure you are wondering how it's possible to use information about maritime and signals to answer potential research questions. Over the next chapter, I will show you how we can identify and collect information on maritime structures, vessels, personnel, and passenger movements, along with ways to uncover the owners behind them. Before we begin, there is some business to take care of in the form of outlining maritime scope and learning key terminology to make the rest a bit easier.

Types of Maritime Entities

The following are types of maritime entities:

VESSELS	OTHER
Container ships	Underwater drones
Bulk carriers	Floating barge

VESSELS	OTHER
Tanker ships	Offshore platforms
Passenger ships	Defensive walls/sluice gates
Naval ships/submarines	Buoys
Offshore ships	Undersea cables
Special-purpose ships	Fishing gear/facilities
Fishing vessels	Offshore wind
Pleasure craft	Restricted zones (reefs, reservoir)
Dredgers	Autonomous spaceport drone ships (ASDSs)
High-speed craft	
Ro-Ro ships	

Vessel Terminology

Part of analyzing maritime is reading through previous reporting, analysis, contracts, and technical documents. Without a firm grasp on the parts that make up a ship, it may be hard to follow the research and apply it to what you are seeing presently in your analysis. Moreover, using the proper terminology when writing your own reports will have a greater impact on the maritime-focused stakeholders presenting you with research questions to answer (see Figure 8.12).[18]

A. **Bow:** The front of the ship, made to cut water as the ship moves.

B. **Stern:** The back of the ship.

C. **Accommodation:** Where the crew live.

D. **Hull:** The part of the ship above and below the waterline.

E. **Freeboard:** The part of the hull above the waterline.

F. **Draught:** The part of the hull that is submerged in water. The more cargo a ship is holding, the greater the draught and the less freeboard will be seen. A ship with no cargo at 8 may be 11 with cargo.

G. **Bridge:** Where the ship is navigated and steered from, where the navigation equipment monitors are held.

H. **Foredeck:** The part of the deck from the Forecastle to the Accommodation.

I. **Forecastle:** The front part of a ship before the mast.

J. **Keel:** The bottom of the ship.

---

[18] https://maritimesa.org/grade-10/
terminology-parts-of-ships-and-equipment-aboard-ships.

K. **Propeller:** A fan-like device that rotates to create thrust and propel a ship forward.

L. **Rudder:** Controlled by the steering system, it turns right or left to steer the vessel.

M. **Main Mast:** Holds lights for night navigation and sometimes radar scanners and electrical equipment.

N. **Radar Scanners:** Attached to the main mast and turns to send out impulses that get picked up by the scanner in the bridge.

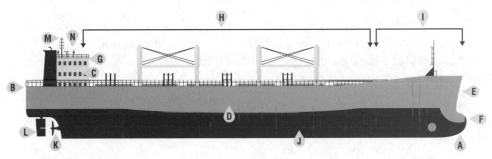

Figure 8.12: Parts of a vessel

Maritime Discovery and Analysis Methods

Let's begin at the beginning. To understand current maritime regulations, movements, and patterns, we must first examine the history behind them. The application of historical context within maritime analysis is extremely important because many of the things that happen are a result of historically significant and politically motivated events.

Traditionally, vessels follow a pattern of operation that is referred to as *economic behavior*, meaning they exist to perform a job and get paid for that job. When a vessel strays from its path extending the trip, which in turn loses profits for the owner, that is abnormal behavior. These types of abnormalities are a red flag for an analyst and are worth digging deeper into. However, when we factor in historical context, suddenly what seems abnormal might actually be normal for that area of the world. For instance, without knowledge of the history surrounding the China-Taiwan tensions,[19] the nine-dash-line,[20] and China's claims over the South China Sea, it would be difficult to understand why vessels might be sailing in odd patterns to avoid conflict within the area. Once context is added, we may see that vessels are forced to take certain routes around an area's economic zone or to avoid things like piracy attacks. As much as I would love everyone to go out and learn the entire history of maritime, I understand that is generally not feasible. My recommendation is to take some time to review

---

[19] www.cfr.org/backgrounder/
china-taiwan-relations-tension-us-policy-biden.
[20] https://time.com/4412191/nine-dash-line-9-south-china-sea.

the history of an area prior to starting your information gathering into it and ask yourself some questions:

- What were the main conflicts, and who were they with?
- How did these conflicts change trade within the region?
- How have ports been used to get supplies to the region?
- What has been the predominant illegal activity regarding vessels and ports in this region?
- Is the area a chokepoint for maritime activity?

There is certainly no singular way to carry out maritime information gathering, and where you begin should be based on the information requests from the stakeholder. I have put together a list of things that I focus on when looking into maritime entities and ownership:

- Vessel paths (present/historically)
- Vessel meetings
- Dark, lost, or abnormal AIS activity
- Patterns of uneconomic activity
- Changing identity and information
- Limited or nonexistent ownership information
- Ownership information (pivot to business intel)
- Facilitator information (freight forwarder, agent)
- Vulnerable technology
- Crew (pivot to subject intel)
- Port calls/cargo unloading

Vessel Paths and Locations

A *vessel path* refers to the route that vessels and other marine entities take while traveling on the sea from one place to another. These routes can be tracked through their broadcasted AIS and GNSS signals that transmit data to a satellite or shore-side base stations detailing the vessel's location, weight, and identification. Web-based analytics tools like marinetraffic[21] and vesselfinder[22] collect this transmitted vessel data to present free near real-time information on their platform showing the movements and details. The live map options allow you to move around the globe and find any type of vessel that is broadcasting and to visualize the path the vessel has traveled. Vessels are not the only maritime entity that broadcast signals, navigational aids like buoys and oil platforms also transmit

---

[21] www.marinetraffic.com.
[22] www.vesselfinder.com.

signals that can be seen in analytics tools. Unfortunately, the largest hindrance to analyzing vessel movements is history.

Historical context regarding maritime is extremely important but likewise are the historic movements of the vessels we analyze. To determine what looks anomalous, we first need access to historical vessel movements so we can compare them with the movements we are seeing presently. Currently, no historical vessel paths exist free for public use.

Tips for Determining Vessel Paths

One way to circumvent the lack of free publicly available historical paths is to rely on other sources for information. I have a few methods that I use regularly to find historical information on vessels without myself having access to the data.

- **Use public disclosures in news stories websites to determine routes:** This method requires using search engines to find targeted information about where the vessel was traveling, end points, who was traveling with it, etc. Additionally, looking at the websites of the owners and operators of the vessel can add context. The news sections on company websites can be a phenomenal resource.

- **Use social media to find other analysts who have detailed information:** Much like querying a search engine to get results, we can query social media platforms for leads about the paths a vessel took. Many analysts just like us are doing the same work through free and pay tools they have access to and then providing the analysis on social media. While it is necessary to vet the information we use, we can certainly use their analysis as a starting point for our own analysis.

- **Use port cameras and ship spotting sites to catch a glimpse of the entity:** We have talked about a few examples where port cameras and ship spotting data has been useful in real world cases. Photos or video can provide verifiable proof that a vessel or marine entity is in a location. Wi-Fi port cameras exist in many ports globally and can be used to see ships coming and going or loading/unloading cargo.

Vessel Meetings

During day-to-day operations, there is often a need to meet up with another vessel for tugging, policing, crew changes, or a transfer of supplies referred to as a *ship-to-ship transfer*. The meeting of two vessels is not itself indicative of illegal activity; however, on some occasions these ship-to-ship transfers are used to transport illegal goods in a way that avoids sanctions and obfuscates activity. Watching and analyzing vessel meetings can give us insights to patterns of activity and what organizations are supplying, refueling, or otherwise supporting these vessels.

Ship-to-Ship (STS) Transfer

An *STS transfer* is when two ships position themselves alongside each other either while moving or stationary for the purpose of transferring goods from one vessel to the other. Typically, the type of cargo that is moved in this way is oil, gas, petroleum, and bulk products like fish. One reason for these transfers could be that the main ship is too large to enter the port so it transfers goods to a smaller vessel that can traverse the port more effectively. Another reason could be that the vessel has an emergency and needs to reduce cargo or the ownership of the cargo changes mid journey so it offloads to another vessel at sea.

A more illicit reason for an STS transfer to take place is skirting sanctions by falsifying documents to record the origin of the goods (usually oil) in another country rather than the sanctioned country. One way to unmask these types of activities is analyze each party within the transaction along with their ownership structure.[23]

Identifying an STS transfer can be done in several ways. First, if we identify what we think is two vessels meeting based on path and length of meeting time (at least an hour), we can attempt to verify it through satellite imagery using EO Browser (see Figure 8.13).[24] By moving around the map we can choose the location that matches the path we found and see if satellite imagery exists for that date and time. Second, we can identify an STS transfer on satellite imagery and then try to tie it to specific vessel paths and vessels in that location at that time. It is a good reminder that AIS is not 100 percent accurate and can be manipulated, so each finding is an assumption until proven.

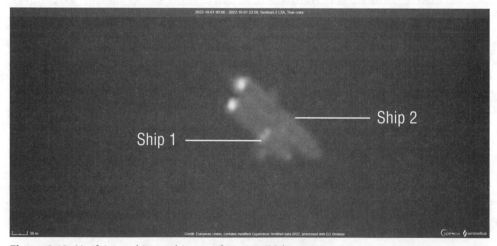

Figure 8.13: Verifying a ship-to-ship transfer using EO browser

---

[23] www.reuters.com/business/energy/
shipping-industry-seeks-combat-dark-oil-transfers-sea-2021-07-13.
[24] www.sentinel-hub.com/explore/eobrowser.

Working from vessel paths and AIS has its downsides. For instance, the following tanker vessels appear like they are meeting, they look close together, the pattern looks abnormally precise, yet if we look on satellite we can see that it is actually Al Basrah Oil Terminal (ABOT) where Iraq fills vessels with oil (see Figures 8.14-8.16).

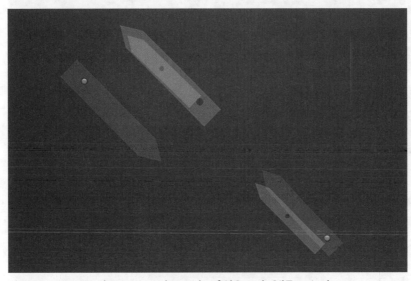

Figure 8.14: Vessels positioned outside of Al Basrah Oil Terminal

Figure 8.15: Satellite view of vessels positioned outside of Al Basrah Oil Terminal

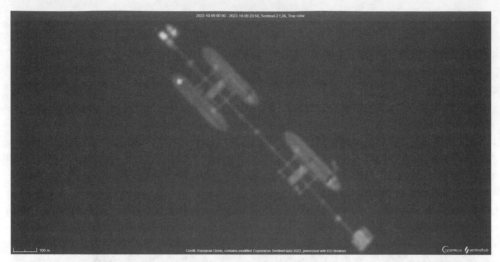

Figure 8.16: Verifying a ship-to-ship transfer using EO browser

Another type of ship "meeting" is used for transferring supplies like fuel and dry stores from a naval auxiliary ship to another naval ship. In the United States, these transfers are called Replenishment At Sea (RAS) or Underway Replenishment (UNREP) (see Figure 8.17). Another type of replenishment is accomplished by air, and we will talk about that in the section of the chapter that deals with aircraft.

Figure 8.17: Replenishment at sea[25]

---
[25] www.dvidshub.net/image/6810714/replenishment-sea.

When talking about any country's navy, it can be hard to track vessels because they turn their AIS off during mission-critical events and vulnerable situations for safety and security. It would be impossible to remain ethical while disclosing ways to track the military that could make the United States vulnerable to attack. However, as a rule of thumb, with any meeting of vessels we can get lucky if we see a public disclosure noting an event and one vessel continues to broadcast while the other remains dark, we can infer they were together and attempt to use satellite imagery to confirm it.

Finally, ships can appear to meet when one vessel is towing or performing maintenance on another vessel or interacting with the crew. For instance, we would see this type of activity when a Coast Guard vessel stops another vessel, when tugboats push or pull larger vessels in for repair, or when they pull barges for rocket launches like we see with the Pegasus, NASA's Barge (see Figure 8.18).

Figure 8.18: Vessel pulling a NASA barge[26]

Port Calls

The normal economic behavior of most commercial vessels is to transport goods from one location to another. The maritime facilities where ships load and unload cargo and passengers is called a *port*. Ports are considered to be critical infrastructure by the U.S. Cybersecurity & Infrastructure Security Agency (CISA) because their assets are "so vital to the United States that their incapacitation

---

[26] www.nasa.gov/centers/marshall/michoud/pegasus-barge-on-pearl-river.

or destruction would have a debilitating effect on security, national economic security, national public health or safety, or any combination thereof."[27]

Modern ports are typically multimodal distribution centers with access to road, rail, and air transportation,[28] and they play an important role in the economy. Within ports are terminals, or checkpoints, where vessels are documented and inspected. Businesses may lease terminals within ports and become terminal operators and terminals may contain many other operations such as storage, tanning, dry cleaning, and gasoline dispensing. It is easy to think of a port as just a place for loading and unloading goods however the larger ports can be seen more like small towns with companies that support the crews and goods on the vessels. Each vessel has a port of registry where it is legally associated, thus giving it a nationality and flag.

When a vessel sails to and stops at a port, we say it is making a port call. These calls can be telling during analysis when we look at the previous port call, the destination port call, the weight before/after the port call, the length of time within the port, and any other vessels it meets with. Once the vessel enters the port, it must berth or park, because ports are complex; they draw up berthing reports in advance to allocate resources and space for the vessel to save time and prevent delays.

Shipping vessels are not the only traffic in a port. Customs and border operations work at all ports of entry to screen foreign visitors, returning citizens, and imported cargo. The Coast Guard also actively patrols ports and waterways conducting inspections, analyzing port security, and enforcing laws.

Tips for Analyzing Ports

Berthing reports, although often drawn up months in advance, are generally available publicly only for the present week. An analyst can use a search engine or the official port website to search for the current berthing reports to gather information about the ships coming and going and, if lucky, the cargo. The following is an example berthing report from Mundra International Container Terminal (see Figure 8.19). You can see it shows the date, along with vessel departures in the last 24 hours, vessels set to arrive (including name, ETA, service, and agent), and ICD Pendency, which is the Indian Customs waiting list. Not all ports make berthing reports public.[29]

---

[27] www.cisa.gov/critical-infrastructure-sectors.

[28] www.porttechnology.org/news/what-are-sea-ports.

[29] portal.dpworldmundra.com:83/BerthinReport/berthingreports.pdf.

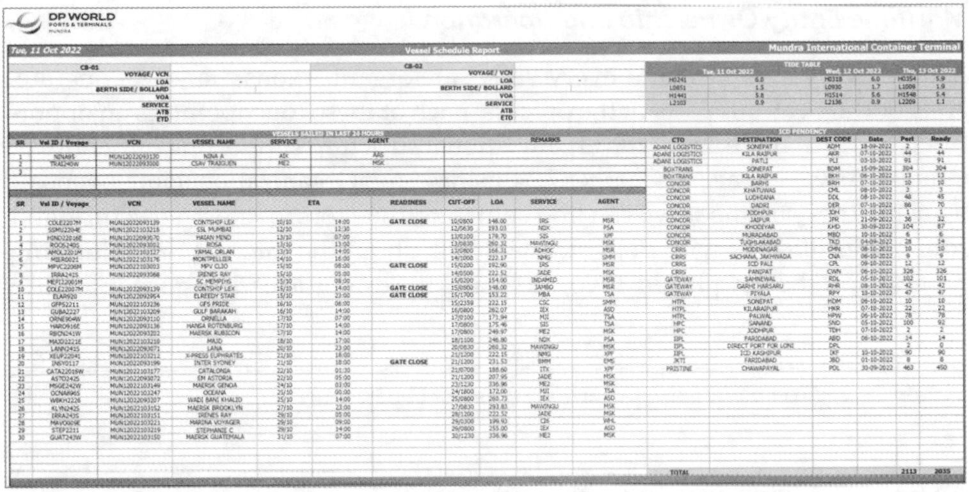

DP WORLD
PORTS & TERMINALS
MUNDRA

Tue, 11 Oct 2022 — Vessel Schedule Report — Mundra International Container Terminal

CB-01		CB-02	
VOYAGE/ VCN		VOYAGE/ VCN	
LOA		LOA	
BERTH SIDE/ BOLLARD		BERTH SIDE/ BOLLARD	
VOA		VOA	
SERVICE		SERVICE	
ATB		ATB	
ETD		ETD	

TIDE TABLE

Tue, 11 Oct 2022		Wed, 12 Oct 2022		Thu, 13 Oct 2022	
H0241	6.0	H0318	6.0	H0354	5.9
L0851	1.5	L0930	1.7	L1009	1.9
H1441	5.8	H1514	5.6	H1548	5.4
L2103	0.9	L2136	0.9	L2209	1.1

VESSELS SAILED IN LAST 24 HOURS

SR	Vsl ID / Voyage	VCN	VESSEL NAME	SERVICE	AGENT	REMARKS
1	NINA95	MUN12022093130	NINA A	AIX	AAS	
2	TRAI240W	MUN12022093008	CSAV TRAIGUEN	ME2	MSK	
3						

SR	Vsl ID / Voyage	VCN	VESSEL NAME	ETA		READINESS	CUT-OFF	LOA	SERVICE	AGENT
1	COLE2207M	MUN12022093139	CONTSHIP LEX	10/10	14:00	GATE CLOSE	10/0800	146.00	IRS	MSR
2	SSMU2204E	MUN12022103218	SSL MUMBAI	12/10	12:30		12/0630	193.03	NDX	PSA
3	HIND2216E	MUN12022093070	HAIAN MIND	13/10	07:00		13/0100	179.70	SIS	XPF
4	ROOS2405	MUN12022093002	ROSA	13/10	13:00		13/0630	260.32	MAWINGU	MSK
5	AMOL2201M	MUN12022103127	YAMAL ORLAN	13/10	14:00		13/0800	164.31	ADHOC	MSR
6	MIER0021	MUN12022103176	MONTPELLIER	14/10	16:00		14/1000	222.17	NMG	SMM
7	MPVC2206M	MUN12022103003	MPV CLIO	15/10	08:00	GATE CLOSE	15/0200	192.90	IRS	MSR
8	IRRA2415	MUN12022093068	IRENES RAY	15/10	05:00		14/0500	222.52	JADE	MSK
9	MEPI22001M		SC MEMPHIS	15/10	08:00		15/0200	154.00	INDAMED	MSR
10	COLE22007M	MUN12022093139	CONTSHIP LEX	15/10	14:00	GATE CLOSE	15/0800	148.00	JAMBO	MSR
11	ELAR920	MUN12022092954	ELREEDY STAR	15/10	23:00	GATE CLOSE	15/1700	153.22	MBA	TSA
12	GFPS2211	MUN12022103236	GFS PRIDE	16/10	06:00		15/2359	222.15	CSC	SMM
13	GUBA2227	MUN12022103209	GULF BARAKAH	16/10	14:00		16/0800	262.07	IEX	ASD
14	ORNE904W	MUN12022093110	ORNELLA	17/10	07:00		17/0100	171.94	MJI	TSA
15	HARO916E	MUN12022093136	HANSA ROTENBURG	17/10	14:00		17/0800	175.46	SIS	TSA
16	RBCN241W	MUN12022093202	MAERSK RUBICON	17/10	14:00		17/0800	249.97	ME2	MSK
17	MAJO2221E	MUN12022103218	MAJD	18/10	17:00		18/1100	246.80	NDX	PSA
18	LANN2415	MUN12022093071	LANA	20/10	23:00		20/0630	260.32	MAWINGU	MSK
19	XEUP22041	MUN12022103212	X-PRESS EUPHRATES	21/10	18:00		21/1200	222.15	NMG	XPF
20	INSY0117	MUN12022093199	INTER SYDNEY	21/10	18:00	GATE CLOSE	21/1200	231.53	BMM	EMS
21	CATA22019W	MUN12022103177	CATALONIA	22/10	01:30		21/0700	188.60	ITX	XPF
22	ASTO2425	MUN12022093072	EM ASTORIA	22/10	05:00		21/1200	207.95	JADE	MSK
23	MSGE242W	MUN12022103149	MAERSK GENOA	24/10	03:00		23/1230	336.96	ME2	MSK
24	OCNA965	MUN12022103247	OCEANA	25/10	00:00		24/1800	172.00	MJI	TSA
25	WBKH2226	MUN12022093207	WADI BANI KHALID	25/10	14:00		25/0800	260.73	IEX	ASD
26	KLYN2425	MUN12022103152	MAERSK BROOKLYN	27/10	23:00		27/0830	293.83	MAWINGU	MSK
27	IRRA2435	MUN12022103151	IRENES RAY	29/10	05:00		28/1200	222.52	JADE	MSK
28	MAVO009E	MUN12022103221	MARINA VOYAGER	29/10	09:00		29/0300	199.93	CIS	WHL
29	STEP2211	MUN12022103219	STEPHANIE C	29/10	14:00		29/0800	255.00	IEX	ASD
30	GUAT243W	MUN12022103150	MAERSK GUATEMALA	31/10	07:00		30/1230	336.96	ME2	MSK

ICD PENDENCY

CTO	DESTINATION	DEST CODE	Date	Perl	Ready
ADANI LOGISTICS	SONEPAT	ADM	18-09-2022	2	2
ADANI LOGISTICS	KILA RAIPUR	AKR	07-10-2022	44	44
ADANI LOGISTICS	PATLI	PLI	03-10-2022	91	91
BOXTRANS	SONEPAT	BOM	15-09-2022	304	304
BOXTRANS	KILA RAIPUR	BKH	06-10-2022	13	13
CONCOR	BARHI	BRH	07-10-2022	10	10
CONCOR	KHATUWAS	CML	08-10-2022	3	3
CONCOR	LUDHIANA	DDL	08-10-2022	48	45
CONCOR	DADRI	DER	07-10-2022	86	70
CONCOR	JODHPUR	JDH	02-10-2022	1	1
CONCOR	JAIPUR	JPR	21-09-2022	36	32
CONCOR	KHODIYAR	KHD	30-09-2022	104	87
CONCOR	MURADABAD	MBD	10-10-2022	6	6
CONCOR	TUGHLAKABAD	TKD	04-09-2022	28	14
CRRS	MODINAGAR	CMN	08-10-2022	10	10
CRRS	SACHANA, JAKHVADA	CNA	06-10-2022	9	9
CRRS	ICD PALI	CPL	09-10-2022	12	12
CRRS	PANIPAT	CWN	06-10-2022	326	326
GATEWAY	SAHNEWAL	RDL	05-10-2022	102	101
GATEWAY	GARHI HARSARU	RHR	08-10-2022	42	42
GATEWAY	PIYALA	RPY	10-10-2022	47	47
HTPL	SONEPAT	HDM	06-10-2022	10	10
HTPL	KILARAIPUR	HKR	07-10-2022	22	22
HTPL	PALWAL	HPW	06-10-2022	78	78
HPC	SANAND	SND	05-10-2022	100	92
HPC	JODHPUR	TDH	07-10-2022	2	2
IIPL	FARIDABAD	ABD	06-10-2022	14	14
IIPL	DIRECT PORT FOR LONI	DPL		2	0
IIPL	ICD KASHIPUR	IKP	10-10-2022	90	90
JKTI	FARIDABAD	JBD	01-10-2022	8	8
PRISTINE	CHAWAPAYAL	POL	30-09-2022	463	450
TOTAL				2113	2035

Figure 8.19: Example berthing report

Ports are also a great place to practice your image and satellite analysis skills. They are great for catching a ship on satellite and port cam imagery because it's often not moving for several hours once berthed. If the vessel path in our free tracking tools shows a vessel is or was recently in port, we can use the EO browser or a search engine to find a webcam to grab a picture or video of it (see Figure 8.20).

Organizational intelligence techniques are also incredibly useful when looking at port and vessel management and operation as well as the supporting businesses working at the port.

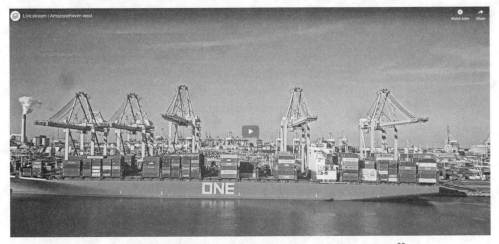

Figure 8.20: Webcam video from the Port of Rotterdam Amazonehaven West[30]

[30] www.youtube.com/embed/M09NaBVPjAI.

Maritime Entity Ownership and Operation

Behind every shipment and every vessel are organizations that own, operate, and contract various parts of the process. Each of these touchpoints is an opportunity to learn more about the organizational structure supporting our entity of interest. As we learned in Chapter 7, "Business and Organizational Intelligence," by using these methods we can find contracts, directors, owners, structure, and sometimes illicit activity markers. Let's talk about the international shipping process and the key players involved using the example of a cargo shipment.[31]

Step 1	An *importer* makes a purchase order for goods.
Step 2	A *freight forwarder*, or agent for the importer, arranges the export of goods, and a *shipping agent* is responsible for handling and transporting the goods. A *freight broker* is responsible for connecting shippers and carriers.
Step 3	A cargo container gets goods loaded into the vessel by *Stevedores*, who employ *Longshoremen* and are overseen by *Port Terminal Operators*.
Step 4	The verified gross mass (VGM) is measured by the *shipper*, and the container is cleared by customs.
Step 5	The container is loaded onto a vessel by *Stevedores*, and a bill of lading, which establishes the contract and receipt between shipper and transportation company, is issued by the *freight forwarder* to the *consignee*, or company that manages the shipment at the destination.
Step 6	The bill of lading is registered on the *vessel manifest declaration*.
Step 7	An arrival notice is issued by the *freight forwarder* to the *consignee* notifying when the shipment will arrive.
Step 8	The arrival notice and bill of lading are paid by the *importer*.
Step 9	The cargo arrives at port and is cleared by a *customs house broker* appointed by the *consignee*.
Step 10	Cargo is removed by *Stevedores*, and the *consignee* picks up the container by truck or rail.

---

[31] https://ppiaf.org/sites/ppiaf.org/files/documents/toolkits/Portoolkit/Toolkit/pdf/modules/09_TOOLKIT_Glossary.pdf.

This is a lot of information seemingly unrelated to OSINT; however, knowing the key stakeholders in the shipping process and who is in a position to possibly facilitate or turn a blind eye to illegal activity is important.

Tips for Analyzing Maritime Entity Ownership and Operations

The process to analyze ownership and operations in the maritime domain is similar to traditional organizational OSINT. Because of the way these cases can quickly become unruly, it is a good practice to begin by developing a link analysis chart in your favorite charting software like Maltego CE. Begin by identifying your vessel or organization of interest and work your way out from that using contracts to identify partnerships, possible cargo shipments, names of shipping agents or port operators, and identities of subjects involved. Public disclosures are a great place to identify funding, exercises, partnerships, and routes. Ship owner websites often list their entire fleet and considerable details about their capabilities, past shipments, and sometimes have tracking for the containers or vessel routes.

Once we have enumerated some of the organizations involved, we can dive in a bit deeper and look at their organizational structure using sites like Open Corporates to determine subsidiaries, headquarters, agents, contact information, and possible linkages between organizations. Developing each of these areas should begin to show any type of interesting, abnormal, or illicit behavior. Doing some simple Google dorks on each entity will bring up news reports, potential other entities, and vessels associated. We can also check each selector we found on the OFAC sanctions list as well as doing a Google dork for "selector" and "sanctions" OR "designation" to find any state and federal-level infractions.

Here are some potential illegal activity examples:

- Sanctions evasions
- Smuggling/trafficking
  - Arms
  - People
  - Drugs
  - Exotic or endangered plants/animals
- Terrorism
- Nuclear materials proliferation
- Illegal fishing
- Shipbreaking
- Pirating
- Hijacking
- Illegal dumping

Maritime Critical Infrastructure and Entity Vulnerabilities

When dealing with maritime critical infrastructure there are several systems and vulnerabilities to be aware of.

Ship-to-Shore Critical Infrastructure

In the maritime domain, Industrial Control System (ICS) is a general term that includes a group of systems like supervisory control and data acquisition (SCADA) systems, distributed control systems (DCS), and programmable logic controllers (PLC).[32] When thinking about maritime systems, we have to consider the vessels themselves, the shore-based systems supporting them, and the systems within the ports. Here are some examples of critical systems:

Vessel

- Engine control room
- Water ingress detection
- Rudder
- Bridge console
- Ship safety system

Port

- Cargo tracking systems
- Shore-based navigation
- Cranes
- Port security
- Automated smart-port systems

Maritime ICS vulnerabilities are no different than shore-based systems all around the world such as outdated operating systems, missing antivirus, poor configurations, default credentials, and unmanaged third-party contractors; they can be exploited in a wide variety of ways using already known techniques (see Figure 8.21). If ICS fails or is exploited, it can have disastrous results including vessel collisions, taking on too much water, incapacitating the navigation or

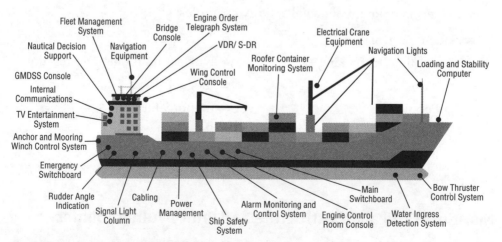

Figure 8.21: Typical vessel industrial control systems

---

[32] https://csrc.nist.gov/glossary/term/industrial_control_system.

safety mechanisms, overwhelming the port and cargo systems, and depending on the size of the port disrupting the supply chain globally.[33]

Many of the systems on a vessel connect and interact with the systems on the shore making all of these systems at risk for exploitation by connection.[34] If the navigation systems on the vessel fail, it could cause the crew to shift to backup plans of navigating by paper charts and radar, collisions, and loss of situational awareness.

As an OSINT analyst, you may be tasked with not exploiting these critical infrastructure vulnerabilities but rather with identifying them for security assessments, red teaming, or intelligence work. The systems on board can be identified through contracts, public disclosures, and even social media walkthrough videos by crew. Once a system name, software, and version numbers are determined, we can use the NIST National Vulnerability Database[35] to determine any vulnerabilities for the specific systems that may be exploited by an adversary and report them to stakeholders.

Many of the systems can also be found on IoT search engines such as Shodan or Censys through a search of the technology name. In the following example I used the name of a Very Small Aperture Terminal (VSAT) system commonly used on vessels, which is a two-way satellite ground station that can transmit and receive data, voice, and video.[36] Searching for 'title: "sailor900" returns results for all Internet-connected Sailor 900 devices showing the open ports available and other vulnerabilities that may exist (see Figure 8.22).

Figure 8.22: Screenshot of Shodan showing sailor 900 devices

---

[33] "ICS Security in Maritime Transportation: A White Paper Examining the Security and Resiliency of Critical Transportation Infrastructure."
[34] www.ics-shipping.org/wp-content/uploads/2021/02/2021-Cyber-Security-Guidelines.pdf.
[35] https://nvd.nist.gov.
[36] www.gartner.com/en/information-technology/glossary/vsat-very-small-aperture-terminal.

Moving on from ship-to-shore critical infrastructure, we should discuss sea-based systems. Undersea cables and pipelines have become very important over the last decade and have been the center of potential sabotage and mysterious cuttings and explosions. Submarine communications cables are cables laid on the sea floor that carry more than 95 percent of international communications data.[37]

According to a report by the Center for Strategic and International Studies (CSIS), undersea cables are vulnerable to both physical and digital attacks with the purpose being to potentially cut military communication, implement targeted Internet access disruption, and/or perform economic sabotage. Digitally, the cables could be vulnerable to a wiretap or disruption and diversion of traffic through exploitation and access to a network system.[38]

Likewise, submarine pipelines are vulnerable to both physical and digital attacks. As I write this chapter, I am watching the news report a potential sabotage attack on the offshore natural gas pipeline Nord Stream that ties Russia and Europe together. Pipelines can be physically cut or destroyed leaking gas and causing international response and environmental disasters.

One way for us to analyze these types of infrastructure is through publicly available infrastructure maps. Subtelforum.com's submarine cable map[39] is my go-to map for undersea cable systems and shows the cable location, name, length, owners, capacity, landing points, and fiber pairs, and provides a URL to the owner site (see Figure 8.23). What I like about this site over the others is that it allows you to filter by the cable-laying vessels that physically lay the cable in the ocean. The vessel filter shows the vessel's location and other details based on its AIS transmissions. This allows me to easily pop over to a vessel tracking site and dig into the vessel paths, taking the vessel name into sanctions lists and looking at them from an organizational intelligence perspective or analyzing the crew.

Figure 8.23: Screenshot of Subtel forum cable map

---

[37] www.csis.org/analysis/
invisible-and-vital-undersea-cables-and-transatlantic-security.
[38] www.csis.org/analysis/
invisible-and-vital-undersea-cables-and-transatlantic-security.
[39] https://subtelforum.com/submarine-cable-map.

For offshore pipelines, it depends on your area of interest which map will work best for you. ArcGIS offers an interactive map that requires an ArcGIS subscription or developer account to access but offers size of pipe, product being transported, owner, and status of the pipeline.[40] The oil platforms themselves are open to similar vulnerabilities as shore-based systems and can be found on maps by searching for

---

"offshore platform map."

Finally, we must talk about the people on board the vessel as a vulnerability. Looking at the crew and passengers crosses into the realm of subject intelligence, and we can assess these people as individuals for their background, motivations, and potential to cause harm intentionally or unintentionally to maritime technology. The biggest vulnerabilities relating to crew are lack of training on technology and security practices leading to attack and the leak of information that can be combined with other open source data that leads to an attack. For OSINT analysts, we will probably come across the latter more often. Crew members tend to post walkthroughs of the engine rooms and navigation area revealing technologies used, paperwork with sensitive information, and even passwords to computer systems on sticky notes.

8.3   Railways

Another critical means of transportation and shipping is by rail. Rail offers many OSINT opportunities, let's look at some.

Introduction to Railway Intelligence

Railways are a globally used and efficient way to transport both freight and people. In 2020, 28 percent of the United States' freight cargo was transported by train. The United States has the most railway track in the world, and the railways themselves are nearly 140,000 route miles across 7 class I railroads, 22 regional railroads, and 584 short line railroads.[41] There are 7 Class I railroads in the United States.

- BNSF Railway Co.
- Canadian National Railway
- Canadian Pacific
- CSX Transportation
- Kansas City Southern Railway Co.
- Norfolk Southern Combined Railroad Subsidiaries
- Union Pacific Railroad Co.

---

[40] www.arcgis.com/home/item.html?id=446f760c682e4750ab6910523b77ff91.
[41] https://railroads.dot.gov/rail-network-development/freight-rail-overview.

Additionally, the freight railways support the Railroads for National Defense Program, which is more than 30,000 miles of commercial rail line that is classified as the Strategic Rail Network and used for mobility and shipment of munitions. If necessary, these railways can be restricted to only military traffic.[42] While the United States may have the most track, China and India move the most passengers per year by rail at roughly 1,550 billion reported in 2019, and Europe's train companies are very profitable with Deutsche Bahn AG being the most significant train company not only in Europe but globally. The most important train companies in Europe are the following:

- Eurostar
- SNCF
- Deutsche Bahn
- Flix Train
- Trenitalia
- Italio
- Renfe

Even though rail itself has been in a steady decline over time, it still serves a valuable position in commuter traffic and multimodal transportation of goods across the globe, which makes it a rich source for OSINT collection. We can apply the skills we have already learned in subject intelligence, social media analysis, imagery analysis and geospatial intelligence, organizational intelligence, and maritime to railway lines to find answers to our intelligence questions.

Types of Railway Entities

These are types of railway entities:

TRAINS	RAILWAY	OTHER
Class I, II, III		
Passenger trains	Heavy rail	Train station
Locomotive	High-speed rail	Train platforms
Road-rail vehicle	Inter-city rail	Switch Gear
Train ferry	Monorail	Bridges
High-speed trains	Mountain rail	Tunnels
Regional trains	Heritage rail	Intermodal Facilities
Inter-city trains	Pateway	
Short-distance trains	Rack rail	
Commuter trains	Tourist rail	

---

[42] https://media.defense.gov/2019/Apr/11/2002115504/-1/-1/0/ 38CRITICALRAILINFRASTRUCTURE.PDF.

TRAINS	RAILWAY	OTHER
Tram	Wagonway	
Rapid transit	Military rail	
Light rail		
Monorail trains		
Railcar		
Automated people movers (APM)		
Subway trains		

Railway Terminology

The following are terms to know:

- **Cab:** Control room of a train with the engine control and crew.
- **Lead Unit:** Locomotive with cab and operation controls
- **Abandonment:** When the freight is so damaged, it is not accepted and is rendered worthless.
- **Absorption:** Switching freight from one carrier to another without an increase in rates.
- **Abstract:** The accounting form used by rail freight for division of revenue.
- **Abstract of Charges:** A report of freight bills issues by a station that is used to total for records.
- **Abstract of Waybills:** A report derived from shipment waybills.
- **Acceptance:** The freight receipt from the consignee of a shipment.
- **Automatic Equipment Identification (AEI):** A trackside system that scans and records encoded information from the side of freight including railcars.
- **Agent:** An individual or organization that connects shippers with carriers.
- **Automatic Block Signal System (ABS):** A series of signals used for railroad communications that divide the rail line into sections called blocks.
- **Automatic Railroad Crossing:** Railroad crossings controlled electronically through a relay in the track.
- **Automatic Train Control System:** A system within the train that involves automatic speed control or reduction such as emergency braking if the engineer fails to respond to an external danger.
- **Classification Yard:** A yard used for organizing railcars by their destination by sending them through switches to the proper tracks.
- **Switching or Shunting:** Sorting rolling stock onto or off of complete trains.

Railway Discovery and Analysis Methods

There are many reasons an OSINT analyst would want to analyze trains, railways, and rail stations. Rail freight shipments, employees, passengers, dispatchers, and organizations are all areas of interest worth looking into. You can scope your work from the initial analysis questions provided by your stakeholder to determine which avenues are the most important to your case. Some things we look at when analyzing railways are the following:

- Train routes
- Intermodal connections (vessel, truck)
- Tracking freight
- Concealed freight (smuggling, arms shipments)
- Ownership information (pivot to business intel)
- Traditional imagery (photos, webcam, video)
- Satellite imagery
- Vulnerable technology
- Operators (pivot to subject intel)
- Vulnerable infrastructure

Additionally, a good starting point for developing insight into a rail network is by learning about the different types of rail yards. Trains use hubs called *classification yards* to route cars to the proper track. Classification yards are divided into different types including flat, gravity, and hump yards.

- **Flat Yard:** Developed on flat or mildly sloped ground, and cars are pushed by a locomotive to their track destination.
- **Gravity Yard:** Developed on sloped ground to let cars roll to their track destination.
- **Hump Yard:** Developed on flat ground where only a small part of the yard is graded. An engine pushes the car to the top of the hump, and it rolls to its track destination.

Visual Identification of Rail Lines

The earliest trainspotter was 14-year-old Fanny Johnson in 1861 who kept a journal of the trains that passed by her home in Westbourne Park London.[43] Train enthusiasts, also known as *railfans*, take photographs, video, and notes about trains as a hobby. Because many railfans strive to take the best photos

---

[43] www.guinnessworldrecords.com/
world-records/685747-first-trainspotter.

they can of the passing trains, they become a handy addition to our analysis when trying to identify a train, rail company, or specific location.

Brand Logos and Colors

One of the fastest ways to identify a train visually is through its logo, the color scheme used on the train, and the shape of the train. Even in black and white it is easy to see the difference between these two trains[44,45] (see Figure 8.24).

Figure 8.24: Examples of rail branding

These are examples of some of the logos and branding (see Figure 8.25):

RAILROAD	LOGO	BRANDING
BNSF Railway Fort Worth, TX	*BNSF* *RAILWAY*	Black, orange, yellow
Canadian National Railway Company Montreal, CA	CN	Red, white, black
CSX Transportation Jacksonville, FL	[CSX]	Blue, yellow
Deutsche Bahn Berlin, GE	DB	Red, white
Trenitalia Rome, IT	*TRENITALIA* GRUPPO FERROVIE DELLO STATO ITALIANE	Red, Grey, black, and red, white, and green

Figure 8.25: Rail company logos

[44] www.getyourguide.com/fiumicino-1715/
fiumicino-airport-leonardo-express-train-ticket-t328786.
[45] commons.wikimedia.org/wiki/File:Union_Pacific_loco.png.

Figure 8.26: QuizTime

Marc Krueger of Quiztime posted this image of a train in March 2020[46] asking where he waited for this train. With no clear logo or names on the side, we need to dig a bit further to figure out what train this is and what platform this could be (see Figure 8.26).

A reverse image search of this photo shows similarly branded train cars in Carnegie Station in Melbourne, Australia. A search engine search of *train lines in Carnegie station Melbourne* turned up a video, and in the video description it reveals that it contains metro train types Comeng and Siemens. Comparing the two train models side-by-side, it is clear that our picture is a Comeng based on the rounded shape of the cars (see Figure 8.27).

Looking at stations in Melbourne, are 218 of them, which is way too many to search through one by one unless necessary. Instead, let's try to narrow it down using our image analysis technique and ask ourselves:[47,48]

Figure 8.27: Siemens and Comeng trains

[46] twitter.com/kollege/status/
1245080313426063361?s=20&t=MXoAakHfYoMe04M40XSc6g.
[47] upload.wikimedia.org/wikipedia/commons/f/f6/Metro_Trains_
Melbourne_Siemens_at_Sunshine.jpg.
[48] upload.wikimedia.org/wikipedia/commons/0/0c/Melboure_Comeng_381M_
Metro.jpg.

- What's in the foreground?
- What's in the background?
- Are there any map markers?

Foreground: Interestingly in two of the three pictures there is a patterned walkway in the foreground, one color on the outside and a stripe on the inside in color its orange, yellow, orange. It seems after looking through images that most of the train stations have this pattern.

Background: In the background there is a curved glass structure that could be the top of the train station roof and a multistory glass walled office building with a satellite on the top.

Map Markers: None

At this point I wasn't ready to just brute-force search every image of Melbourne train stations, so I used a search engine to search

---

"Live rail maps Australia"

---

and found `anytrip.com.au`[49] with real-time information. Zooming in on the Melbourne area, it showed me only two stations, Southern Cross Station and

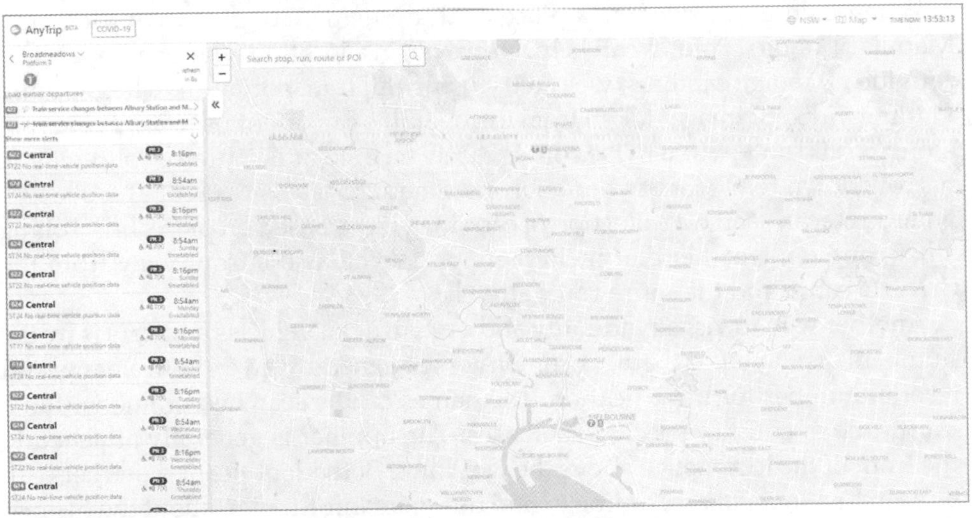

Figure 8.28: Stations on Live rail map

Broadmeadows (see Figure 8.28).

I searched each name in a search engine, and Broadmeadows returned an image with the orange path with the stripe, a curved glass roof, and a several story building with glass sections. Using just a cropped image of a train and working from its branding colors, we were able to geolocate the exact spot the photo was taken (see Figure 8.29).[50]

---

[49] `https://anytrip.com.au`.
[50] `upload.wikimedia.org/wikipedia/commons/c/c2/Suburban_platforms_at_Broadmeadows_station%2C_Melbourne.jpg`.

Figure 8.29: Exact spot photo was taken

When trying to geolocate a place or thing using Google Street View and Mapillary, photo captures can help. However, in a location where these services provide no image captures, we can try using rail transportation to help us out. Finding video or images taken from inside trains can orient us to a specific spot along a rail route. Since these routes rarely change, it is a pretty solid way to narrow down the focus of your analysis. One such site is `railcabrides.com`,[51] where you can search a collection of cab ride videos based on place, line, rolling stock, or even weather that include maps as well as the front view from the driver's cabin and the entire route stretch.

Another way to visually identify and organize rail vehicles and cars is by the numbers displayed on them. Locomotives are generally given both a name and a serial number for identification. The names can be searched online within a multitude of country-specific databases. The number is generally attached to the front of the locomotive above the windows. Both identification markers can be searched in databases online to find out more information about the history, locations of use, and ownership changes behind the locomotive (see Figure 8.30).[52]

---

[51] `https://railcabrides.com/en`.
[52] `www.up.com/heritage/fleet/streamliners/index.htm`.

Figure 8.30: Identification marker on front of train

The number on a train car has several names. In the UK it is referred to as a Train Reporting Number; in the United States it is called the Rolling Stock Identification Number or Reporting Mark. In its current state, there is no global standard for these numbers, and they vary across time, which makes it nearly impossible to generalize. I will use the U.S. system as an example, but the rest should be somewhat similar. In North America, Reporting Marks are issued by the Association of American Railroads (AAR) and made up of one to five letters indicating ownership, with the first letter matching the initial letter of the railroad name. The letters are followed by up to six digits that indicate the place in the fleet. If a reporting mark ends in an X, it indicates a private company owns the car, a U indicates intermodal containers, and a Z refers to trailer-on-flatcar. Lists of these serial number codes by country can be found online relatively easy.

In the following image, we see SHPX 462477; using a search engine to search SHPX I determined that the owner is American Railcar Leasing, LLC, but their old name was Shippers Car Line (thus the S as the first letter of the Serial Number) (see Figure 8.31).[53]

---

[53] www.wikiwand.com/en/Reporting_mark#Media/File:Train-connections .jpg.

Figure 8.31: Identification marker on side of train car

Railway Routes and Schedules

Now that we can identify a train by its identification markers and branding, let's discuss some ways to identify tracks, routes, and schedules to enhance our analysis.

Tips for Analyzing Railways and Train Routes

Global railway systems can be found on a number of free to access and often interactive maps like OpenRailwayMap[54] that show details such as infrastructure, max speed per line, signaling, electrification, and track gauge (see Figure 8.32). There are also country, city, rail line, and historical maps of railways that we can use to answer questions like "What railroad delivers freight to this specific region north to south?" and "what is the most likely commuter train station a subject would use?" and "What is the most likely route a smuggler would use?"

The benefit of looking at a specific rail line's maps is that many of them are interactive and offer live tracking of their trains. Geops has a live train tracker[55] that integrates public transport and mobility along with transit maps, vehicle positions, and other information (see Figure 8.33). It does have some countries that it doesn't track, but it is nice to have several in one spot versus searching out the specific maps. You can watch the trains move in real time across the map.

---

[54] www.openrailwaymap.org.
[55] https://mobility.portal.geops.io/en.

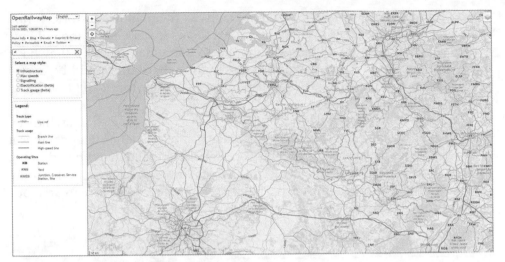

Figure 8.32: Open railway map

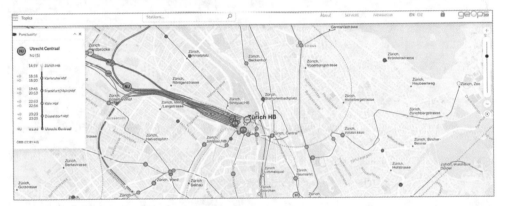

Figure 8.33: Geops

Railway maps and train tracking can be used to pivot to further information. The following are some examples of ways we can move forward from knowing the train route or path:

Use Street View, Mapillary, or satellite imagery to get a visual of the train or parts of the track.

Leverage social media to find a precise location example: using train tracking and TikTok or Snapchat to find a spot along the route

Tips for Analyzing Train Schedules, Passengers, and Cargo

Hand in hand with railway routes are the schedules that keep trains running on time and getting to their destination. Schedules are not hard to find and are readily available on train station or rail line websites. Historical train schedules are a bit harder to find. I do know that Deutsche Bahn allows historical train schedule searches back several months, so it seems to depend on the rail line. Schedules are meant to be public data, though, so what value do they have to OSINT analysts? The following is a scenario where this could be useful information to have access to that also integrates other forms of OSINT like subject intelligence:

A crime is committed, and you know the suspect traveled by rail on the day of the crime. Using train schedules, you may be able to determine whether it was feasible for the suspect to accomplish. Enriching that data with additional information using a site like TravelTime[56] that allows you to enter a location, a time frame, and mode of transportation, we can now establish an area our suspect could have traveled in the time they had (see Figure 8.34).

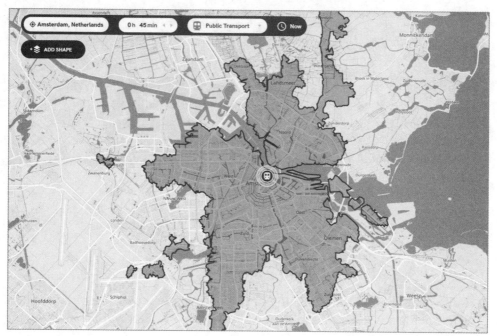

Figure 8.34: Traveltime

Most trains are not fully automatic and require people to operate the equipment and help passengers or cargo get to where it is going. Surprisingly, very few people are required to operate a train although even in fully automatic trains some employees remain for safety. A freight train could run with a certified engineer who drives the train; a conductor who handles on board operation and safety of the train including record keeping, repairs, ticketing, coupling/decoupling; and the brake operator who works as an assistant to the conductor. In addition to the workers on board, commuter trains also carry passengers.

---

[56] https://app.traveltime.com.

Freight

Freight movement by rail is an ordinary component of the supply chain. The ability to recognize the type of cargo inside a railcar based on its type can be useful in anticipating where it is headed or where it came from. The shipments, depending on content, are carried within eight different types of railcars.

- **Boxcar:** The most common type of railcar has a roof and sliding doors, used for palletized and bulk shipments.
- **Hopper Cars:** Loaded from the top with side release doors, used to transport loose commodities like salt, sand, and coal.
- **Flat Cars:** A flat open deck made of wood or steel made for carrying large cargo like lumber, machinery, intermodal containers.
- **Tank Cars:** Long tubes with a valve on top made for carrying liquid like oil, chemicals, and petroleum.
- **Gondolas:** Low sides and an open top for carrying dense bulk cargo like gravel, scrap metal, and waste.
- **Coil Cars:** Cylindrical-shaped gondola car used to transport metal coils and tubing.
- **Refrigerator Cars:** Specially designed for keeping cargo like milk or frozen meat at its required temperature.
- **Specialty Cars:** Cars shaped for a specific commodity including ballast cars, side dumps, and auto racks.

Tracking the train itself is much easier than tracking the railcars and cargo. To track cargo, it requires knowing the container number along with the bill of lading, booking number, and shipping line. Rarely do we ever have all the information available for online tracking of a train shipment through the cargo number. It is possible, however, to combine data sources such as train schedules, public disclosures, social media, and photos to track cargo visually.

Railway Entity Ownership and Operation

Now let's learn about how we can integrate the information provided through railway ownership and operation into our OSINT analysis.

Tips for Analyzing Railway Entity Ownership and Operations

Railway ownership and operations can be split into two main buckets: freight train shipping (generally intermodal) and passenger travel. In intermodal shipping there are several points of contact in the shipping, ownership, and operation of the train and the cargo that we can analyze using business intelligence methods including railroad logistics companies, drayage, and shippers.

Step 1	If the freight arrives via international modal, it would first be transloaded from a shipping container on a vessel to a rail car at a transload, cross-docking, or distributions center facility.
Step 2	The railroad takes the container from the origin rail ramp to the destination ramp or the closest intermodal railyard to its destination.
Step 3	The container is then off-loaded onto a truck or trucks, and an intermodal driver continues the journey.

- **Intermodal Marketing Companies (IMCs)** maintain contracts with the Class I railroads for access to a large pool of equipment and draymen.
- **Asset-Based Intermodal Carriers** own their fleet and drayage operations.
- **Asset-Lite Intermodal Carriers** have access to both the railroad's equipment and some of their own.
- **Resellers** rely on asset carriers and IMCs to move the loads and are brokers.

To gain more context about the railroads and operation, we can use contracts, and corporate business databases to determine ownership, partnerships, subsidiaries, and discretions. Using the methods of social media analysis and disclosures, we can gain information about agreements and partnerships.

Railway Critical Infrastructure and Entity Vulnerabilities

As we learned previously about maritime entities, the rail system is also made up of industrial control systems, SCADA, and PLCs that keep the trains running either while operated or automatically. There are a lot of reasons that trains and their systems are targeted, and the more modernized and digitized they become, the more vulnerable they are to attack. The many railway control systems are present on board, within train stations, and even alongside railway tracks to facilitate the smooth operations of rail systems (see Figure 8.35). Rail is considered to be critical infrastructure because if the rail systems are disrupted or sabotaged, it could have a ripple effect on the economy.

When thinking about railway systems, we have to consider the trains themselves, the track-based systems supporting them, and the systems within the stations. Here are some examples of critical systems:

Train

- Interlocking signaling systems
- Train safety system
- Positive train control (PTC)
- Continuous-based train control (CBTC)

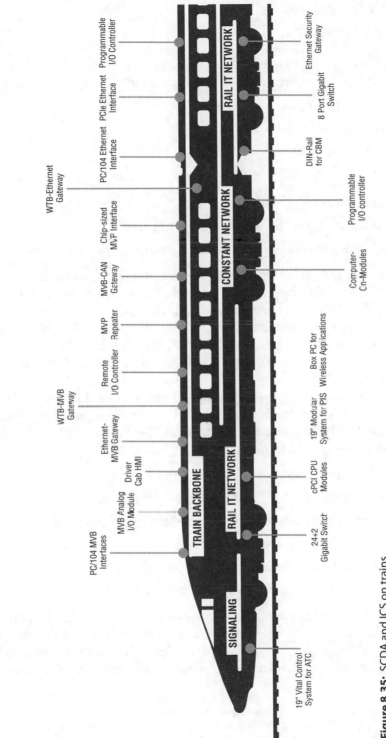

Figure 8.35: SCDA and ICS on trains

- Cab signaling
- Automatic train control (ATC)

Trackside

- RFID Trackside AEI readers
- IoT sensors (temp, vibration, pressure)
- Controlling and switching tracks
- Wayside equipment

Station

- Railcar monitoring solutions
- Rail control systems (platforms, tracks, lines)
- Intermodal connections systems (freight monitoring)

According to CISA, the critical infrastructure of mass transit and passenger rail includes "terminals, operational systems, and supporting infrastructure for passenger services by transit buses, trolleybuses, monorail, heavy rail—also known as subways or metros—light rail, passenger rail, and vanpool/rideshare." And freight rail has more than 138,000 miles of railroad (including U.S. military designated), more than 1.33 million freight cars, and approximately 20,000 locomotives.[57]

When it comes to trains, there are many systems on board that could be vulnerable to exploits. Locomotives have onboard control systems to help optimize the speed, fuel, and transitions the train makes. The components of these systems perform several important functions.[58]

- Centralized traffic control
- Communication to and from trains and wayside units
- Train control technology (signals, coded circuits, transceivers)
- Location monitoring or positioning
- Vital onboard computer systems for dispatch
- SCADA control system for overhead third rail power supply

Trains also have railway safety systems that communicate track status and condition information to the engineers. Some trains such as remote-controlled locomotives and high-speed trains are driverless and remotely operated via radio or infrared signals transmitted by device. Some trains are even outfitted

---

[57] www.cisa.gov/transportation-systems-sector.
[58] https://railroads.dot.gov/sites/fra.dot.gov/files/2020-06/Cyber%20Security%20Risk%20Management-A_0.pdf.

with sensors that visualize things like cars or people on the tracks and adjust speed accordingly for safety.

Dispatch centers are 24/7 locations for directing and organizing train traffic. The technology used at these centers varies but are referred to as *centralized traffic control* systems using VHF/UHF. They have automated systems as well such as traffic control and intuitive train routing systems to protect workers and direct traffic (see Figure 8.36).

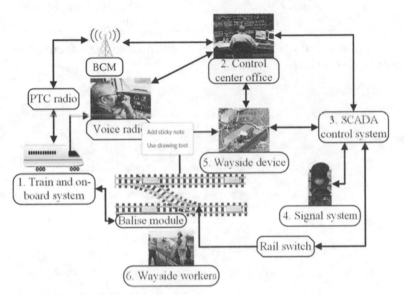

Figure 8.36: Trackside technology

Trackside and bridge/tunnel technology is just as integral to the safe and smooth operation of a railroad as control systems. In freight, the rail cars often have an RFID Automatic Equipment Identification (AEI) tag that gets read by trackside readers, and this data gets collected and shared through contract life-cycle management (CLM) systems to allow real-time tracking of cargo. Bridges use radio-controlled technology to move positions for trains to enter.

When viewing these technologies through an OSINT lens, it is not about physically exploiting these systems but rather identifying the vulnerabilities that could lead to an exploitation by an attacker, gathering the information, and reporting it to key stakeholders. All of the above mentioned technologies fall victim to the same default credentials, external connections, and user errors that any system does. Some examples of potential attacks on these systems are as follows[59]:

---

[59] https://railroads.dot.gov/sites/fra.dot.gov/files/2020-06/
Cyber%20Security%20Risk%20Management-A_0.pdf.

SYSTEM	ATTACK	POSSIBLE RESULTS
Train control system	Remotely control train, manipulate sensors	Delay, stranded, collisions
Automatic stop	Data compromise	Wrong train stop, stranding
Communication systems	Compromise signaling	Collisions, fail-safe
Transit system	Compromised SCADA system	Unable to communicate with devices, disruption of operations

This critical technology can also sometimes be found publicly facing the Internet with tools like Shodan (see Figure 8.37).

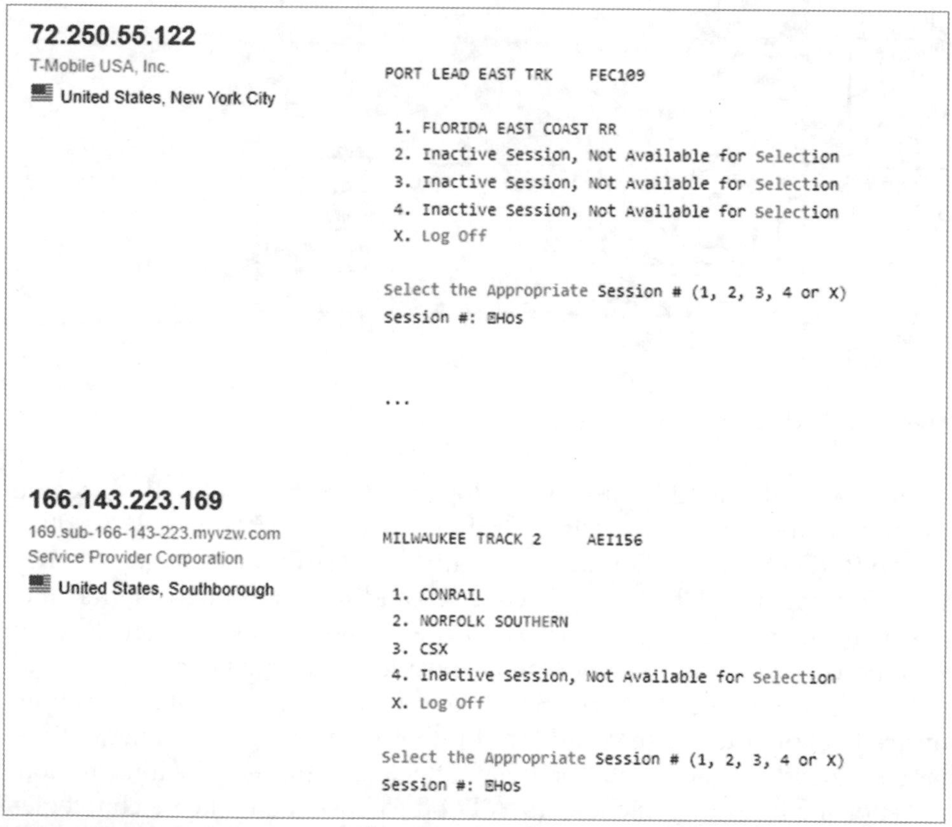

```
72.250.55.122
T-Mobile USA, Inc.
🇺🇸 United States, New York City

                                   PORT LEAD EAST TRK    FEC109

                                   1. FLORIDA EAST COAST RR
                                   2. Inactive Session, Not Available for Selection
                                   3. Inactive Session, Not Available for Selection
                                   4. Inactive Session, Not Available for Selection
                                   X. Log Off


                                   Select the Appropriate Session # (1, 2, 3, 4 or X)
                                   Session #: ⌷Hos



                                   ...



166.143.223.169
169.sub-166-143-223.myvzw.com
Service Provider Corporation
🇺🇸 United States, Southborough

                                   MILWAUKEE TRACK 2     AEI156

                                   1. CONRAIL
                                   2. NORFOLK SOUTHERN
                                   3. CSX
                                   4. Inactive Session, Not Available for Selection
                                   X. Log Off

                                   Select the Appropriate Session # (1, 2, 3, 4 or X)
                                   Session #: ⌷Hos
```

Figure 8.37: Shodan screenshot showing track technology

Additionally, passenger trains and train stations have been used throughout history for terrorist attacks including the 1995 sarin attacks in Tokyo that injured 6,252 people, the 10 simultaneous explosions at Madrid Atocha Railway in Madrid in 2004 injuring 2,050 people, and the 2016 suicide bombing in Maalbeek Metro Station in Brussels injuring 200 people. Security on trains and in their systems is a huge issue because of the long stretches of railway they travel across. Constantly inspecting and monitoring every part of a track is near impossible. Many countries have asked railfans to help keep the railroads safe by reporting any unusual behavior they see, with some railroads even instituting rail safety programs.

8.4 Aircraft

Similar to vessels and rail, air travel and transportation is highly critical to the global economy. Let's look at some ways to integrate air analysis into your OSINT.

Introduction to Aircraft Intelligence

Since the first successful powered flights in the 1900s by Gustave Whitehead and the Wright brothers, air travel has grown to be an integral method of transportation within our society. Presently, there are nearly 45,000 flights per day in the United States with many of those flights being commercial jets. These jets travel across the world at speeds of up to 500 to 600 mph (804 kmh) transporting hundreds of passengers as well as cargo. Much of the world's shipping relies on air cargo transport; by value it accounts for nearly 35 percent of the world's trade.[60] Even if you have never personally set foot on an aircraft, you have most likely still encountered them. We see planes travel overhead to and from airports, news helicopters circle over traffic accidents providing footage for news stations, commercial planes transport our mail and the products we purchase from all over the world, and military planes transport much needed supplies to troops. The heavy integration of air transportation within our society means that there is an abundance of opportunities to collect information on and around aircraft; further, there could be devastating consequences if air travel is purposefully disrupted, degraded, or manipulated by an adversary.

Because information collection from open sources is often the first step in exploitation, understanding what information a person can find on aircraft, personnel, passengers, routes, and cargo can help us to better protect this critical infrastructure. Looking at aircraft and airports through the lens of intelligence, we can identify subjects and entities, develop patterns of life relationships, understand direct or beneficial ownership of business structures and assets, and track routes. The data points we can collect help answer a variety of research questions and use cases. First let's look at the three main categories of aircraft we will talk about in this book:

- **Commercial Aircraft:** This refers primarily to civil aircraft that is used for a job in return for payment. Some examples include a helicopter used for sightseeing tours, a photographer flying a drone over a wedding ceremony, and a commercial jet transporting hundreds of passengers.

---

[60] www.iata.org/en/programs/cargo/sustainability/benefits.

- **Private Aircraft:** This type of aircraft is not for charter but can carry passengers and cargo for personal use. Examples include private jets, medical helicopters, and personal light aircraft.

- **Government Aircraft:** These are both fixed and rotary wing craft used by the many facets of government including armed forces, law enforcement, and federal, state, and local government offices. Aircraft in this category include political transportation, military drones, search and rescue aircraft, and fighter jets.

Understanding the categories of aircraft can help us to more effectively implement targeted analysis based on our needs. In the previous chapters on maritime and rail intelligence, we learned that much of the information gathered and analyzed in these areas is in support of developing context behind what we discover.

Military aircraft are an integral part of tracking and analyzing geopolitical events and movements around the world, providing context often in near real time. Although not strictly military-related, reports of unmanned aerial vehicle sightings to the FAA by pilots, citizens, and law enforcement have increased significantly over the past two years, with more than 100 reports per month in the United States.[61] The ability to use open-source information to detect, track, and identify ownership of reconnaissance aircraft and weapons of war is invaluable.

While knowing the category of aircraft helps us quickly identify potential uses, such as commercial, government, or private, knowledge of the specific types of aircraft that exist, and the correct names for their parts and systems, will help narrow the scope of your analysis even further by providing specific keywords we can then query.

Types of Aircraft

AIRPLANE	OTHER
No Engine (Glider)	**Unmanned Aircraft**
Examples:	*Examples:*
▪ Air100 Arsenal	▪ Fixed-wing drone
	▪ Single-rotor drone
	▪ Multi-rotor drone
	▪ Fixed-wing Hybrid VTOL
	▪ Hobby planes

---

[61] www.faa.gov/uas/resources/public_records/uas_sightings_report.

AIRPLANE	OTHER
Single-Engine	**Spaceplane**
Examples:	*Example:*
■ Cessna Skylane	■ X-37B
■ Beechcraft Bonanza	
■ Piper Cherokee	
Multi-Engine	**Rotorcraft**
Examples:	*Examples:*
■ Piper Seminole (twin-engine)	■ Helicopter (monocopter)
■ Dassault Falcon (three-engine)	■ Helicopter (twin rotor)
■ Boeing 747 (four-engine)	■ Autogyro
■ Antanov AN-225 Mriya (six-engine)	■ Gyrodyne
	■ Rotor kite
Single-Engine Seaplane	**Powered Lift**
Example:	*Example:*
■ DeHavilland Turbo Beaver	■ Boeing V-22 Osprey
Multi-Engine Seaplane:	
Example:	
■ Aircam w/ amphibious floats	

Source: www.naa.edu/sectors-of-aviation/Aviation Terminology

Parts of a Typical Jet

Figure 8.38 shows the parts of a typical jet.

Here are terms to know:

- **Aileron:** The hinged portion on the back edge of an airplane wing that can be adjusted to facilitate banking and turning.
- **Cockpit:** The area near the front where the pilot(s) and crew sit that contains the instruments to control the aircraft.
- **Elevator:** A flight control surface near the rear of an aircraft that controls the pitch or lateral axis movement.
- **Jet Engine:** The part of the aircraft that thrusts the plane forward allowing it to gain enough speed to lift off. Aircraft can have up to six engines.
- **Flaps:** Hinged panels on the back edge of the aircraft wings that increase and decrease surface area when moved to get more lift.

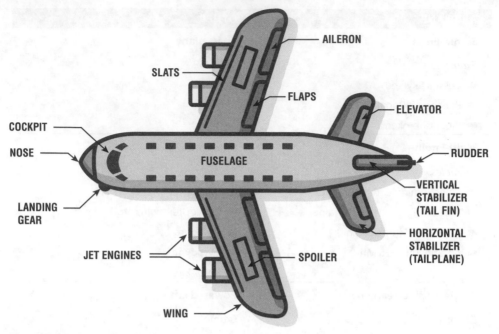

Figure 8.38: Parts of a jet

- **Fuselage:** The hollow main body of the aircraft which holds crew, passengers, or cargo.

- **Landing Gear:** Supports the aircraft during takeoff, landing, taxiing, and being parked. Can be various equipment such as wheels, floats, and skis.

- **Nose (Radome):** Conically shaped cap on the front of the aircraft that is shaped to minimize drag and protects sensitive equipment such as weather radar.

- **Rudder:** A movable flight control surface on the back edge of the vertical stabilizer to control yaw on the vertical axis.

- **Slats:** Extendable, lift devices on the front edge of the wings that increase lift at low speed.

- **Spoiler:** A hinged flight control surface on the top face of the wings that when deployed slow the aircraft or help with descent.

- **Stabilizers:** A movable control surface on the vertical tail fin and the horizontal tailplane that keeps the aircraft flying straight and prevents pitching.

- **Wing:** A streamlined fin that creates lift when moved rapidly through the air.

Aircraft and Air Travel Terminology

Here are more terms:

Air Traffic Control (ATC): Specialists who monitor aircraft by radar and transponder from within a control tower to ensure the aircraft remains in its assigned airspace and prevents collisions, provides pilot support, and organizes air traffic.

Concourse (Terminal): The area within an airport where passengers purchase tickets, check luggage, and go through security before boarding an aircraft.

Federal Aviation Administration (FAA): A United States Department of Transportation organization for regulating and enforcing standards for manufacturing, operating, and maintaining aircraft.

Flight Recorder (Black Box): A shoebox-sized electronic recording device inside an aircraft to facilitate the analysis of an accident or incident.

Gate: The area within an airport terminal where passengers board the aircraft.

International Civil Aviation Organization (ICAO): A United Nations agency established by the International Civil Aviation Convention that focuses on air traffic coordination, airspace regulations, aircraft registration, safety, and sustainability.

ICAO ID: Aircraft are assigned a unique 24-bit address, or "hex code," used to identify an aircraft using their Mode-S transponder. These addresses can be represented in hexadecimal, octal, and decimal notations. The ranges of numbers are reserved and allocated to countries by the ICAO for domestic distribution through the appropriate national means, like the Department of Transportation in the United States. Identifying trends in contiguous numeric ranges can help to identify who owns aircraft not otherwise listed in public sources. For example, the U.S. Air Force blocks generally begin with "AE." Therefore, an enumerated address beginning with AE is likely operated by the United States Air Force, U.S. Navy, U.S. Marines, U.S. Coast Guard, or U.S. Army.

Pilot in Command (PIC): The person ultimately responsible for the safety and operation of the aircraft during flight.

Runway (Tarmac): A defined location, usually a strip made of dirt, grass, asphalt, or concrete, that aircraft use for takeoff and landing.

Runway Number: Number designations 1 to 36 on the runway based on the compass bearing the runway is oriented with.

Squawk Code: A four-digit code from 0000 to 7777 used to identify different aircraft and that work with Mode A, C, and S transponders. Some squawk codes are reserved for emergencies and other important communication.

Stand: An area reserved for maintenance, emplaning, and deplaning passengers and crew.

Transponder: Normally a pair of redundant electronic devices within the cockpit of an aircraft that transmit static identifying information and dynamic in-flight data to provide situational awareness to other pilots and air traffic controllers.

Very High Frequency Omnidirectional Range (VOR): A short-range navigation system that when received by an aircraft can help it determine its position through radio signals. The Tactical Air Navigation System (TACAN) is a similar beaconing system used primarily for military aircraft.

Aircraft Discovery and Analysis Methods

Now that you have a solid knowledge of aircraft parts and terminology that will be useful when collecting information from open sources, let's move on to learning how to research and analyze aircraft and their associated entities.

One of the more well-known OSINT analyses into aircraft in the last decade is the 2014 investigation and subsequent podcast by the Netherlands-based investigative journalism group, Bellingcat, and the intelligence they gathered on the downing of Malaysian Airlines Flight 17 (MH17). The passenger flight departed from Amsterdam on July 17, 2014, with 298 people on board to Kuala Lampur. Ukraine authorities lost contact with the flight at 33,000 feet 30 miles outside of the Russia-Ukraine border. Debris was soon located, and footage began to emerge of the crash site in Donetsk. Bellingcat launched an investigation into the crash finding footage of a Buk missile launcher being transported through Donetsk on the day MH17 went down.[62] Using a combination of social media posts revealing videos of the Buk launcher being transported and unloaded as well as satellite imagery and photographs provided by news reporters on-site, they were able to estimate the path and verify the origin of the Buk missile to the 53rd Anti-Aircraft Missile Brigade. Ultimately the Dutch Safety Board and Dutch Joint Investigation Team concluded the airliner was downed by a Buk surface-air-missile that was launched from Donetsk, a pro-Russian separatist-controlled territory.[63]

The Bellingcat example shows one clear way that OSINT can be used to answer a research question "What happened to flight MH17?" and through open-source tracking, geolocation, visual identification, social media, and public aviation information we can develop a theory and attempt to prove or disprove it. Had Bellingcat analysts been unable to establish what normal patterns of aircraft activity looked like when beginning this investigation, it could have

---

[62] www.bellingcat.com/wp-content/uploads/2015/10/
MH17-The-Open-Source-Evidence-EN.pdf.
[63] www.onderzoeksraad.nl/nl/media/inline/2019/1/10/prem_rapport_
mh_17_en_interactief2.pdf.

been harder to spot the abnormal activity, and their theory may have been completely different.

Patterns can be telling when looking at an airplane's trajectory. All aircraft are required to follow ATC flight pattern regulations, but more than that, personal planes can reveal the patterns of where a subject lives, commercial planes can divulge the customers that repeatedly receive shipments of cargo, and private jets can expose the secret getaway locations for politicians and celebrities. Similarly, these patterns extend to the passengers and crew who reliably will make the decision to fly to meetings during business hours to make it home to their families on the nights and weekends. When we pair these patterns with concepts like identification and geolocation techniques, we can begin to tell a story about the aircraft. The following are some of the typical items I look for when researching aircraft:

- Aircraft markings
- Air fleet records
- Air registrations
- Call signs
- Dark, lost, or abnormal transponder activity
- FAA Registry NOTAMs, TFRs
- Facilitator information (freight forwarder, agent)
- Flight patterns or abnormal flight paths

- ICAO hex number
- Modex
- Ownership information
- Passengers and crew
- Patterns of uneconomic activity
- Seat plans
- Serial numbers (MSN)
- Tail numbers
- Visual confirmation (social media, plane spotters)
- Vulnerable technology

Identifying Aircraft

Although aircraft are regulated across the world by differing regulation bodies, within the United States, aircraft are regulated by the Federal Aviation Administration (FAA). The FAA governs air travel, authorizes aircraft and personnel, sets airport standards, and protects U.S. assets during commercial spacecraft launches or reentry. Examples of similar agencies that support the same functions of the FAA are the European Union Aviation Safety Agency (EASA), the Luftfahrt-Bundesamt (LBA, "Federal Aviation Office") in Germany, and the Civil Aviation Bureau in Japan. These regulation bodies require specific markings and registrations for aircraft to legally fly within their airspace. We can use these registration details along with other visual and physical identification markers to identify an aircraft of interest.

Aircraft Registration Code (N Number)

Mandated by the international convention, the aircraft registration code is a unique code included on the certificate of registration. The registration must always be kept within the aircraft during operation, and the code is also affixed to the exterior of all civil aircraft. Although this code can change throughout the lifetime of the aircraft, it can be registered in only one jurisdiction at a time. Many countries also require the registration code to be imprinted on a permanent fireproof plate and mounted on the fuselage to help identify the aircraft after a fire or crash.

In the United States, the registration numbers are referred to as the N number because they begin with an N and have one to two numbers followed by one to two letters for a total of up to five characters. In the following image, the aircraft has the registration code F-BCNL; we know because it doesn't start with an N that this is not a U.S. aircraft (see Figure 8.39). A quick search engine query shows it is registered in France. For a quick list of all the national registration prefixes, you can consult Section 1: Nationality Marks, 7340.2L on the FAA website.[64]

In the case of military aircraft, they are often not provided with the civil registration code, but rather they use tail codes and serial numbers. The exception to this would be government-owned nonmilitary aircraft assigned civil registrations.

Figure 8.39: Aircraft Registration Number, Photo by Daniel Eledut on Unsplash

---

[64] www.faa.gov/air_traffic/publications/atpubs/cnt_html/chap4_section_1.html.

Call Signs

The origin of an aircraft's call sign varies, but for general aircraft it is a unique identifier derived from the registration (N number) or tail number. In the United States, call signs are spoken using the International Civil Aviation Organization (ICAO) phonetic alphabet to avoid mistakes from letters that sound similar. While most aircraft have a single call sign, U.S. commercial aircraft have registered call signs for each company. and typically it will be the designated company name followed by the flight number. However, some companies use unique call signs that relate to the brand. For instance, Republic Airlines in Indianapolis uses "Brickyard" in reference to the Indy 500 race, Dragon Airlines in Hong Kong uses "Dragon," and before their merger with American Airlines, US Airways was known as "Cactus" because they were based in Phoenix, Arizona. A database of all FAA airline call signs can be found at 123atc.com.[65]

If we start with a call sign as a selector, we can use it to search databases and query search engines to find additional details on the aircraft. Additionally, call signs can be useful when listening to ATC communications to help quickly identify the aircraft they are referring to.

Make/Model

Just like an automobile can be identified by its make (brand) and model (specific vehicle model), aircraft can be identified by the manufacturer's name and model numbers. For instance, the Cessna 172 Skyhawk is manufactured by the Cessna Aircraft Company, and the mode is the 172 Skyhawk. Using identifiers like logos, model names, paint schemes, and vehicle shape, we can potentially identify the make and model of an aircraft within imagery. In the military, it varies by country as they all use their own designation systems such as the U.S. Modex.

Manufacturer Serial Number

The manufacturer serial number (MSN) is a unique code given to an aircraft many times before manufacturing begins. This serial number is used to identify specific manufactured parts on an aircraft such as airframes and to designate their airworthiness. Each manufacturer has a different format for MSNs, but generally they are incremental numbers. The military uses MSNs to uniquely identify their aircraft, and the number is printed on the fin or the rudders of the craft (for example, MSN 1742). The FAA offers a Serial Number Inquiry (see Figure 8.40).[66] The MSN is important for quality control and can be used to trace parts of an aircraft back in case of an accident or incident where defects might be the cause.

---

[65] https://123atc.com/call-signs.
[66] https://registry.faa.gov/aircraftinquiry/Search/SerialNumberInquiry.

Figure 8.40: Photo by Stephanie Klepacki on Unsplash

Nonregistration Markings

One highly visible way that an aircraft can be identified is through the commercial branding on the outside of the fuselage, nose, or tail. The branding colors and logo are large and easily seen from the ground at low altitudes. Because branding is vastly easier to spot from a distance than a registration number, it can be helpful to know and recognize some of the larger airline colors and branding. Luckily, there is no need to memorize the branding because it is readily available through search queries like "red, blue, yellow" and "branding" and "aircraft," which will return options we can view on the Images tab.

An insignia is another form of mark on an aircraft and is primarily used on military aircraft to identify the nation, branch, and service that it belongs to. Much like branding, the insignia is traditionally featured on the sides of the fuselage, tops and bottoms of the wings, and the fin and rudder; however, placement and look can vary (see Figures 8.41-8.42). A detailed list of military aircraft insignia both present and historic can be found through search engine queries or at `Military-history.fandom.com`.[67]

Branding of Southwest commercial aircraft in the U.S[68]

Figure 8.41: Photo by Lukas Souza on Unsplash

Military insignia showing dark outer circle, white middle, and dark inside, which is France. The OH airfield code Escadrille d'Avions Legers d'Appui = Light Support Airplanes Squadron 5/72 based in Colomb-Bechar in 1957-1958[69]

Figure 8.42: Photo by Daniel Eledut on Unsplash

---

[67] https://military-history.fandom.com/wiki/Military_aircraft_insignia.
[68] Photo by Lukas Souza on Unsplash.
[69] Photo by Daniel Eledut on Unsplash.

Modex

A *modex* is a two- to three-digit US Navy and Marine Corps number used to identify a squadron's mission and the specific aircraft within the squadron. It's usually painted on the nose, fin tip, and flaps. The following example shows the tail code FF with 192d FW underneath. FF refers to First Flight or "1st Fighter Wing," and the 192d stands for 192D (192nd) Wing, which is a unit of the Virginia Air National Guard in the United States Air Force (see Figure 8.43).

Tail Code FF Modex code 192d FW

Figure 8.43: Photo by Todd Macdonald on Unsplash[70]

Name

Aircraft naming may be a personal choice, or, in the case of airliners, they may be named according to company naming conventions. For commercial aircraft, names and informal nicknames typically refer to landmarks, city, or region identifiers such as "Flying Kangaroo." Private and personal aircraft are usually named after their owner's interests, while military aircraft are given nicknames for identifying characteristics such as "warthog" and "viper." Modern aircraft often have names printed on the nose, and historic aircraft such as World War II aircraft have nicknames printed conspicuously on the fuselage. The name is a searchable feature if registered, but if not registered, it can be displayed in imagery and detailed in plane spotter records or public disclosures.

Shape and Features

It is possible to use the shape of the aircraft and its parts to identify them; an acronym used for visual identification of an aircraft by the U.S. military is WEFT,

---

[70] Photo by Todd MacDonald on Unsplash.

which stands for wing, engine, fuselage, and tail fins.[71] Using the configurations of aircraft parts, we are better able to visually narrow down and possibly even correctly identify aircraft.

WING

Wing Configurations (see Figures 8.44-8.47):

1. Fixed wing: wings are permanently positioned on the aircraft.

a. High-mounted

b. Mid-mounted

c. Low-mounted

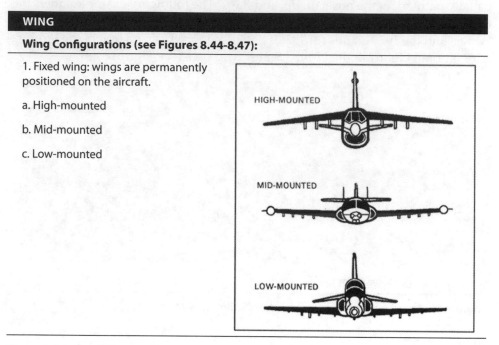

Figure 8.44: Fixed Wing positions

2. Variable Geometry: wings can transition in angle from high to low.

a. High-mounted

b. Mid-to-low-mounted

c. Low-mounted

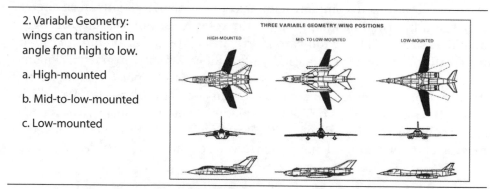

Figure 8.45: Variable geometry

---

[71] irp.fas.org/doddir/army/tc3-01-80.pdf.

3. Rotary

a. Single

b. Dual

c. Coaxial

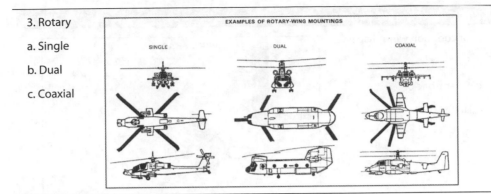

Figure 8.46: Rotary wing

WING TAPERS

Gradual taper of wing width to wing tip

a. untapered

b. Forward tapered

c. Swept-back

d. Backward tapered

e. Diamond shaped

f. Swept-back and tapered

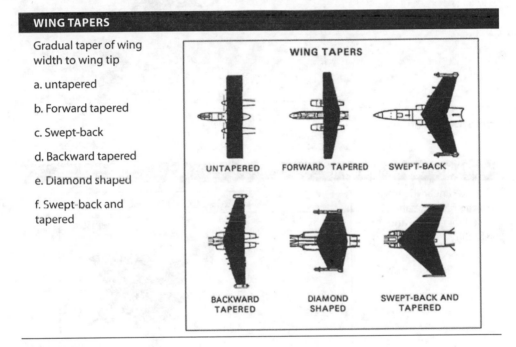

Figure 8.47: Wing tapers

WING SHAPES (SEE FIGURE 8.48):

Four common wing shapes:

a. Straight

b. Swept-back

c. Delta

d. Semidelta

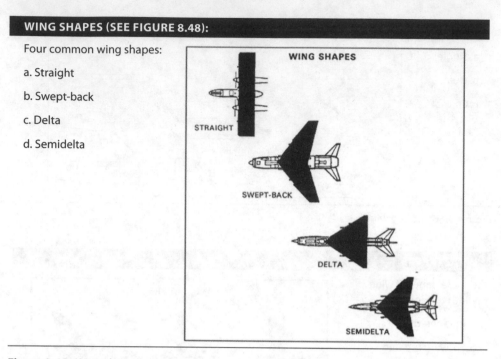

Figure 8.48: Wing shapes

CANARDS (SEE FIGURE 8.49):

Located near the front of the fuselage and used for control and stability

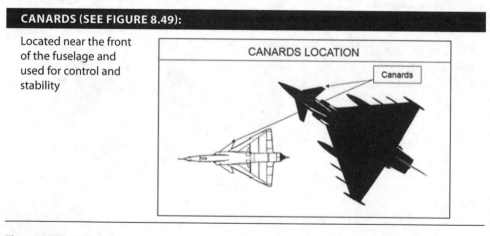

Figure 8.49: Canards

WING SLANTS (SEE FIGURE 8.50):

The vertical angle of the wing

a. Positive

b. Negative

c. Wing tip

d. No slant

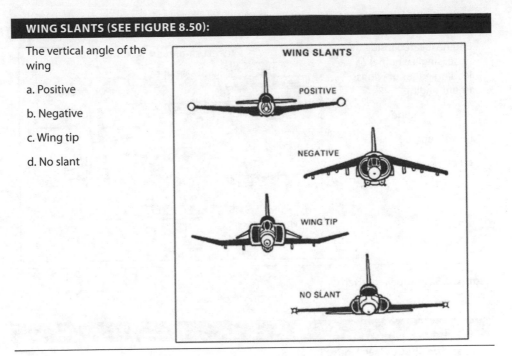

Figure 8.50: Wing slants

ENGINE

Jet Engine (see Figure 8.51):

Engine Is mounted inside or faired into the fuselage.

a. Single-engine

b. Twin-engine

c. Three-engine

d. Four-engine

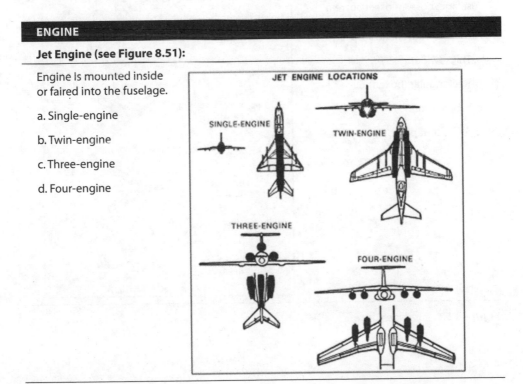

Figure 8.51: Jet engines

PROPELLER DRIVEN (SEE FIGURE 8.52):

Engine located inside the nose (single-engine) or leading edges of wings (multi-engine)

a. Single-engine

b. Twin-engine

c. Four-engine

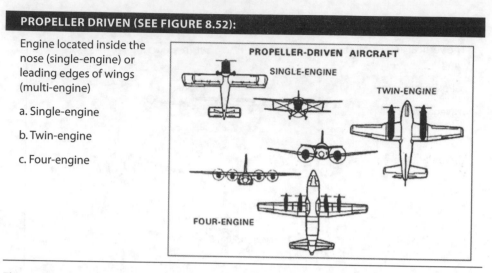

Figure 8.52: Propeller driven

FUSELAGE

Fuselage Shapes (see Figure 8.53):

Three main sections of the fuselage: nose, midsection, rear section and tail. Four main examples of fuselage shapes:

a. Thick (wide)

b. Rectangular (boxed)

c. Tubular (round)

d. Slender (tapered)

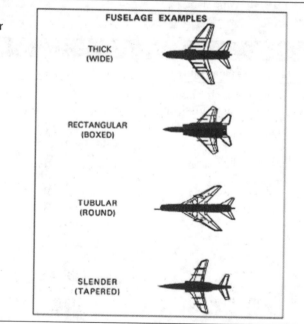

Figure 8.53: Fuselage shape

CANOPY SHAPES (SEE FIGURE 8.54):

Three examples of cockpit canopy shapes:

a. Stepped

b. Flush

c. Bubble

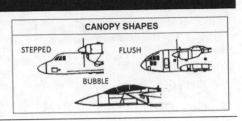

Figure 8.54: Canopy shape

TAIL FINS

Number of Tail Fins (see Figure 8.55):

Four examples of single and multiple tail fins:

a. Single

b. Double

c. Triple

d. Quadruple with Radar

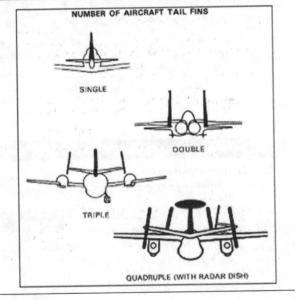

Figure 8.55: Number of tail fins

FIN SHAPES (SEE FIGURE 8.56):

Tail fins are located on the aft sections of the fuselage.

a. Round tip

b. Blunt tip

c. Curved tip

d. Equal taper with square tip

e. Back taper with square tip

f. Swept-back with blunt tip

g. Round

h. Oval

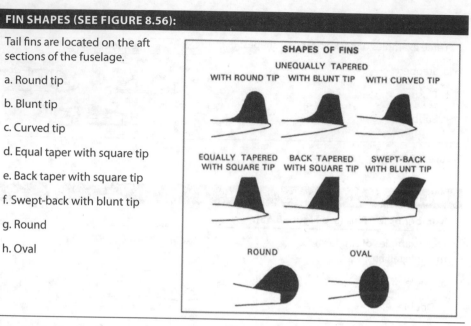

Figure 8.56: Fin shapes

TAIL FLAT DESIGN (SEE FIGURE 8.57):

Tail flats are located on the aft sections of the fuselage.

a. Back tapered with square tips

b. Back tapered with round tips

c. Equally tapered with blunt tips

d. Unequally tapered and swept-back with sq tips

e. Equally tapered with square tips

f. Delta-shaped with blunt tips

g. Rectangular

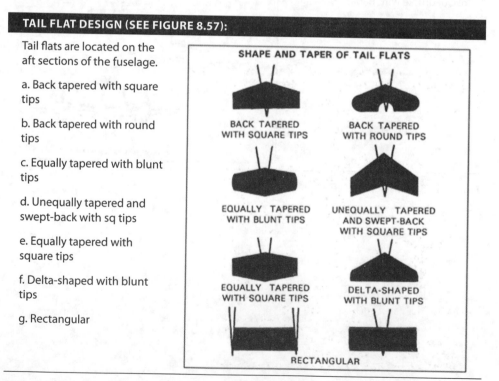

Figure 8.57: Tail flat design

TAIL FLAT LOCATION (SEE FIGURE 8.58):

Tail flat locations vary with the fuselage.

a. Low-mounted on tail

b. Mid-mounted on tail

c. High-mounted on tail

d. Low-mounted on fuselage

e. Mid-mounted on fuselage

f. High-mounted on fuselage

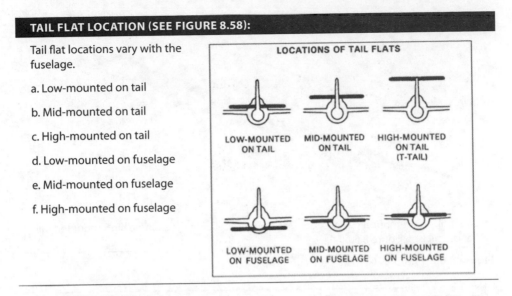

Figure 8.58: Tail flat location

Now let's examine 3 photos of aircraft to determine their physical details that may provide context to their identification.

Looks like mid-mounted wings with no slant, four jet engines with what appears to be a stepped nose (see Figure 8.59)[72]

Figure 8.59: Photo by Kevin Hackert on Unsplash

---

[72] Photo by Kevin Hackert on Unsplash.

Looks like high-mounted wings, no slant, twin propellor engine, single high-mounted tail flat on tail (see Figure 8.60)[73]

Figure 8.60: Photo by Gerhard Crous on Unsplash

Looks like mid-to-low mounted wings, set back and tapered, semi-delta, with canards, and bubble cockpit (see Figure 8.61)[74]

Figure 8.61: Photo by Jatin Singh on Unsplash

Unmanned aerial vehicles (UAVs) are classified based on wings and rotor into six groups: fixed wing, tricopter, hexacopter, single rotor, fixed-wing hybrid VTOL, and quadcopter. We can use their silhouettes to attempt to identify them (see Figure 8.62).[75]

---

[73] Photo by gerhard crous on Unsplash.
[74] Photo by gerhard crous on Unsplash.
[75] www.dronesurvivalguide.org.

Figure 8.62: Drone survival guide

Below are three examples of drone types with varying physical characteristics and silhouettes (see Figures 8.63-8.65):

DJ Mavic 2 Quadcopter[76]

Figure 8.63: DJ Mavic 2 Quadcopter

---

[76] www.google.com/url?sa=i&url=https%3A%2F%2Fstore.dji.com%2Fguides%2Flandscape-photography-with-mavic-2-pro%2F&psig=AOvVaw2SFi5IiU5Ta P1SxXHyNlhb&ust=1667067587293000&source=images&cd=vfe&ved=0CA0Qjhx qFwoTCNivy-3Eg_sCFQAAAAAdAAAAABAO.

MQ1 predator[77]

Figure 8.64: MQ1 Predator

Sentinel[78]

Figure 8.65: Sentinel

Other Key Visual Identifiers

The overall shape of an aircraft is a great identifier, but the shape and configuration of the aircraft's elements can also be used to identify the make and model. Some examples of this include the number and position of exit doors on the fuselage, the design of the engine housing, and the shape of the windows on the cockpit (see Figures 8.66-8.68).[79]

---

[77] https://en.wikipedia.org/wiki/File:MQ-1_Predator,_armed_with_AGM-114_Hellfire_missiles.jpg.

[78] https://upload.wikimedia.org/wikipedia/commons/6/60/RQ-170_art_impression.jpg.

[79] https://simpleflying.com/commercial-aircraft-identification/#:~:text=There%20are%20several%20things%20to,and%20fuselage%20layout%2Fexit%20doors.

Boeing 747 cockpit[80]

Figure 8.66: Boeing 747 cockpit

Turkish Airlines[81]

Figure 8.67: Turkish Airlines engine

ANA-Boeing 747-8 Dreamliner[82]

Figure 8.68: ANA-Boeing 747-8 Dreamliner

One method I often use to match aircraft images and gather additional detail and context are plane spotter databases. Hobby spotters love to provide detailed information about their aircraft, including photos, videos, news, and local sightings. Some plane spotters even focus on a specific detail of planes such as catching registration numbers on all the planes they spot or only aircraft from a brand they like. `Planespotting.net`[83] is one of the more well-known plane spotting databases, and because of the large following, it's possible to follow their hashtag on social media for addition insight: #planespotters.

---

[80] www.google.com/url?sa=i&url=https%3A%2F%2Fcommons.wikimedia
.org%2Fwiki%2FFile%3ABoing_747_Jumbo_front_cockpit_windows
.jpg&psig=AOvVaw2Xa7rYJ_pWWUSpFV4oDoLH&ust=1667069808579000&source
=images&cd=vfe&ved=0CA0QjhxqFwoTCLCzqJDNg_sCFQAAAAAdAAAAABAEpro%2F
&psig=AOvVaw2SFi5IiU5TaP1SxXHyNlhb&ust=1667067587293000&source=ima
ges&cd=vfe&ved=0CA0QjhxqFwoTCNivy-3Eg_sCFQAAAAAdAAAAABAO.

[81] Photo by Adam Dardour on Unsplash.

[82] Photo by jet dela cruz on Unsplash.

[83] www.planespotters.net.

Because plane spotters are often positioned at airports and airfields when collecting photos and videos, they can obtain high-resolution close-up images of aircraft, sometimes from multiple angles. Plane spotter databases can also be a useful tool when tracking flight paths where the aircraft transponder has gone dark. If we can get a photo of the aircraft during the time it is dark, we could verify its location when a transponder couldn't.

Flight Paths and Locations

Flight paths are the routes identified through location identification pings from an aircraft or ground station VOR that tracks an aircraft during takeoff, flight, and landings. Similar to the way maritime and rail transportation entities communicate, aircraft are required to transmit positioning and altitude signals to ground stations for safety and collision avoidance.

As aircraft transmit signals, tools such as FlightRadar24,[84] ADSBExchange,[85] and FlightAware[86] collect these signals and make them available through easy-to-view platforms that display movement and details in near real time. ADSBExchange, unlike the other options, is an enthusiast-run platform, and therefore most features are free for us to access. The live map is overlaid on OpenStreetMap[87] so you can move around the world and see planes that are currently transmitting signals. This platform primarily uses ADS-B and MLAT data to obtain aircraft positions. Another advantage of using ADSBx is that they do not block undisclosed military aircraft like other platforms (although military aircraft may use fake IDs) and do not presume where the aircraft should be.

Many of the flight tracking platforms sell USB software-defined radio receivers that hobbyists can set up on Raspberry Pi computers, connect an antenna, and track nearby flights. The website uses these "feeder sites" to collect aircraft location information and geolocate aircraft using multilateration, or "MLAT"; four time-synchronized feeder sites are needed at one location to multilaterate (triangulate, but with four points) the aircraft location in three dimensions. I built a Flight Aware Raspberry Pi tracker for home use to track flights to and from the nearby airport. The best part about owning a transponder is that many of the platforms will provide you with a full account for free as long as your transponder is live.

Unfortunately, while we can track real-time flights using these platforms, historical tracking remains hidden behind a pay wall that may be too costly for individual researchers. As an analyst, the main benefit to having historical flight data is the ability to track paths over time, compare aircraft, and look for

---

[84] www.flightradar24.com.
[85] www.adsbexchange.com.
[86] https://flightaware.com.
[87] www.openstreetmap.org/#map=5/38.007/-95.844.

anomalies. Canadian research consultant and flight tracking enthusiast Steffan Watkins[88] says the best way to get historical data on a budget is to pay only when you need it and buy directly from the data owner to minimize costs. Whether you're buying historical data or using free real-time data, there are some telltale signs of unusual activity to look out for that can affect your analysis.

According to Watkins, the following are some anomalous things to keep an eye out for when monitoring aircraft paths:

- State-registered aircraft that suddenly fly internationally
- A transponder that goes dark and then reappears in a different location
- Identity manipulations (incorrect numbering ABCD1234)
- Downgrades from precise location transmissions (ADS-B) to transmissions lacking latitude and longitudinal data
  (Mode-S)

It is important to note that, as with most satellite and radio transmission tracking, the anomalies we see do not always equate to illicit activity or intentional obfuscation. A dark transponder could just be an equipment malfunction, and a strange path could indicate an emergency requiring a quick change of direction.

Tips for Monitoring and Analyzing Aircraft Routes

Finding planes on the live map seems relatively easy, but there are a few tricks to understanding their movements, limitations, and behavior. First let's tackle some of the basic information that can be pulled from the flight tracking platforms:

- Name
- Call sign
- Hex
- Type
- Squawk
- Groundspeed
- Altitude
- Position
- Signal source
- Photos
- Airline logo
- Departure/arrival city

Check Many Different Flight Tracking Sites

As we learned, the platform ingests data from different feeder locations around the world. If an area has feeders from only one source platform, aircraft in that area will appear only on that platform. Note that low-flying aircraft often go undetected by trackers, and this can be used as a method of concealment.

---

[88] https://twitter.com/steffanwatkins.

Use Social Media To Find Other Analysts Researching Similar Information

Twitter is full of great analysts doing aviation and OSINT analysis. You can use this to improve your own analysis and find new pivot points. By studying aircraft and following a series of analysts conducting OSINT in an area of interest, you can often gain insight and access satellite imagery and flight paths you would otherwise have to pay for. Try searching for a specific aircraft name, number, or make/model and consider maintaining a TweetDeck by region or project to organize research, and create information boards for quick lookup of new data.

Use Airport Cameras And Plane Spotting Sites To Catch A Glimpse Of The Aircraft

Many airports and highways have Internet-enabled cameras used for traffic reporting, weather, and general awareness. Depending on their proximity to an airport, we can use these cameras to capture images of aircraft picking up passengers, taxiing on the runway, landing, or taking off. Webcams facilitate being able to capture visual imagery and verify the location of an aircraft all over the world. To locate webcams, we can use Google dorks such as "airport name" and "webcam" or use a webcam site like `Windy.com`.

Use Public Disclosures In News Stories And Websites To Determine Routes

We may use information disclosed by airlines, websites, documents and even messages to collect details about suspected aircraft routes. Nancy Pelosi, for example, flew to Taiwan earlier this year, and many details about the trip and plane have been made public; these details allowed analysts to trace the flight path and make predictions about routes.

Search Flights By Airport

You can get additional information beyond the flight tracking platforms by tracking your flight the traditional way, through the airport. Airportia[89] is a website used for searching flights by airline, flight number, or trending flights (see Figure 8.69). Airport information lookup can provide additional context to tracked flight routes, indicating expected arrival/departure times, whether flights have been delayed or canceled, and departure and arrival gates.

---

[89] `www.airportia.com`.

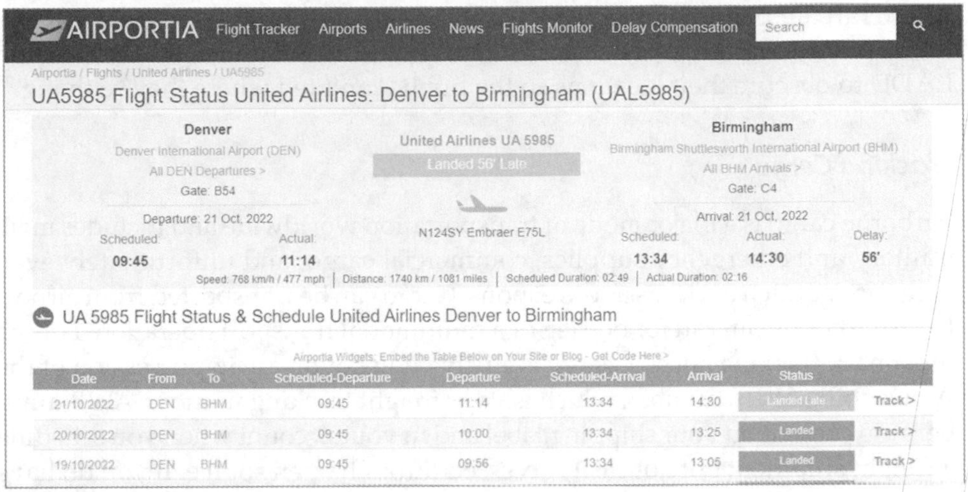

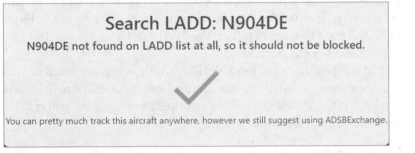

Figure 8.69: Airportia

Limiting Aircraft Data Displayed and Private ICAO Addresses Listings

If an aircraft is part of the Limited Aircraft Data Displayed (LADD) list, it means that the aircraft data is for FAA use only and is not available to third parties, including flight tracking providers. The FAA has a website dedicated to LADD applications located at `ladd.faa.gov`.[90] Here, an aircraft can be registered on the LADD list; however, unless FAA source blocking is added, LADD only blocks flights through the FAA system, and third parties are still able to capture the aircraft ICAO address. Alternatively, aircraft can be registered for Private ICAO Addressing (PIA) to broadcast a PIA address out on the ADS-B out transmission instead of their true ICAO aircraft address. In other words, LADD blocks transmissions from being seen, while PIA (U.S. only) provides a fake identity that flight trackers will see. To search the LADD list, we can use `laddlist.com` and enter a tail number or call sign to see if it is blocked (see Figure 8.70).

Search LADD: N904DE

N904DE not found on LADD list at all, so it should not be blocked.

✓

You can pretty much track this aircraft anywhere, however we still suggest using ADSBExchange.

Figure 8.70: LADD

---

[90] `https://ladd.faa.gov`.

Aircraft are placed on the LADD or PIA list for several reasons, some illicit. Many planes owned by politicians, churches, and even influencers are listed on LADD to obscure their locations so the public can't tell where they're flying.[91]

Tracking Cargo

Airborne cargo is a major mode of transportation worldwide and includes mail, military and emergency supplies, commercial cargo, and unfortunately even illegal cargo such as drugs and weapons. Cargo can be transported from airport to airport or by aircraft for one leg of a multimodal transport operation. For the most part, tracking specific cargo is elusive unless you are in possession of the Airwaybill (AWB) number, which is your freight tracking number. AWB numbers are present on your shipping label and in your account when you schedule a freight shipment but not easily accessed through open source. If you do have access to an AWB number, it is possible to search by airline using Utopiax .com.[92] Otherwise, one possibility is to use OSINT data obtained from other sectors of the multimodal transport chain such as rail and shipping, which can provide information about buyers and consignees. For reported and publicized shipments, you may be able to find information about actual shipments and planned movements on company websites, contracts, news, and social media.

Notice to Air Missions (NOTAMs)

According to faa.gov, NOTAMs are "notices containing essential information for personnel involved in flight operations." In other words, they are notifications alerting aircraft pilots and airports to potential hazards along routes and locations. Examples of NOTAMs include closed runways, flocks of birds, military maneuvers, and flights with important people. In the United States we can check active commercial and private NOTAMs through the FAA NOTAM Search at notams.aim.faa.gov.[93] The search allows you to query the database by flight path, geography, location, allows you to sort by date, and even provides an archive search. Events and incidents may result in Temporary Flight Restrictions (TFR), these TFRs are listed on the NOTAMs and also on the FAA TFR list at tfr.faa.gov/tfr2/list.html.[94]

Unfortunately, it can be difficult to read NOTAMs unless you are familiar with all the abbreviations used for weather, clouds, and other forms of restrictions. Fortunately, the FAA NOTAMs search offers a plain-language translation of the majority of their NOTAMs (see Figure 8.71).

---

[91] www.propublica.org/article/
off-the-radar-private-planes-hidden-from-public-view-040810.
[92] www.utopiax.org/index.html.
[93] https://notams.aim.faa.gov/notamSearch/nsapp.html#.
[94] https://tfr.faa.gov/tfr2/list.html.

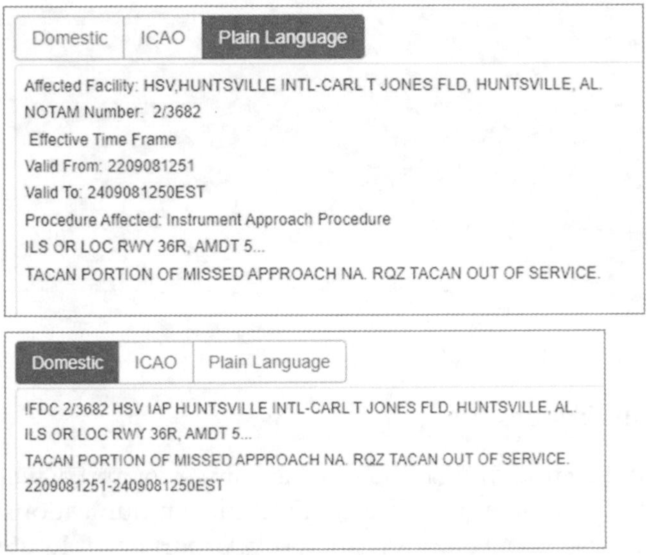

Domestic	ICAO	Plain Language

Affected Facility: HSV,HUNTSVILLE INTL-CARL T JONES FLD, HUNTSVILLE, AL.

NOTAM Number: 2/3682

 Effective Time Frame

Valid From: 2209081251

Valid To: 2409081250EST

Procedure Affected: Instrument Approach Procedure

ILS OR LOC RWY 36R, AMDT 5...

TACAN PORTION OF MISSED APPROACH NA. RQZ TACAN OUT OF SERVICE.

Domestic	ICAO	Plain Language

!FDC 2/3682 HSV IAP HUNTSVILLE INTL-CARL T JONES FLD, HUNTSVILLE, AL.

ILS OR LOC RWY 36R, AMDT 5...

TACAN PORTION OF MISSED APPROACH NA. RQZ TACAN OUT OF SERVICE.

2209081251-2409081250EST

Figure 8.71: NOTAMs

For defense NOTAMs for the Air Force, Army, Navy, Marines, etc., you can use the Defense Internet NOTAM Service (DINS) at `notams.faa.gov/dinsQueryWeb/`.[95] DINS provides advanced NOTAM features such as North Atlantic Track, Pacific Track, and Special Notices (see Figure 8.72).

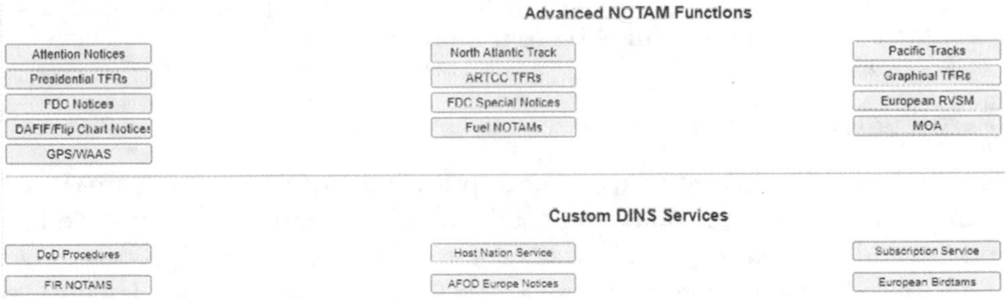

Advanced NOTAM Functions

Attention Notices	North Atlantic Track	Pacific Tracks
Presidential TFRs	ARTCC TFRs	Graphical TFRs
FDC Notices	FDC Special Notices	European RVSM
DAFIF/Flip Chart Notices	Fuel NOTAMs	MOA
GPS/WAAS		

Custom DINS Services

DoD Procedures	Host Nation Service	Subscription Service
FIR NOTAMS	AFOD Europe Notices	European Birdtams

Figure 8.72: NOTAMs for Military

NOTAMs are used worldwide to ensure the safety of pilots, passengers, and people on the ground. Many, if not all, NOTAMs are published online, and you can find them using official sources for the country in question. An example of an exceptionally useful NOTAMs map comes from Norway, where UAS Norway worked with `safetofly.com` to develop an interactive map with layers showing NOTAMs, airspace, and restricted areas (see Figure 8.73).

---

[95] `www.notams.faa.gov/dinsQueryWeb`.

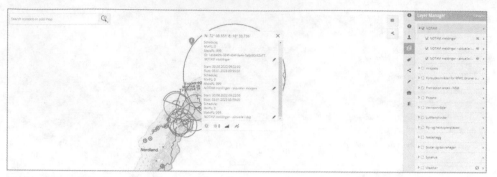

Figure 8.73: safetofly

Air Traffic Control Communications

It is possible with a VHF and UHF airband radio, scanner, or web or app player like `LiveATC.net`[96] to listen to pilot and Air Traffic Control communications. Live ATC allows the user to search for communications by Airport or Air Route Traffic Control Center (ARTCC) Code as well as by frequency such as 124.400. Coverage for these services work much like flight tracking and use feeder sites to provide the data, so if no one is feeding data from an area of interest, there might be no communications available. For an OSINT analyst the value of these live feeds is context and disclosure information that may not otherwise be known. Names, routes, locations, concerns, cargo, and purpose are all things that could be revealed verbally. Using aircraft terminology learned in this section can assist in interpreting ATC communications.

Aerodromes

In the days before paved runways and sprawling airports, landing areas were simply grass with limited take-off and landing directions. Aerodromes, on the other hand, were larger and allowed takeoff and landing in all directions. Over time, Aerodrome became an umbrella term for all, as most grasslands gave way to airports, air force bases, airfields, and airstrips. Although it is rarely used, it remains a legal term in many parts of the world.

Airport

An airport is a place where aircraft take off and land with a system of runways, buildings, and facilities for the passengers and crew. Airports can be regional, national, and international.

---

[96] `www.liveatc.net`.

Airports can be given an International Air Transport (IATA) code, which is a unique designation for a specific airport; an ICAO Airport Code; an FAA Location Identifier (LID); and a World Meteorological Organization (WMO) code for a weather station.

Airports are a great place to collect OSINT. The size of the building, and its connection to world travel, offers many possibilities. Focusing on passengers and crew, subject intelligence techniques can be used to examine social media accounts and build a pattern of life on our subjects. We can learn specific details about passenger trips such as their home city, destination, and length of stay from their social media posts. Consider the number of phones that come through the airport every hour and connect to Wi-Fi; there is a lot of information we can gather from captured SSIDs and MAC addresses. If we need to examine the airline, we can use business intelligence techniques to research data on who owns the airline, who profits, and what subsidiaries fall within their corporate structure. We can even use other transportation intelligence techniques as airports often rely on additional transportation methods for passengers such as speed rail or trams that we could gather information on using railway information.

Air Base

An air base is a location where aircraft take off, land, and receive maintenance and are given similar codes to airports (IATA, ICAO, FAA LID, and WMO) (see Figure 8.74). Typically, air bases are used for the military and civil seaplane bases. Using web queries, we can find the history of an air base and details about past and present squadrons and units that were stationed there. Contracts and business intelligence techniques can provide interesting information about companies who provide service to the bases, and social media leaks from service members can reveal the inner workings of the base.

Figure 8.74: Air base

Airfield

Airfields are typically used by small aircraft to take off, land, and undergo maintenance (see Figure 8.75). Airfields are more secluded and private than major airports and lack many of the amenities. Like airbases, airfields can be used for both civil and military aircraft and are given similar codes (IATA, ICAO, FAA LID, WMO). California's Moffett Field is an example of an airfield; it is a joint civilian-military airfield and is located adjacent to a National Guard Air Force base.

Figure 8.75: Airfield

Airstrip

An airstrip is a strip of cleared land that serves as a runway for small aircraft to take off and land in remote locations. Airstrips do not have the comforts of airports and usually only have refueling facilities. While airstrips themselves are generally not a huge resource for OSINT, they can be and often are used in illicit and clandestine activities that can then be analyzed using OSINT methods.

One use of these strips is to transport drugs like cocaine on small commercial planes from locations like Southern Mexico, the Amazon, and Guatemala. Author and analyst at USNI News, H.I Sutton, wrote an article on his website, Covert Shores, about Narco Planes in 2020[97] illustrating the possibilities of taking off and landing on a small strip and noted the possibility that business jets could fly from clandestine airstrips with ease.

---

[97] www.hisutton.com/Narco-Aircraft-101.html.

Using seed data like a tip, news reports, or historical activity in the area, along with satellite imagery, it could be possible to find and track illegal airstrip activity. Another method shown to be useful in tracking drug traffic on small planes in this area is through satellite fire identification. In 2020, the *Washington Post* reported that traffickers in Guatemala had set fire to an aircraft after removing drugs to hide evidence and other trafficking aircraft has been found burning after crash landing. Furthermore, illicit landing strips are typically built by these groups through razing parts of the jungle with fire.[98] To identify fires in these remote areas, we can use the NASA Fire Information for Resource Management System (FIRMS).[99] FIRMS generously provides both a current and historical fire search for free use. Let's take a deeper look at one of the possible airstrip locations used for drug transport.

The *Washington Post* article outlined an increase of fires near "Laguna del Tigre National Park, Guatemala." Using FIRMS, we can narrow the time down to May 2020 where there appear to be quite a few fires burning in this area. FIRMS doesn't allow us to zoom in and get a real clear view of the area so we can switch over to Google Earth and match up the location of the fire. The satellite imagery from Google Earth shows what looks to be an airstrip right off the main road in Laguna del Tigre. The size and shape of the strip of land along with the location seem to match up to reports of drug trafficking by airstrip (see Figure 8.76).

Geolocation and Imagery Analysis of Aircraft

Image analysis techniques such as examining context, foreground, background, map markers, and using trial and error along with visual identification techniques we learned for aircraft like WEFT can help you explore images, video, and satellite imagery of aerodromes and aircraft. Let's look at a scenario where we can practice these techniques to identify an aircraft.

As with any OSINT analysis, the steps we take should coincide with the intelligence cycle that we learned about in Part I (see Figure 8.77).

During our faux analysis, we received feedback from our stakeholder and a new question based on a 2021 satellite image we collected during the collection phase showing Guangzhou Shadi Airbase in China and revealing several aircraft positioned on the tarmac (see Figure 8.78). She asked, "Can we identify aircraft at the bottom of this satellite image and what it is used for?"

Using this question as a guide, we restart the intelligence cycle and begin collection and analysis using techniques like WEFT and imagery analysis.

---

[98] www.washingtonpost.com/world/2020/07/05/
guatemala-cocaine-trafficking-laguna-del-tigre.
[99] https://firms.modaps.eosdis.nasa.gov/map.

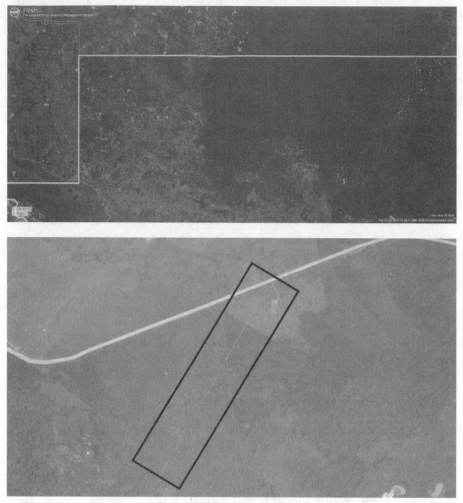

Figure 8.76: Airstrip Google Earth 17.55731,-90.82303

First, we must answer these basic imagery analysis questions:

- **Context:** This is an air force base in China, and these military aircraft are not out of place here

- **Foreground:** The foreground has a hangar just off the edge of the image. We can also see the aircraft in question that appears different than the others.

- **Background:** Nothing significant.

- **Map Markings:** None.

- **Trial and Error:** We will use WEFT to identify the aircraft.

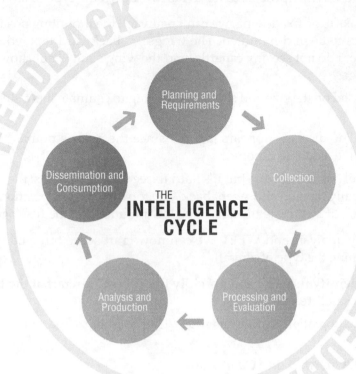

Figure 8.77: The intelligence cycle

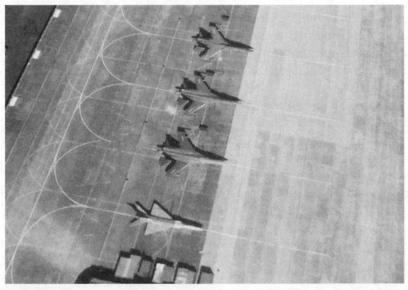

Figure 8.78: Guangzhou Shadi Airbase

Next, let's use the WEFT process to try to narrow down the type of aircraft.

- **Wings:** Looks to be fixed-wing; we can't really tell the mounting position but appears to be mid-mounted. The wings are backward tapered in a delta-shape. I do not see any canards, and the wing slant is not showing in this image.

- **Engine:** Based on the size and shape, I am going to estimate it is a single-jet engine.

- **Fuselage:** The fuselage appears tapered since the nose is pointed and seems to have a bubble canopy.

- **Tail:** The tail has a single fin, but it's hard to see what shape it is; the flats look unequally tapered and swept back. The top view makes positioning hard to see, but I estimate the flats to be low mounted on the fuselage.

Using imagery analysis and WEFT, we can now craft some targeted web queries to determine the type of aircraft.

Q: "Can we identify the type and possibly the specific aircraft at the bottom of this satellite image?"

A: It appears to potentially be a Chengdu J-7C or a similar variation.

Aviation Entity Ownership and Operation

Now that we have some knowledge of what we are visually looking for when analyzing aircraft let's take a look at who owns and operates them.

Tips for Analyzing Aviation Entity Ownership and Operations

From airliners and military helicopters to personal drones and suborbital space shuttles, every aircraft is owned and operated by an individual or an organization. Finding organizational information such as names, companies, subsidiaries, and partnerships can inform on the people, processes, and profits, surrounding aircraft.

In the United States, all aircraft must be registered with the FAA, and therefore searching the FAA registry is a good place to start. Selectors such as name, number, and make/model are required inputs to use FAA search and return results. Another option is to pull the hex or registration number from a flight tracker and paste it into a search engine.

In this example, I grabbed a random registration number "N308ME" belonging to a helicopter. Running the registration number through the FAA search I discovered that it is a Eurocopter EC-635 owned by Wintrust Asset Finance Inc. Pivoting to a flight tracker, I was able to view some past flights from this aircraft that indicate that this could be a medical flight helicopter. To verify, let's dig further into the company by querying a search engine for

---

"Wintrust Asset Finance and helicopter."

This search took me to a page that revealed in 2021 Wintrust launched a new aviation finance group. Following that search, I queried *N308ME* and *helicopter* and found an image of the helicopter on `jetphotos.com`, which tagged the location as York Hospital, Pennsylvania. This made contextual sense because the current location of the helicopter on the flight tracker is leaving from York, Pennsylvania (see Figure 8.79).

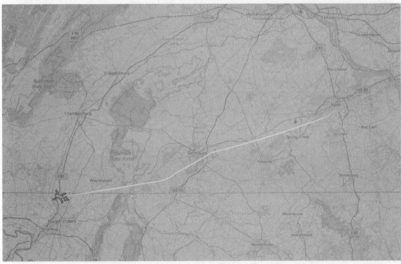

Figure 8.79: Wellspan Helicopter

In the image I noticed that the side of the helicopter says "Wellspan," so a quick query of

---

"wellspan and helicopter"

---

revealed that the company Wellspan Wellflight primarily operates in three counties which includes York, Pennsylvania.

Continuing my search I queried Opencorporates.com for *Wellspan*, which showed through corporate records that the company is presently registered in York, Pennsylvania, and one of its previous names was York Health System. This is a simple example, but it's easy to see how valuable these types of searches are when trying to understand the context of anomalous flight patterns or uncover possible illegal activity.

Another form of important aircraft business is freight transportation. We touched a bit on tracking commercial cargo, but I believe that to fully understand how to effectively analyze these scenarios, we must understand the points in the process where humans can interact or interfere.

The following is a typical example of the process commercial air cargo takes and the businesses along the way that could have an impact on the cargo:[100]

Step 1	A *customer* makes a purchase order for goods.
Step 2	A *freight forwarder* arranges and plans the routing, confirms capacity, and arranges pickup of freight.
Step 3	A freight forwarding truck delivers goods to the cargo handling agent at the carrier. Waybill information, security screening needs, and ETA are provided ahead of arrival.
Step 4	Airport cargo and ground handling personnel verify security clearance on goods and perform a ready-for carriage check.
Step 5	Airport cargo and ground handling personnel prepare cargo by clearing through security again (X-ray, explosive trace detection [ETD]), piece count, and integrity check.
Step 6	Loaded unit load devices (ULDs) are moved to a secure area by a warehouse operator, and upon loading they are transferred to a ramp handler.
Step 7	ULDs are loaded per the load plan; electronic flight manifests are updated and mailed with the loading and carriage information before departure.
Step 8	Upon landing the airport cargo and ground handlers unload cargo to a warehouse, check them in, and hand them over to forwarders.

---

[100] www.iata.org/en/publications/newsletters/iata-knowledge-hub/what-to-know-about-air-cargo-handling.

Step 9	The forwarder collects the goods from the carrier and moves it to the forwarder hub to be unloaded and checked before being turned over to the consignee.

Step 10	Forwarder loads the cargo onto a truck at the forwarder hub, creates a run sheet and delivers the cargo to the consignee.

Aviation Critical Infrastructure and Entity Vulnerabilities

Industrial control systems in aviation and aerospace are often used to assemble, manufacture, and repair the extremely large and complex parts to allow them to be lifted into place. Additionally, many modern airports have SCADA-controlled sensors and controllers used for everything from car parking and building control to baggage image weight identification (BIWIS) and navigational aids.[101] Another extremely important area where OT systems are employed are for the de-icing capabilities on an aircraft that prevent dangerous ice buildup. This process is regulated through OT sensors and if disrupted could potentially cause an aircraft to crash.

Some additional examples of aircraft and airport OT systems include the following[102]:

- Ramp and jetway systems
- Baggage transportation
- Electronic signage
- Aircraft fuel pump regulation (bad mixture/explosion)

OT systems in aircraft and airports fall victim to the same vulnerabilities that critical infrastructure and OT systems on land do. Many of these systems are outdated, using default credentials, with existing vulnerabilities and no updates or patches for them. It is possible for an adversary to use these vulnerabilities, which can be searched for each OT system on the NIST Vulnerability Database. With the number of passengers inside of aircraft and airports taking photos and video and posting to social media, it wouldn't be difficult to locate a system panel or manufacturer's name within them.

---

[101] www.vtscada.com/airport-solutions-overview.
[102] www.darkreading.com/vulnerabilities---threats/airports-andoperational-technology-4-attack-scenarios-/a/d-id/1334282.

8.5 Automobiles

We have covered all of the major transportation methods from vessels to rail and aircraft, now let's take a look at one of the most important methods of transportation and shipping- Automobiles.

Introduction to Automotive Intelligence

Since the early 1900s automobiles have awarded people the freedom and independence to travel, shop, and work away from home. In 2022, there are about 1.446 billion cars in the world and roughly 284 million vehicles operating in the United States. Most towns and cities within the United States have grown around the automobile, and the many parking garages, highways, and bridges facilitate their movements. In direct opposition to cities such as Copenhagen, Denmark, that focus on pedestrian and bike transportation, 91.5 percent of households in the United States own at least one vehicle. The American Trucking Associations reported in 2021 that there were 3.49 million truck drivers employed in the United States alone. This means there is great potential for using automobiles to monitor a subject's pattern of life, track supply chain shipments, and harvest organizational and technical information.

Because there are so many variations of and uses for automobiles, let's take a moment to learn some of the important types along with some keywords we may encounter while gathering information.

Types of Automobile Entities

These are the types:

PERSONAL	COMMERCIAL	SPECIAL USE	MILITARY
Motorcycle	Bus	Ambulance	Ballast tractor
Car	Semi-truck	Firetruck	Combat vehicles
Truck	Taxi	Heavy haulers	Tactical vehicles
SUV	Flatbed truck	Law Enforcement vehicles	Recon vehicles
Jeep	Dump truck	Farm equipment	Anti-aircraft weapons
Trailer	Cement truck	Limousine	Air defense artillery
Camper	Box truck		Tank
Motorhome	Logging truck		Tracked vehicles

PERSONAL	COMMERCIAL	SPECIAL USE	MILITARY
Van	Garbage truck		Logistics/support
Fifth wheel	Tow truck		
Electric Vehicles			

Automobile Terminology

Here are the terms to know:

Make: When we talk about the make of a vehicle, we are referring to the brand. For instance, Nissan, Ford, and Chevrolet are all the make of vehicles.

Model: The model of a vehicle is the specific model within the brand (Nissan *Alitma*, Ford *Explorer*, Chevrolet *Trax*).

Vehicle Registration: Some countries such as the United States and EU require that a vehicle be officially registered with the government tying an owner to a vehicle. Registration often certifies that a vehicle is appropriate for road travel.

Vehicle Identification Number (VIN): A VIN is a unique code for a single automobile and cannot be changed. The VIN is printed inside the driver's side door of most vehicles or where the windshield meets the dashboard. No other vehicle will have the same VIN.

Vehicle Registration Plate: Also referred to as a license plate or number plate, this is a metal tag that is placed on the front, back, or both front and back of a vehicle. The license plate displays a registered code associating it with the vehicle or vehicle owner. License plates also feature unique designs and markings by location that can help identify the origin.

Driver's License: This is an official document that authorizes a person to operate a vehicle. Licenses vary depending on the class of vehicle (motorcycle, bus, semi-truck). Driver's licenses vary by location, so one country or state may have different legal rules for obtaining a license, and the appearance would be different. In the United States, we use driver's licenses as an official identification method, and the Real-ID can be used for domestic travel. Licenses feature a unique ID number to the user and typically require renewal over time.

Vehicle Title: A title is a document issued by the government that proves ownership of a vehicle and contains information about both vehicle and owner.

Automobile Discovery and Analysis Methods

Analyzing cases that include automobiles often requires the capability to identify them visually from photos, video, and satellite imagery, as well as the ability to uncover their ownership through primary source documents and identification markings. An example of a situation where identifying a vehicle might be part of your case could be a request from a stakeholder to find the owner of a vehicle based on a Google Street View photo and a partial license plate number using only open source. We can employ several techniques for identifying automobiles that we will learn in this chapter and combine them with imagery analysis, subject intelligence, and information from primary source documents to answer the question. The following are some key things we look at when researching automobiles:

- Make/model
- VIN
- License plate number/design
- Name of owner/operator
- Markings/customizations

- Vehicle history
- Pattern of life
- Equipment damage, loss, theft
- Special uses

Identifying Automobiles

Identifying automobiles relies heavily on the visual aspects of the vehicles. Let's look at some of the key ways in which we can make an identification.

Make/Model

The make of an automobile refers to the specific brand of the vehicle, while model refers to the model within that brand. For example, Chevrolet would be the make of the vehicle, while Tahoe would be the model. The make and model of a car can be found through search engines by querying unique features of the automobile. If you have a photo or a video, you can perform a reverse image search using a still shot and a search engine to scour the Web for similar-looking vehicles. You can also upload a photo of the vehicle to the site `Carnet.ai`,[103] which uses AI to recognize make and model of an automobile within several degrees of accuracy.

License Plate Number/Design

A license plate is the officially registered and required sign displayed on the front and/or back of a motor vehicle that connects an owner to a vehicle. Of course, a license plate could be removed from one vehicle and switched to another, but if

---

[103] `Carnet.ai`.

it was checked in official databases, it would come up as belonging to a vehicle of a different make and model. While law enforcement can run a plate to verify ownership and check for vehicle theft, the public does not have access to search official databases for a plate number. Luckily, using OSINT techniques there are a few ways to extract information from license plates using open sources.

Civilians can use search engine queries to look for the plate number and any associated details available to the public. Sometimes we get lucky and the plate number is posted in a forum or on a website with additional context. There are sites like Platesmania.com[104] that are databases of user-submitted license plate photos that can be queried by country and plate. Faxvin.com[105] is a site to help get history on a car before purchase, and a user can look up license plates if they know both the number and state of registration. If we find a plate on Platesmania.com, we can also enter it into Faxvin to get the VIN, make, model, year, trim, style/body, engine, place of manufacture, and age. Sometimes we can even use social media for searching license plate numbers even if the license plate is never mentioned in the post. With optical character recognition (OCR) and metadata the platform will "read" the license plate within the photo and return images of the vehicle.

World License Plates

License plates around the world have unique designs, colors, and shapes that can be used in image analysis and geolocation to determine where a vehicle is. In the United States, license plates vary by state and often have the state slogan and an image representative of the state (see Figure 8.80). Each state may have more than one variation of the state license plate. For instance, Tennessee is the Volunteer State, and the 2022 license plate features Tennessee colors, the shape of the state, and website, with a choice of the "In God We Trust" option. The state of Montana offers 14 options for license plate designs as of 2022 from agriculture and forestry to youth groups.[106] The standard plate has five variations, with consulate, farming, vintage, and other vehicles having slightly differing plates.

In addition to plate design variations, in the United States we also have personalized or vanity plate options. The owner of the vehicle can pay a fee to choose the numbers and letters that go on the plate. Generally, this is a phrase, initials, or something meaningful to the owner.

---

[104] http://platesmania.com.

[105] www.faxvin.com/license-plate-lookup.

[106] https://dojmt.gov/driving/plate-designs-and-fees.

Figure 8.80: U.S. License plate examples

European plates look different than U.S. plates; they are skinnier in size, they are less focused on the artwork, and because many countries require them to be on the front and back of the vehicle, they will be slightly different (see Figure 8.81). In France, the license plate has the EU circle and stars along with France's international code on the left and on the right inside the blue strip is the coat of arms of the French region and a number combination of the region department. The Philippine license plate is a simpler design with just black on white numbering.

Figure 8.81: European License plate examples

With all of the variations of plates across the world, databases of imagery are the best way search through them to quickly and efficiently compare and verify our license plate in question. Using a database like `Worldlicenseplates.com`,[107] we can search not only current license plates by location but also historical ones.

Vehicle Identification Number

The *VIN* is a unique 17-digit code that never changes and is assigned to every automobile and printed within the driver's side door and on the dashboard by the windshield. There are several ways we could end up with a VIN code during analysis: it could be included in the initial ask from stakeholders, we could have found it in an up close photo or video of a vehicle, or maybe it was the secondary data found when searching a license plate.

However you come across a VIN, because of the uniqueness of the number, it can be difficult to pull further information from it without paying a fee for a vehicle history report. One step we can take that costs us nothing is using a process of analyzing the numbers to decode the VIN (see Figure 8.82). It is important to note here that vehicles between the 1950s and 1980 cannot be decoded by this method.[108] You can also perform the decoding automatically using the National Highway Traffic Safety Administration (NHTSA) VIN Decoder at `vpic.nhtsa.dot.gov/decoder/Decoder`.

Digit 1: Indicates the country of origin.

Digit 2: Indicates the manufacturer, usually the first letter of the manufacturer's name.

Digit 3: Combined with the first two digits, indicates the vehicle type or World Manufacturer Identifier (WMI). The list of WMI codes is available on Wikipedia.[109] WMI searches can be performed at the HNTSA Manufacturers Information Database at `vpic.nhtsa.dot.gov/mid`.

Digits 4–9: Describe the model, transmission, restraint system, engine code, and body type and position 9 is the check digit to detect invalid VINs.

Digit 10: The 10th position indicates model year (B-Y=1981-2000). The VIN does not use I, O, Q, U, or Z. From 2001 to 2009, the numbers 1 through 9 were used in place of letters. The alphabet started over from A in 2010 and will continue until 2030.

Digit 11: Indicates the manufacturing plant based on plant code.

Digits 12–17: Indicates the production number received at assembly.

---

[107] www.worldlicenseplates.com.

[108] www.edmunds.com/how-to/how-to-quickly-decode-your-vin.html.

[109] https://en.wikipedia.org/wiki/Vehicle_identification_number#List_of_common_WMI.

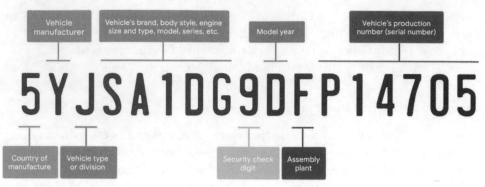

Figure 8.82: VIN breakdown

Name of Owner/Operator

The vehicle owner is the person who has officially registered as the owner or who is in possession of the vehicle lawfully, and an operator is a person using a vehicle to perform a task. There are times when we may be asked to connect a vehicle to a specific owner or operator through open source collection and analysis. An example would be a case where a person in a vehicle has potentially witnessed a major crime and needs to be found using only visual identifiers as a starting point. Another example is that during political conflict between countries, heavy equipment is spotted constructing something suspicious. Video of the equipment was posted to social media, and now you have been asked to identify the organization who owns equipment.

Markings

Vehicle markings have many meanings and goals across personal, commercial, and government automobiles. Many of the markings are informative and indicate proper usage and designations, while for personal vehicles the purpose is more for art and individuality. The varying functions of vehicle markings can provide us with important information about the individual or organization. Using information derived from analyzing vehicle markings, we can potentially determine ownership, manufacturing location, services it performs, and even the military unit it supports. I have broken the types of markings into Personal, Commercial, and Military.

- **Personal:** Markings on personal use vehicles could include the branding logo, custom painted imagery, front license plates, license plate frames, window clings, food delivery decals/magnets, and stickers. Stickers on vehicles are used around the world for verification that the vehicle has been tested for emissions and inspection, as well as used for proof of payment in zone parking and general parking permits which may be able to lead you to a region, city, or zone that uses that particular sticker.

- **Commercial:** Markings on commercial vehicles such as tractor trailers include car make, organizational branding, the legal name or trade name of the business entity that owns or controls the vehicle, U.S. Department of Transportation number, hazardous materials placards, custom graphics including painted or wrapped vehicles, phone numbers, slogans, and unit numbers if the company has more than one vehicle.

- **Military:** U.S. military vehicles are required to have a visible unit designation and bumper numbers, which are a set of numbers and letters on both the front and back of a vehicle for unique identification. The markings are split into four positions.[110]

  ○ Major command, organization, or activity

  ○ Intermediate organization or activity

  ○ Unit that operates the vehicle

  ○ The vehicle number

Military vehicles are regularly marked with national symbols to signify the nation the vehicle belongs to, which in the United States can be seen with the Army White Star logo. Operational markings are also present on military vehicles to help identify the units during operations. These markings could include stripes, simple designs, names, and geometric figures. Sometimes markings can even be spraypainted on during conflict. We saw the Russian military in Ukraine begin painting a Z on the sides of vehicles, which has become a symbol of Russian Support during the invasion. Vehicle camouflage can be queried on the Internet and matched to a vehicle because the patterns vary by country. This is a great way to potentially match a military vehicle to a nation using a photo or video.

Safety markings are used for hazardous material transportation and usually list FLAMMABLE or NO SMOKING with a determined reflective stripe pattern, while technical markings display things like tire pressure, max speed, and weight classification. The weight plates are affixed to the front of the vehicle to show max weight for crossing a bridge; these are usually yellow circles with a number on it for weight. Ambulance markings such as the red cross symbol are displayed on the left and right sides and rear as well as the roof and marked above the windshield. The registration markings on military vehicles, at least in the United States, indicate vehicle category such as tank or tractor, as well as the vehicle production number.

Special Use

The term *special use vehicle* covers a vast range of automobiles from heavy equipment and public transportation to police vehicles. Each of these vehicles will have

---

[110] https://gear-report.com/wp-content/uploads/2017/03/
TB-43-0209-Color-Markings-And-Camouflage.pdf.

special marking regulations based on their industry. Some of the more general markings found on these vehicles are hazard notices, unit markings, custom wraps with advertising, and unit numbers such as police cars and ambulances.

Shape and Features

When attempting to identify a vehicle, there are several unique features we can take note of that can help us determine what kind of automobile we are looking at. Identification may be necessary when we are provided images, video, satellite imagery, and even heat maps. Understanding some quick methods for identification can speed up the process.

- **Size:** This is probably the easiest to spot and use to rule out vehicles that don't fit the size description. Visually matching an automobile to similar sizes within its class should help to narrow down the focus.

- **Shape:** The shape of an automobile is generally tied to the model and purpose of the vehicle. For instance, passenger cars have roughly seven main body types (sedan, hatchback, SUV, MUV, coupe, convertible, pickup truck), and every year the model of the automobile will change along with its shape to stay modern. Heavy equipment manufacturers also create different models by year that can be determined by overall shape and features, but they may change less often.
  Being able to quickly identify a vehicle based on the shape and verify it through a query of the models across the years is useful. This tactic is similar across the various types of vehicles including military and commercial.

- **Color:** Try to determine the color of the automobile. Does the shade or color exist in the type of vehicle you estimate it to be? Is the vehicle painted or wrapped in a specific company branding you can identify? If it is a military vehicle, can you identify the type of camo that is used?

- **Symmetry:** Examine whether the automobile is symmetrical from the left to the right and front to back. Especially in military vehicles this can be an indication of where an engine is located, which could help to identify it.

- **Roof Shape:** This is especially useful from above in satellite view to help discern specific vehicle types based on roof or hull shape. Does the roof have a rack, or does the military vehicle have openings, a soft top, or equipment on the roof? Is there a turret for mounting weapons, what is the shape and position?

- **Engine and Exhaust Location:** Can you see steam from the exhaust on a specific portion of the vehicle indicating the exhaust might be positioned there? Can you tell from the shape of the body or from heat maps where the engine is located?

- **Traction:** Is the vehicle wheeled? How many wheels does it have, are they evenly spaced, small/large, does the vehicle have a track or part track, bogie wheels?
- **Customizations:** Do you see any custom additions on the vehicle like a body kit, custom paint or wrap, exhaust, etc., that might be an indication as to who owns the vehicle.

Vehicle History

The history of an automobile can be pulled from what is called a *vehicle history report*. These reports are meant to protect consumers from fraud and from buying an unsafe or stolen vehicle. The reports contain data on previous owners, title status, mileage, recalls, previous accidents, damage, and repairs to the vehicle. Pulling vehicle history reports can also provide VIN numbers that can be pivoted from to find more information.

Pattern of Life

Pattern of life may seem to be an odd identifier for vehicles, but often the routes and patterns they take can help to determine their use. For instance, if we see a vehicle go from the main place of residence then to a restaurant, before driving to another home several times a week we could surmise it could be a food delivery driver. Likewise, a dark SUV parked suspiciously in a covert area to watch traffic might be an unmarked police car.

Equipment Damage, Loss, Theft

Sometimes it is useful to document vehicle damage, theft, and loss to estimate the rest of the fleet or to understand pattern of life that we see. During the invasion of Ukraine, several groups have developed lists to track the destruction of military equipment[111] such as tanks to give a real-life view of battle losses and how many remain active.

Tips for Monitoring and Analyzing Automobile Routes

There are many reasons we may want to track the route of an automobile. We spoke previously about pattern of life, which involves tracking the subject operating a vehicle, commercial vehicles such as intermodal trucking companies could be a way to track cargo shipments from one location to another, and special-use vehicles such as construction equipment can indicate an organization behind land development that we may be researching.

---

[111] `www.oryxspioenkop.com/2022/02/`
`attack-on-europe-documenting-equipment.html`.

Visually Track

Because personal automobile tracking is difficult without placing a physical tracker on a vehicle (which is not OSINT) and freight tracking involves pay sites, it is beneficial to track automobiles by sight. Use webcams, satellite, social media, and videos/images to track location over time based on patterns.

Live publicly accessible webcams around the world are a great way to capture visuals on an automobile without having to be there physically. Cameras are attached to poles near highways, on overpasses, and on buildings to gather streaming video of road traffic for use by news stations and local government. The cameras tend to focus on intersections, heavy traffic areas, and stretches of roads where accidents are prevalent. Sometimes the public puts up their own traffic cameras; one of my favorite web cameras is the 11 foot 8 bridge also known as the Can Opener Bridge. This camera was placed in 2008 by Jurgen Henn at his office at Brightleaf Square facing a railroad trestle in Durham, NC. Henn wanted to capture the many trucks who ignore the height limit sign, flashing lights, and massive steel crash beams to wreck into the bridge.[112] Using web camera footage both live and historical not only allows us to see hilarious videos like 11 foot 8 bridge, but they can help us to catch a vehicle on a timestamped video at a specific location (see Figure 8.83).

Figure 8.83: Copyright Jürgen Henn – 11foot8.com

---

[112] youtu.be/iB4_fxVjJ80.

Use Social Media

Social media can be used as a method to identify and track vehicles through user posts and geotags. Lots of vehicle owners are proud of their personal automobiles and take pictures and video in front of or inside their cars to post on their social media. Browsing through a subject's social media can reveal the car make and model and sometimes even a full or partial license plate.

TikTok can be a wonderful resource for seeing a subject's driving routes, travel plans, and new car purchases. By expanding our social media search out to a subject's friends, family, and colleagues, we may be able to find additional subject vehicle photos including new angles. Focusing on commercial automobiles, we can use the ownership or operational organization's social media accounts to search for imagery of their fleet of vehicles. This may not reveal license plate numbers but can show branding and the vehicle make and model that the organization uses for their work.

Similarly, branches of the armed forces maintain social media pages for talking about present exercises or public outreach. Sometimes within the posts from these official accounts, as well as unofficial personal accounts, we can see details showing vehicles with clear identification and markings outlining the specific units the vehicles belong to. Commercial vehicles often have both private and public GPS trackers, and drivers share their locations and routes through sites like `locatoweb.com/en`[113] allowing anyone to track their routes in real-time to stay in touch with family and friends. Another way drivers share their travel and daily lives with their family is through personal blogging platforms. We can sometimes get lucky and find detailed routes and trip plans on the personal blogs of drivers.

Use Auto Enthusiast and Specialty Sites for Additional Details

Just like shipspotters and railfans, there are automobile enthusiasts who love photographing and discussing cars. Some enthusiasts maintain public websites, forums, and databases of vehicle information. We can use these public resources to gather specific information about an automobile such as body, paint color, and technology by make and model. Hobbyists may keep a record of all the vehicles they interact with on a day-to-day basis including history, images, and video showing emblems and license plates, etc. Some automobile hobbyists focus only on historical vehicles, some on heavy equipment, and others on historical military vehicles.

---

[113] `https://locatoweb.com/en`.

Use Public Disclosures in News Stories and Websites to Determine Routes

Using the information disclosed within news stories and company websites we can find detailed information on an organization's vehicle fleet, routes, customers, drivers, and more.

Automobile Entity Ownership and Operation

Understanding the ownership and operation of commercial and special-use automobiles is one way to begin to unravel various use cases such as supply chain analysis, tracking, and verification. Freight movement and supply chain are key reasons behind the daily activity of many commercial vehicles. Analyzing freight transportation requires a bit of knowledge surrounding keywords and the steps taken from freight order to freight delivery, including the organizations interacting with the freight along the way. The following are some important terms to know before starting your analysis:

- **Full Truckload:** The entire trailer is needed for the shipment.
- **Less Than Truckload:** Only part of a trailer is needed, so goods may be transported along with goods from another shipper.
- **Intermodal Shipment:** A shipment that uses more than one mode of transportation without touching the cargo (vessel to train to truck).
- **Container Chassis:** A trailer for transporting ocean containers over the road in an intermodal shipment.
- **Multimodal Shipment:** A shipment where more than one mode of transportation is used, and the goods are opened and moved to a second mode of transportation.

Basic Steps Used in Freight Transportation by Vehicle

Step 1	A *buyer* or *agent* makes a purchase order for goods.
Step 2	A *freight forwarder* organizes with a transportation company to pick up a shipment, and a bill of lading is created for the shipment.
Step 3	The *shipping company* picks up the goods and transports them to a central distribution point.
Step 4	Items are checked for damage, and if exporting internationally, a *customs broker* would need to clear cargo.
Step 5	A *freight forwarder* receives all documents and bills and works with the buyer and shipper to ensure payment is made.
Step 6	The *shipping company* picks up the goods from the distribution point and transports it to the destination or next stop in an intermodal or multimodal journey.

During the process of transporting freight by vehicle there are many steps where different individuals and organizations have their hands on the money, goods, and vehicles. Each of these touchpoints along the way can be researched for their connections and possible corruption. By using company record databases like open corporates, sanctions and designations reporting, and subject intelligence techniques, we can begin to unravel the connections between people and organizations revealing motives. Another method of analysis is utilizing public disclosures related to each organization to discover further connections, lawsuits, or discretions. We can also look at freight-related database sites like `Truckingdatabase.com`,[114] which contains the registration, contact, driver, and commodity data on interstate and noninterstate truck and bus companies operating within the United States that have registered with the Federal Motor Carry Safety Administration (FCMA). FCMA offers a safety research database as well that can be used to check for previous driving infractions at `ai.fmcsa.dot.gov/SMS`.[115]

Automobile Security and Technology

A modern car is a complex computing system on wheels made up of many important systems. These systems are important because a failure can stop the operation of the vehicle or create a dangerous safety hazard. Examples of automotive critical systems are airbags, sensors, anti-lock brakes, engine, active safety, and accelerator. Critical automotive systems are the primary reason OSINT analysts are interested in researching automotive technology (see Figure 8.84)

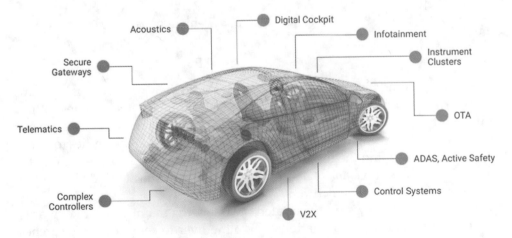

Figure 8.84: Technology within an automobile

---

[114] `https://truckingdatabase.com`.
[115] `https://ai.fmcsa.dot.gov/SMS`.

Uncovering vulnerabilities in any technology within a vehicle could like-wise expose the critical systems technology allowing for tracking or even full control of the vehicle. Of course, we are analysts and not hackers, so we would never access a computer system on board an automobile, but what we can do is determine the vulnerabilities through open-source analysis and present them to stakeholders to act on.

Within a vehicle, the controller area network (CAN) bus is a communications protocol enabling communications to electronic control units (ECUs) or nodes. The nodes are all interconnected through the CAN bus and can send messages to each other in the form of an ID stating priority of the message, along with a CAN message. Higher-priority messages are sent first allowing microcontrollers and devices to communicate. For instance, a message from the anti-lock brakes or the steering system would be labeled higher priority than the infotainment center. Unfortunately, the existing security features built into the CAN bus are primarily designed to ensure reliable communication, not cybersecurity. There-fore, the network cannot be effectively protected from cyberattacks.[116]

Automobiles suffer from the same cybersecurity issues that we see in all forms of control systems; the CAN works as a broadcast network capturing messages, but the data is not encrypted. Interception of that data could lead to breaches of driver PII and ultimately loss of trust in the manufacturer. The following are some examples of possible attacks:

- Multimedia attack
- Malicious node
- Bluetooth
- Wi-Fi
- Keyless entry

- Immobilizer
- Tire pressure monitoring system (TPMS)
- Vehicular ad hoc net-work (VANET)
- GPS

Knowing the adversary attack surface along with the various critical systems on board an automobile assists us with developing targeted queries to find information. Plainly, understanding what is possible can help us figure out how an adversary might pivot to that data. We can use search engines to query system names to find the top manufacturers for those products. Searching for terms like *canbus* and *automotive* and *telematics* is great start to find automotive specific electronics manufacturers.[117]

When I ran my own search, I located the following manufacturer keywords: Cellco, vodapone, and kpn national. Pivoting over to censys.io,[118] I searched for *telematics*, which returned many results, but I was looking for one of the

---

[116] www.ncbi.nlm.nih.gov/pmc/articles/PMC7219335.
[117] https://dl.acm.org/doi/pdf/10.1145/3538969.3543802.
[118] https://search.censys.io.

manufacturer keywords I had found previously (see Figure 8.85). Telemetric gateway units (TGUs) are used heavily in trucking to track the units in the fleet.

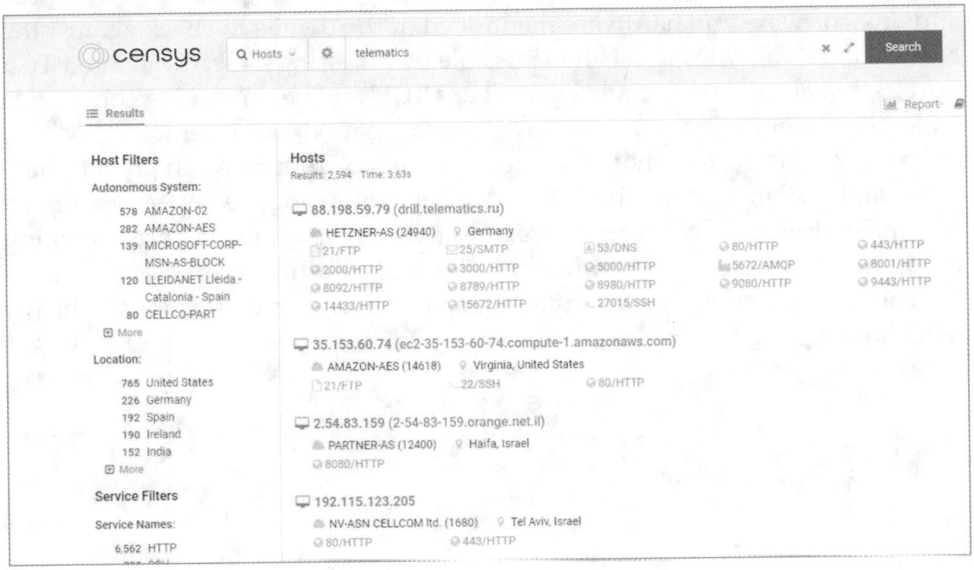

Figure 8.85: Telematics searched in `Censys.io`

I located several results that had the name CELLCOM Ltd. In the title I randomly chose a CELLCOM from the list, and when I looked closely at the details, I noticed Trimble Telematics was listed in the HTML title (see Figure 8.86). A quick search engine query for that business name revealed they make fleet management software.

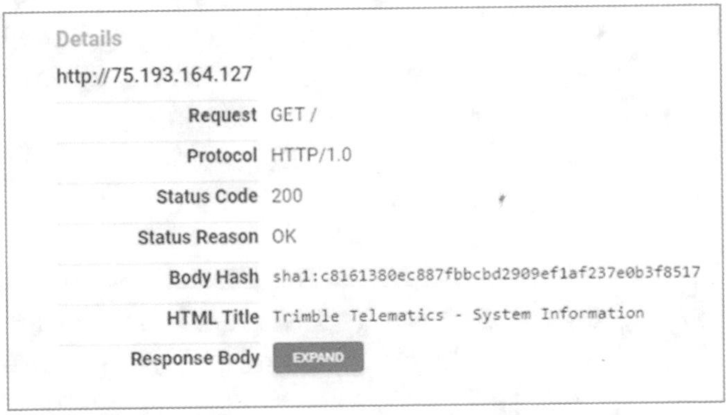

Figure 8.86: Trimble Telematics in `Censys.io`

Using a similar methodology, you can work by curating a list of keywords, querying them on `Censys.io`, and then matching the results with known automobile technologies. Taking it one step further you could note the open ports, and any software and hardware mentioned in the details to check against the NIST Vulnerability Database. It is possible by accessing a GPS system on TCP port 23 that an adversary could connect to a TGU and begin making commands and gathering information on the owner and location of the vehicle.[119]

This example goes to show how doing some up-front research on manufacturers and systems to develop a solid list of keywords can speed up your research and make it more effective. Because automobiles big and small are becoming more interconnected, these vulnerabilities will continue to exist across all of the categories of automobiles from personal cars and tractor trailers to heavy machinery.

---

[119] `http://jcarlosnorte.com/security/2016/03/06/`
`hacking-tachographs-from-the-internets.html`.

CHAPTER 9

Critical Infrastructure and Industrial Intelligence

9.1 Overview of Critical Infrastructure and Industrial Intelligence

The following figures from the United States in 2022 are just a small fraction of the critical manufacturing and infrastructure across the country and the world:

  140,000+ miles of freight railroad track

  1,689 chemical product manufacturing businesses

  987 energy plants

  19,622 airports

  3,000,000+ miles of gas pipelines

  More than 4,000,000 miles of roads

  100,000+ defense industrial base manufacturers

  360 shipping ports

  361,617,000,000 mobile subscribers

  2,721 data centers

Damage to critical infrastructure can have a catastrophic effect on the population and their ability to receive supplies, communications, and energy, as well as to move to safety. In 1996, President Bill Clinton signed Executive Order 13010 to define the term *critical infrastructures* within policy for the first time stating that the systems are "so vital that their incapacity or destruction would have a debilitating impact on the defense economic security of the United States."[1] Since then, the Cybersecurity and Infrastructure Security Agency (CISA), founded in 2018, has defined the sectors of critical infrastructure and key resources (CIKR) as follows[2]:

- Chemical
- Commercial
- Communications
- Critical manufacturing
- Dams
- Defense industrial base
- Emergency services
- Energy

- Financial services
- Food and agriculture
- Government facilities
- Healthcare and public health
- Information technology
- Nuclear reactors, materials, and waste
- Transportation
- Water and wastewater

Critical infrastructure (CI) threats have been around long before attackers were able to cripple industries with ransomware. Mother Nature is the original threat to our infrastructure with hurricanes, fires, floods, and earthquakes. We have most likely all been an unwilling participant in Mother Nature's lightning strikes to the power grid. Back in the dead of winter in 2018, I spent a week freezing in my house in the mountains of Pennsylvania due to ice weighing down and breaking power lines cutting the power to the entire town.

However, Mother Nature is not the only threat we face; many critical infrastructure and industrial manufacturing systems suffer from obsolete or unpatched software/hardware, default credentials, vulnerable third-party technologies, and more. As technology became more and more integrated into our critical systems and daily lives, it became an enticing target for attacks. This fact was brought abruptly to the forefront on September 11, 2001, when the attack on the United States using transportation pushed the topic of critical infrastructure threats to the top of the federal priorities list. This issue doesn't stop at the border of the United States; many countries rely on the infrastructure and manufacturing from other countries to survive. We got a glimpse of what the degradation of the supply chain would look like in 2019 with the Coronavirus outbreak nearly

---

[1] Executive Order 13010, Federal Register, Vol. 61, No. 138, July 17, 1996.
[2] www.cisa.gov/critical-infrastructure-sectors.

halting production and transportation of key supplies from countries like China with shipping ports backing up for weeks. With the perceived lack of toilet paper being received in the United States, there was a run on purchases that depleted the supply in stores causing the purchase of bidets to surge.[3] We have also seen the effects of critical infrastructure attacks in the attack on Ukraine in 2022. The fire at the Chernobyl reactor was a critical target that would have affected the entire world. We have also witnessed how the degradation of communications technology such as bombings targeting cell phone radio towers has the potential to isolate an entire country.

Manufacturing and industrial companies may be a less critical target than a nuclear power plant in terms of protecting lives; however, I would argue we should protect it the same way. Consider a scenario in which all the ballistic missile defense systems for an entire country are built using the same technology and that technology requires a specific electronic chip manufactured in a single plant. If that plant was hacked and proprietary schematics were stolen, if the plant was locked down by ransomware, or even if the machine was physically tampered with, the chips could no longer be manufactured causing huge delays and potentially a national security issue.

Attacks on critical infrastructure are increasing,[4] and what we can provide as OSINT analysts is value through the information we can collect and turn into intelligence to prevent against such attacks and system failures. *Critical infrastructure and industrial intelligence* is a term I use for the analysis and collection of information regarding industrial, manufacturing, and CI systems. Something we must consider when doing this type of analysis is that historically many of the digital attacks on systems begin with reconnaissance using the same open-source intelligence techniques we use. The *ICS Cyber Kill Chain* developed by Michael J. Assante and Robert M. Lee[5] and adapted to ICS based on the Lockheed Martin Cyber Kill Chain™ was designed to aid in decision-making for better detecting and responding to adversary intrusions[6] and bolsters the value of OSINT regarding ICS. In the Planning phase of the ICS Cyber Kill Chain (see Figure 9.1), reconnaissance is listed as the very first step in the intrusion process for attackers. Understanding how and why an adversary gathers information on CI and industrial systems will ultimately help us to provide stakeholders with better solutions for protecting them.

---

[3] www.npr.org/2020/03/22/819891957/bidets-gain-u-s-popularity-during-the-coronavirus-crisis.

[4] www.cisa.gov/uscert/sites/default/files/ICSJWG-Archive/QNL_JUN_2022/OT%20Security%20Incidents%20in%202021%20Trends%20&%20Analyses_FINAL_s508c.pdf.

[5] https://sansorg.egnyte.com/dl/HHa9fCekmc.

[6] Eric M. Hutchins, Michael J. Cloppert, and Rohan M. Amin, Ph.D., "Intelligence-Driven Computer Network Defense Informed by Analysis of Adversary Campaigns and Intrusion Kill Chains," www.lockheedmartin.com/content/dam/lockheed/data/corporate/documents/LM-White-Paper-Intel-Driven-Defense.pdf.

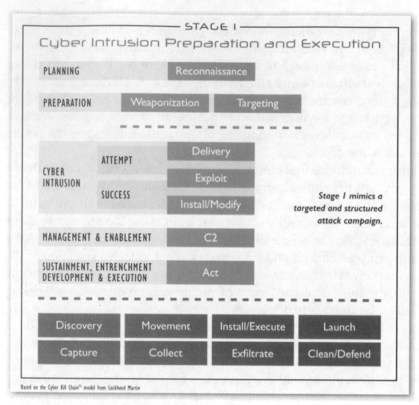

Figure 9.1: ICS Cyber Kill Chain

A watershed moment in digital attacks on critical infrastructure came back in Iran in 2010. International Atomic Energy Agency inspectors were visiting the Natanz uranium enrichment plant when they realized to their complete confusion, the centrifuges used to enrich uranium gas were failing. Shortly after, in Iran, a Belarusian security firm was called to fix a group of computers mysteriously crashing and restarting over and over.

In 2009, the world's first digital weapon, an undiscovered operation known as Stuxnet, was being perfected to manipulate Siemen's control systems that manipulate the speed of centrifuges in the Natanz enrichment plant. The attack had been designed to be spread through infected USB flash drives. To infect the computers on the inside of the plant, the attackers first infected the computers of third-party companies connected to the Iranian nuclear program hoping to make them unknowingly transport the infected USB drives inside the facility. One by one the companies fell victim to Stuxnet before reaching the intended target. In the next five months the functioning enrichment centrifuges at the plant dropped by 984.[7]

Experts speculated that the attack on the nuclear facilities was a joint operation, and in June 2012 the chief Washington correspondent for the *New York Times* published an article describing the Stuxnet worm as part of operation Olympic Games, a joint operation between Israel and the United States to prevent or delay Iran's development of weapons-grade uranium.[8] The operation had been successful; however, in 2010 the worm had spread beyond the enrichment plant and could then be found and downloaded by anyone with programming knowledge on the Internet, which begs the question can the United States defend its own critical infrastructure from a similar cyber weapon?[9]

There is no doubt that countries like Russia and China have cyber weapon capabilities to manufacture and manipulate their own malware and penetrate infrastructure and energy targets.[10] In an effort to protect our own infrastructure from these attacks, an OSINT analyst can provide value through being able to spot the signs of an attack in publicly available information, trace actors through their disclosures, and think like an adversary to develop adversary simulations.

Typically, adversary collection on CI and industrial/manufacturing systems focuses on two key areas.

- Uncovering proprietary data and processes
  - Corporate espionage
  - Physical attack
  - Digital attack
- Uncovering vulnerable systems including pumps, regulators, pipelines, manufacturing robots, etc.
  - Physical attack
  - Digital attack

To accomplish this as an adversary would, a typical analysis for an OSINT analyst working in critical infrastructure and industrial intelligence might look like an adversary simulation on a company based on the requirements from your stakeholder. This type of analysis could involve looking at both the physical space and digital footprint for that company from the perspective of an attacker and providing a report outlining potential weak points, OPSEC mistakes, and vulnerabilities in their structure and processes. Another type of analysis could

---

[7] www.wired.com/2014/11/countdown-to-zero-day-stuxnet.
[8] www.nytimes.com/2012/06/01/world/middleeast/
obama-ordered-wave-of-cyberattacks-against-iran
.html?pagewanted=1&_r=1.
[9] https://k1project.columbia.edu/news/stuxnet.
[10] https://crsreports.congress.gov/product/pdf/IF/IF11718.

be to view a whole region, area, or infrastructure sector and determine the weak points and vulnerabilities in the way it is set up. For instance, does only one single company provide energy for a whole city? What happens if someone were to target that company?

In the cold winter of December 2022, more than 38,000 people were without power after two substations were intentionally targeted in Moore County, North Carolina. This was, however, not a digital attack on infrastructure but rather a physical attack on several substations with a gunfire attack on the equipment.[11] This is a great example of how it isn't always necessary for an attacker to use complex digital attacks if they have performed reconnaissance and targeted their attacks to have the most impact; a few well-placed bullets can do the trick. As of this writing, there have been no arrests in connection with the substation attacks.

What Is Operational Technology?

Operational technology (OT) is hardware and software that detects or causes change by directly monitoring and/or controlling industrial equipment, facilities, processes, and events. OT is an encompassing term for the systems that keep our critical infrastructure working properly. The many systems that the term OT is referring to are as follows:

- **Industrial Control Systems (ICSs)** are used to control processes such as manufacturing and production. These systems include SCADA, DCS, and PLC.[12] Because of the interconnectedness of ICS and its peripheral devices, it is an enticing target for attackers.

- **Distributed Control Systems (DCSs)** are computerized control systems for a process or plant, typically with many loops and distributed autonomous control throughout the system, but without central operator supervision.

- **Supervisory Control and Data Acquisition (SCADA)** is an architecture that controls computers, communications, and interfaces for the supervision of machines and their processes. SCADA encompasses other devices like PLCs that communicate with other machinery or systems. The PIPEDREAM toolkit targets ICS and SCADA devices to manipulate the speed of motors, identify network components, brute-force PLC passwords, start and stop processes, limit access to ICS systems, bypass firewalls, and make PLCs unavailable.[13]

---

[11] www.cnn.com/us/live-news/power-outage-north-carolina-updates/index.html.

[12] https://csrc.nist.gov/glossary/term/industrial_control_system.

[13] https://hub.dragos.com/hubfs/116-Whitepapers/Dragos_ChernoviteWP_v2b.pdf?hsLang=en.

- **Programmable Logic Controllers (PLCs)** control processes in manufacturing such as machines, robots, and assembly lines that all require reliability in their function. The "evil PLC" attack weaponizes PLC controllers so the attacker can enter a workstation and pivot to all other PLCs on the network to start and stop processes or access sensitive systems.[14]

- **Remote Terminal Units (RTUs)** are electronic devices that connect hardware to DCS and SCADA systems within an industrial control system.

What Is IoT and IIoT?

The Internet of Things (IoT) is a connected network of objects that contain technologies like software and sensors for exchanging data with other devices connected with the Internet. IoT devices can be everyday household items like refrigerators and televisions but are also heavily integrated into many industrial settings where they control sensors and devices that monitor and manage critical technology. This is called *Industrial IoT (IIoT)*.

IoT has grown to be one of the most popular technologies because it has been integrated with nearly every aspect of our lives; it also plays a huge role in the integration of technology with the OT systems used in critical infrastructure, manufacturing, and supply chains. IoT devices maintain and monitor processes, including monitoring events and making adjustments as well as monitoring other devices within industrial systems. For instance, in manufacturing, IIoT smart sensors can regulate temperatures and adjust the machines to optimize product manufacturing. IoT devices can automatically dock a vessel in a smart port, track a train across the country using devices alongside the track, and track your luggage through an airport on a flight and to your destination. IoT devices are used in the energy sector for things like smart grids, alerts for repairs, and predictive meters for disasters.

The convergence of IoT and OT systems is important because without the proper functioning of these systems, we would lack fresh water, energy, safety, and security. Each system is made of systems, and each relies on the next for proper functioning to sustain society. Proper maintenance of the electric grid requires functioning IoT sensors, the supply chain relies on the functioning of the grid to move cargo across the world, businesses and homes rely on the supply chain to bring parts for manufacturing and supplies for survival, and it goes on. As convenient as the interconnectedness of the world has become, it can also pose problems due to lack of segmenting, default credentials, and access to the Internet.

---

[14] https://thehackernews.com/2022/08/
new-evil-plc-attack-weaponizes-plcs-to.html.

In London in 2017, Nicole Eagan, the CEO of cybersecurity company Darktrace, recounted an attack where a North America casino network was illegally accessed through an aquarium thermometer in the lobby that was connected to the Internet.[15] The thermometer was set up to monitor the temperature of the tank as well as the food and cleanliness of the water. The attackers were able to enter the network through a vulnerability in the thermometer and move laterally through the network to the high-roller database, pulling 10 GB of data and sending it to a device in Finland. While a casino is certainly not as critical as an oil pipeline, it stands as an example of how an attacker can move laterally through a seemingly benign IoT technology to a more critical system. Because of the impact an OT attack would have on society and the known connections between OT and IoT devices, they have both become targets for strategic attacks that are often used to further political, economic, and foreign agendas. Some of the tactics and techniques used by attackers are as follows:

- **Industrial Espionage** is where an attacker targets a specific organization to illegally exfiltrate proprietary information about a manufacturing process, formula, or specification for the purpose of gaining a business advantage or to pass information to a foreign government. Industrial espionage can be in the form of hacked and exfiltrated information, an insider threat, or physical access by an attacker on site.

- **Ransomware** is a digital way to hold a system hostage using malware until a ransom payment is made. Ransomware can severely impact a supply chain because goods won't arrive on time, manufacturing can be set back, and this can cause safety issues with critical infrastructure. In 2021, 56 percent of companies that fell victim to ransomware paid the ransom to limit their downtime.[16]

- **Degradation or Destruction** is where a system is accessed and digitally or physically damaged for the purpose of causing harm or destruction. For example, adjustments in temperature, pumps, and motor speed can be turned to an unhelpful setting to cause destruction. Things could be turned off or on to make the machines run in a way that it wouldn't normally run.

One of the most relevant events related to critical infrastructure and IoT security in the last 5 years is the ransomware attack on Colonial Pipeline in

---

[15] www.washingtonpost.com/news/innovations/wp/2017/07/21/how-a-fish-tank-helped-hack-a-casino.

[16] www.kaspersky.com/about/press-releases/2021_over-half-of-ransomware-victims-pay-the-ransom-but-only-a-quarter-see-their-full-data-returned.

May 2021. Owned by the Colonial Pipeline Company, the Colonial Pipeline consists of three tubes from the U.S. Gulf Coast to the U.S. East Coast and moves more than 2.5 million barrels of jet fuel, diesel, and gasoline through a day; it is the largest pipeline system for refined oil in the United States. On May 6, the DarkSide[17] group used publicly available information to locate a legacy VPN system setup without multifactor authentication in place. The group used a single password to access the Colonial systems, steal 100 GB of data, and infect the network with ransomware. Ultimately Colonial paid the $4.4 million ransom to DarkSide to obtain the key to decrypt their infrastructure, but the financial systems were down for 5 days causing a fuel shortage on the East Coast of the United States. Crypto wallet research has shown that $90 million in other bitcoin ransom payments had been made to DarkSide and their affiliates in 2021. In this example, the attacker used OSINT password enumeration techniques that we learned earlier in this book in order to access the system and place ransomware. Imagine the value that you could provide to a company like Colonial Pipeline that is looking for an assessment on how their publicly available information can be used against them. Having knowledge of how these systems work, connect, and are exploited will benefit you when you are in the Planning phase of analysis into CI, OT, and IoT technologies.

The following are a few examples of potential questions you may receive from your stakeholder:

- Can you find any actionable information about the hacker group that attacked the system?
- Could you provide a report on any vulnerabilities you find about the systems in open source information?
- Has any proprietary information or code been leaked?
- Are any of the employees a potential insider threat?

9.2   Methods for the Analysis of Critical Infrastructure, OT, and IoT Systems

In order to begin analyzing critical infrastructure and the related systems, we can implement specific methodology for identifying, tracking, and understanding CI. Below is a pivot chart example showing several ways in which we can pivot through CI information (see Figure 9.2).

---

[17] www.state.gov/reward-offers-for-information-to-bring-darkside-ransomware-variant-co-conspirators-to-justice.

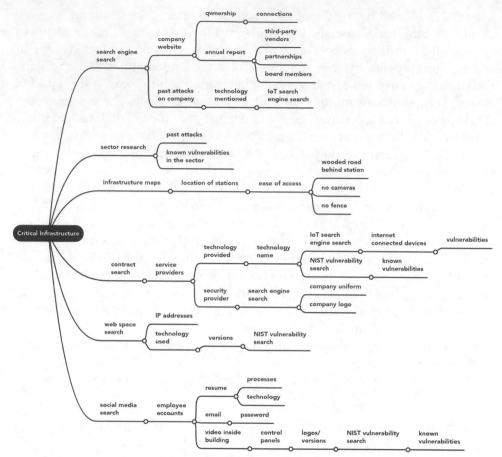

Figure 9.2: Pivot chart of critical infrastructure

Planning the Analysis

Using the intelligence cycle as the driver for our analysis, we should rely on the Planning and Requirements phase along with feedback from any previous information gathering to determine the focus of our analysis. Depending on the stakeholder questions and requirements, the direction of the analysis is likely to include one or more of the following avenues (see Figure 9.3).

Five Possible Information Gathering Avenues

Here are the five avenues:

- Looking at a specific area (country, city, town, etc.)
- Looking at a specific company (Colonial Pipeline, Pennsylvania, Power and Light)
- Looking at a specific sector (energy, manufacturing, supply chain)

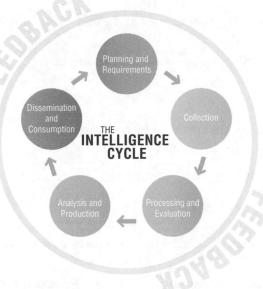

Figure 9.3: The Intelligence cycle

- Looking at a specific technology (oil pipelines, Rockwell systems)
- Looking at an APT and their attacks on a critical infrastructure, OT, or IoT system

Using a funneling approach similar to what is used in law enforcement interrogation (see Figure 9.4), we can narrow the focus of our requirements and questions alongside the stakeholder. The process of funneling begins with determining the avenue of information gathering. For our example, let's use "Looking at a specific area." Baselining requires developing a starting point using historical data, and from there we then ask open ended questions to establish a wide scope before narrowing the focus further. Eventually we layer in questions to fill in the gaps and we are able to systematically plan our approach.

Q: Can we identify vulnerabilities in the energy sector for Brussels, Belgium?

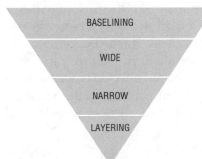

Figure 9.4: The funneling approach for narrowing information

Baselining

- Can we determine the key energy companies in the area? Does anything stand out?
- Does the area rely on a specific grid, technology, or company?

Starting Wide

- Where is the infrastructure located for the key companies?
- Who has access to the systems?
- What are the problems if those systems go down?

Narrowing Focus

- What are the selectors associated with the people who have access to the systems?
- What are the physical points of access to a system or infrastructure?
- What are the network points of access?

Layering

- Are any usernames, passwords, or other identifying selectors found in breaches?
- Do any systems have open ports or known vulnerabilities?

Visualizations

Visualizations like maps and trackers can help us to understand the landscape and to trace the routes and layouts of critical infrastructure around the world. We can use visualizations to enrich our analysis, add useful graphics to our reports, and gain a deeper understanding of an area without having to be there physically.

A good example of when a visualization may be useful is during an analysis when I uncovered the GPS coordinates of more than 100 IoT devices within a city. I wanted to be able to visualize them on a map to see any patterns and clustering. In Chapter 2, "The Intelligence Cycle," we learned about several tools for documentation such as Maltego and Google Earth that we can use to create our own visualizations based on data we have collected. I was able to effectively plot all of the IoT devices on a map by uploading them in Google Earth, which helped me to quickly see where most of the devices were located and provide a good visualization in a written report.

Additionally, we can utilize the many tools, visualizations, and maps that have been created by the community to aid us in our analysis. Analysts and organizations focused on specific regions or sectors develop visualizations to help keep track of their work or to put out tippers and alerts. Sometimes, companies have maps of their service locations for their customers that we can use for our analysis.

Plotting Locations with Google Earth Pro

Using Google Earth Pro, it is possible to upload data from a spreadsheet to automatically plot the points on the map and visualize the data. This is especially useful if you have a list of GPS coordinates and want to plot them to look for patterns or anomalies.

Step 1: Download Google Earth Pro.[18]

Step 2: Begin with a spreadsheet of data.

Google Earth requires latitude and longitude coordinates for each point, so we need to manipulate the spreadsheet we have or develop a new one with coordinates. The following is an example of how to set up your spreadsheet. Google Earth will use the spreadsheet column headers to parse the data within Earth, so be sure to have at least a map ID, name, and latitude/longitude coordinates (see Figure 9.5).

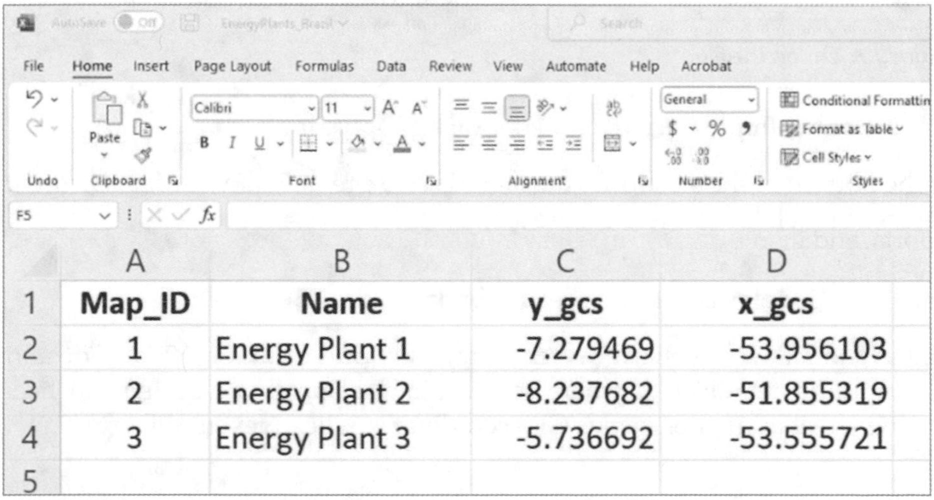

	A	B	C	D
1	**Map_ID**	**Name**	**y_gcs**	**x_gcs**
2	1	Energy Plant 1	-7.279469	-53.956103
3	2	Energy Plant 2	-8.237682	-51.855319
4	3	Energy Plant 3	-5.736692	-53.555721
5				

Figure 9.5: Spreadsheet list

---

[18] www.google.com/earth/about/versions/#earth-pro.

Alternatively, your spreadsheet could be street addresses rather than GPS coordinates; if that is the case, they all must be written in identical address formats.

Step 3: Save your spreadsheet as a tab-delimited text file (see Figure 9.6).

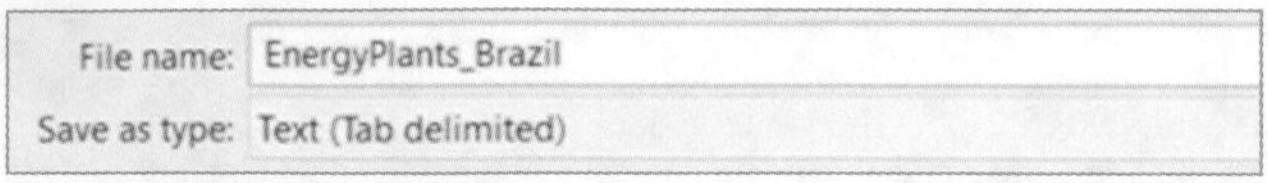

File name:	EnergyPlants_Brazil
Save as type:	Text (Tab delimited)

Figure 9.6: Save as a text file

Step 4: Open Google Earth and import the tab-delimited file.

Select File ➪ Import ➪ Open and open the tab-delimited file we saved in the previous step (see Figure 9.7).

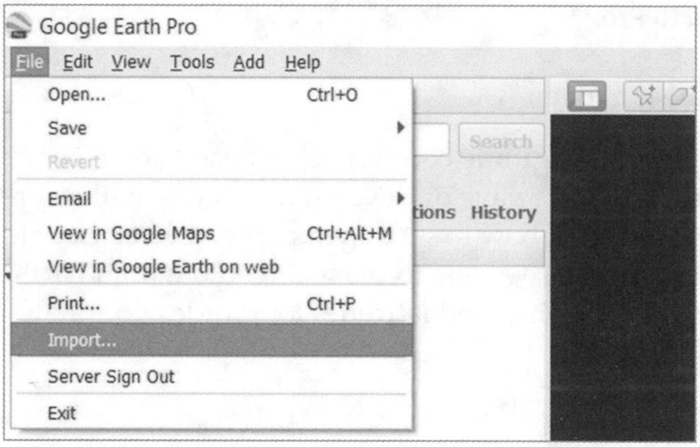

Figure 9.7: import the file

Step 5: Use the Import Wizard to guide you through importing.

At the bottom of the window, you should see a preview of your file; ensure it matches and click Next (see Figure 9.8).

Step 6: Tell Google Earth how to read your data.

We have to tell Google Earth which columns to pull from for (Y) latitude and (X) longitude data. Here is where you would also specify if your spreadsheet is using street addresses versus GPS coordinates. Click Next (see Figure 9.9).

Step 7: Specify field types (optional).

If you need to specify a field type for each column, you can do that next; then click Finish (see Figure 9.10).

Step 8: Specify a style template.

Earth will ask you to specify a style template; click Yes. Here you will be able to select the icons, colors, and height for your plotted points. I selected the thumbtack icon and hit OK (see Figures 9.11–9.12).

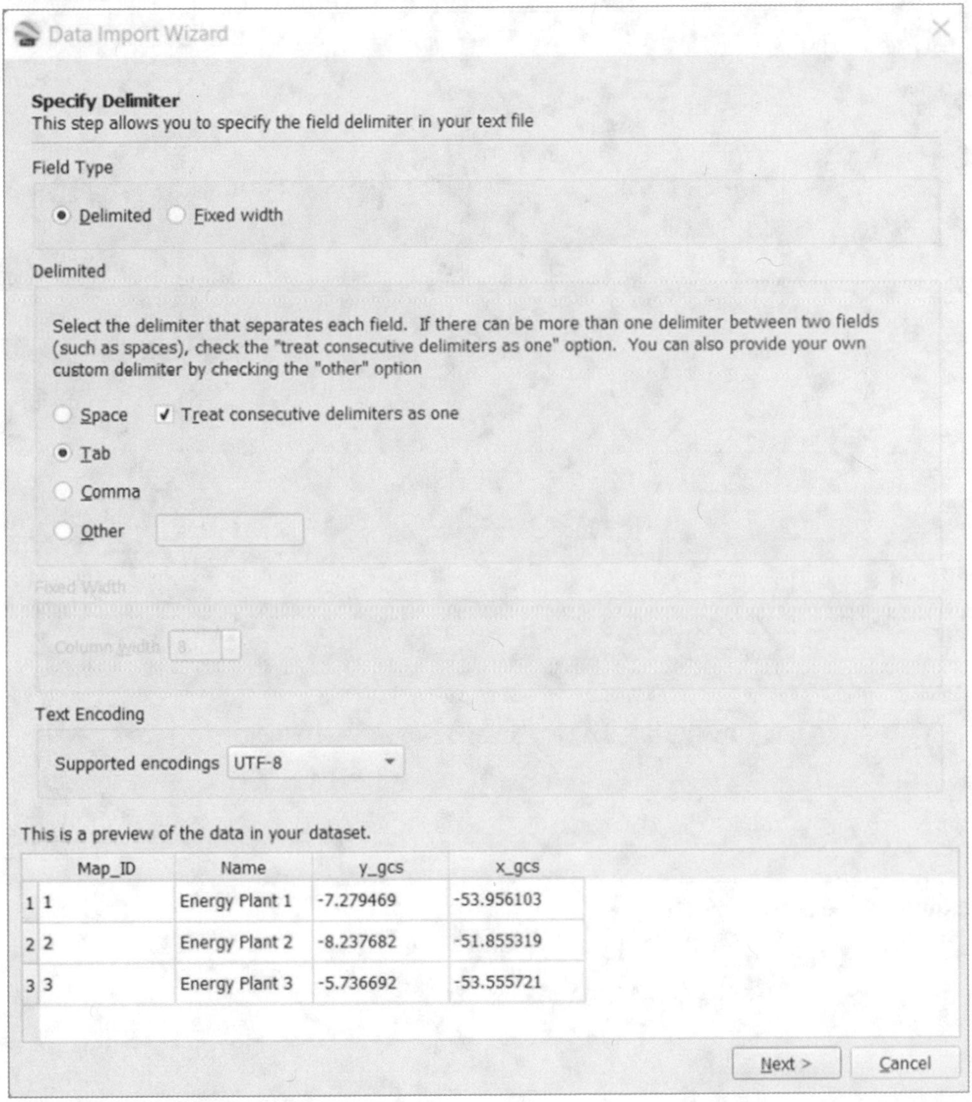

Figure 9.8: Preview file

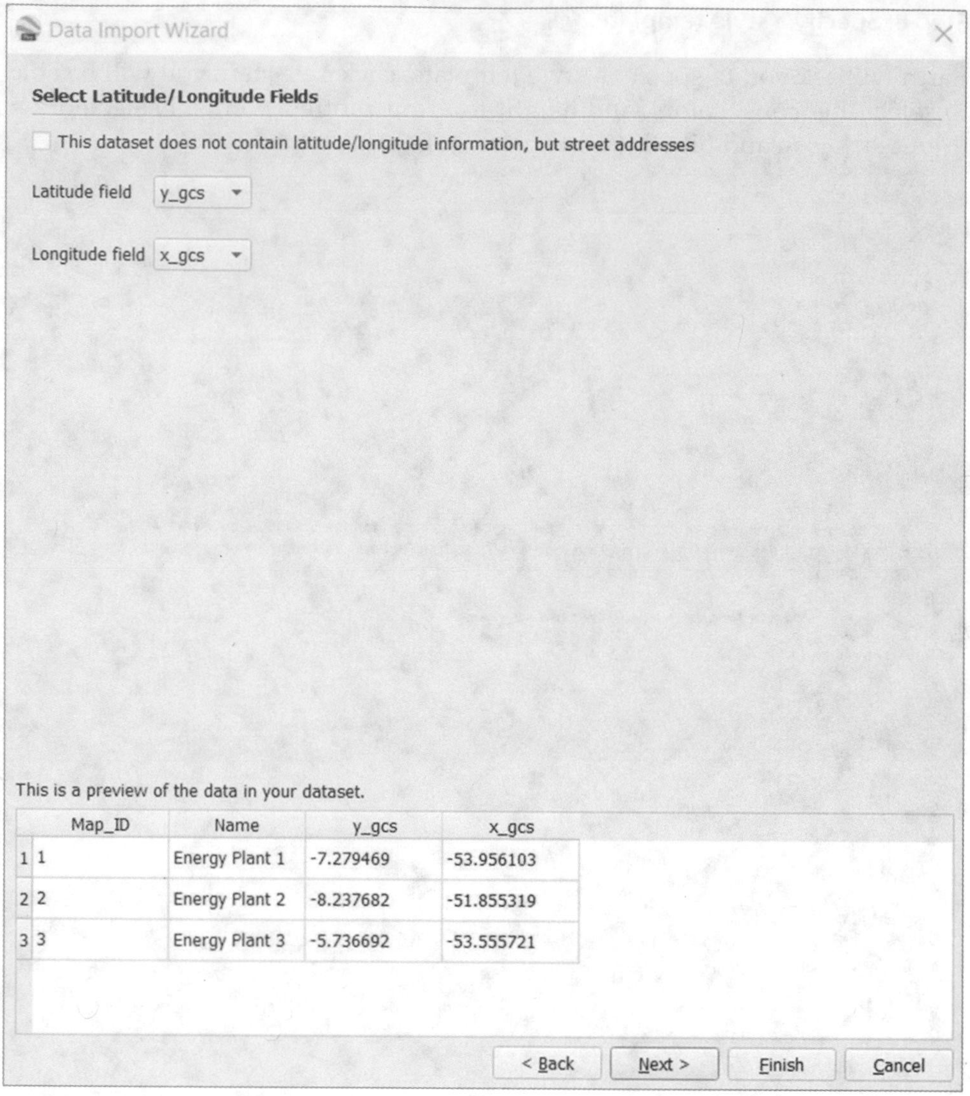

Figure 9.9: Select columns

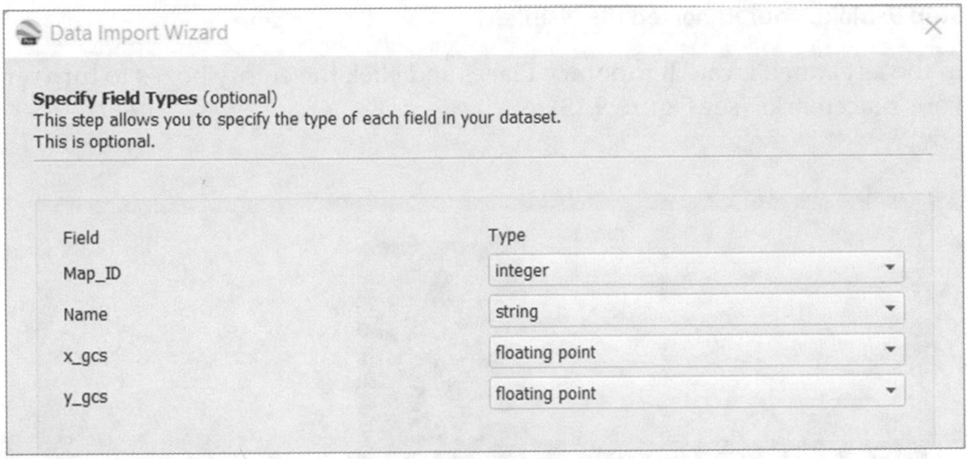

Figure 9.10: Specify field type

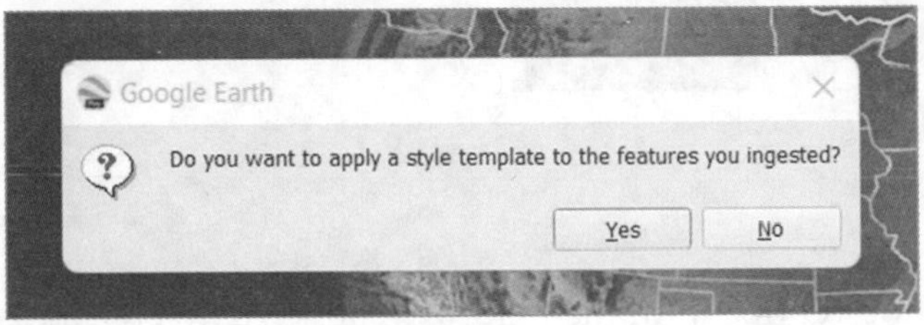

Figure 9.11: Apply template

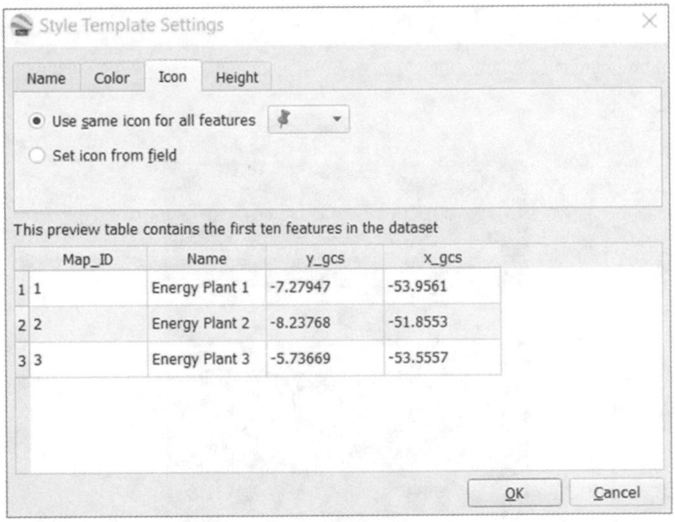

Figure 9.12: Select icon

Step 9: Make your imported file visible.

In the left panel, locate Temporary Places and click the empty boxes to turn on your placemarks (see Figure 9.13).

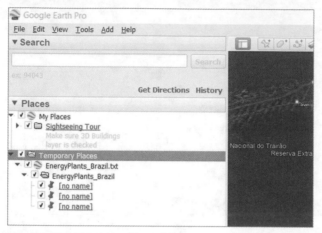

Figure 9.13: Make your file visible

Step 10: View and save.

Now your GPS locations should appear on the map. We can save this file as a KMZ file by right-clicking Temporary Places and saving as a KMZ so that it can be reused at a later date, sent to other analysts, or integrated into other tools (see Figure 9.14).

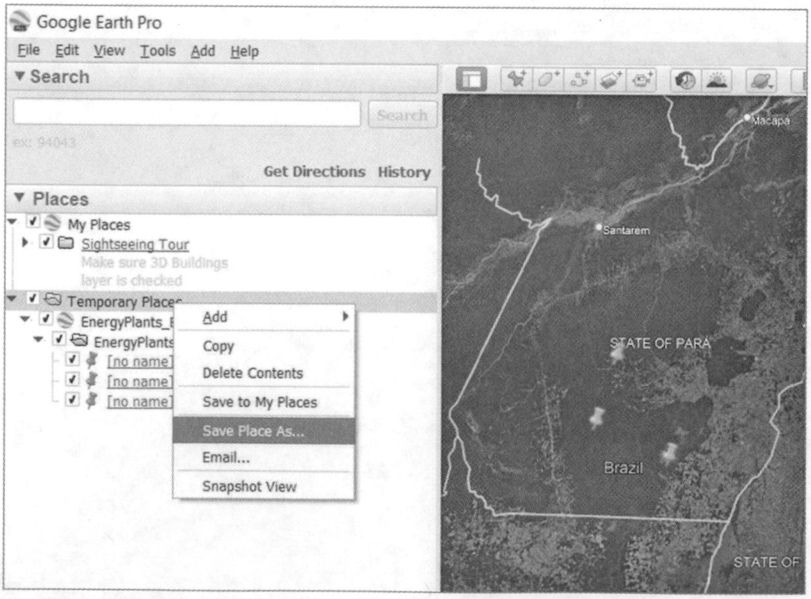

Figure 9.14: Save your place

Using Premade Visualizations

Tools and premade visualizations can be super handy to an analyst because they remove the time spent in developing our own visualization. Many great maps and trackers are even developed and hosted by the providers and government organizations themselves for public awareness. We can use these maps as a guide to help baseline activity and providers in regions or sectors of critical infrastructure and industrial manufacturing or to integrate them as a source in our own systems.

We must be careful when using maps and trackers developed by someone else because we never know their biases and motivations, so we have to independently verify the data we see rather than take it as the full truth. In the following sections, I have provided some examples of tools and visualizations to illustrate the types of data that can be found through simple targeted search engine searches. Consider your case and tailor your searches appropriately (for example, "oil pipeline" and "map" and "Mexico" or "defense industrial" and "map").

Government

Government map resources are pretty easy to find if we know where to look because they make much of the information public. Government visualization resources exist for critical sectors such as transportation, electricity lines, pipelines, and more. Many government maps use ArcGIS as a platform such as all the categories on the Homeland Infrastructure Foundation-Level Data (HIFLD) page[19] or on the United States Energy and Information Administration's Energy Atlas at `eia.gov/maps`.[20] Each of these categories leads to an ArcGIS map that can be explored and adjusted for your requirements (see Figures 9.15-9.16).

Provider

Provider data maps are straight from the company itself; this would be specific energy company maps or mapped locations of manufacturing plants. These can be found on the company websites, or they can be found through search engine searches such as "Company" and "map" or "company" and "location" and "pipeline" and "map." These visualizations can be useful in determining which companies hold a majority stake over an area and the locations of their infrastructure. One example is the company Norsk Petroleum in Norway that offers an interactive map[21] from its website showing information such as field name, operator, owners, and reserves (see Figure 9.17).

---

[19] U.S. Department of Homeland Security / `https://hifld-geoplatform.opendata.arcgis.com/` / last accessed 15 February 2023.
[20] `www.eia.gov/maps`.
[21] `www.norskpetroleum.no/en/interactive-map-quick-downloads/interactive-map`.

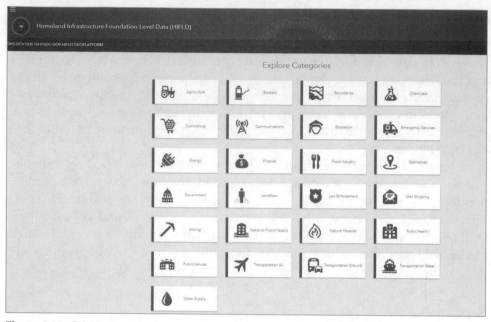

Figure 9.15: EIA Maps

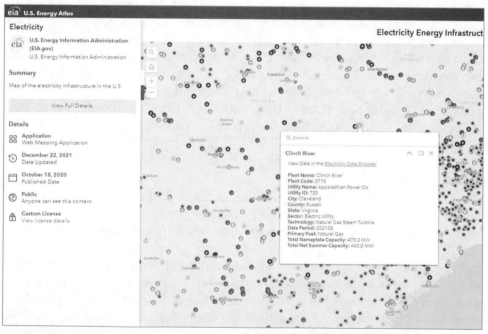

Figure 9.16: EIA Map

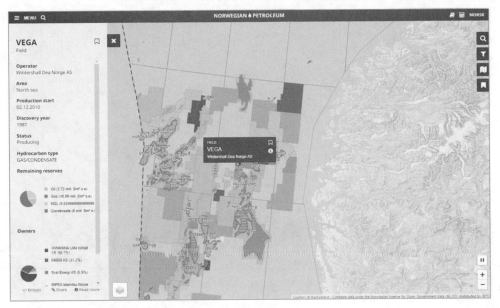

Figure 9.17: Norsk Petroleum map

We also can see a map of thermal power plant locations on the website for the JERA company in Japan.[22] Clicking each one reveals more information about each station and the capabilities. While not as detailed as the Norsk Petroleum map, it does lay out all the locations in one single view allowing us to focus our energy on deeper analysis (see Figure 9.18).

Watchdogs and Analysts

Beyond government agencies and specific providers exist think tanks, research bodies, watchdog groups, and analysts like us who are curious about infrastructure and what exists. Quite a few of the organizations and a few focused analysts have developed their own maps and trackers for monitoring a specific sector of critical infrastructure or manufacturing. Again, it is good to reiterate here that we can't always be fully aware of the motivations and biases for their research, so we have to independently verify any information that becomes key to our analysis. An example of an analyst-driven platform is `oilmap.xyz`,[23] which is a world oil map maintained for the purpose of expanding academic research and providing awareness to the general public (see Figure 9.19).

---

[22] `www.jera.co.jp/english/business/thermal-power.`
[23] `www.oilmap.xyz.`

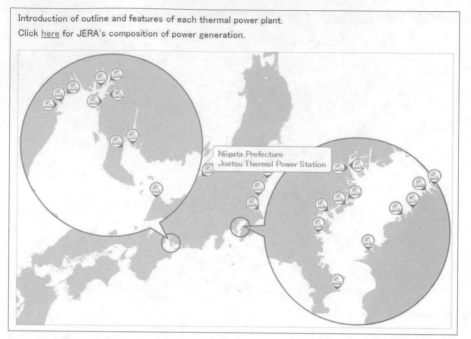

Introduction of outline and features of each thermal power plant.
Click here for JERA's composition of power generation.

Niigata Prefecture
Joetsu Thermal Power Station

Figure 9.18: JERA company map

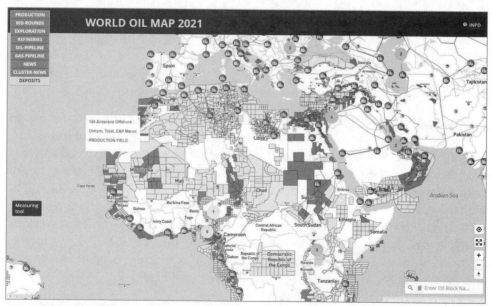

Figure 9.19: World oil map

Another organization is the World Association of Nuclear Operators (WANO), a nonprofit organization for the safety and reliability of nuclear power. WANO has a world map[24] on its website that shows all of its members and where the nuclear plant is located along with some information about the plant itself that could be used for further research (see Figure 9.20).

Figure 9.20: WANO world map

For digging into the industrial sector, we can look for maps like the Defense Industrial Base map[25] provided by ARMSCOM, which is an international media platform for the aerospace and defense industry with a database of "more than 4,000 companies acting in 3,400 defense sectors." The global map shows companies across the world and their details. The map itself is a bit finicky, but it gives you a good idea of what you can find when applying your own search criteria (see Figure 9.21).

---

[24] www.wano.info/members/wano-world-map.
[25] www.armscom.net/world-defense-industry-map.

Figure 9.21: Defense Industrial Base Map

Public Disclosures

Here are some public disclosure examples that you can integrate into your daily analysis to gain insights into Critical Infrastructure.

Contracts

Contracts are an excellent way to find information about companies because they show the teaming, partnerships, and services provided. By using contracts through a free source like usaspending.gov, we can find details about the specific technology used within the company, version numbers, and sometimes even schematics. Here is a sample pivot chart for how I would begin to analyze CI contracts (see Figure 9.22):

Social Media

Social media can be a great source to gather images and insight for specific systems. Often the details found include panels, switches, and stations with brand names and version numbers that can then be researched in NIST for vulnerabilities.

TikTok is great for video walkthroughs of technology, and using keywords like *SCADA*, *ICS*, and *control room* can get you some extremely detailed insider information about the systems in critical infrastructure such as oil platforms and industrial manufacturing (see Figures 9.23-9.24).

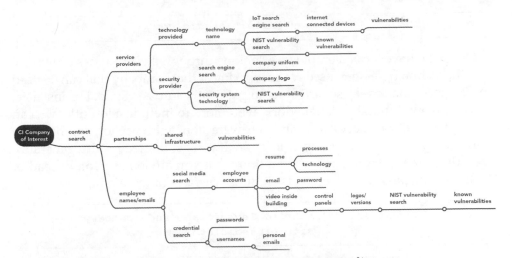

Figure 9.22: Pivot chart showing a critical infrastructure company of interest

Figure 9.23: TikTok

Figure 9.24: TikTok

LinkedIn can be used to find people who have high-level access to systems and also people who work on these systems that provide details in their job description. You can use a simple Google dork to find résumés or people working at the company of interest. Using this dork can provide a refined list of people who have noted the company on their résumé or in their description. One benefit of using a dork over the built-in LinkedIn search is that you are not required to log in to see basic information, which will prevent the subject from being alerted.

```
"Company" site:Linkedin.com
```

Once you have located employees, looking through their résumés can reveal specific technologies they used while working at that company that can be used for targeted attacks like spearfishing to gain entry into a system. For instance, if we narrow down the Google dork even more to include a job title, we can attempt to find specific software and hardware along with version numbers that are used on that specific system or location. If you get limited results, generalize the title a bit and try again until you find what you are looking for. Instead of *Industrial Engineering Technician*, I might use *engineer* or *technician*.

```
"Industrial Engineering Technician" and "company"
site:Linkedin.com
```

Job Advertisements

We can use job listings and advertisements from the company to figure out what types of industrial systems are being used to manufacture or run the systems within the company. There are a few dorks useful for this type of search.

If you know the company but not the job title, use this:

```
"company name" and "job"
```

If you know the company and job title, use this:

```
"company name" and "job title"
```

If you know the system you are looking for information on, use this:

```
"company name" and "job" and "system name"
```

Company Disclosures

The company or organization itself can disclose details on its website or social media about teaming, partnerships, and shareholders, and the annual report can reveal tons of information about how the company is structured and where any weak points may exist. What are they concerned about?

An example of what can be done with this information could be that your task is to gather information about a specific company's systems and tell them what you can find from an adversarial perspective. To begin with, we can research the company website for any details within their annual reports, files, and website contents that might give us any hints about the layout, structure, systems, and software/hardware the company uses.

Moving over to USASpending.gov, we check out the contracts for the company that mention that system using targeted searching. In the contracts we notice that another company has provided an annual servicing of the system we are interested in. Perhaps the system manufactures an integral part that isn't made at any other plant, so shutting the system down would be catastrophic.

In the contract documents we can see software and versions mentioned for this system, the mechanical workings of the machine, and the panel configurations. Looking on social media and searching for the system name, we can find people from other companies doing a walkthrough of how they use the machine, so now we know how it works and what parts are important. We can gather further information on the system from résumés and job listings to figure out which parts of the machine may be vulnerable.

Hopping over to NIST, we can check each system, software, hardware, and versions for any vulnerabilities that have been noted. Additionally, we can try to use Censys and Shodan to see if the system has public-facing endpoints accessible to the Internet that can be used to find vulnerabilities.

Infrastructure Search Tools

In previous chapters, we learned techniques for integrating Internet of Things search tools like Shodan for finding transportation device information, cameras, and more. Now, we are specifically focusing on methods for uncovering critical infrastructure and Internet-connected industrial control devices. There are a few options for these types of searches, and as time goes on, I am positive more will be added to your repertoire. Since we have already learned about Shodan, let's look at two other tools we can use: Censys.io and Kamerka.io.

Censys.io

Censys is a web-based tool developed by scientists from the University of Michigan that searches and identifies Internet-connected devices and IoT/IIoT along with industrial control systems and platforms. The purpose of Censys was to make the Internet more secure, and even CISA wrote a white paper about how Censys can be useful for "attack surface reduction."[26] The main differences between Censys and Shodan are that Censys is free to use with no limits on searching, and the creators claim the searches are more precise with providing specific vulnerabilities for each device.

---

[26] www.cisa.gov/sites/default/files/publications/Censys_ Technical_508c.pdf.

Kamerka

Kamerka is an industrial control system and IoT device search tool developed by researcher Wojciech.[27] Initially developed for locating Internet-connected surveillance cameras, it has since been expanded to focus more on ICS and IoT devices. Much like Censys, it passively gathers information through the API's for Shodan, WHOISXML, and Binary Edge and geolocates based on the device response and geotagged information. Some things that can be found through Kamerka include the following:

- Cameras
- Printers
- ICS/SCADA
- MQTT sensors
- RTSP-based video streams
- Social media geolocation details

Kamerka Lite Version

Kamerka Lite[28] is a GUI-based statistical view of devices that are found in the latest scan and viewable by country and device as well as being mildly searchable. No download is required for this version, and it is accessible through the website `lite.kamerka.io`. It is definitely a lighter version than the Python-based full version, but this will give you a quick look at some overall statistics of a region (see Figures 9.25-9.26).

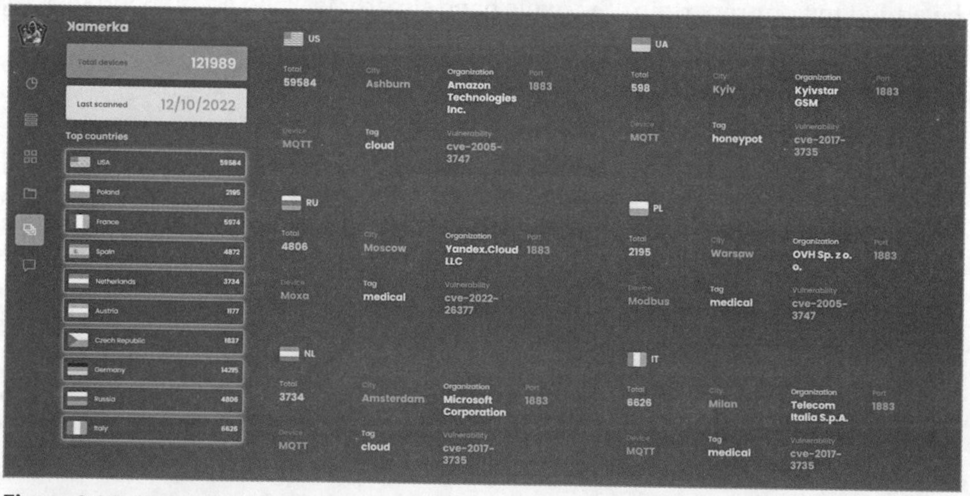

Figure 9.25: Kamerka Lite

---

[27] `https://twitter.com/the_wojciech`.
[28] Offensive OSINT / `https://lite.kamerka.io/`/last accessed February 15, 2023.

Figure 9.26: Kamerka Lite

Kamerka Full Version

The full version of Kamerka can be found at `github.com/woj-ciech/Kamerka-GUI` and is written in Python. Although not as easily accessible to a beginner in OSINT who has no knowledge of Linux or Python, the full version of this tool does open up some useful search options for industrial control systems and IoT devices that I think are worth exploring. Instructions for install can be found on the GitHub page, and it requires several API keys to work. Once installed, the full version of Kamerka lets you search for industrial control and IoT devices by country and by specific coordinates (see Figure 9.27).

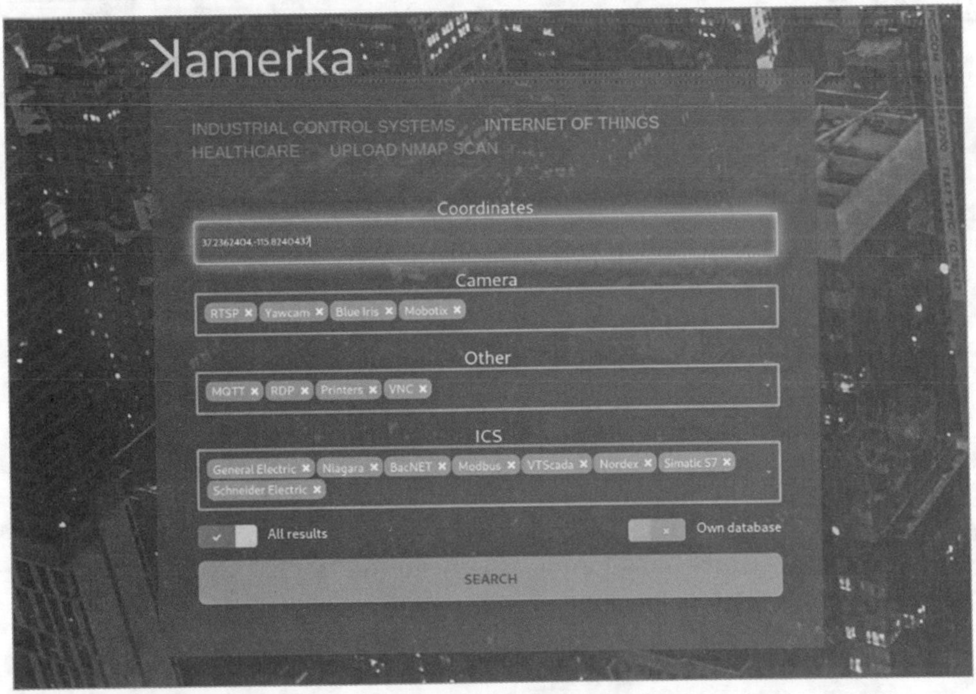

Figure 9.27: Kamerka Full

With the Google Maps API key installed, there is also a maps feature that shows all found systems and devices on a map with details and statistics and also geolocation possibilities (see Figure 9.28).

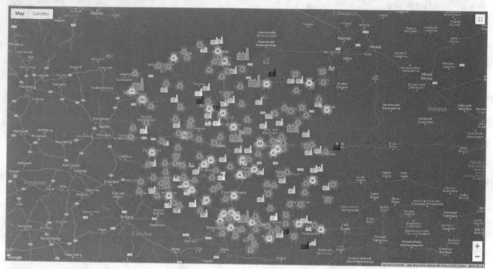

Figure 9.28: Kamerka full

9.3 Wireless

The following is wireless-related information that you can use to analyze critical infrastructure.

Overview of Wireless Networks

A *wireless network* is a computer network that allows devices to remain interconnected to each other and typically to the Internet but remain untethered by any cables. Devices that connect to wireless networks include mobile phones, televisions, laptops, and printers. This is what allows you to pick up your laptop and walk into another room without losing your connection.

A wireless computer network that links two or more devices in a co-located area through one or more access points is called a *wireless local-area network (WLAN)*. One type of WLAN is a wireless technology called *Wi-Fi* that allows nearby devices to communicate through radio waves. Because many of our devices are connected through Wi-Fi at our home, in the office, or at the gym, they are nearly always transmitting a signal to and from a nearby router. Even when not connected to our home, work, or coffee shop Wi-Fi, our devices, by default, will be searching for these wireless networks, broadcasting beacons creating a history of what we have connected to for anyone that can translate the information.

Because the signal travels through the air, our data can be intercepted, or bits of information can be transmitted along with like location data. To use many of the apps and technologies on our mobile phones for checking the weather or getting local deals for the grocery store, we are required to turn on Location Services. Location Services lets the apps on our devices know where we are located based on our GPS coordinates, but that data could also be used to pinpoint the location of a subject or gather information on the places and people they interact with. One way that law enforcement pinpoints the location of a person is through mobile network towers. Wireless networks can be our typical Wi-Fi but also includes mobile/cellular networks, GPS, or any other interconnected devices which transmit data without wires.

Mobile Networks

If you have watched any cop dramas in the last decade, you will no doubt be familiar with the term *mobile phone triangulation* as a means of determining a mobile phone location at the time of a crime. A *mobile network* is a network of mobile phone radio towers distributed over cells of land that are served by at least one base transceiver. The difference between Wi-Fi and a mobile network is that the mobile network uses towers instead of routers. When you hear *mobile phone triangulation*, what that means is by using several mobile towers they can measure the delay of a mobile signal back to each tower to triangulate a phone's position. As civilians, we don't have access to mobile phone data, but we could have access to a mobile phone's cellular IP address or MAC address that could tell us a lot about the location of a phone. IP addresses are sometimes stored when creating accounts and so they can be found within breach data.

How Accurate Is Tracking a Mobile Phone by Cellular IP Address?

In late 2019, Ghislaine Maxwell, the socialite girlfriend of convicted pedophile Jeffrey Epstein, was being sought by the FBI for her involvement in the crimes. Maxwell was reported by news outlets to be hiding out in a family friend's Pennsylvania farmhouse. OSINT analysts on Twitter began feverishly attempting to track her down and were reporting that her location was found through a mobile phone's cellular IP address. There was a heated debate about whether the IP address associated with a mobile phone could be seen as accurate and whether it should be posted as verified information, so I wanted to quickly examine why this may not be an accurate way to pinpoint location.

OSINT analysts Matthias Wilson and Steven Harris wrote a great set of blog posts on the geolocation of mobile phones based on cellular IP addresses[29] that discuss the unreliability of this type of IP addresses in geolocation due to the limitations of the IPv4 protocol. The shortage of Ipv4 addresses means that many websites use the same static IP address, devices use dynamic or changing IP addresses, and on mobile you are most likely connecting to a network that is sharing an IP address with thousands of users at a time while also changing dynamically as often as every few seconds.[30]

Of course, we can always try to geolocate an IP address using a tool like Maxmind,[31] one of the leading IP geolocation companies in the world, but as the writers point out, digging into Maxmind's own Accuracy Reports shows how many IPs are incorrectly resolved to an address.[32] The reason for the inaccuracy is that the ISPs are reallocating IP addresses based on network demand versus geographic area. When a user drives through an area, they may constantly reconnect to new towers and new cells as the signal strength fades, but because the user never actually detaches from the network, they could keep the same IP address the whole drive. If you were to turn off your phone or set it to airplane mode for a set amount of time determined by the provider, detaching your IMSI identification number from the network, a new cellular IP will be issued to your device. While geolocation and triangulation of mobile phones through the mobile network may be best left to law enforcement and intelligence agencies, tracking Wi-Fi signals is a tactic more available to the average person. Attackers can create cheap wardriving Wi-Fi reconnaissance tools for less than $20 to search for unsecured wireless networks and capture information or gain unauthorized access to the network.

War Driving

Wardriving is the act of searching for and mapping Wi-Fi networks in an area, usually collected by an antenna while driving a car. The term comes from the 1983 movie *WarGames* with Matthew Broderick who in the movie performs war dialing, which is dialing many phone numbers at a time to find a working modem. Wardriving is seen as a modern evolution of wardialing.

Wardrivers are trying to discover wireless networks as they drive through an area for the purpose of mapping networks including encryption type. The data can be uploaded to websites or apps that build maps of available Wi-Fi networks within an area. One of these websites is `wigle.net`. Because wardriving is considered active collection, we as OSINT analysts would not be doing

---

[29] https://keyfindings.blog/2020/07/05/ geolocating-mobiles-phones-based-on-ips.

[30] www.cs.yale.edu/homes/mahesh/papers/ephemera-imc09.pdf.

[31] www.maxmind.com.

[32] www.maxmind.com/en/geoip2-city-accuracy-comparison.

it; however, we can access the data once it is uploaded to a public site, which we will talk about shortly. If an attacker were to find your vulnerable network through wardriving, they could gain access, exfiltrate data, or install malware. Wardrivers also record the network details to upload them to publicly accessible platforms for mapping wireless signals.

Wardriving may seem like an intrusive activity used only by criminals; however, in a tale seemingly ripped right from the movies and recently documented in the Netflix series *Web of Make Believe:* Death, Lies, and the Internet, this is proved false. The notorious IRS scammer Daniel Rigmaiden was profiting thousands of dollars off of illegally filing tax returns for dead people for 10 years[33] until being arrested in 2008 and charged with 35 counts of wire fraud, 35 counts of aggravated identity theft, and several other miscellaneous charges. While his crimes themselves are interesting, what is relevant to this book is the way in which he was caught.

Because law enforcement was trying to find Rigmaiden, they used a now controversial tool called a *stingray*. The stingray simulates a cell phone tower and forces a subject's cell phone to connect to it instead of the cellular network. The trouble with this tool is that it doesn't target a specific phone; it will allow all phones in the area to connect, which is a breach of privacy for all of the other people. In 2008, law enforcement agencies were actively using the stingray for cases, but due to Non Disclosure Agreements, the tool was not disclosed.

Rigmaiden and his lawyer built a case with research from his jail cell in Arizona and the library in the facility before passing the information onto the ACLU. Rigmaiden filed a motion to suppress his case on the grounds that his Fourth Amendment rights had been violated, which was ultimately denied. By this point the research had been passed on to the *Wall Street Journal* making the use of this technology publicly known.

We in the OSINT field have to rely on historical collection of network information to try to place networks or devices, while law enforcement can create a real-time map of device active in a target area. As OSINT analysts we cannot participate in wardriving because it is active collection of information; however, we can use the information uploaded to the public map platforms.

So far the wireless networks we have discussed are long-range communications with mobile phones and computer networks. However, these networks can be short range only as well. *Bluetooth* is a common type of wireless radio technology that enables the exchange of data between different devices in close range. Used as an alternative to wired connections, it typically allows connections up to about 10 meters. This type of short-range connection is used with things such as earbuds, mobile phones, printers, and fitness watches, many of which travel with us wherever we go.

---

[33] www.bustle.com/entertainment/
where-daniel-rigmaiden-is-now-web-of-make-believe.

Because Bluetooth integrates with so many of our personal and professional devices that are used as we move around in our day-to-day routines, they can leave a traceable footprint of where we go and how long we are there. If you open the Bluetooth menu on your phone, how many devices show up in range around you? Do any have unique names like "Dave's Fitness Watch" or "Company HP printer" that could indicate what they are? In the same way that your phone picks up the signals around you, wardrivers may drive through an area and pick up those same signals, log them, and upload them to a mapping website. A user can then go to the site, and if they were trying to determine where Dave lived on the street, they could infer his location based on the name of the Bluetooth connection. This is also where fitness trackers fit into the equation. We learned in pattern of life analysis that by using sites like Strava, fitness watches can track a person's location based on the Bluetooth and location-based connection.

Low-Power Wide-Area Networks

A low-power wide-area network (LPWAN) is a wireless network that connects and operates up to 10 kilometers. The main use for LPWANs is in smart communities and industrial settings because they are low powered and run for nearly 20 years. One specific type of LPWAN that is used is called LoRaWAN.

Long Range Radio (LoRa)

LoRa is a wireless protocol that was designed for low-power and long-range communications like M2M and IoT networks to connect several applications on the same network. LoRaWAN is a low-power, wide-area networking protocol that is built on top of the LoRa protocol to manage communications between devices and gateways.

A common use for LoRaWAN is in smart communities and industrial spaces to connect low-powered IoT devices such as water-level sensors to send the information to a central administrator. A device can connect to a network using LoRaWAN through over-the-air-activation, which requires a network and application session key and activation by personalization, which means the device is hard-coded with keys, making it less secure but easier to access.

The value of understanding what LPWAN and LoRaWan networks are is in case you are working on an OSINT analysis into critical infrastructure for a city that runs on LoRaWan for major sensors and detectors around the city that might have vulnerabilities that we can identify in order to prevent the city from losing connectivity to important devices. I have performed analysis where social media imagery from the installer of LoRaWAN devices has shown the technology inside and allowed me to find specific manufacturers of the critical components within the device.

Wireless SSID, BSSID, MAC

Understanding what makes up a wireless signal and the associated identifiers can be useful to OSINT analysts for determining things such as location, identity, owner, and often even inferred information based on the naming conventions of identifiers. Once we know what to look for, we can easily pivot to finding useful data relating to our analysis. The key identifiers for wireless networks are the SSID, BSSID, and MAC address.

Service Set Identifier (SSID)

This is the name of your network that you connect to. If you open your computer and try to connect to the Internet, a list of nearby SSIDs will show up that you can pick from. This is often where people get creative and name their networks "FBI Van." The purpose of the SSID is to properly route the packets to the correct WLAN.

Basic Service Set Identifier (BSSID)

Consider the layout of a typical office; you may be familiar with the wireless access point cones on the ceiling so that the network reaches around the whole building. To route the packets to the correct access point within the WLAN when multiple access points exist, the network uses an identifier called a BSSID. Generally, users are unaware of which BSSID they are connecting to, but when you move your laptop from one room to another, your BSS can change because it is covered by a different access point. If a user has a hidden Wi-Fi network that is not publicly broadcasting their SSID, you may still be able to pick up the BSSID.

Extended Service Set Identifier (ESSID)

This is a 6-byte electronic marker that identifies a set of BBSIDs that have the same SSID.

Media Access Control (MAC) Address

A MAC address is a 12-digit (6 bytes or 48 bits) hexadecimal unique identifier for each device that connects to a network. In OSINT we can use the prefix, or first seven digits, of the MAC address to determine the manufacturer. Each manufacturer registers MAC prefixes from the IEEE and often maintains an online list that can be found through a search engine query of "manufacturer name" and "MAC prefix" showing each prefix they use. If you don't know the specific manufacturer, you can use a site like `maclookup.app/macaddress`.

For example, if we look at the following MAC address, we can see the prefix is ffc22c, and on the right would be the identification number for the specific device (see Figure 9.29):

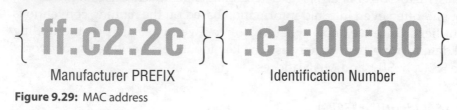

ff:c2:2c
:c1:00:00
Manufacturer PREFIX
Identification Number

Figure 9.29: MAC address

By using `maclookup.app` or any similar MAC search tools, we can see that the prefix belongs to Apple, Inc., and it provides the range for the addresses. This information can be useful for determining what kind of device an entity or subject is using and what vulnerabilities may exist for them (see Figures 9.30-9.31).

Apple, Inc.
Vendor
Details
OUI: F8:FF:C2
Vendor name: Apple, Inc.
Address:
1 Infinite Loop
Cupertino CA 95014
US.
Assignment Type MA-L
Mac Address Block Large (previously named OUI). Number of address 2^24 (~16 Million)
Initial registration: 10 September 2019

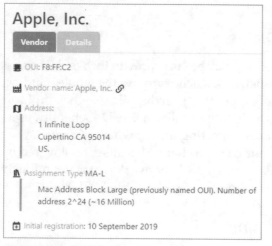

Figure 9.30: MAC lookup

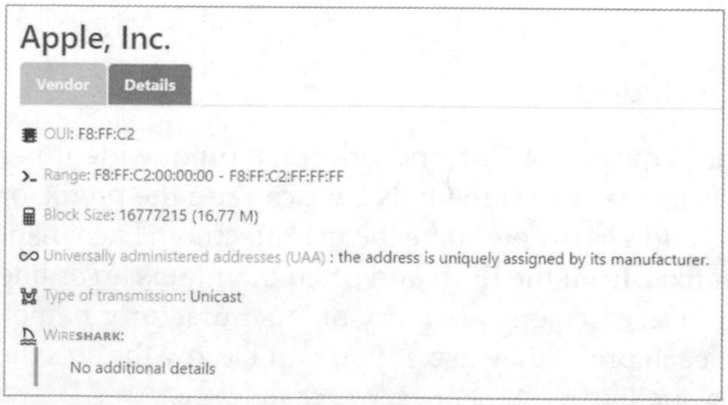

Apple, Inc.
Vendor
Details
OUI: F8:FF:C2
Range: F8:FF:C2:00:00:00 - F8:FF:C2:FF:FF:FF
Block Size: 16777215 (16.77 M)
Universally administered addresses (UAA) : the address is uniquely assigned by its manufacturer.
Type of transmission: Unicast
WIRESHARK:
No additional details

Figure 9.31: MAC lookup

Understanding the main components and identifiers for wireless communications is a great starting point for any analysis into wireless. This is also a good time for an OPSEC reminder about your own information being available through your wireless connection. Be sure to turn off location services, and use a VPN and a VM when possible, to avoid being tied to a wireless connection.

9.4   Methods for Analyzing Wireless Networks

We should utilize the Planning and Requirements phase along with feedback from any previous analysis to determine the focus of our analysis. We also want to determine whether we will have legal access to third-party ingested network data. Depending on the stakeholder questions and requirements, the direction of the analysis is likely to include one or more of the following avenues (see Figure 9.32).

Information Gathering Techniques

Here are some pivots for wireless network information gathering

- Finding an identifier that leads to a subject
- Finding an identifier that leads to an organization
- Finding an identifier that infers use (ex. Printer1)
- Uncovering an identifier that leads to a device vulnerability
- Plotting connections over time to determine pattern of life

By implementing the funneling approach we used for critical infrastructure, we can narrow the focus of our requirements and questions alongside the stakeholder. For this example of funneling, let's use 'Finding an identifier that leads to an organization."

For the use case, baselining for this question might involve doing historical research on the types of technology used within the organization to develop a starting point. From there we then ask open-ended questions to establish a wide scope before narrowing the focus further. Eventually we layer in questions to fill in the gaps, and we are able to systematically plan our approach (see Figure 9.33).

Q: Can we identify a wireless network that is part of a specific organizations network?

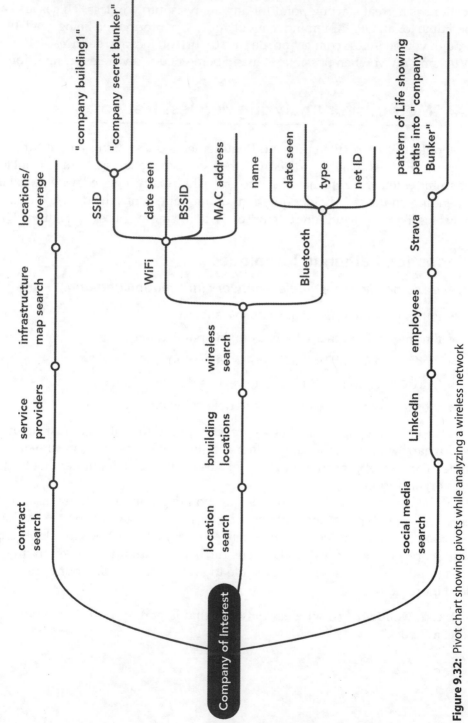

Figure 9.32: Pivot chart showing pivots while analyzing a wireless network

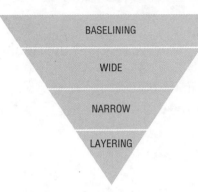

Figure 9.33: Funnel technique

Baselining

For baselining wireless networks, we must identify what the network has looked like over time so we can distinguish patterns or variations. One example for why baselining can be useful is if we are analyzing the wireless providers in a certain location that have been the same for the last 15 years and suddenly one changes.

I would want to know about the new company and the history with the old company. I would also want to know if something happened that made them switch providers, perhaps a lawsuit or a contract ending. Focusing on our question "Can we identify a wireless network that is part of an organizations network?" some examples of questions we may be trying to answer with baselining could be as follows:

- Does the organization have any history with wireless companies?

- Do any contracts exist between the organization and wireless companies?

- Does the organization have any history with manufacturers of wireless devices (such as HP or Xerox printers).

A resource that I have found to be great for baselining is Open Signal,[34] an independent reporting company that develops market insight reports for world communications and networks. The website lets you pick a region and gather insights and information based on location and market.

Starting Wide

- Can we find any wireless signals in the area of the organization?

- Can we find any Bluetooth signals nearby?

- Is there a location the employees frequent (restaurant, bar, coffee shop)?

---

[34] www.opensignal.com.

Narrowing Focus

- Can we find any wireless SSIDs that indicate a connection to the organization?
- Can we find any technology mentioned in the SSIDs?
- Can we find any wireless signals that can be tied to employees?
- What is the MAC address of the device?

Layering

- Do any of the technologies listed have known vulnerabilities?
- What is the MCC, MNC, CID, and radio type?
- What vendor is the MAC address tied to?

Wi-Fi Searching Techniques

Many of the tools and techniques related to wireless analysis utilize diagrams and maps to show where towers are located or where signals have been noted. I am going to dive into a few tools as an example of the types of data that can be found and what we as analysts can do with it.

WiGLE

WiGLE is a well-known wireless network search engine and visualization tool used for analyzing Wi-Fi, Bluetooth, and cell data. WiGLE has both basic and advanced search options that allow you to search by the following:

- Address
- GPS coordinates
- SSID
- BSSID
- Time
- Cell Operator, LAC, or network
- Base station
- Network name
- MAC address

A typical search in WiGLE looks like a map with SSIDs showing the location where a wardriver has recorded the signal and uploaded it to WiGLE. When using this tool, it is important to understand the limitations in accuracy and location of data. WiGLE data is entirely dependent on wardrivers to upload the data they collect, and this means that the information we see may not be the most up-to-date. An area may show no SSIDs at all, but this doesn't mean none exist. It may just mean that the area was never scanned and uploaded.

Additionally, do not take the location of the SSID as verifiable proof the device was seen in that precise location on the map. Wireless signals can travel far, especially in areas without a lot of buildings to bounce off of. If you trust the location of the SSID as fact, it could lead to inaccuracies in your analysis. Instead, use WiGLE and tools like it as a guide to develop pivot points for further analysis (see Figure 9.34).

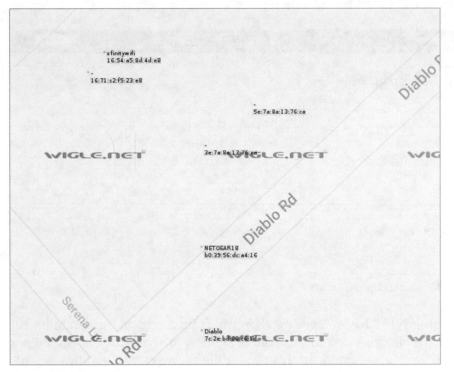

Figure 9.34: WiGLE

WiGLE not only shows the SSIDs but also the MAC addresses of the devices based on region or specific search criteria. I recommend creating an account so that you can access the advanced search options. Here you can see what a search query result looks like (see Figure 9.35). We get quite a bit of information we can pull from for further analysis. One thing we can do is take the MAC address out to additional tools such as macaddress.io to dig into them deeper.

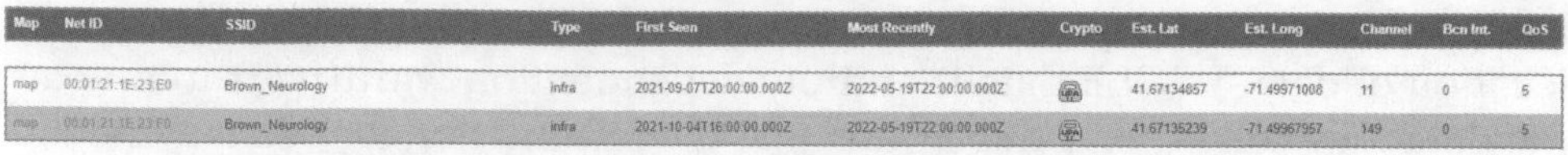

Map	Net ID	SSID	Type	First Seen	Most Recently	Crypto	Est. Lat	Est. Long	Channel	Bcns Int.	QoS
map	00:01:21:1E:23:E0	Brown_Neurology	infra	2021-05-07T20:00:00.000Z	2022-05-19T22:00:00.000Z	🔒	41.67134057	-71.49971008	11	0	5
map	00:01:21:1E:23:E0	Brown_Neurology	infra	2021-10-04T16:00:00.000Z	2022-05-19T22:00:00.000Z	🔒	41.67136239	-71.49967957	149	0	5

Figure 9.35: WiGLE screenshot of a search query result

In this screenshot, you can see how those two images should go together.

Looking at the previous MAC address in `macaddress.io`, we get information about the vendor being WatchGuard Tech Inc., and the address details show that it is a virtual server. If I was running an OSINT assessment on this organization for publicly available information that could possibly be used against them, I would take this information over to the NIST Vulnerability Database to search for known vulnerabilities (see Figure 9.36).

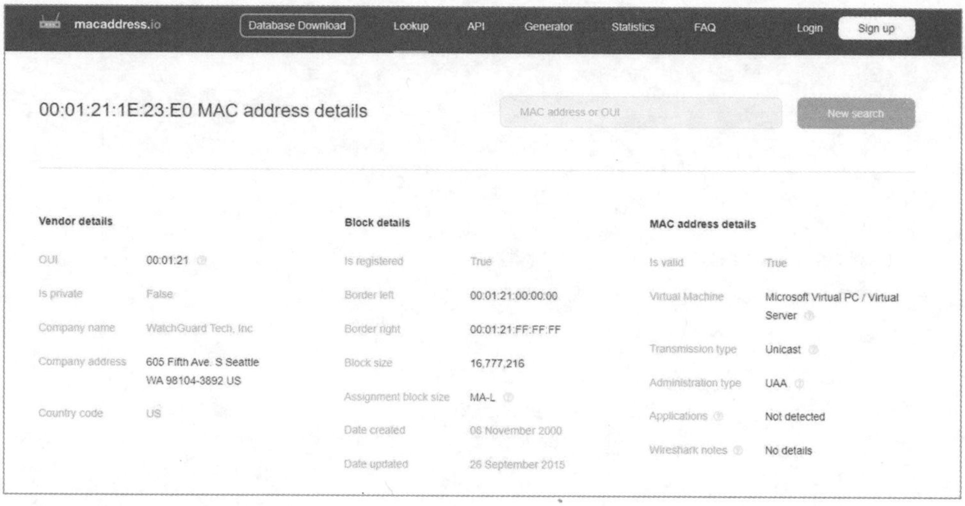

Figure 9.36: `macaddress.io`

Searching NIST for *Watchguard Tech* brings up a critical vulnerability on Watchguard Firebox that allows a remote attacker to access the system. With a bit more digging, we could surely uncover the exact systems that this organization is using through contracts or public disclosures (see Figure 9.37).

Another method we can use with WiGLE is narrowing down information until we make useful connections. For example:

- Our subject of interest is a businesswoman at Company X.
- By using WiGLE, we collect all wireless signals from the area around Company X during the timeframe of her employment.
- The businesswoman posts on social media that she was at a conference in Dallas, Texas, on November 1, 2022.

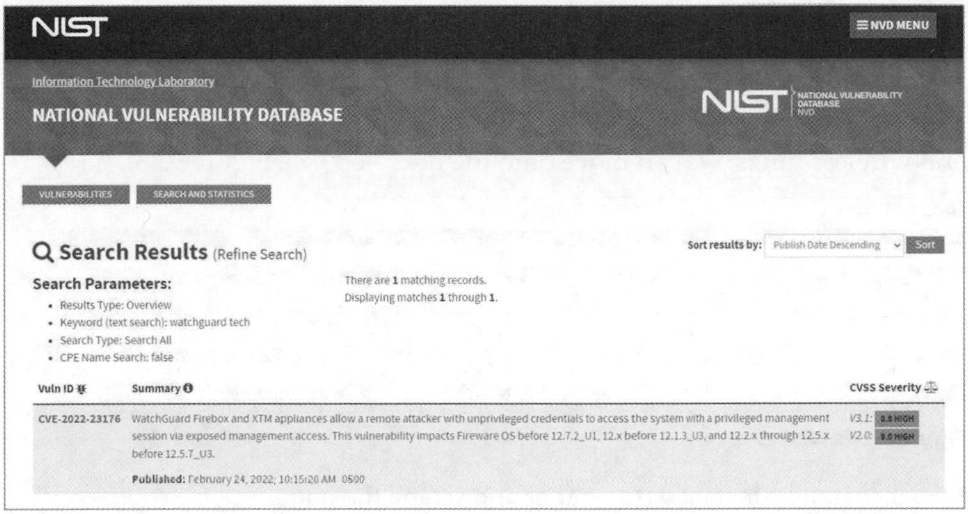

Figure 9.37: NIST database

- We can now look at WiGLE in the area of the hotel and the conference on November 1, 2022.

- Looking at SSIDs that only show up at only two or more of those locations can help us to:

  - Develop a more specific profile on our subject.
  - Gather information such as a MAC address that can be used by law enforcement.
  - Develop a more detailed pattern of life analysis for the subject.

If I am trying to establish a pattern of life for a device, and by proxy a human who is using/carrying the device, I need a way to extract the WiGLE data for a specific entry and track it over time. Luckily, this job is fairly easy using Google Earth Pro and an exported CSV from WiGLE.

Plotting Wireless Locations with Google Earth Pro

Tracking the pattern of life for devices can be a great way to identify clustering patterns of activity that may reveal key locations (work, home, gym) for an individual. Looking at more than one device can help us to visualize convergence of activity between the individuals such as going to the same office or living in the same home. With the variance of locations based on Wi-Fi signal in mind, we can track pattern of life using Google Earth Pro and WiGLE.

Step 1: Download Google Earth Pro.[35]

Step 2: Make a WiGLE account and find data.

Once you make an account and have a specific device or devices showing several wireless pings, we can move onto the next step (see Figure 9.38).

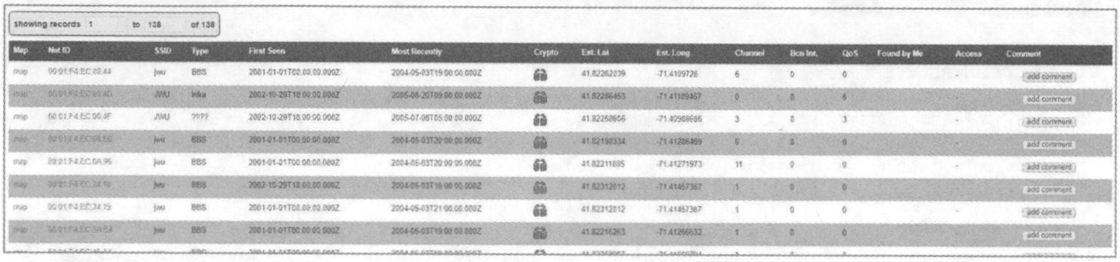

Figure 9.38: Wireless pings

Step 3: Install an instant data scraper and scrape the page.

Once installed, click the Instant Data Scraper plug-in[36] and scrape the contents of the page. For this example, I then deselected all of the columns that weren't important to me and left the Latitude and Longitude. Save it as a CSV file (see Figure 9.39).

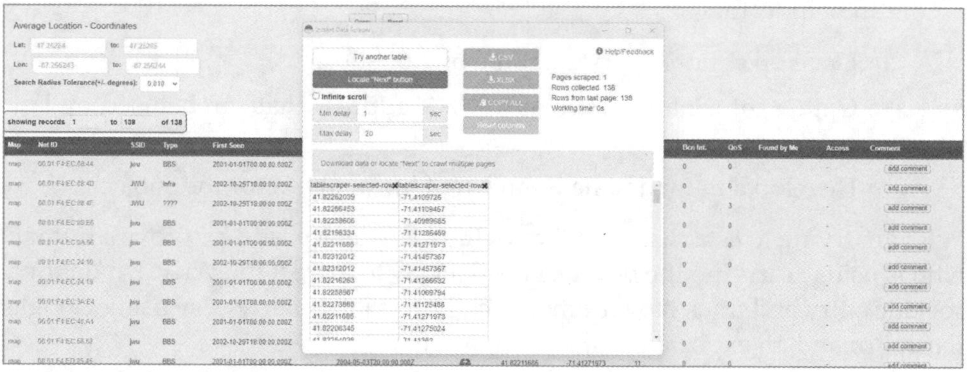

Figure 9.39: Using Instant Data Scraper

Step 4: Follow the importing steps from page 13 for Google Earth plotting.

Step 5: Analyze your plotted map.

Once the device pings have been plotted on the map, we can use visual clustering to attempt to figure out where this device spends time. From here we

---

[35] www.google.com/earth/about/versions/#earth-pro.
[36] https://chrome.google.com/webstore/detail/instant-data-scraper/ofaokhiedipichpaobibbnahnkdoiiah?hl=en-US.

can pivot to analyzing the places on the map or even attempt to uncover who owns the device (see Figure 9.40).

Figure 9.40: Plotted wireless pings

While WiGLE is certainly not the only Wi-Fi search tool out there, now that you see what is possible and the pivots that can be made with the data, you can better use the other tools.

Tower Searching Techniques

There are times when you might need to know where mobile towers are located and information about each one. This method would be useful when performing an analysis of critical infrastructure in a specific region, for instance, determining if a city maintains communications in an emergency if an entire provider was taken offline. Using OSINT, we can assess towers and infrastructure based on contracts, public disclosures, and identification tools.

Sites like OpenCellID.org, the world's largest open database of cell towers, and Cellmapper.net[37] have global cell tower information that can give insights to the technology and identifying information of each tower (see Figures 9.41-9.42).

---

[37] CellMapper / www.cellmapper.net//last accessed February 15, 2023.

Figure 9.41: OpenCellID

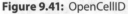

Figure 9.42: Cellmapper

Below is a reference for possible pivots through wireless and cell data sources based on an area of interest (see Figure 9.43).

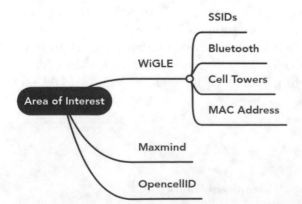

Figure 9.43: Pivot chart focused on wireless and cellular activity stemming from an area of interest

Financial Intelligence

10.1   Overview

Financial intelligence (FININT) is the collection, monitoring, and reporting on the finances of entities to understand their current actions and predict future actions. The typical functions of FININT are to identify crimes such as money laundering, tax evasion, and financing criminal or terrorist organizations. The analysis of data can include looking through large amounts of transaction data and identifying people and entities involved with specific activity. Of course, as OSINT analysts, we many times do not have access to bank transaction histories and must rely on open sources to follow the money. Some examples of things we would be looking for from an OSINT perspective with financial intelligence are as follows:

- Tying people to specific accounts
- Noting large/strange purchases
- Identifying high-risk behavior
- Discovering patterns of activity that indicate safe havens
- Detecting individuals committing card fraud, drug trafficking, or money laundering
- Determining terror cell relationships from their crypto transactions

Financial Organizations

There are several financial intelligence organizations worth knowing.

Financial Intelligence Units

Financial Intelligence Units (FIUs) are investigative units within each country for the collection and analysis of raw transaction reports and suspicious activity reports (SARs) provided by banks of money laundering, terrorist financing, and criminal activity. FIUs are also responsible for disseminating the results of their analysis sometimes with other countries through intergovernmental networks.

Financial Crimes Enforcement Network

A Financial Crimes Enforcement Network (FinCEN) is a government bureau that is administered by the U.S. Department of Treasury and operates both domestically and internationally to protect the financial system from illegal activity, combat money laundering, and enhance national security through disseminating intelligence throughout the network. Additionally, they write the anti-money laundering rules for more than 100,000 financial institutions. If a SAR has been filed, FinCEN is prohibited from disclosing any person involved in the transaction per their documentation.[1]

The Financial Action Task Force

The Financial Action Task Force (FATF) is an international and intergovernmental watchdog organization for global money laundering and terrorist financing. The organization developed the FATF Standards for a coordinated global response to help authorities fight human trafficking, illegal drugs, terrorism, and other money-driven crimes. FATF provides several publications that are useful for analysts including the FATF Standards,[2] recommendations, and reports on specific locations and situations (for example, "Money Laundering from Fentanyl and Synthetic Opioids"[3]).

---

[1] www.fincen.gov/disclosure-prohibited#:~:text=The%20disclosure%20 prohibition%20includes%20providing,notify%20FinCEN%20of%20the%20 request.

[2] www.fatf-gafi.org/publications/fatfrecommendations/documents/ fatf-recommendations.html.

[3] www.fatf-gafi.org/publications/methodsandtrends/documents/ money-laundering-fentanyl-synthetic-opioids.html.

The Federal Deposit Insurance Corporation

The Federal Deposit Insurance Corporation (FDIC)[4] is an agency created by Congress that insures financial deposits in the case of bank failure and oversees the banking industry to protect consumers. An FDIC Certificate ID is a unique number assigned by each institution to each depository by the FDIC. The FDIC website hosts an "Analysis" section full of financial research that we can use to gain a better understanding of the financial industry. The site also offers a suite of data tools and searchable databases of U.S. bank information that is great to use as an authoritative source including institution financial reports, deposit market share reports, and the Bank Find Suite.[5]

The Bank Find Suite[6] offers the following ways to search FDIC data records (see Figure 10.1):

- Institutions by name and location
  - Find the FDIC Certificate ID
- Historical bank data since 1934
- Bank failure and assistance data
- Financial reports
- Peer group comparisons
- A summary of branch deposits

International Monetary Fund

The International Monetary Fund (IMF) includes 189 member countries, and its purpose is to support economic policies to promote financial stability for its members. The IMF focuses on identifying risk to its member counties including money laundering and other financial crimes. IMF produces useful reports like the World Economic Outlook Report[7] as well as publications and working papers on various regional-specific financial issues.

Federal Financial Institutions Examination Council

The Federal Financial Institutions Examination Council (FFIEC) produces the BSA/AML Examination Manual and Procedures that is located on their FFIEC InfoBase and is considered the anti-money launderer's bible[8] because it shows

---

[4] `www.fdic.gov`.
[5] `www.fdic.gov/resources/data-tools`.
[6] Federal Deposit Insurance Corporation (FDIC) / https://banks.data.fdic.gov/bankfind-suite/ /last accessed Feb 16, 2022.
[7] `www.imf.org/en/publications/weo`.
[8] `https://bsaaml.ffiec.gov`.

what regulators look for compliance-wise from financial institutions in addition to the red flags to look for in banking practices. While many of us do not have access to a financial institution's records, we can use this document to help target our analysis and identify similar red flags in our subjects and entities.

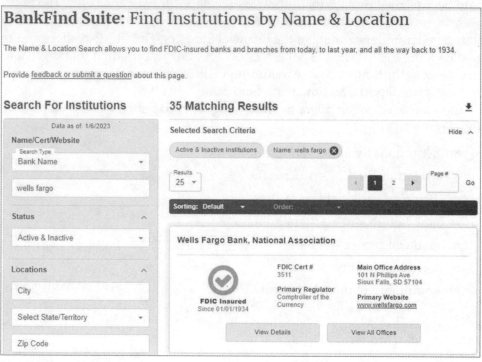

Figure 10.1: Bankfind

The Office of Foreign Assets Control

The Office of Foreign Assets Control (OFAC) is an enforcement agency arm of the U.S. Department of the Treasury. We talked extensively about OFAC across several chapters in the book, including Chapter 7, "Business and Organizational Intelligence," and OFAC is the financial resource that I use the most in my everyday work routine.

For this chapter, I will focus on it as a resource for revealing and understanding financial crimes. OFAC provides analysts with reporting and information on organized crime as well as a search for any information that may be included in sanctions (crypto wallet, names, addresses, organizations, vehicle identification, etc.). Because of the strong connection between organized crime and financial crime, we must explore how and why criminal organizations use financial crime.

10.2   Financial Crime and Organized Crime, Together Forever <3

The oldest known organized crime group is considered to be the Japanese Yakuza who have been operational since roughly 1612 (that's more than 300 years!). Their humble beginnings included members selling poorly made products at markets to turn a profit; in the 1900s they grew to 184,000 members who controlled businesses and engaged in loan sharking, drug trafficking, smuggling, and political corruption.[9]

If the path of the Yakuza sounds familiar, it's because the U.S. La Cosa Nostra followed a similar route. The Italian American crime families took advantage of labor wars and national alcohol prohibition from 1919 to 1933 to seize control of labor unions where they rigged bids and fixed profits. For decades the La Cosa Nostra was able to run illegal gambling rings, loan sharking, and drug trafficking and sway political opinion without a second glance from the FBI.[10] It has been written that by 1925, criminal "Lucky" Luciano was making $4 million personal profit each year through[11] bootlegging and illegal gambling, which amounts to roughly $68,000,000 in 2023. The majority of organized crime is in the form of a financial crime because the objective of the organizations is ultimately power and profit.

According to the United Nations Office on Drugs and Crime (UNODOC),[12] the most prominent forms of organized crime are:

- Money laundering
- Asset misappropriation
- Counterfeiting and contraband
- Fraud and extortion
- Human trafficking
- Cybercrime

All of the forms of crime listed here have one thing in common: using a criminal activity for financial gain. Organized crime can be focused on a specific region, or they can position their groups across borders in several different nations where they become known as *transnational criminal organizations*.

---

[9] www.ojp.gov/ncjrs/virtual-library/abstracts/
yakuza-past-and-present.
[10] www.journals.uchicago.edu/doi/10.1086/706895.
[11] Brian Robb (2014). *A Brief History of Gangsters*. Robinson. ISBN 978-1472110688.
[12] www.unodc.org/e4j/en/organized-crime/module-4/key-issues/
intro.html.

Transnational Criminal Organizations

Transnational criminal organizations (TCOs) are organizations committing crime that is coordinated and perpetrated across national borders and involving people from several countries to facilitate illegal business using violence and corruption.[13] An example of a TCO is the Mara Salvatrucha (MS-13) gang that can be found in Canada, El Salvador, Mexico, and the United States. Formed by Salvadorian immigrants, some of its members had been trained in guerilla warfare, and they are known for their use of fear and violence for intimidation. The transnational crimes they are associated with include weapons smuggling, drug trafficking, human trafficking, and stolen vehicle trafficking[14] across national borders. When researching TCOs, we can use OFAC as a great starting point because they provide detailed reporting on TCOs[15] including press charts showing the organization layout and key players.[16] The following is an example of a press chart for the Kinahan Organized Crime Group (KOCG) or the Kinahan Cartel, a TCO operating out of Ireland, Spain, and the UAE and involved in trafficking drugs and firearms as well as laundering money using Dubai as a facilitation hub (see Figure 10.2).[17]

Interestingly, the Kinahans fell victim to a social media gaffe in 2020 leading to OFAC sanctions of the seven key Kinahan members after heavyweight champion Tyson Fury mentioned Daniel Kinahan three times on a viral video clip.[18]

"I'm just after getting off the phone with Daniel Kinahan. He just informed me that the biggest fight in British boxing history has just been agreed. A big shoutout to Dan, he got this done, literally over the line. The two-fight deal, Tyson Fury versus Anthony Joshua, next year," Fury, one of the world's most famous boxers, says in the June 2020 video clip. "So a big thank you Dan for getting this deal over the line. All the best, God bless you all, and see you soon, peace out."

While the Kinahan's connection to boxing may have put the crosshairs on the organization, they had already been on the radar of national law organizations like Interpol. The International Police Organization (INTERPOL) has a searchable database of their "Red Notices" which are formal requests to law

---

[13] www.dni.gov/files/documents/NIC_toc_foldout.pdf.
[14] www.ojp.gov/ncjrs/virtual-library/abstracts/ms-13-gang-profile.
[15] https://home.treasury.gov/policy-issues/financial-sanctions/ sanctions-programs-and-country-information/ transnational-criminal-organizations.
[16] https://home.treasury.gov/system/files/126/20220411_ kinahan_tco.pdf.
[17] https://home.treasury.gov/news/press-releases/jy0713.
[18] U.S. Department of the Treasury / www.vice.com/en/article/93bxaz/kinahan-cartel/ last accessed 15 February 2023.

enforcement agencies worldwide to find and arrest a person (see Figure 10.3). While Red Notices note wanted individuals, they are not warrants, and so a member country may apply their own laws around the arrests. Red Notices provide key details about the individual such as photograph, date of birth, nationality, and charges.

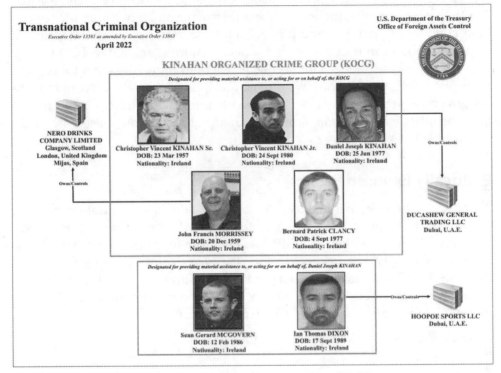

Figure 10.2: Press chart for the Kinahan Organized Crime Group (KOCG)

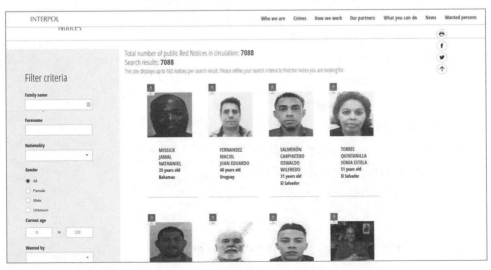

Figure 10.3: Red Notice database

As organized crime groups, TCOs use violence, illegal sales, and corruption for profit, making them a danger not just to the nations they work from but to the world.

As an OSINT analyst, especially with a focus on financial crime, you may notice that some of your work will cross paths with TCOs because of their wide influence on entire regions of the world. Being able to effectively research TCOs, their sphere of influence, and how they make and move their money can help you identify patterns and pivots from your data. Knowing the tactics of a specific group can lead you from financial patterns back to the TCO to help prevent trafficking, money laundering, illegal migration, illegal gambling, and corruption. Illegal operations will often target individuals who hold an influential government position or a person who has influence within a community to look the other way to certain crimes. In financial regulation, these potentially corruptible individuals are called *politically exposed persons*.

Politically Exposed Person

A politically exposed person (PEP) is someone who is susceptible to bribery, corruption, or illegal activity based on their important position or community influence.[19] Being classified as a PEP does not mean they have committed illegal acts but rather they are working in roles related to government, legislation, executive, judiciary, diplomatic, military, financial institutions, and the immediate family members or business partners of those who may be influenced. People in the following roles can become an exposed person:

- People who work in government roles
  - Diplomats
  - Parliament
  - Head of state
  - Presidential team
- Judiciary roles
  - Supreme court
  - Constitutional court
  - Judicial bodies
- State-owned enterprises (SOEs)
  - Board members (past and present)
  - C-suite level employees

---

[19] www.fatf-gafi.org/documents/documents/peps-r12-r22.html.

- High-level job positions
  - ○ Central finance employees
  - ○ High-ranking officers in the armed forces
  - ○ International sports committees
- Close associates and relatives of a PEP
  - ○ Parents
  - ○ Children
  - ○ Immediate, second-, and third-tier family members
  - ○ Business partners
  - ○ Sole beneficiaries
  - ○ Joint ownership members

The OCCRP investigation into a Mexican prosecutor leading an investigation into Romanian gangs by Attila Biro, Lilia Saúl Rodriguez, and Jonny Wrate outlines a great example of the usefulness of a PEP to organized crime.[20] A former member of the Riviera Maya gang was stabbed by other members of the gang, and the Mexican state prosecutor Jonathan Medina Nava refused to look at them as possible suspects. In 2021, Medina Nava's bank account was frozen by Mexican financial investigators after they noted several transactions linked to the gang. A former associate of gang leader Forian Tudor told reporters that Medina Nava had received gifts of $5,000 to 6,000 USD a month. While Medina Nava's connections to Tudor and Riviera Maya have not been proven in court, nor has he been charged with a crime, the case stands as an example of how a person in power can be corrupted. The corruption of PEPs can take many forms including gifts, protection, and nepotism, and while it doesn't always begin with organized crime, it can lead to things like money laundering, embezzlement, and fraud that can be tracked and traced through financial intelligence.

Anti-Money Laundering

Anti-money laundering (AML) is the fight against money laundering, a financial crime that involves moving criminally earned illicit proceeds and hiding its source so that it appears to be legitimate. AML involves the investigation, analysis, and monitoring of financial institutions, PEPs, and entities for suspicious or illegal activity that may indicate money laundering. To understand anti-money laundering, we must first understand the process of laundering money.

---

[20] www.occrp.org/en/how-a-crew-of-romanian-criminals-conquered-the-world-of-atm-skimming/mexican-prosecutor-who-led-investigations-into-violent-crimes-of-romanian-gang-is-accused-of-being-on-their-payroll.

In the AMC show *Breaking Bad*, the main character Walter White, a high school chemistry teacher, makes roughly $80 million[21] in a scheme to sell methamphetamine (initially) to pay for his cancer treatments. As White brings in increasingly larger amounts of money, it is suggested that to make it more believable that a failed chemistry teacher would have large sums of cash, he hides the source of the money through a front company. Essentially, Walter and his wife, Skylar, purchase a car wash to "launder" the illicit funds through a legal car wash business and turn it into "clean" profits.

For money laundering to work, it generally involves a three-step process of placement, layering, and integration.

1. **Placement: Walter buys a car wash.**
   This is where illegal or "dirty" funds are introduced into the financial system to be "washed" by disguising where it came from. Examples include the following:

   - Paying debt with illegal funds

   - Smurfing or depositing small amounts to avoid the reporting threshold

   - Buying foreign currency with illegal funds

2. **Layering: Skylar "cooks" the books to hide the inflow of money.**
   To make the laundering activity harder to notice, the activities are obscured through strategic movement of money to add layers of legitimacy. Layering could include the following:

   - Investing in legitimate businesses

   - Moving funds between financial institutions

   - Selling high-value goods

3. **Integration: The Whites launder through their car wash profits.**
   Now the dirty money is integrated back into the economy as legal tender from legitimate sources. Once legitimized, the money is returned to the criminal through what appears to be a legitimate transaction.

For their crime, the White's use the structuring method, which involves breaking up transactions into smaller amounts and entering them into the carwash books to legitimize them. Skylar, with her background in accounting, broke the transactions up and then entered them into the car wash financials to make them appear like normal customer payments.

In an attempt to prevent this type of criminal activity, governments including financial institutions, public entities such as police departments, and intelligence

---

[21] https://money.cnn.com/2013/09/27/news/economy/breaking-bad-profit/index.html#:~:text=Walter%20White%20may%20be%20fictional,has%20accumulated%20by%20cooking%20crank.

have developed regulations, compliance mandates, and processes to find and report money laundering. A specific due diligence process used in financial monitoring called *know your customer (KYC)* is key in determining customer risk.

KYC is a process used by financial companies to check and verify the identity of a customer and the risk associated to doing business with them. Ultimately, by verifying the identity of a customer and the intentions behind the accounts they hold, they can prevent money laundering, fraud, and terrorist financing and continue to monitor the accounts over time for suspicious activity. To comply with AML laws, institutions must verify a customer's identity through ID cards, biometrics, facial recognition, and/or documents. In the United States, we have also established the Bank Secrecy Act (BSA) of 1970, which is enforced by the financial crimes enforcement network (FINCEN), followed soon after by the formation of the Financial Action Task Force (FATF) to develop and maintain international regulations and standards to prevent money laundering and other criminal activity such as terrorist financing.

Because money laundering is linked so heavily with the financing of terrorism, if we can spot the patterns and signs of these situations through open source analysis, we can potentially assist with the counter financing of terrorism.

The Counter Financing of Terrorism

The *counter financing of terrorism (CFT)*, also known as *countering the financing of terrorism*, focuses on preventing or restricting the movement of money to terrorist organizations through government regulations, laws, and other means. Analysts working in CFT uncover the source and destination of funds that support terrorist activity to try to prevent the activities from occurring. The analysis focuses on financial entities, organizations, and businesses, and they regulate, monitor, and disseminate reporting. CFT is spearheaded by the FATF for sharing and creating policies to prevent the concealment of laundering and other illegal financing techniques. Funds for terrorism often come from legitimate sources like religious organizations or businesses as well as illegal sources like corruption and trafficking, which are also the basis for funds laundered before being used for terrorism funding. The U.S. Treasury Department puts out a report called the National Terrorist Financing Risk Assessment (NTFRA)[22] that identifies the terrorism financing threats, risks, and vulnerabilities to the United States. While this document is U.S. focused, many of the concepts and reporting can be applied to other first-world countries.

Racha Farhat, a dual Lebanese and U.S. citizen, pled guilty in 2021 for participating in a decade-long money laundering conspiracy to ship electronic equipment to a television station owned by Hizballah in Lebanon. According to the U.S. Department of Justice, Farhat received money from a co-conspirator

---

[22] 2022-National-Terrorist-Financing-Risk-Assessment.pdf.

located in Lebanon that she used to purchase equipment in the United States to ship the items overseas. The co-conspirator provided $175,000 of goods to the Hizballah-owned television station. Farhat received the money through wire transfers, which were sent to third-party bank accounts controlled by Farhat, and she actively participated in concealing the origins of the money.[23]

While much of traditional financial crime analysis involves examining bank records and transactions, which is not necessarily something that an OSINT analyst has access to, the value that open-source intelligence can provide is from looking at the problems from the perspective of the adversary and the access to open-source data often outside of the government purview due to time or access roadblocks. Additionally, locating financial transactions and connecting payments and accounts to people and organizations can help enrich other analysis by providing additional context and avenues for analysis once you pass the reporting on. There are times when we will not have access to the same information that our governments may have, so by providing the added context, we may enrich their ongoing analysis.

Many OSINT financial cases begin with a key piece of information outside of the financial realm that allows us to pivot into it. For example, I have worked on cases where the initial piece of data is nothing more than a username that has been implicated in illegal activity. With the username I was able to tie together their other social media, link the username to a person, and note windfall purchases that the subject posted on social media. This is the same for CF cases where we are attempting to tie financial transactions to a subject of interest; often we begin with a name or a purchase, and using OSINT techniques for financials, cryptocurrency, businesses, and subjects we can reveal the following:

- People and organizations involved
- PEPs tangentially involved
- Financial transactions
- Cryptocurrency wallets
- Notable windfalls (new car, new house, jewelry)
- Potential money laundering schemes
- Trade-based money laundering schemes
- Tax evasion and fraud
- Embezzlement

---

[23] www.justice.gov/usao-edva/pr/
dual-lebanese-us-citizen-pleads-guilty-money-laundering-and-tax-offenses.

Tax Evasion, Tax Fraud, and Embezzlement

Tax evasion is where a person or entity uses tactics like deceit or concealment to avoid paying taxes or to greatly reduce their taxes. One of the largest cases of tax evasion in the United States is telecommunications entrepreneur Walter Anderson who was indicted in 2005 for evading $200 million in federal and local taxes using offshore corporations and accounts to conceal income from collectors. In September 2008, Anderson pled guilty to two counts of tax evasion and one count of fraud while admitting to hiding hundreds of millions of dollars from the IRS between 1998 and 1999. In addition to these crimes, Anderson was linked to at least seven other aliases with forged identification and manuals on how to create fake IDs and hide from the government.[24] While Anderson certainly committed *tax evasion*, the act of knowingly submitting false information through methods like overstating expenses, not reporting income, or not filing taxes at all is tax fraud.

A bigger example of tax fraud in recent months is the collapse of FTX. In late 2022, the cryptocurrency exchange FTX collapsed, and its founder and former CEO Sam Bankman-Fried was extradited from the Bahamas as FTX filed for bankruptcy. In November, FTX sought a bailout from Binance to fix a liquidity crisis. After performing due diligence, Binance walked away from the acquisition deal. Bankman-Fried was then replaced by a court-appointed CEO who then filed for bankruptcy causing investors to lose billions of dollars that will not be entirely recoupable. On November 12, FTX reported an alleged hack of up to $477 million before Bankman-Fried was arrested in the Bahamas and jailed on charges of fraud. In a court hearing on December 22, 2022, a federal judge released him on $250 million, the largest bond in history. On January 3, Bankman-Fried pleaded not guilty to all criminal charges, and he currently awaits trial.[25] The appointed CEO John Ray told the U.S. House Committee that FTX practiced "no bookkeeping" and "it was old-fashioned embezzlement."[26]

Embezzlement is where funds are intentionally misused and misappropriated by someone trusted to manage them. An example of embezzlement is a *Ponzi scheme*, which is an investment fraud where the funds from new investors pay the current investors with promises of low risks and high rewards. One of the most famous Ponzi schemes was the Bernie Madoff scandal where he defrauded thousands of investors guaranteeing 50 percent returns but depositing their money in his personal bank account. Another lesser known example of embezzlement is when comedian Dane Cook's half-brother Darryl McCauley

---

[24] www.nytimes.com/2006/09/09/business/09evade.html.

[25] www.wsj.com/articles/
ftx-and-sam-bankman-fried-your-guide-to-the-crypto-crash-
11669375609.

[26] www.nytimes.com/2022/12/14/business/dealbook/
ftx-sbf-charges-extradition.html.

stole $12 million while managing Cook's business. McCauley was sentenced to 6 years in prison and 16 years of probation for transferring millions from Cook's business accounts to his personal accounts through wire transfers and checks.[27] Again, as OSINT analysts we would usually not have access to financial records, but by using open-source intelligence sources, we may have been able to recognize windfalls posted in McCauley's social media posts or other personal disclosures leading us to the potential of embezzlement.

Learning how to spot red flags and indicators within our cases that might mean tax fraud, tax evasion, embezzlement, and other similar types of white-collar crimes can help to identify criminals and collect information that can be used by law enforcement and intelligence agencies as evidence to enable legal action. There are some key financial identifiers and methods like derogatory search strings that we can use in OSINT to find financial information.

10.3   Methods for Analysis

Because we are OSINT analysts, not financial analysts, unless we are employed in a job that provides access to closed financial sources, our analysis must come from publicly available information. This means that many of the resources for traditional financial analysis involve the same tools and methodologies we have learned about in previous chapters of this book. Below is an example of how analysis might look for a financial case beginning with a username (see Figure 10.4).

Your specific requirements within your financial analysis should determine where to start digging, but for many analysts, understanding the banking landscape, basic financial crimes, how to trace the flow of money, and how to analyze subjects of interest will be integral to achieving the end goal of catching illegal activity. Many of the starting points for a financial analysis you will already be familiar with (username, email, phone number, subject name); the difference will be the pivots from that point on that focus on finding financially related connections, motivations, and information. We can drill down into the financial connections by asking ourselves questions to narrow the focus.

- Does your subject or entity of interest have ties to organized crime?
- Is your subject a PEP?
- Does your entity or subject match their lifestyle?
- Do they seem to be experiencing a windfall of money?
  - Can we determine through OSINT where it came from?

---

[27] www.cnn.com/2010/SHOWBIZ/celebrity.news.gossip/12/06/dane.cook .restitution/index.html.

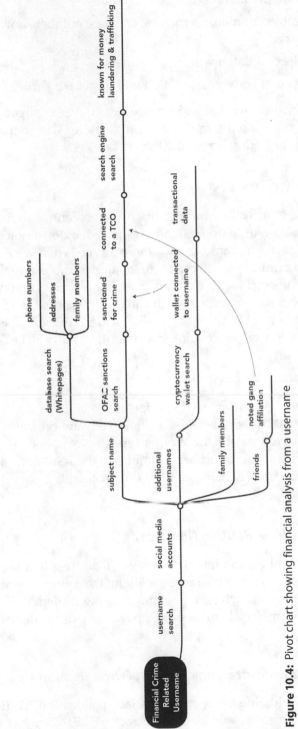

Figure 10.4: Pivot chart showing financial analysis from a username

- Are there any indications on social media?
- Does the subject's email, usernames, or phone number show up on forums, pages, or ads?
- Is the subject affiliated with any businesses?
- Is the subject or activity associated with organized crime?

By asking ourselves targeted questions, we can develop targeted search strategies using financial identifiers and resources along with derogatory search strings to find information across the Internet.

Financial Identifiers

Because banks are incredibly important and often central to financial crimes analysis, it can be useful to understand the breadth of terminology and identifiers used in reference to banking and transactions. When we pair terms with the key financial crimes, we can craft search queries and examine databases of information for the exact focus of our analysis. For example, if you are exploring a case where a bad actor is selling credit card information illegally on the Dark Web, it would be helpful to know what a BIN and SWIFT are. The following are some of the frequently referenced financial identifiers that will be useful to know.

Issuer Identification Number

The issuer identification number (IIN) refers to the first few digits of a payment card number issued by a financial institution. They are typically the first eight digits found on a credit, debit, or another type of payment card.

The issuer identification number is unique to the issuer and its partnering network provider. The IIN helps identify the processing network used for the card's transactions.

Routing Number (ABA Routing Numbers)

A bank routing number is a nine-digit numerical address that identifies a bank and allows it to send and receive money. Without the routing number, we would have no way of knowing where the money is being routed to. These numbers are used for wire transfers, bank deposits, payments, direct deposits, and other transactions.

Society for Worldwide Interbank Financial Organization

The Society for Worldwide Interbank Financial Organization (SWIFT) codes and BIC codes are interchangeable identifiers; each SWIFT code has a handle that is referred to as a BIC, which is important in figuring out where a wire came from or went to. The Bank Identifier Code (BIC) is an 8- to 11-character code identifying a bank and is used to transfer money from one bank to the other. Typical bank SWIFT codes follow this pattern:

AAAABBCCDDD
    AAAA: Shortened bank name
    BB: Country code of the bank
    CC: Location of bank's headquarters
    DDD (optional): Branch code, which may be replaced with XXX or removed

Here is an example for the Bank of America, London:

BOFAGB22XXX

- BOFA is for Bank of America.

- GB is for the country (Great Britain).

- 22 is the location code.

- XXX is the branch code.

To search BIC codes, try the Swift Online BIC Search tool at `swift.com/bsl`,[28] which according to the site provides access to BIC data but does not indicate whether a BIC is connected to the SWIFT network; it indicates only the institution name, descriptions, and identifiers (see Figure 10.5).

Value-Added Tax

Value-Added Tax (VAT) is a consumption tax that is added onto a product at each stage of the supply chain and used in many countries but not the United States. Because each business has to register for VAT, we can use databases to perform searches on subjects and entities to gather information such as subject names, business names, addresses, VAT status, and more. One such database is `vat-search.eu`[29] that you can access with a free account (see Figure 10.6).

BIN-Bank Identification Number

A bank identification number (BIN) is the first six to eight numbers seen on a bank, credit, or debit card that identifies the financial institution where the card is from. The purpose is to match the bank transactions with the financial institution to help identify fraudulent or stolen cards. Using a free site like `binlist.io`, you can determine what network the BIN belongs to, the level of

---

[28] `www2.swift.com/bsl`.
[29] VAT-Search / `https://vat-search.eu//` last accessed February 15, 2023.

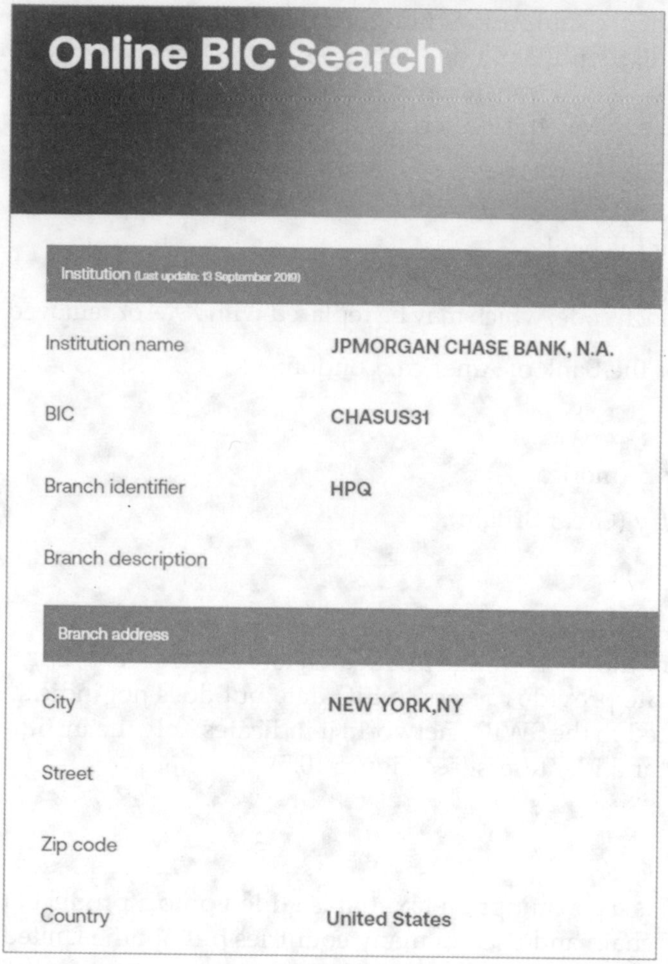

Figure 10.5: Online BIC search

the card that can indicate status, the type of card (credit or debit), the country, and the bank it is issued from. Another option is to use `binlist.net`, which provides additional details on whether the card is prepaid, which can be used as an indicator for possible money laundering (see Figure 10.7).

If you need to identify a bank, you can narrow down the search using the Wiki List of Banks[30] and searching by continent, super continent, or specifiers like largest banks or systemically important banks. Using the wiki, we can uncover information on a bank's branches, subsidiaries, and directors, as well as curated lists of systemically important banks (see Figure 10.8).

---

[30] Wikimedia Foundation, Inc. / https://en.wikipedia.org/wiki/Lists_of_banks/ last accessed February 15, 2023.

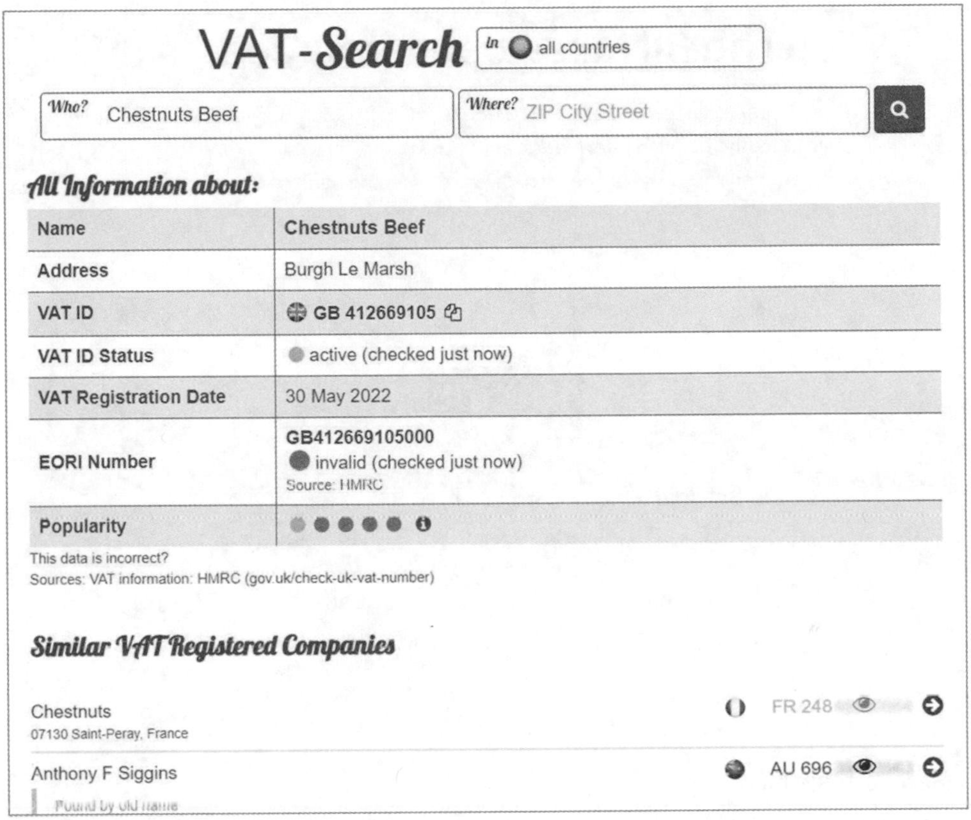

Figure 10.6: VAT search

Using the information pulled from the wiki, we can pivot to a more reliable authoritative source. For instance, we can pull subsidiary information from the wiki on a bank of interest and check against OpenCorporates or CorporationWiki to locate the additional business identifiers and people associated with the bank. Much of this type of analysis will hop back and forth between business intelligence, subject intelligence, and financial intelligence, leading to derogatory information, public disclosures, sanctioned entities, and PEPs.

Identifiers are most useful when you have a location to tie them to as all regions and countries have differing rules and regulations for financial institutions. By using location-based resources, we can research financial crimes, country codes, and currencies for a specific area.

Location-Based Resources

Regardless of the country you are analyzing, you will want to know as much as possible about their financial laws, regulations, and prevalent criminal activity by region. Each country is internationally recognized by an ISO country code,

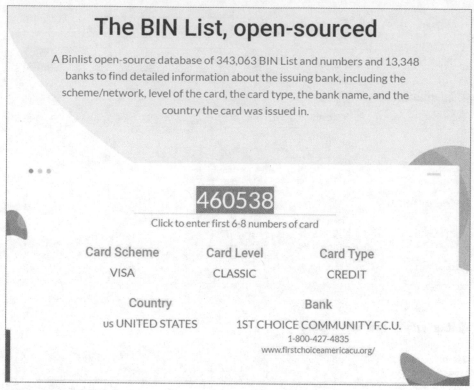

Figure 10.7: BIN list

which is a two- or three-letter combination, much like an acronym, that is used to identify a country or state.

Searching the Internet for *ISO country codes* will reveal several lists to use, but I like to use `nationsonline.org/oneworld/country_code_list`.[31] While knowing a country's codes is not essential to your case, it can help you to quickly identify countries within financial documents that will only list countries by their ISO codes. Knowing the prevalent crime and risks for a country of interest can make it easier to determine the type of crime you should keep an eye out for. If you are analyzing a region that is primarily known for money laundering and drug trafficking, for example, you can frontload your analysis with localized research that may help you better focus your efforts.

By using the Global Anti-Money Laundering tool KnowYourCountry,[32] you can find country-specific reporting on FATF status, sanctions, blacklists, bribery rating, and the economy as well as visualization tools such as their World Risk Map,[33] screening tools, and information on narcotics (see Figure 10.9).

---

[31] www.nationsonline.org/oneworld/country_code_list.htm.

[32] www.knowyourcountry.com.

[33] www.knowyourcountry.com/information-centre/world-risk-map.

Lists of banks

From Wikipedia, the free encyclopedia

Lists of banks are contained in the following articles:

> **Contents** [hide]
>
> 1 By continent
> 2 By super continent or intercontinental region
> 3 Other lists
> 4 See also

By continent   [edit]

- **List of banks in Africa** – Each country in Africa has a list of banks operating in that country
- **List of banks in Asia** – Asia has a list of banks operating in that country
- **List of banks in the Americas** – Each country in the Americas has a list of banks with operations in that country
- **List of banks in Europe** – Each country in Europe has a list of banks operating in that country
- **List of banks in Oceania** – Each country in Oceania has a list of banks operating in that country

By super continent or intercontinental region   [edit]

- **List of banks in the Arab world** – Each Arab country has a list of banks operating in that country
- **List of largest banks in Southeast Asia** – Each country in Southeast Asia has a list of banks with operations in that country

Other lists   [edit]

- **List of international banking institutions** – List of international and multilateral financial institutions
- **List of systemically important banks** – List of banks deemed systemically important by at least one major regulator
- **List of largest banks** – List of largest banks as measured by market capitalization and total assets on balance sheet
- **List of investment banks** – List of investment banks and brokerages

See also   [edit]

- List of oldest banks in continuous operation

Figure 10.8: List of Banks

Along with understanding the risks by country, we should be able to recognize the look of international currency, their codes, and where certain types of currency are used across the world. A scenario where recognizing currency could be useful is if you located an image or video on social media of drugs, guns, and money, you could quickly estimate where the photo may have been taken by the type of currency in the photo. For this you can use a resource like the List of Circulating Currencies Wiki (see Figure 10.10),[34] or I have had luck using a search engine to target specific keywords to find the information I need such as *currency* and *Russia*. The wiki provides an alphabetical listing of currencies, abbreviations, ISO codes, units, and links to images of the currency that you can compare to what might be found in a social media, website, or Dark Web image.

---

[34] Wikimedia Foundation, Inc. / `https://en.wikipedia.org/wiki/List_of_circulating_currencies` / last accessed February 15, 2023.

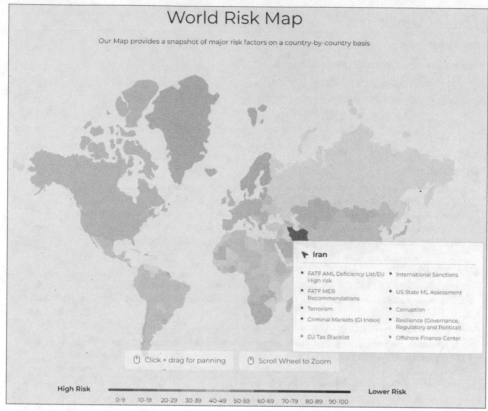

Figure 10.9: World Risk Map

State or territory [1]	Currency [1][2]	Symbol[b] or Abbrev.[3]	ISO code[2]	Fractional unit	Number to basic
Abkhazia	Abkhazian apsar[R]	(none)	(none)	(none)	(none)
	Russian ruble	₽	RUB	Kopeck	100
Afghanistan	Afghan afghani	Af or Afs (pl.)	AFN	Pul	100
Akrotiri and Dhekelia	Euro	€	EUR	Cent	100
Albania	Albanian lek	Lek	ALL	Qintar	100
Alderney	Alderney pound[R]	£	(none)	Penny	100
	Sterling banknotes are issued by the Bank of England and by some banks in Scotland and Northern Ireland (incl. Danske Bank). Laws on legal tender vary between various jurisdictions. [4]	£	GBP	Penny	100
	Guernsey pound	£	(none)	Penny	100

Figure 10.10: List of Circulating Currencies Wiki

Drug Financing Analysis Resources

Our financial analysis may often lead us into forums on the Dark Web, and even in the clear Web on social media discussions about drugs that may use slang and code words that we need to know to follow the conversation. The U.S. Drug Enforcement Administration (DEA) provides documents and information that outlines the most recently used slang and code words used by buyers/sellers. Sometimes we can even see these code words being used on public payment systems like Venmo where users can comment along with a purchase. Additionally, the dea.gov site provides information on growing narcotics threats and guides on the most common misused drugs.[35] The DEA also offers a National Drug Threat Assessment (NDTA) that lists the threats posed to the United States through trafficking and drugs. This resource provides information on transnational crime as well as photos of how the drugs were trafficked.

We can also check the Controlled Substances List for a listing of illegal or limited distribution drugs within the United States. Using the FDA Approved Drug List, we can determine which drugs are available without a prescription and which medications are restricted along with their basic ingredients. If you live outside of the United States, the International Narcotics Control Board[36] provides a list of internationally controlled substances, and the United Nations has an office on Drugs and Crime[37] at unodc.org that provides additional information on international drug control conventions as well as the going street prices for drugs in specific regions.

For instances where you run across images of drugs for sale and need to quickly identify them, the DEA has a Drug Images Gallery[38] that shows images of bottles, labels, pills, and more.

At a state level, there might be a need for analysts to understand marijuana legalization and track licensed cannabis sellers. Because these laws change so often, my best recommendation is to do a search engine query for *state+marijuana legalization*. Marijuana-related businesses (MRBs) are required to be licensed in the locations they operate, and those licenses should be searchable in state databases.

Looking at a screenshot from the now defunct Dark Web marketplace Silk Road,[39] you can see the listings of drugs with photos, names, sometimes slang words used to describe the drugs (see Figure 10.11). Using the drug resources we learned about, we can do analysis into packaging, type, color, and naming schemes that may indicate a known pattern that traces back to a specific group of people. Remember that the resources and tools can change, but the methodology used to solve a problem will remain the same no matter what task we are performing in OSINT.

---

[35] www.dea.gov/documents/2022/2022-12/2022-12-02/drugs-abuse-2022.
[36] www.incb.org/incb/en/narcotic-drugs/index.html.
[37] www.unodc.org/unodc/en/commissions/CND/Mandate_Functions/ Mandate-and-Functions_Scheduling.html.
[38] www.dea.gov/media-gallery/drug-images.
[39] Yahoo / www.engadget.com/2015-05-22-silk-road-survival-deep-web-alex-winter.html/ last accessed February 15, 2023.

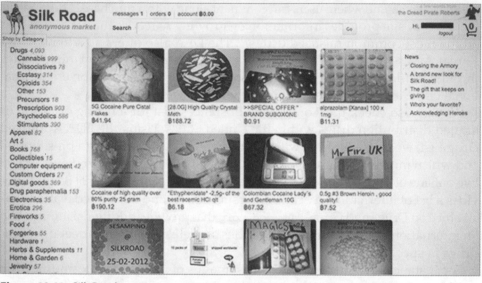

Figure 10.11: Silk Road

Organized Crime Analysis Resources

If you think you may be dealing with an organized crime group, it can be use-ful to perform background research using resources like the Organized Crime Wiki,[40] which gives a pretty good jumping-off point for learning about different criminal organizations and their illegal money making schemes. For gang-specific information, I have found the National Gang Center's Information Exchange[41] to be a phenomenal resource. Through the website you can sign up as law enforce-ment, researchers/policy makers, or direct service to exchange ideas, opinions, and interest in gang identification, indicators, activities, trainings, and jobs.

The DEA's Wanted Fugitives Database[42] at `dea.gov/fugitives` is a good place to start analyzing, and it will give you a physical description of the person, any aliases, a photo, and what they were charged with. This information can also be found through a search engine query.

Many analysts tend to focus on South America when analyzing the financing of drug trafficking. Insight Crime[43] provides country trafficking reports that will help you keep up on the activities of cartels and gangs along with political corruption in the area that have an impact on financial crime activities. The Global Organized Crime Index at `ocindex.net` is a tool that measures organized crime in a country and assesses their resilience to criminal activity, placing it on an easy-to-read map (see Figure 10.12).

---

[40] https://en.wikipedia.org/wiki/Organized_crime.
[41] https://nationalgangcenter.ojp.gov/ganginfo.
[42] www.dea.gov/fugitives/all.
[43] https://insightcrime.org.

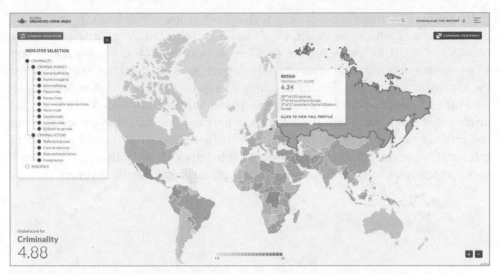

Figure 10.12: Global organized crime index

What this research can provide is insight into the crime by region so that if you are performing analysis in an area, you will know the key players to look into first before broadening your search.

Negative News String Searching

Now that we have a good grasp on banking and financial crime terminology and the available resources for finding further information, we can use what we have learned to start crafting specific search engine strings to look for derogatory information about the entity or subject. We can create a string of search terms using keywords and terminology to run against our entity/subject of interest. For example, the following query can be run in Google (but would need to be adjusted for other search engines based on their string logic) to search for a specific ENTITY in conjunction with other keywords from this chapter to determine if there is any derogatory information online that we can use in our analysis:

> **"ENTITY NAME"** AND **"arrest"** OR **"conviction"** OR **"criminal"** OR **"fraud"** OR **"lawsuit"** OR **"money+launder"** OR **"ofac"** OR **"ponzi"** OR **"terrorist"** OR **"violation"** OR **"honorary+consul"** OR **"consul"** OR **"panama+papers"** OR **"embezzlement"** OR **"evasion"** OR **"occrp"**

This type of search string can be adjusted to look for whichever keywords or crimes you are looking for, but this will give you a good starting point for developing your own. At the start of a project, I will search using a similar search string to begin to narrow the focus of my analysis.

By using the methodology and techniques from subject intelligence and business intelligence, we can apply it to financial intelligence analysis using tools like OCCRP, Open Corporates, Corporation Wiki, and `Whatsmyname.app` to garner pivot points and answer analysis questions outlined in the intelligence cycle prior to the project. Financial crimes can be incredibly complex not only to pull off as a criminal but for us to then unravel. Often the analysis into financial crimes will reach across multiple teams with true financial analysts identifying the initial criminal activity, OSINT analysts identifying assets and additional information, and then all the teams working together along with digital currency focused analysts to trace the source and destination of the illicit funds.

CHAPTER 11

Cryptocurrency

11.1   Overview of Cryptocurrency

If you had invested only $1,000 in Bitcoin in 2010 when it first launched, you could have $354,947,000.00 today.[1] Originally dubbed cyber currencies in the 1980s before being reintroduced as Bitcoin in 2008, *cryptocurrency* is an alternative form of payment. It is a digital currency that uses encryption algorithms to conduct transactions. Cryptocurrency exists only virtually, and in most cases there is no centralized authority that maintains or manages value like there is with fiat currency. While "centralized" cryptocurrencies issued by governments and/or businesses do exist, "decentralized" currencies distribute these management tasks across users via the Internet. Unlike government-issued currencies, there is no legislated value for cryptocurrency; it is worth whatever people are willing to pay for it.

While cryptocurrency tends to have a negative connotation for being attached to illicit activity, for many it is used in the same way a typical bank account would be used to buy and sell goods and services. However, as an OSINT analyst, you will most likely encounter the illicit sides of cryptocurrency for the purpose of analyzing and understanding the motivation, tactics, and procedures of cryptocurrency crimes such as fraud, scams, trafficking, and money laundering.

---

[1] https://bitcoinfomo.club.

In 2014, a cryptocurrency Ponzi scheme using the company OneCoin was perpetrated by founders Ruja Ignatova and Sebastian Greenwood. OneCoin was a centralized currency hosted on the servers of Bulgarian offshore company OneCoin LTD. The company used a data entry scam to simulate transactions that were not registered with the blockchain and never mined. OneCoin recruiters received commissions for recruiting other individuals to purchase cryptocurrency educational packages for 100 euros to 118 euros.[2] Greenwood was the leader of the educational package scheme and made approximately 20 million euros a month for his role in the multilevel marketing scheme. The Justice Department stated that more than 3 million people invested in the fraudulent cryptocurrency packages that incentivized people to purchase OneCoin tokens that generated coins that went into your account under the assumption those coins would turn back into euros.[3] Investors could watch their money rise on the OneCoin website as they invested more and more money. Until one investor who began to question the investments was told by the leaders of her OneCoin group that the "blockchain" for the coins was actually a SQL Server database.

In May 2022, Ignatova, dubbed the "Cryptoqueen" by a podcast about her crimes, was added to the Europol Most Wanted Fugitives List for being the driving force and inventor of OneCoin. She remains on the run today, but BBC reporters believe she may be hiding in the EU under a fake identity.[4] Using this case as an example to show the relevance of cryptocurrency to an OSINT analyst, we can use subject intelligence techniques to uncover their previous fraudulent histories and connections, we can use business intelligence to reveal the offshore accounts used, and we can use financial intelligence to understand depth of the fraud and analyze any available cryptocurrency transactions. But before we get too into the weeds, we have to learn more about how cryptocurrency works and the methods used to maintain security and provenance in transactions through basic cryptography.

Cryptography is the practice of using mathematical and computational methods to encode and decode data. Cryptocurrency uses encryption algorithms or mathematical formulas that scramble input text into cipher text and only with a key can be reorganized back into readable text. Much in the same way you would be required to sign a check at the bank to verify your identity before cashing it, cryptography can be used to ensure the authenticity of the transactions, senders, and receivers. This security along with the transactional freedom and lack of government regulation are all reasons people choose to use cryptocurrency as a payment method.

---

[2] https://yle.fi/a/3-8743590.

[3] www.justice.gov/usao-sdny/press-release/file/1141981/download.

[4] www.bbc.com/news/stories-50435014.

Now that you know the "why" behind using digital currency, let's learn about how cryptocurrency is utilized and how it gets from one place to another.

The Basics of Cryptocurrency

Before jumping into the analysis of cryptocurrency, let's take a look at the basics.

How Is Cryptocurrency Used and Transferred?

Although cryptocurrency is a digital asset, it can be used in many places the same way other common forms of payment like cash and debit are used. You can now pay your bills with cryptocurrency either directly or through a third-party cryptocurrency payment processor like Bitpay.[5]

The following are a few of the major companies and stores that accept Bitcoin as a form of payment in 2023:

- AT&T
- Microsoft
- Wikipedia
- Starbucks
- Airbnb

To pay for services or products with cryptocurrency, either you would select "pay with cryptocurrency" at checkout or owners can transfer cryptocurrency to another person by logging into their wallet account where you hold the currency and sending the appropriate amount to the receiver's wallet address. What happens is that you are digitally signing the hash of the last transaction, and then the public key of the next owner is added to the end of the coin. The payee can then verify the chain of ownership as well as the signatures. Once the cryptocurrency is transferred, typically, it can't be reversed or canceled due to the nature of cryptocurrency protocols unless you happen to be able to identify the receiver and they kindly return the funds. Unless you are using a privacy coin like Monero, or a private blockchain, all of the transactions sent from your wallet will be viewable to the public. This also means that you can view another owner's wallets and their transactions including dates, names, amounts, and other juicy details that can be helpful to an analyst. Getting a baseline of knowledge on how cryptocurrency wallets and transactions normally look can be a good way to train yourself to notice when a transaction or set of transactions might be abnormal.

---

[5] https://bitpay.com/directory.

What Is a Cryptocurrency Wallet?

Cryptocurrency wallets can be hardware-based, software-based, or cloud-based, and they store your private encryption keys that give you access to your cryptocurrencies and allow you to send and receive currency. There are apps like Coinbase Wallet that store your private keys and facilitate the sending, receiving, and spending of your currency. However, your cryptocurrency wallets don't work like a physical wallet; they don't store your currency but rather allow you access to your currency that exists within the blockchain.

To access your cloud-based cryptocurrency wallet, you will need your wallet address, password, and any secondary authentication you have activated. For hardware-based access to your wallet, the private keys are stored in a physical device like a hard drive. The very obvious downside to these types of access is that if you lose your hard drive or forget your wallet password, you would lose access to all of your money. For some, this loss has been in the millions of dollars.

In 2013, James Howells from Newport, Wales, threw away what he thought was a blank hard drive, but he had actually tossed a hard drive containing the private keys to 7,500 Bitcoins, which would be worth more than $280 million today. In a last-ditch effort to find the lost hard drive he begged local officials to let him fund the excavation of the landfill and offered 25 percent of the money to a COVID relief fund, but he has so far been unsuccessful to convince them.[6] In a similarly depressing case, Stefan Thomas, a programmer in San Francisco, lost a tiny slip of paper several years ago with his password for his small but rugged hard drive known as an IronKey that holds the private keys to his digital wallet and 7,002 Bitcoin, or roughly $300 million today.[7]

If you do know your password and have access to your wallet, you can send and receive currency, and to do this, you will need a cryptocurrency address. You can think of a cryptocurrency address like a traditional bank account. Under your identity at a traditional bank, you can hold multiple accounts (checking, savings, vacation fund), and each of these accounts gets their own account number. When you need to add or remove funds from your savings account, you will need the account number.

Similarly, a cryptocurrency wallet holds multiple addresses for each blockchain like Bitcoin, Ethereum, Litecoin, etc. To receive or send funds using that account, you will need the account number, and in cryptocurrency to send money from a wallet you will need an address to send funds from and an address for the

---

[6] www.cnbc.com/2021/01/15/
uk-man-makes-last-ditch-effort-to-recover-lost-bitcoin-hard-drive.html.
[7] www.nytimes.com/2021/01/12/technology/
bitcoin-passwords-wallets-fortunes.html.

receiver to send funds to. For example, you and I could both have an Ethereum wallet with two addresses. If you want to send funds from your Ethereum address 1 to my Ethereum address 2, you would need to know both addresses so that the funds can be routed properly. An example address looks like this: 0x71C7656EC7ab88b098defB751B7401B5f6d8976F.

YOU	ME
Ethereum Address 1	Ethereum Address 1
Ethereum Address 2	Ethereum Address 2

Even though there is a potential to lose your cryptocurrency, these added mechanisms for security and anti-counterfeiting are in part why people are drawn to currency on the blockchain rather than centralized traditional banks.

What Is Blockchain?

Blockchain is a distributed digital ledger that stores encoded transactions and is maintained by a network of computers and can be considered centralized or decentralized based on the use case (see Figure 11.1). Blockchain is a set of individual "blocks" of data that are chained together with each block containing transactions that have been verified by each member in the network. As data is added, a new "block" is created and verified by each node in the chain. Each node agrees upon the contents and updates their version of the blockchain ledger to be identical, making it nearly impossible to forge transaction history because one single node cannot make changes without oversight and agreement by all. The beginning of each block contains the hash of the previous block, thus forming the chain. If a rogue node decided to forge a transaction in block 10, the hash of block 10 would change, and thus no longer match the block 10 hash included at the beginning of block 11. The network would recognize something is wrong, trash that copy of the chain, and replace it with a validated one. In this way, not only can we detect when changes have been made to the chain, we can see exactly where it occurred and fix it (see Figure 11.2).

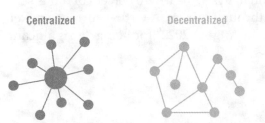

Figure 11.1: Centralized and decentralized networks

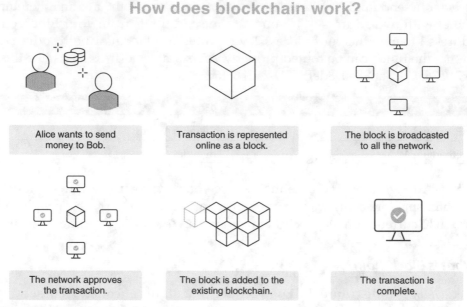

Figure 11.2: How blockchain works

To succeed in forging a blockchain transaction, not only would a node have to control 51 percent of the entire network (to gain consensus), they would have to rehash the block with the forged transaction *and* every block afterwards *and* do it faster than every other node. In the case of BTC, new blocks are mined every 10 minutes, so they better be quick too. The further back the forged transaction is, the more computing power it would take to hash every subsequent block. This verification of data is done by a network of nodes that receive a reward for recording and validating this data, called *mining*. Blockchain and smart contracts can also allow for the embedding of *provenance* to fully document the history of something like an NFT to prove legitimacy.

When someone sends cryptocurrency from one account to another, it leaves a public data trail within the blockchain that analysts can use to trace the flow of money sometimes directly to the identity of a person. To hide this public transaction history on the blockchain, "mixing" services have been developed. According to a recent report from Chainalysis,[8] nearly 10 percent of funds sent from illicit wallet addresses are sent through mixers. A virtual currency mixer called Tornado Cash was sanctioned in August 2022[9] for being "a significant

---

[8] https://blog.chainalysis.com/reports/
crypto-mixer-criminal-volume-2022.
[9] https://home.treasury.gov/news/press-releases/jy0916.

threat to national security" as a means to launder more than $7 billion. According to the U.S. Department of the Treasury, the laundered money includes more than $455 million stolen by the sanctioned North Korean state-sponsored Lazarus Group from the 2022 Harmony Bridge and Nomad Heists. The decision to sanction Tornado Cash has drawn criticism for what is seen as a significant overstep by the government for a legitimate service that is also used for legal purposes.[10] There are obvious limitations for using the blockchain to maintain privacy through transactions and headaches for regulators who find it difficult to scrutinize decentralized platforms. For security and privacy-focused users, sometimes the type of currency used can provide the anonymity in transactions.

Types of Cryptocurrencies

Presently there are more than 20,000 different types of cryptocurrencies in use, but with the volatility of the market (like with Bitcoin dropping 65 percent in early 2022) many have collapsed into bankruptcy or worse. Terra LUNA's UST stablecoin fell 99.9 percent and collapsed in 2022 triggering a landslide of other collapses ultimately costing investors $33 billion.[11] While some coins seemingly pop up and then disappear overnight, there are many that are worth getting to know due to their popularity with users. The most popular cryptocurrency is of course Bitcoin, which was launched in 2009, soon followed in 2011 by alternative cryptocurrencies called *altcoins*. Because each coin or token is different, they have varying levels of privacy and verification methods as well as address identifiers associated with them that we can consider when analyzing transactions and accounts.

Coin and Token Quick Reference

Here is a quick reference:

Coin: A digital currency such as Bitcoin that runs on its own blockchain and is used primarily for payment.

- **Altcoin:** Means "alternative coin" and is all cryptocurrency other than Bitcoin.
- **Stablecoin:** Cryptocurrency whose value is tied to another "stable" asset like the U.S. dollar.
- **Memecoin:** Cryptocurrency inspired by Internet jokes and memes.

---

[10] https://time.com/6205143/tornado-cash-us-crypto-ban.
[11] https://beincrypto.com/worst-losses-before-ftx-chainalysis.

Tokens: Tradeable assets that run on another network's blockchain. Rather than being "mined" like coins, they're "minted" through smart contracts.

- **Value Tokens:** Objects of value
- **NFTs:** No inherent value
- **Security Tokens:** Ownership of an asset such as equity in a company
- **Utility Tokens:** Gives users the right to perform actions on a blockchain or network

Bitcoin

Bitcoin (BTC) is the most well-known cryptocurrency in the world. Bitcoin uses a decentralized ledger system (blockchain) and is secured by proof-of-work consensus. The history of Bitcoin began in 2008 when a person using the fake name Satoshi Nakamoto announced the creation of a peer-to-peer electronic cash system. Initially, Bitcoin was created to be a P2P payment system, but as it has increased in value, it is accepted as payment at stores and used as investments. Bitcoin has a finite number of coins available that generate demand; the maximum supply of Bitcoin is $21 million. Bitcoin is considered *fungible*, which means the currency is interchangeable, divisible, and uniform. To recognize Bitcoin addresses, look for an address that begins with a 1, 3, or bc1 such as 3J98t1WpEZ73CNmQviecrnyiWrnqRhWNLy.

Ether

Ether (ETH) is the cryptocurrency that uses the Ethereum blockchain. Ether is uncapped and has an infinite amount of coins that can be created. In addition, it also supports smart contracts that execute automatically when conditions are met. Ethereum addresses are 42-characters long with an 0x in the beginning: 0x71C7656EC7ab88b098defB751B7401B5f6d8976F.

Binance

Binance (BNB) is native to the binance blockchain, and transaction fees are reduced for users who pay in BNB, which drives the adoption of the coin. Binance Coin was initially issued as am ERC-20 token on the Ethereum blockchain before launching its own Binance Chain in 2019 known as BNB Beacon Chain. Therefore, older BNB on the Ethereum blockchain begin with addresses starting with a 0x, while newer BNB addresses on the BNB Beacon chain start with bnb.

Tether

Tether (USDT) is a stablecoin, which means it is less volatile because it is linked to external assets such as U.S. dollars. Tether was initially issued on the Bitcoin blockchain but can now be on any Tether-supported chain (Bitcoin, Ethereum, EOS, Tron, Algorand, and OMG Network blockchains). Tether addresses can be recognized for starting with a T: TR7NHqjeKQxGTCi8q8ZY4pL8otSzgjLj6t.

Solana

Solana (SOL) is native to the Solana platform on blockchain, and the draw is that it can perform 50,000 transactions per second. It is great for investors who trade fast. A Solana address is 32 to 44 characters and does not start with a specific character like Bitcoin or Ethereum: HN7cABqLq46Es1jh92dQQisAq662SmxELLLsHHe4YWrH.

Dogecoin

Dogecoin (DOGE), based on the technology of Litecoin, was created as a joke and is considered a meme coin. Dogecoin has no set limit of coins that can be mined or created, meaning there is an endless supply of Dogecoin. You can recognize a Dogecoin address as starting with the letter D:DLCDJhnh6aGotar 6b182jpzbNEyXb3C361.

Monero (XMR)

Monero is a privacy-focused cryptocurrency that is specifically configured for anonymity. The identity of senders and recipients and the transaction amounts are privacy-focused and disguise the addresses used. Mining of Monero works a bit differently as well, and everyone is viewed as equal with an equal opportunity to mine. Additionally, Monero is considered fungible, meaning it is interchangeable (one XMR can be swapped for one XMR with no difference), divisible (you can have portions of an XMR), and uniform (as in each XMR is not unique). Monero has a reputation because of its anonymity of being used for malicious or illicit activities in an attempt to evade law enforcement. A Monero address is a set of 95 characters starting with a 4 or an 8; if it starts with an 8, it is a subaddress:

4AdUndXHHZ6cfufTMvppY6JwXNouMBzSkbLYfpAV5Usx3sk
xNgYeYTRj5UzqtReoS44qo9mtmXCqY45DJ852K5Jv2684Rge

888tNkZrPN6JsEgekjMnABU4TBzc2Dt29EPAvkRxbANsAnjyPbb3iQ1Y
BRk1UXcdRsiKc9dh

I fully recognize the overwhelming amount of knowledge required to under-stand cryptocurrency, how it works, and how to analyze it. My goal with this chapter is not to overwhelm you but rather to give you a quick overview of the key cryptocurrencies and to provide some keywords that you can utilize to quickly find what you need during your analysis. Now let's pivot into a brief overview of the mining and verification process, which can help make sense of some of the individual actions and motivations for your subject of interest.

What Is Cryptocurrency Mining and Minting?

The process used by Bitcoin and some other cryptocurrencies for generating new coins and verifying transactions is called *cryptocurrency mining*.[12] However, this is a bit more complicated depending on the verification mechanism used, which determines whether the cryptocurrency is mined or minted. Tokens are also created through a similar yet separate process called *minting* (see Figure 11.3).

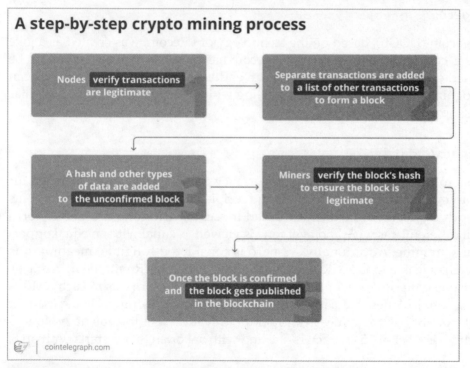

Figure 11.3: `Cointelgraph.com` step-by-step crypto mining process

---

[12] `www.coinbase.com/learn/crypto-basics/what-is-mining`.

As we learned, a blockchain is a chain of linked blocks of transactional data including hashes. After the block is created, a list of all transactions including the new block get compiled, which prevents the expenditure of the same digital currency twice, called *double-spending*. Once the ledger is verified, it cannot be changed or corrupted, and when enough transactions have been added to the block header, information gets added along with the hash of the previous block and a new hash.

Network miners verify the hash to ensure that the unconfirmed block is valid and that proof has been completed. This final step means the miner will be rewarded based on the specific blockchain requirements, and the block will be added to the blockchain. Because mining cryptocurrency uses a lot of computational power, people will sometimes combine their computing power into what is called a *mining pool*, and if the pool receives the reward, it is split among the members. The blockchain and mining process are meant to ensure that transactions are valid and to prevent counterfeit and fraud because no single user can change something without the whole chain agreeing. One way that criminals are getting around the security of blockchain is through vulnerabilities in blockchain bridges.

Because of the interoperability of incompatible blockchains, if a user needs to move assets from one blockchain to another, they may need to use a *blockchain bridge*, which takes a token from one type of wallet, wraps it, and converts it to a token that is usable by another blockchain. For example, if John wants to send a Solana coin to Jane's Ethereum wallet, John would use a bridge, and Jane would receive a wrapped bridge version of a Solana coin that has been converted to an ERC-20 token.[13] Bad actors have learned that they can exploit the vulnerabilities in the bridges for profit. In February 2022, a vulnerability was found in the smart contract code for the popular bridge Wormhole Crypto. The hacker was able to mint 120,000 wrapped Ethereum on Solana (weETH) worth more than $320 million without putting up the necessary equivalent collateral to bridge.[14] This type of activity is exactly why validation is so important in typical blockchain transactions. The techniques that miners use in verifying each transaction is called *proof*, and there are many different types of this proof including proof of work, proof of stake, and proof of time.

Types of Verification

In a traditional centralized system like a bank database, an administrator can update and maintain the database; however, with public blockchain, they are

---

[13] www.coindesk.com/learn/
what-are-blockchain-bridges-and-how-do-they-work.
[14] www.coindesk.com/tech/2022/02/02/
blockchain-bridge-wormhole-suffers-possible-exploit-worth-
over-250m.

decentralized and constantly changing, so they need a secure and functional mechanism to achieve an agreement on a data value, trust, and security. These types of secure decentralized verification used for cryptocurrency are called *consensus mechanisms*. For OSINT analysis, understanding the types of verification may help determine where to look for more information. Proof of space indicates the existence of storage such as an S3 bucket, while proof of work can point you toward mining pools to look for additional data.

Proof of work (PoW)

Proof of work is where a node, using a *ton* of computing power, races to be the first to find the correct cryptographic "hash" for the block potentially being added to the blockchain. The hash is added to the end of that block and the beginning of the next block as a security feature to maintain the integrity of the blockchain. The hash is sent out and "validated" by the rest of the network, and then the block is accepted.

Advantages

- Incentivization, which increases power/security
- Impractical to sabotage a blockchain

Disadvantages

- Energy intensive
- Hard to scale to a large number of transactions for some blockchains
- Longer processing time

Proof of Stake (PoS)

Proof of stake passes the responsibility for the maintenance of the public ledger to a randomly selected node based on the amount of cryptocurrency each node has in the pool of cryptocurrency and the length of time it has been there. The purpose of PoS is to reward the most invested participants to incentivize against compromising the network they are financially invested in. In PoS, coins are not mined, but they are validated, and then new blocks are minted.

Advantages

- Fast processing time
- Less energy intensive

Disadvantages

- Incentivizes cryptocurrency hoarding; however, some mechanisms do have a cap for staking

While proof of work and proof of stake are the most prevalent consensum mechanisms, there are some others such as the following:

Proof of Capacity uses a node's hard drive space to determine the rights to mine on the network.

Proof of Activity is a hybrid of proof of work and proof of stake and first requires miners to compete with compute power and randomly selects a node based on cryptocurrency they own.

Proof of Burn makes participants show proof that they have sent coins to a verifiable and unspendable address and consumes little resources.

Proof of Time chooses a participant based on how long they have been active on the network and their reputation.

Public Blockchains vs. Private Blockchains

Two types of blockchain exist: public and private. *Public blockchains* are available for anyone to participate in (read, write, audit) the data. Even though the blockchain is public, it is still decentralized so that no one person controls the nodes. On the other hand, a *private blockchain* is controlled internally by a group or organization, and it decides who gets invited. Unlike a public blockchain, the private blockchain has the authority to go back and change the blockchain and functions much like a storage system spread across many nodes for security.

Why Tracking Cryptocurrency Matters

Being able to track and understand the movement of cryptocurrency is crucial to the discovery of associations between entities, subjects, and products or services they purchase using digital currency. Reading the transactions back and forth between wallets can tell us a lot about a person's habits and connections, and in some cases the patterns can lead to uncovering illicit activity. While certainly not all cryptocurrency transactions are illegal, the privacy afforded through cryptocurrency is happily enjoyed by criminals online.

Some of the most prevalent forms of illicit activity associated with cryptocurrency are money laundering, fraud, and for-profit trade of child sexual abuse material (CSAM). One misconception about cryptocurrency is that it is explicitly used for digital crimes; however, it can be a part of *any* crime of monetary value. The Government Accountability Office (GAO) posted a report in 2022 stating that federal data indicated that digital currencies are being increasingly used in offline activities such as human and drug trafficking.[15] In financial analysis,

---

[15] www.gao.gov/blog/virtual-currency-use-human-and-drug-trafficking-increases-so-do-challenges-federal-law-enforcement#:~:text=Federal%20data%20indicate%20that%20virtual,prevent%20and%20discover%20these%20crimes.

an often used phrase is "follow the money," and by the end of this chapter you will have learned the techniques to begin tackling real cryptocurrency cases. We talked before about how organized crime uses money laundering as a technique for masking the source of illicit funds. Would you be surprised if I told you that money can be laundered through cryptocurrency transactions?

Money Laundering

Operation Crypto Runner was a multiyear Organized Crime Drug Enforcement Task Force (OCDETF) investigation into transnational money laundering networks running romance scams, business email compromises, and other fraud schemes and then laundering the funds through cryptocurrency. Twenty-one people were indicted on charges that involved drug sales on the Dark Web, counterfeit pharmaceuticals, and shell companies. In the majority of the cases, the indicted subject was receiving victim funds, exchanging the cash for cryptocurrency, and sending it to foreign co-conspirators who structured deposits to avoid detection and laundered profits through hundreds of layered transactions.[16]

Government oversight of decentralized digital currency to avoid fraud and illicit activity is not easy. The regulation of cryptocurrency is a hotly debated topic because while you can regulate the businesses and entities that accept and send cryptocurrency, you cannot effectively regulate the currency itself any more than you could regulate people trading cash or gold on the street. While traditional AML laws seek to prevent the "layering" process, in cryptocurrency, the illicit funds may be transferred through hundreds of cryptocurrency addresses before being cashed out at a cryptocurrency exchange. Unlike a traditional bank account, hundreds of cryptocurrency wallet addresses can be opened without any proof of identity such as a passport or driver's license. While some analysts may have access to paid tools that allow them to discern where funds originated and to analyze risk based on past risky transactions, many of us are only working with publicly available information

The use of money laundering schemes using cryptocurrency has risen in tandem with the increase in drug trafficking. In Brooklyn, New York, a man named Mustafa Goklu was arrested after posting an advertisement to `localbitcoins.com` offering to convert a user's Bitcoin (BTC) to U.S. currency for a fee.[17] Goklu was observed outside a coffee shop meeting known narcotics traffickers in his Mercedes-Benz. The trafficker would transfer BTC to Goklu's cryptocurrency wallet in exchange for somewhere between $5,000 to $133,000 in

---

[16] www.justice.gov/usao-edtx/pr/eastern-district-texas-announces-multi-year-investigation-transnational-cryptocurrency.
[17] www.dea.gov/press-releases/2022/10/11/queens-man-convicted-laundering-bitcoin-and-operating-unlicensed-money.

addition to a 7 to 8 percent commission fee. While Goklu's operation wasn't very complex, most large-scale money laundering operations require networks of professional money launderers. A good friend in financial intelligence once told me "it takes a village to develop a large-scale criminal operation, and it takes a village to dismantle it," which is why we should do our part and learn some methods for recognizing patterns that may point to illicit activity.

Recognizing Patterns in Transactions

If I asked you to close your eyes right now and picture what OSINT analysis looks like, I wager most of you would think of the exact same meme from *Always Sunny in Philadelphia* of Charlie Day and his board of red string (see Figure 11.4). However, what the red string truly creates is an analog link analysis chart. Sometimes in law enforcement cases, the links would be connecting places on a map where crimes have taken place in an effort to use spatial analysis to spot patterns or centralized locations. When we look at cybercurrency transactional data, we are trying to see patterns in the source and destination of money, the amounts transferred, and the manner in which the funds are transferred.

Figure 11.4: FX image from Always Sunny in Philadelphia

A common pattern in money laundering is a process called *layering*. The purpose of layering is to make it difficult to trace the flow of funds and the source of assets. In cryptocurrency, layering is done using many transactions, mixers or tumblers, dark markets, and peer-to-peer exchanges (see Figure 11.5).

A *mixer* or *tumbler* is a service used for obscuring the source of funds to make it completely anonymous by pooling cryptocurrency from multiple owners, mixing it together, and then sending each owner "clean" cryptocurrency. Using a mixer makes it difficult for investigators to track the flow of money, which is why it was a perfect way to make money for Larry Dean Harmon, owner of Helix a Dark Web cryptocurrency laundering service.[18] From 2014 to 2017, Helix partnered with Darknet markets including infamous Alphabay, Cloud 9, and Evolution to launder bitcoin generated from illegal drugs, guns, and child pornography. Harmon would allow customers to send Bitcoin to specified recipients for a fee where it would be pooled and "mixed" and then returned "clean." Over the three years Helix was operational, Harmon laundered more than 350,000 BTC, which at the time was equal to $300 million (see Figure 11.6).[19]

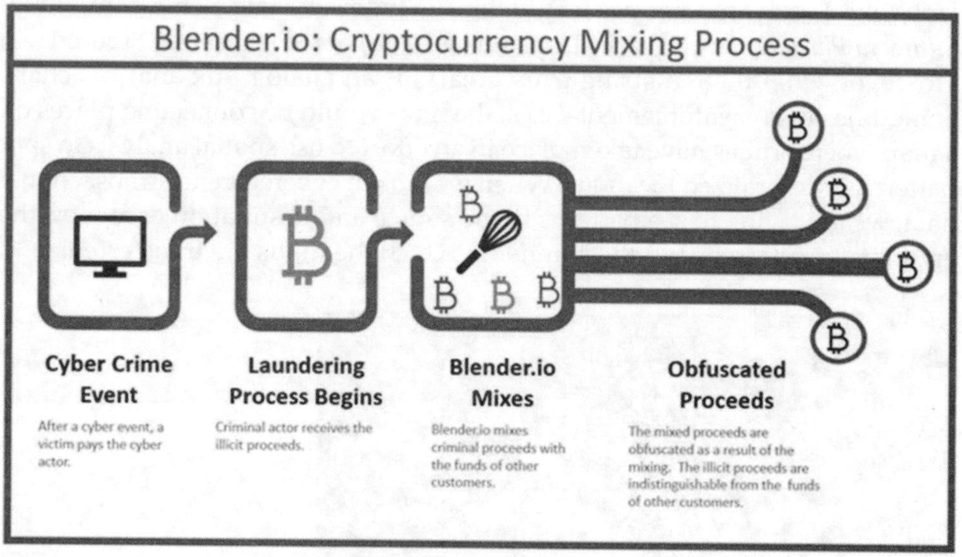

Figure 11.5: `Blender.io` cryptocurrency mixing process

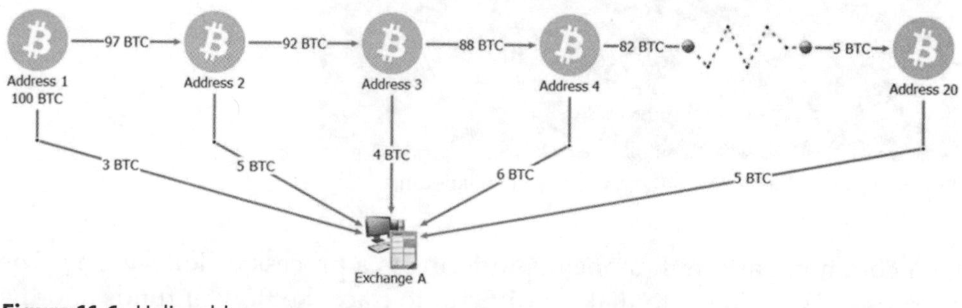

Figure 11.6: Helix addresses

[18] `www.justice.gov/opa/pr/ohio-resident-pleads-guilty-operating-darknet-based-bitcoin-mixer-laundered-over-300-million`.

[19] `www.justice.gov/opa/press-release/file/1425346/download`.

Another way to hide the source of cryptocurrency funds is through what is called a peel chain. A *peel chain* is a method used to obfuscate cryptocurrency transactions through a long series of small transactions that are "peeled" from the wallet and directed to exchanges where the money can be exchanged for fiat currency. The small amounts in the transactions typically do not trigger mandatory reporting or throw up red flags.

A good example of how a peel chain is used in illicit activity is the case of Chinese nationals Tian Yinyin and Li Jiadong who were charged in 202 for laundering more than $100 million in cryptocurrency funds. The funds in question primarily came from a hack of digital currency by North Korean actors in 2018.[20] Tian and Li laundered the money by using a peel chain and sending funds to many accounts across four exchanges and hundreds of automated transactions until the funds were placed into two new exchanges. Due to the complexity of transactions, peel chains are often automated through scripts to prevent loss of funds. Once the cryptocurrency was "clean," the North Korean actors converted the alt coins into Bitcoins to obscure the source of the money even further. Tian linked a commercial bank Guangfa Bank (CGB) to one of his digital currency accounts allowing him to deposit nearly $35 million profit into his account. Li linked nine commercial bank accounts to his digital currency account and made 2,000 total deposits totaling $32,848,567. In addition to these transactions, Tian used a U.S. exchange to trade Bitcoin for prepaid Apple iTunes gift cards, which is a common method to launder money that requires no ID.[21] The figure on the following is an example of what the peel chain and money laundering scheme looked like for Tian Yinyin's accounts (see Figure 11.7):

Peel chains are not the only transactional method to obscure the source of funds; another is called a *coin join* where multiple users sign a digital smart contract to mix their coins together to anonymize the source and destination of Bitcoin. When we analyze transactions and accounts for signs of money laundering, we must keep in mind that money laundering is a method of trying to conceal funds produced by other types of criminal activity. Fraud is considered a predicate crime for money laundering, meaning it is the reason illicit funds are generated that need to then be laundered. The same concept holds true for activity such as illegal drug and weapons sales, and the trading of child sexual assault/exploitation material.

Fraud, Illegal Sales, and CSAM/CSEM

Because of the perceived anonymity provided through the use of cryptocurrency and especially privacy-focused services like mixers, blenders, and privacy

[20] www.justice.gov/opa/pr/two-chinese-nationals-charged-laundering-over-100-million-cryptocurrency-exchange-hack.
[21] https://ciphertrace.com/chinese-linked-dprk-laundering-analysis.

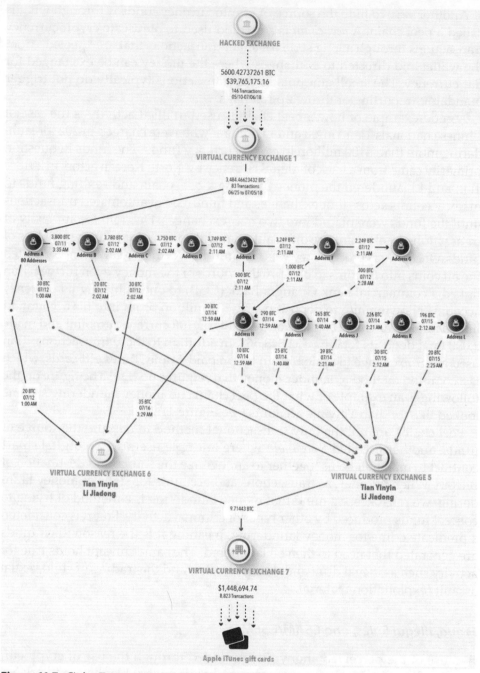

Figure 11.7: CipherTrace example of Tian Yinyin's accounts

coins like Monero, online users feel protected and even comfortable committing illegal acts. One extremely interesting case of fraud using cryptocurrency that stands out to me is Anne-Elisabeth and her husband, Tom Hagen, a prominent businessman in Lørenskog, Norway. In 2018, Anne-Elisabeth went missing leaving little forensic evidence behind and no sign of forced entry to the couple's home. Tom revealed to police that he received a ransom letter demanding $10 million in Monero for her return. After years with no leads, police arrested her husband Tom in 2020 for killing and aiding and abetting the murder of his wife Anne-Elizabeth.

Surprisingly, another man was arrested with Tom, a 30-year old man using the fake identity, Ole Henrik Golf, purchased from the Dark Web site CardPass. Law enforcement revealed that crypto services were used to obscure the movement of funds in the kidnapping, and after police helped Tom pay $1.4 million in ransom, all communication stopped. Tom was subsequently released 11 days after his arrest and has never been charged with any crimes, denying any involvement in his wife's disappearance. Anne-Elizabeth is still missing with no information about whether she is alive.[22,23] Using the Dark Web, it is possible to purchase fake identities like passports and driver's licenses that a person could use to hide who they truly are when perpetuating a fraud, and whole markets exist for the purpose of selling these types of illegal documents.

As an individual looking to commit a fraudulent and illegal act online, using Dark Web marketplaces and masking your identity and purchases through privacy coins, mixers, VPNs, and privacy emails is commonplace. This tactic is used for purchasing drugs, weapons, and unfortunately child exploitation material. According to the Internet Watch Foundation (IWF) the number of websites accepting cryptocurrency in return for child sexual abuse material (CSAM) has more than doubled every year since 2018.[24] It's a sick game of whack-a-mole, and when investigators shut down one child abuse network, two more will pop up and facilitate their crimes through untraceable cryptocurrency transactions.

Many think their transactions can never be traced back to them, like the 2017 Matthew Falder case outlined in the book *Tracers in the Dark* by Andy Greenberg.[25] Falder, a Manchester-based academic, would pretend to be a female artist soliciting nude photos from strangers online and then threaten to

---

[22] www.esquire.com/uk/culture/a41088769/who-is-anne-elisabeth-hagen-the-lorenskog-disappearance-true-story.

[23] www.nytimes.com/2020/04/28/world/europe/tom-hagen-murder-anne-elisabeth-hagen.html.

[24] www.iwf.org.uk/about-us/who-we-are/annual-report-2021.

[25] www.amazon.com/Tracers-Dark-Global-Crime-Cryptocurrency/dp/0385548095?asc_campaign=&asc_source=&asc_refurl=https%3A%2F%2Fwww.wired.com%2Fstory%2Ftracers-in-the-dark-welcome-to-video-crypto-anonymity-myth%2F&tag=w050b-20&ascsubtag=6245f57dc7f67532c5aa5310.

expose the images to their family and friends unless they recorded themselves performing depraved acts including self-injury and sexual abuse. When arrested by the UK's National Crime Agency (NCA), considered their equivalent to the FBI, they found he was a registered member of a site called "Welcome to Video."

Welcome to Video sold users access to a large library of constantly updated child sexual abuse videos in exchange for Bitcoin payments. An NCA agent then contacted Chainanalysis, a company that developed techniques for de-anonymizing Bitcoin users through watching the coins move through the blockchain until reaching an address that could be tied to a real person. Using a crypto-tracing tool called Reactor, they quickly uncovered nearly the entire network of users, many of whom sent payments to Welcome to Video straight from their personal wallets with no attempt to anonymize the transactions.

Through transactional analysis, they were able to trace the cash-outs to two exchanges in South Korea, but because the site with 250,000 videos appeared to be one of the biggest repositories of CSAM videos law enforcement had ever seen, they needed to take faster action than just pulling down the server in South Korea. On a hunch, one investigator logged into Welcome to Video and right-clicked the page to view page source. There it was, an IP address within the HTML showing the unprotected physical location of where the Welcome to Video server was physically hosted. The mistake the administrator made was that the site was hosted on Tor, but the images on the site pulled from their computer without being routed through the anonymizing platform Tor. The investigation team painstakingly traced each user on the blockchain to try to establish the true identity of the men. Finally, they got a warrant for 23-year-old South Korean Son Jong-woo's Gmail accounts and exchange records based on his cash-outs of the proceeds from the site.

After the investigation and arrests and numerous suicides of users from Welcome to Video including academics and daycare workers, the site was finally seized by authorities in 2019.[26] In October 2019, Jong Woo Son was indicted on nine counts for his operation of the insidious child exploitation site Welcome to Video.[27] Jong Woo Son and the countless other users of the site failed to understand that the Dark Web and the use of cryptocurrency does not inherently provide anonymity to users. OSINT analysts can implement tracing techniques to follow both the money and the user's actions back to a point where their identity could be revealed. I have talked about the Dark Web and the reliance on it for both legal use such as journalism in repressed regions but also for illegal activities, but let's look at it a bit closer to understand how analysts use it to find information.

---

[26] www.wired.com/story/ tracers-in-the-dark-welcome-to-video-crypto-anonymity-myth.
[27] www.justice.gov/opa/pr/south-korean-national-and-hundreds-others-charged-worldwide-takedown-largest-darknet-child.

11.2   The Dark Web

Now let's turn to cryptocurrency and the Dark Web.

Overview of the Dark Web

To fully realize the ways in which cryptocurrency is used, we have to talk about the different parts of the Internet and specifically the Dark Web. We learned in the beginning of this book that the Internet is being indexed and crawled all the time by indexers like Google who capture the data to allow us to easily search through it. The part of the Web where indexers are able to perform this task is called the *Clear Web*. However, there are places on the Internet where these indexers are unable or unallowed to access called the Deep Web and Dark Web (see Figure 11.8).

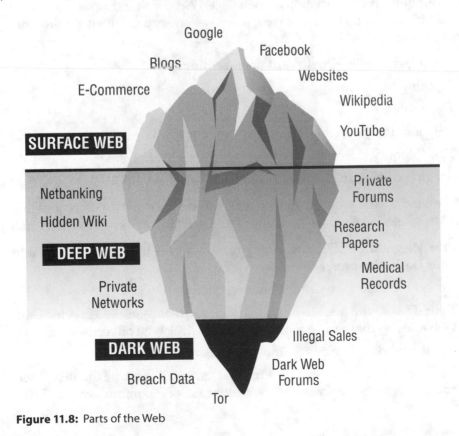

Figure 11.8: Parts of the Web

The *Deep Web* is a part of the Web where the content owners have blocked crawlers from indexing their data, or the data is behind a paywall or sign-in page preventing indexing. Typical Deep Web material could be medical records, legal documents, confidential pages, and government resources; the Deep Web is estimated to be roughly 96 percent of the Internet. The 5 percent of the Internet called the *Dark Web* is a part of the Deep Web that is not only inaccessible to indexers but also to those with a regular browser. To access the Dark Web, users need to use a special browser like Tor because it is *intended* to be hidden from the rest of the Internet.

The Deep Web is generally only talked about in a negative light regarding its use for illicit or illegal activity such as the sale of drugs, weapons, and CSAM. However, the Dark Web serves legitimate and legal purposes such as news organization websites that may be banned in certain regions like ProPublica, some clear websites like Facebook also have Deep Web sites, and journalists and whistleblowers often use the Dark Web to communicate anonymously with their sources. It's important that we not view all sites and users on the Dark Web as criminals. As an analyst, following users and activity into the Dark Web can be tricky due to the requirements for anonymity, special browsers, and marketplace requirements. Consider that in many cases you can find enough information about your subject or entity in the open Clear Web. If you do end up having to chase the rabbit into the Dark Web, there is some typical illicit activity that you may come across.

- Buying and selling credit card data (carding)
- Hacking/ransomware as a service
- Drug sales
- Weapons (although this is almost always done by law enforcement as bait)
- Fake identity information (passport, driver's license, etc.)
- Trading child sexual abuse material (CSAM)

If, for example, your project requirements have you searching for users engaging in illicit drug sales on the Dark Web, you would need to follow several steps first:

1. Practice good OPSEC, ensuring your identity is in no way attached to your Dark Web presence.
2. Access the Dark Web using a browser such as Tor.
3. To find sales, you need to find a marketplace that requires a specific Dark Web address that can be found on lists or Clear Web advertisements.
4. Use the marketplace ads to find your sellers of interest.
5. Discover pivot points and patterns that may lead to a true identity (usernames, cryptocurrency wallets, social media, and communication IDs).

Much of the illegal activity that takes place on the Dark Web happens in Darknet marketplaces where a seller is able to post advertisements for potential buyers including drugs, weapons, CSAM, and hacking for hire, some of which are scams themselves.

Darknet Marketplaces

Darknet markets are black markets on the Dark Web for selling and buying legal and illegal products (often scams) using cryptocurrency to anonymize the sales for both sellers and buyers. To access a marketplace, you will need to have an onion link (a specific link used to access Tor sites) , which typically you can find posted in an ad, forum, or website on the Clear Web.

Also, there are maintained lists of onion link sources like dark.fail that provide the current links for marketplaces, forums, and sites, or analysts can use trusted resources like the Hunchly Dark Web Report at www.hunch.ly/darkweb-osint that provides weekly reporting on marketplaces including their onion links.

Once you have a link to a marketplace, it does not necessarily guarantee your entry. If you are a vendor trying to create listings in a new market, some will require a referral, proof of reputation, proof of a crime, or even cash deposit. As a buyer, making an account can also have similar requirements, making it hard to use a newly created research account for Darknet marketplace research. If you know you will be performing a lot of this type of analysis, do yourself a favor and begin curating a research account now so that it has been around longer and appears more trustworthy. Yet other marketplaces will be entirely off-limits to us as OSINT analysts because they demand proof, which would mean committing a crime or interacting with other users in an active way (see Figure 11.9).

Once a vendor has been approved to sell on a marketplace, generally they will post an advertisement with a photo of the product along with a description, any good reviews, and instructions for how they accept payment and how the goods will be delivered to the buyer. Listings often include usable OSINT information such as a privacy email, WhatsApp address, clear website addresses, and Pretty Good Privacy (PGP) encryption keys that can all be individually analyzed using the same techniques we have learned throughout the book. If a purchase and shipment has been successful, the buyer leaves a review, which then adds a rating to the seller's account giving them a good reputation and proving they are not scamming. Marketplace sales can net huge profits for vendors like Maximilian Schmidt, the 19-year-old German teenager running a drug empire from his bedroom in his mom's house.

Schmidt, known on the Dark Web as Shiny_Flakes, openly sold hundreds of kilos of cocaine, LSD, meth, marijuana, MDMA, and hash worldwide using several Darknet markets. For payment he accepted cryptocurrency, and for shipping he would order a taxi using a burner SIM card and take them to package station 45 near his house. A mistake of insufficient postage on a package initially tipped off investigators, and the routine of the narcotics dead drops by a courier from the Netherlands every Thursday led law enforcement to arrest the courier, which kicked off a raid on Schmidt's residence that was filled with drugs. A document that was open on his laptop at the time of arrest listed the logins for all of his servers.[28] Maximillian was sentenced to seven years in a juvenile detention center and was released in 2019 after serving more than half of the sentence; however, authorities suspect he is still trafficking drugs online and are actively investigating him. To me, shipping always seemed like it would be the weak point in the chain of illegal online sales, but the Dark Web also provides education for buyers and sellers through forums that offer techniques for avoiding detection while shipping.

Figure 11.9: Hydra marketplace

While Shiny_Flakes may have run a drug empire, his operation as a vendor is miniscule compared to the entire Dark Web marketplace known as AlphaBay. In 2017, AlphaBay, a major source of fentanyl and heroin distribution along with fraudulent IDs, firearms, toxic chemicals, and malware, was seized by the United States in cooperation with at least six other countries in secret two prong operation known as Operation Bayonet. Alpha02 AKA Alexandre Cazes was arrested in Thailand for creating and administering the marketplace. He

---

[28] www.vice.com/en/article/pgan8z/
how-police-busted-shiny-flakes-germanys-biggest-online-drug-market.

was indicted on several counts, and his assets were frozen including millions in cryptocurrency that are the profits from AlphaBay's illegal dealings. At the time of the site's takedown, the market had more than 250,000 listings for illegal drugs and chemicals and was the largest marketplace at the time.[29]

When AlphaBay went offline, Dutch police working on the second prong of the investigation noticed users rising on AlphaBay's rival marketplace, Hansa. The investigations team was noting thousands of cryptocurrency transactions due to the influx of new members from AlphaBay. When Operation Bayonet came to light with the seizure of AlphaBay and the suicide of Alexandre Cazes in a Thai jail cell, the operation into the Hansa marketplace was almost revealed. Little did users know that the German police had arrested the administrators of Hansa, and the Dutch police were impersonating them to collect information about the users, vendors, and staff on the marketplace. After police ran Hansa for 27 days, they were finally pressured by prosecutors to shut down the site having surveilled 27,000 transactions, seizing 1,200 Bitcoins worth tens of millions of dollars, and collecting data on more than 420,000 users and more than 10,000 home addresses sowing fear across the Dark Web.[30]

These thrilling tales of cat-and-mouse games between law enforcement and criminals and the profits they make illustrates how understanding the Dark Web will continue to play a huge role in cryptocurrency analysis. Knowing the history of cryptocurrency, how it is moved, and how it is used is only half the battle; the other half is learning the methods for analyzing it from publicly available information.

11.3 Methods for Cryptocurrency Analysis

Now that we have learned a bit about cryptocurrency and how it is used let's look at some analysis methods.

Where to Begin?

Because cryptocurrency use is rooted in anonymity and many coins like Monero are specifically used to mask the identity and address of the user, it can be hard to analyze cryptocurrency transactions. For this book I want to narrow the process down to three main starting point and how to work through the analysis for each:

- Starting with a subject of interest
- Starting with a wallet of interest
- Starting with a transaction of interest

---

[29] www.justice.gov/opa/pr/alphabay-largest-online-dark-market-shut-down.
[30] www.wired.com/story/alphabay-series-part-6-endgame.

Once you have the requirements as agreed upon by the stakeholder of the project, you can begin the funneling process of information for each starting point.

Starting with a Subject of Interest

Q: Can we tie a subject to a cryptocurrency wallet (see Figure 11.10)?

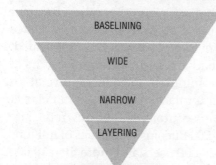

Figure 11.10: Funnel method

Baselining

- Are there any historically relevant cases tied to the subject?
- What information do we already know?

Starting Wide

- Does the subject's name appear in NFT search results?
- Does the subject's name appear in wallet search results?
- Does the Subject disclose any wallet addresses?

Personal disclosure

Personal disclosure remains one of the most important ways to gather information in OSINT. Some examples of how wallet addresses can be disclosed through a subject are as follows:

- Using the address to collect donations on their website. This happens with politically affiliated or fraudulent groups collecting donations.
- Posting the address in Clear Web or Dark Web forums where their username can be tied to an identity.
- Using a cryptocurrency wallet and personally identifying themselves through a name, email address, username, etc.

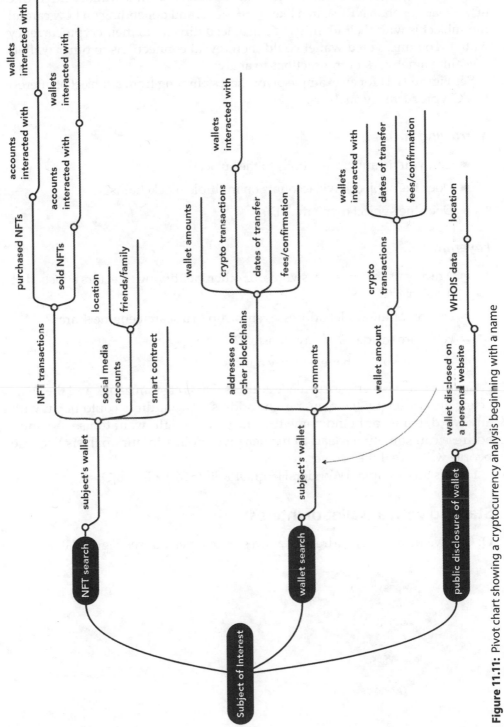

Figure 11.11: Pivot chart showing a cryptocurrency analysis beginning with a name

For example, the name of a subject can be searched in a wallet search like `etherscan.io` or an NFT search like `opensea.io`, and depending on how careful the subject is with their identity, this may lead directly to their cryptocurrency wallet. The uncovered wallet could then reveal connections to other wallets revealing a network of transactions to analyze.

See Figure 11.11 for an example pivot chart stemming from a subject of interest in a Cryptocurrency analysis.

Narrowing Focus

- Can you tie any transactions to the subject?
- Does the subject have accounts on multiple blockchains?
- Does the subject own any NFTs?

Layering

- Are any usernames, passwords, or other identifying selectors attached to the subject?
- Do any of the wallet addresses show up in a search engine search?
- What are the dates of any transfers?
- Does the subject have a vanity address?

A *vanity address* is a cryptocurrency address that is customizable, and the characters are chosen by the owner of the address. The address could begin with any word, name, or brand name that the owner might want to use. A vanity address can sometimes lead to further pivot points in our analysis because people will reveal themselves.

Here is an example: 1WondersHHqnDPRSfiZ5GXJ8Gk9dbjO.

Starting with a Wallet of Interest

Q: Can we tie a wallet address or addresses to a person (see Figure 11.12)?

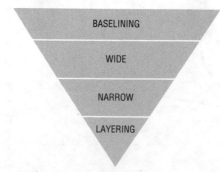

Figure 11.12: Funnel method

Baselining

- Are there any historically relevant cases we can use to get ideas?
- What information do we already know?
- Does the address(es) have any history?

Starting Wide

- Do any of the wallet addresses appear on the Dark Web?
- Do any of the wallet addresses appear in wallet search results?
- Do any of the wallet accounts disclose an identity?
- Do any of the associated transactions lead to an identity?

Narrowing Focus

- Do the addresses appear in search engine results?
- Do the addresses appear in a sanctions search?
- Are the addresses tied to any illicit sales advertisements?

Layering

- Are any usernames, passwords, or other identifying selectors attached to the addresses or wallet?
- What are the dates of any transfers?
- Do the receivers in the transactions reveal their identity?
- Do the wallets appear on other blockchains?
- If the address is used on the Dark Web for payment, is it tied to any social media or communication accounts (WhatsApp, email, etc.)?

When looking at addresses and wallets, bear in mind there are privacy-focused options that will make the source harder to determine. Ultimately, with a privacy-focused cryptocurrency, we are hoping for an OPSEC mistake by the owner that will tie the address back to the owner's real identity.

Privacy-Focused Cryptocurrency

While Bitcoin is public, we have learned that Monero is privacy-focused and thus intrinsically harder to track.

Public Cryptocurrency

If we focus here on Bitcoin because it is the oldest active public cryptocurrencies and because all Bitcoin transactions are public, traceable, and stored within the

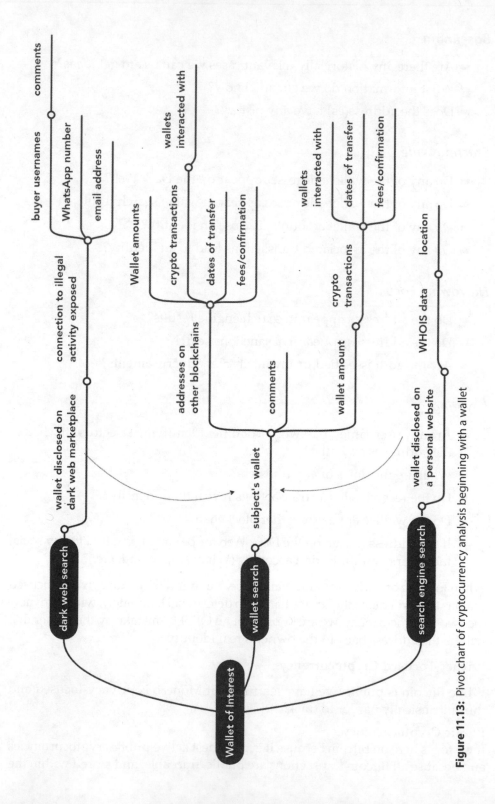

Figure 11.13: Pivot chart of cryptocurrency analysis beginning with a wallet

Bitcoin network, there is information we are able to access for each address. Each Bitcoin address is unique to its wallet, and although we are unable to see the owner of the address, we can see the following:

- Bitcoin wallet balance
- Transaction history
    - Amount sent
    - Address sent from
    - Date of transfer
    - Address of receiver
    - Any fees
    - Confirmations

See Figure 11.13 for an example pivot chart stemming from a wallet of interest in a Cryptocurrency analysis.

Tracing Cash-Outs at the Exchange Point

According to veteran OSINT analyst and cryptocurrency tracing expert @sinwindie, the most effective way to analyze cryptocurrency transactions is to track them back to the cash-out point or exchange to reveal a person of interest. The disclosures available will depend on the specific blockchain; some exchanges like ETH have their wallets noted as belonging to a specific exchange.

Let's look at an example of address tracing with a known "bad" cryptocurrency wallet in Etherscan.io (see Figure 11.14).

Known Bad Address: 0x098B716B8Aaf21512996dC57EB0615e2383E2f96

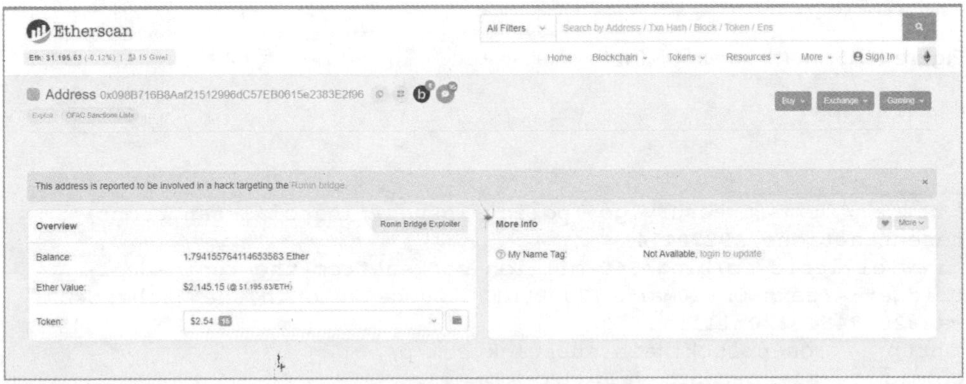

Figure 11.14: Tracing a "bad" wallet in Etherscan.io

Right from the start we can see something is wrong with this address because Etherscan gives it the labels "Exploit" and "OFAC Sanctions List." If we search this wallet address on the U.S. Department of the Treasury website,[31] we find out that the wallet has been added to the North Korea Designation Update for Specially Designated Nationals. The exploit listed on the Etherscan page is the "Ronin Bridge Exploiter," which the Treasury Department associated to the North Korean group named Lazarus Group. On March 29, 2022, the Ronin Network divulged that 173,600 Ether (ETH) and 25.5 million USD coins were stolen from the Ronin cross-chain bridge with the total being $540 million (see Figure 11.15).[32,33]

North Korea Designation Update

04/14/2022

SPECIALLY DESIGNATED NATIONALS LIST UPDATE

The following changes have been made to OFAC's SDN List:

LAZARUS GROUP (a.k.a. "APPLEWORM"; a.k.a. "APT-C-26"; a.k.a. "GROUP 77"; a.k.a. "GUARDIANS OF PEACE"; a.k.a. "HIDDEN COBRA"; a.k.a. "OFFICE 91"; a.k.a. "RED DOT"; a.k.a. "TEMP.HERMIT"; a.k.a. "THE NEW ROMANTIC CYBER ARMY TEAM"; a.k.a. "WHOIS HACKING TEAM"; a.k.a. "ZINC"), Potonggang District, Pyongyang, Korea, North; Secondary sanctions risk: North Korea Sanctions Regulations, sections 510.201 and 510.210; Transactions Prohibited For Persons Owned or Controlled By U.S. Financial Institutions: North Korea Sanctions Regulations section 510.214 [DPRK3]. -to- LAZARUS GROUP (a.k.a. "APPLEWORM"; a.k.a. "APT-C-26"; a.k.a. "GROUP 77"; a.k.a. "GUARDIANS OF PEACE"; a.k.a. "HIDDEN COBRA"; a.k.a. "OFFICE 91"; a.k.a. "RED DOT"; a.k.a. "TEMP.HERMIT"; a.k.a. "THE NEW ROMANTIC CYBER ARMY TEAM"; a.k.a. "WHOIS HACKING TEAM"; a.k.a. "ZINC"), Potonggang District, Pyongyang, Korea, North; Digital Currency Address - ETH 0x098B716B8Aaf21512996dC57EB0615e2383E2f96; Secondary sanctions risk: North Korea Sanctions Regulations, sections 510.201 and 510.210; Transactions Prohibited For Persons Owned or Controlled By U.S. Financial Institutions: North Korea Sanctions Regulations section 510.214 [DPRK3].

Figure 11.15: North Korea SDN list

---

[31] https://home.treasury.gov/policy-issues/financial-sanctions/recent-actions/20220414.

[32] www.elliptic.co/blog/540-million-stolen-from-the-ronin-defi-bridge#:~:text=On%20March%2029th%2C%20the%20Ronin,the%20theft%20was%20%24540%20million.

[33] https://roninblockchain.substack.com/p/community-alert-ronin-validators?s=r.

Looking back at the Etherscan image, we see an icon next to the address with an 8 next to it, indicating the other tokens that the same wallet address was holding including the following:

- Binance Smart Chain (BSC)
- Polygon (MATIC)
- Fantom (FTM)
- Avalanche C-Chain
- Moonbeam (GLMR)
- Boba (BOBA)
- Ropsten Testnet
- Polygon Mumbai Testnet

We can also see the balance of this wallet is 1.794155764114653583 Ether at a value of $2,144.97. This attacker used hacked private keys to forge fake withdrawals through two transactions, one of which is shown here where the attacker transferred 173,600 Wrapped Ethereum (WETH) (see Figure 11.16):

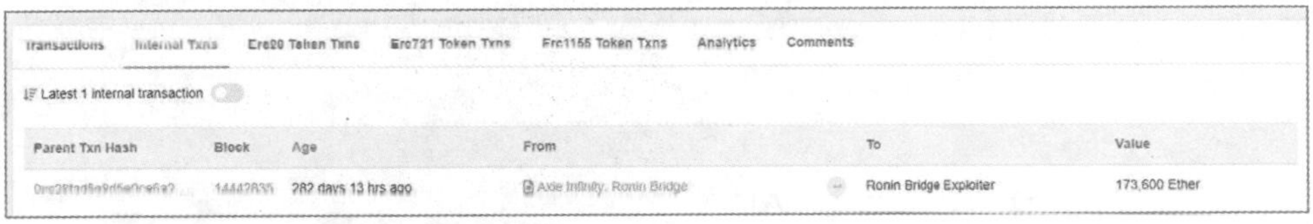

Figure 11.16: Transfer of wrapped ethereum

By using the freely available charts within Etherscan, we can get an overview of the balance history for the wallet address. With a quick look, we can see when a big cash-out has happened or a big influx of money possibly indicating illicit activity. In March, there was a huge spike in Ethereum transactions for this address, which directly corresponds to when the Ronin Network had 173,600 Ether (ETH) stolen (see Figures 11.17-11.18). Seeing variances in visual data can offer clues to what is going on in the accounts when we are able to add context with additional open-source information.

Following Cryptocurrency Mining Scripts

Cryptocurrency mining scripts are functions that are placed on a website and use a website visitor's CPU to mine cryptocurrency and when the block is validated the visitor is rewarded with cryptocurrency. Typically, Monero is used as the cryptocurrency of choice because of its anonymity. It is sometimes possible to find

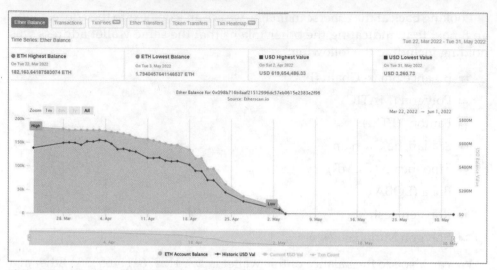

Figure 11.17: Tracking wallet balance over time

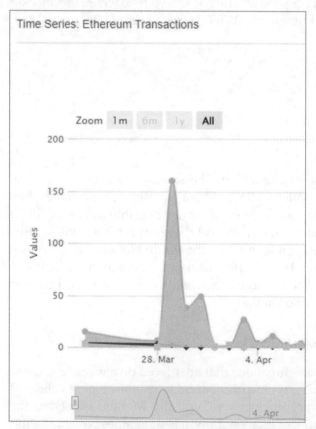

Figure 11.18: Narrowing wallet in on anomalous days

and view the scripts on public code repositories like Docker, Gitlab, and GitHub or in threat intel reports that can contain information such as the following:

- Username
- Password
- Mining pool
- Worker ID

Starting with a Transaction of Interest

Starting with a cryptocurrency transaction, our goal might be to determine the wallets involved in the transaction as well as the owners of the wallets. We can use *transaction mapping* techniques to trace financial transactions to their exchange endpoints.

Q: Can we tie a transaction to a subject (see Figure 11.19)?

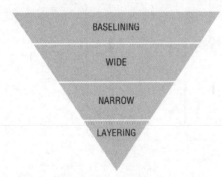

Figure 11.19: Funnel method

Baselining

- Are there any historically relevant cases we can use to get ideas?
- What information do we already know?
- Does the address have any history?

Starting Wide

- Do you have the wallet address tied to the transaction through a wallet search?
- Are there other transactions?
- Do any of the wallet accounts disclose an identity?
- Do any of the associated transactions lead to an identity?

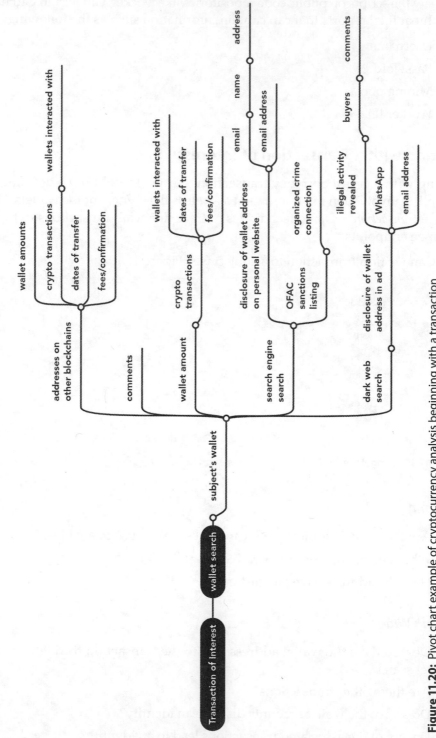

Figure 11.20: Pivot chart example of cryptocurrency analysis beginning with a transaction

Narrowing Focus

- Is the address tied to other blockchains?
- Which addresses do the transactions go to?
- Is there a pattern to the payment amounts?
- Can any of the addresses be found in a search engine search?

Layering

- Are any usernames, passwords, or other identifying selectors attached to the addresses or wallet?
- What are the dates of any transfers?
- Do the addresses appear on the Dark Web?
- Do the addresses appear on a website along with personal disclosures?
- If the address is used on the Dark Web for payment, is it tied to any social media or communication accounts (WhatsApp, email, etc.)?

See Figure 11.20 for an example pivot chart stemming from a transaction of interest in a Cryptocurrency analysis.

CHAPTER 12

Non-fungible Tokens

12.1   Overview of Non-fungible Tokens

We previously discussed fungible tokens like Bitcoin or Litecoin that are not unique and have no distinguishing marks like a serial number. Now we turn to non-fungible items, which are wholly unique and indivisible like a house, car, or piece of artwork. *Non-fungible tokens (NFTs)* are one-of-a-kind cryptocurrency items that store data such as digital artwork or an academic title and cannot be duplicated. NFTs are often bought and sold on dedicated marketplaces like `opensea.io` and `rarible.com` and work on what are called *smart contracts*. A smart contract is a program used to execute an agreement between a buyer and seller, and typically the output will vary depending on the input.

Smart contracts control things such as royalties, rarity, and collections for NFTs, and ultimately, they determine how you are allowed to use your NFT and how much it will resell for. Finally, a person's ownership of an NFT is dependent entirely on their possession of the private key and the NFT; if someone steals the private key and transfers the NFT to their own wallet, the NFT will now belong to them.

A good example of NFTs while analyzing a crime is to revisit the Ronin Explorer exploit wallet address from Chapter 11, "Cryptocurrency." If we examine the wallet, we can see the owner purchased NFTs as well (see Figures 12.1-12.2).

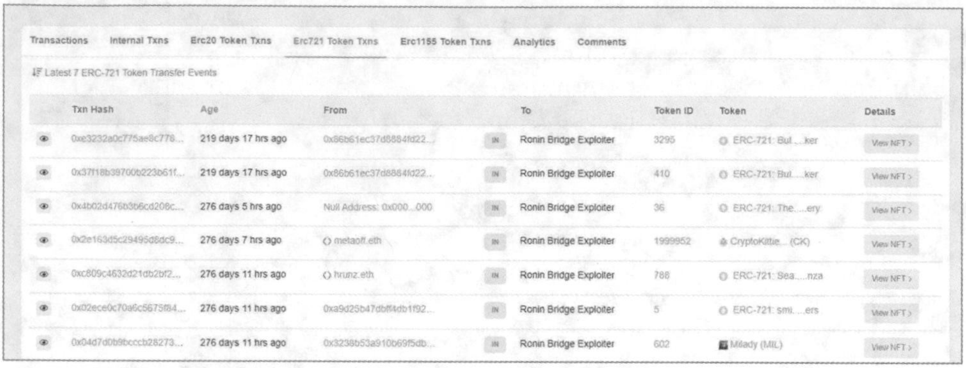

Figure 12.1: Ronin Explorer wallet address transactions

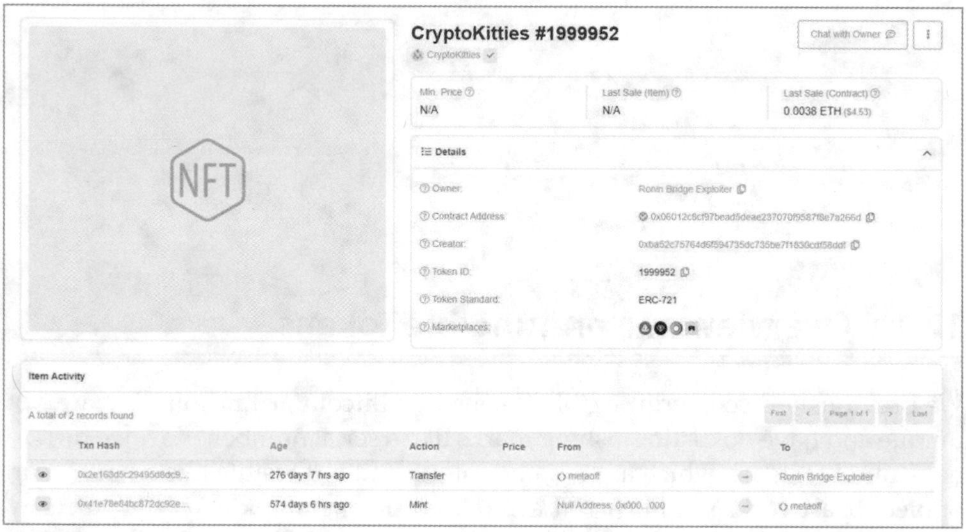

Figure 12.2: NFT details

NFT Crimes

Let's now explore some specific crimes that are seen regarding NFTs and the transactions.

Ponzi Schemes and Rug Pulls

A *Ponzi scheme* is a trick used to get investors to invest money in something with the promise of high returns, but in reality, each new investor is paying the existing investor while the people behind the scheme get rich. NFTs are attractive for Ponzi schemes because of the difficulty in valuing an NFT and the perceived value from marketing driving up the price. Similarly, a *rug pull* is where cryptocurrency developers lure in early investors and then abruptly abandon the project either running away with the funds or selling off their investments and draining investor funds.

Fake NFTs

In this scam, valueless *fake NFTs* are created for cheap, and then the owners convince everyone the NFTs are rare and desirable by getting influencers and celebrities to post on social media about it. The price of the NFTs is driven up rapidly, and then the owners sell them off for a large profit leaving the new owners with a worthless NFT. Because anyone can create an ERC-721 token, there is no guarantee it will be worth anything.

Get Rich Quick

Someone creates an NFT, claims it is rare and worth lots of money, and sells it to a consumer at a much higher value than it is actually worth.

Phishing

The phishing scam is like a traditional phish where a fake message is sent to the wallet owner from an exchange, business, or wallet provider. The message usually contains a link that tricks the user into putting their credentials in, and then the scammer can steal the funds from the wallet.

12.2   Methods for Analyzing NFTs

Now that we have learned what NFTs are and how they are used for both good and bad, let's look at how we can analyze them for OSINT.

By Wallet Number or Address

Much like other forms of cryptocurrency, NFT marketplaces will let you search users by their wallet numbers, which can often lead to the following:

- Wallet transaction activity
- Owner's other accounts
- Owner's online presence
- Owner's identity

One way to search for wallet addresses is by using a site called `Opensea.io` (see Figure 12.3).[1] Opensea is a site that allows you to search, collect, and sell NFTs, and for us it is useful because we can search by user and wallet number. This number can be searched on multiple marketplace accounts to see if we can find any similarities.

Figure 12.3: User BenColefax on `opensea.io`

As an example, if I copy the wallet number for this user on Opensea and search it in `etherscan.io`, I can see the balance of the wallet, the value in Ether, and multiple transactions. At the top by the wallet number it shows other chains where this wallet number shows up (see Figure 12.4).

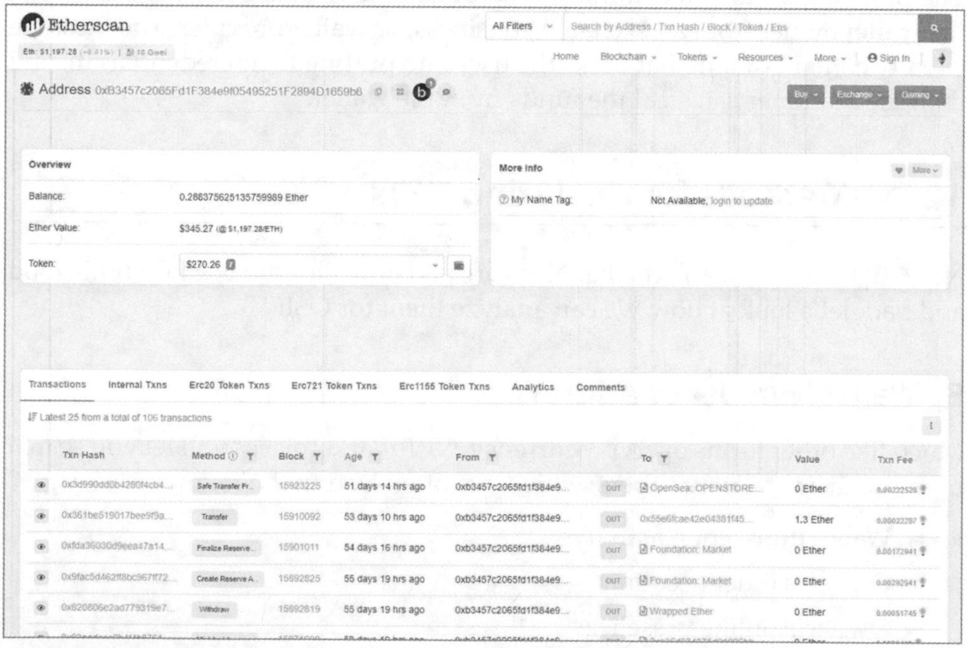

Figure 12.4: Wallet details based on wallet ID search in `etherscan.io`

---

[1] `https://opensea.io`.

This number also shows up on PolygonScan. Polygon (MATIC) is another token that uses the Ethereum blockchain and connects their products, increasing scalability and flexibility without sacrificing security. There are roughly 10 billion tokens for MATIC, and most have already been issued. We could explore these other chains for details that may reveal the person's identity or connections to other wallets (see Figure 12.5).

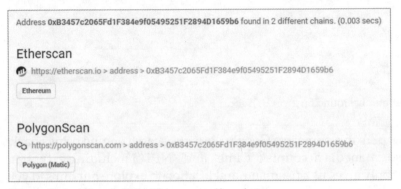

Figure 12.5: Other wallet addresses on other chains

If we hop over to another top marketplace for NFTs, `Rarible.com`, we can search for the same wallet number to see if this wallet is connected to anything for sale/sold on that marketplace (see Figure 12.6). Looking on other marketplaces might reveal disclosures that alone mean very little but combined can provide our subject's personal information.

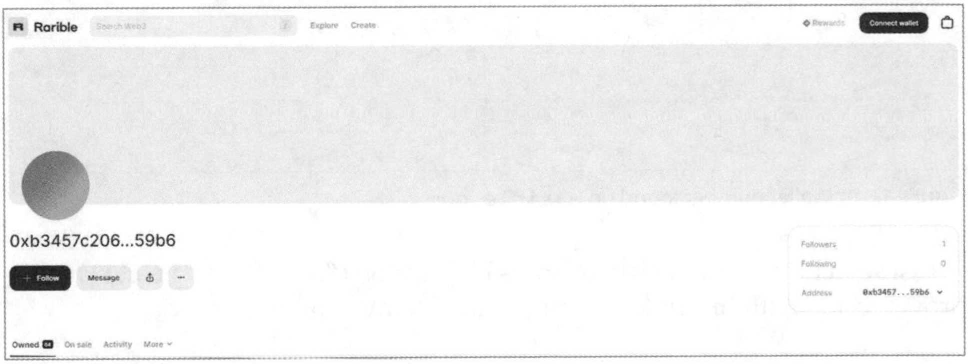

Figure 12.6: Wallet number found on `Rarible.com`

On Rarible we can see this wallet ties to an account that owns several NFTs, and if we click Activity, we see NFTs that match the style of our original account, and we also see the same name (see Figure 12.7). Having the name is a very good lead, but I wouldn't expect to see a name available with more nefarious transactions, so you might have to get creative to find personal account information.

Figure 12.7: Wallet number found on `Rarible.com`

Searching this person's name in a Google dork in a search engine brings back many of their social media accounts ("name" and "NFT") including a Twitter account that not only gives us a username and location to explore but links to yet another marketplace (see Figure 12.8): Foundation App. By using `Whatsmyname .app` to search for the username found on Twitter, I was able to find a YouTube account with a photo of the arts and a link to an Instagram account. So, you can see a bit how pivoting works from an NFT to a subject of interest.

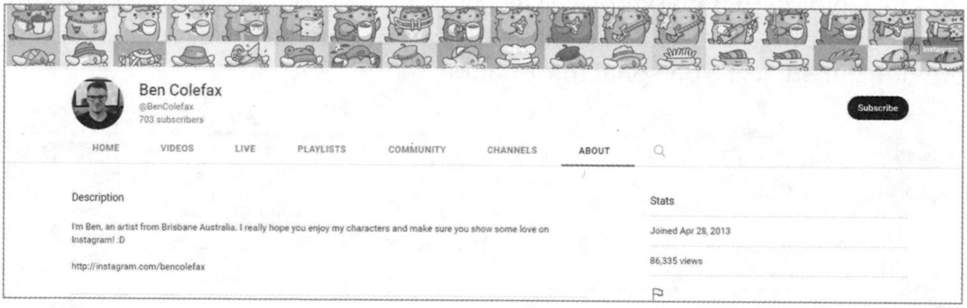

Figure 12.8: Wallet number found on `Rarible.com`

Just searching the artist's name plus his location (*"NAME" + "LOCATION"*) provided me with his LinkedIn page and Udemy course.

By Image

Another method to locate a subject of interest from an NFT is by image searching, specifically reverse image searching. If we have an image of an NFT, we can reverse search it to find other places on the Internet where the image exists.

Using the same account as earlier, I reverse searched one of the images and ended up finding the artist's website (see Figure 12.9). Unfortunately, the website no longer exists, and the WHOIS records were privacy covered.

Figure 12.9: Reverse image searching an NFT

Another tool that @sinwindie clued me into is NFT Finder,[2] which lets you search text or drop an image into the search to find similar NFTs (see Figure 12.10).

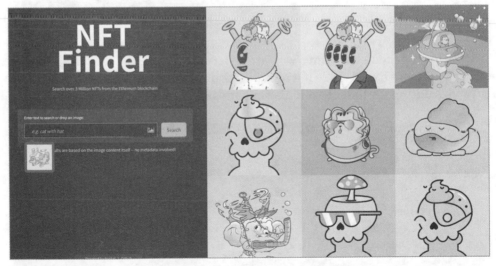

Figure 12.10: NFT finder

---

[2] www.nyckel.com/nft-finder/?%20NFT%20Finder.

What Is ENS?

Looking at another account on Opensea, we see another identifier above the wallet number that ends in `.eth`. The `.eth` is for the Ethereum Name Service (ENS), which is a naming service for a blockchain similar to the Domain Name System (DNS) (see Figure 12.11). Much like DNS, it maps machine-readable identifiers to human-readable names; for example, we use URLs rather than some obnoxiously long number. This makes them easier to remember like a website. These ENS names can be purchased with a wallet on Ethereum and linked to wallets, making wallet addresses easier to remember than a random string of digits.

Figure 12.11: NFT finder

By using the Ethereum Name Service app (`app.ens.domains`), we can search the `.eth` address we found to see if it provides additional associations. This example provides addresses for both a registrant and a controller (see Figure 12.12).

Figure 12.12: Ethereum name service

If we then search the registrant and controller on `etherscan.io`, we can see the value of the wallet, any NFTs they own, and any transactions in their history. Sometimes we can get lucky and use the same `.eth` address in a search engine query to find it listed in the profiles of Instagram, Twitter, and other social media where the artist is trying to sell their product. This may lead to revealing the identity of the wallet owner.

Look for Metadata

In the same way that we have previously found data hidden in imagery, we can find the digital information or metadata in NFT files. The metadata in an NFT is information that the author decides is significant to include. To get a bit technical, the NFT's metadata is often saved in the InterPlanetary File System (IPFS), which is a P2P system that preserves multimedia files. When an NFT is created, a random number is generated, assigned, and kept in the metadata. We can view an NFT's metadata, confirm its ownership, and track the transactions using `etherscan.io`, but to view the metadata of a smart contract that controls an NFT, we have to inspect the smart contract under Details to find the following:

- NFT token ID
- Contract address
- Status of NFT metadata
- NFT encoding protocol
- Blockchain housing the NFT

While financial research and cryptocurrency analysis require some advanced OSINT tradecraft techniques, this type of analysis is certainly something that can be achieved at all levels. Much of the background information for how these technologies and financial systems work can be found online, and with a bit of experience and trial and error, you can be performing financial OSINT!

CHAPTER 13

What's Next?

13.1 Thank You for Diving In with Me

Where do I even begin to wrap up this book? I feel like we were just getting to know each other and now it's already time for you go out into the world. When I first dreamt up the concept for *Deep Dive* more than a year ago, I had one goal in mind: *to develop a resource focused on methodology and tradecraft for new and senior OSINT analysts to be able to apply to their current work.*

I truly hope that this book will be a long lasting and valuable resource for you. By limiting the references to tools throughout this book, I was able to spotlight the methodology that should be valuable no matter which tools are used. I know there are quite a few of you that love lists of tools, and for you I will be maintaining a list of resources on my website at `raebaker.net/resources`. If you find yourself yearning for more OSINT learning resources, there is a huge community of analysts on Twitter, Youtube, and Discord. Another great resource for OSINT is analyst blogs, some of which I mentioned throughout the book. If you want to keep up-to-date with my YouTube training videos, blog, and conference talks, you can sign up for my newsletter on `raebaker.net`. Remember that everyone starts somewhere and that your present is someone else's beginning.

Important Reminders

Now that you have read through this book, here are some reminders as you begin to tackle real-world cases.

Take Care of Yourself

Depending on your role, you may encounter cases that take a heavy emotional toll and it is not always clear to us when we are experiencing depression. Be sure to speak to someone regularly if you deal with any traumatic cases and take care of yourself, physically and emotionally. Always remember that *you are not alone*; an entire OSINT community is out there rooting for you and maybe would drop everything to help a fellow analyst. In Part I, "Foundational OSINT," of this book there are resources for help; please use them immediately if you are feeling like you need to talk. Ensure that you take care of yourself by taking breaks often, getting up and moving, talking with other people, and eating right.

Use Your Skill for Good

Information itself is not inherently bad, but what we do with that information can be. In this field you will come in contact with personal data, and you will learn OSINT tradecraft, which can be quite powerful. You may be faced with situations that force you to choose between helping or harming someone. I implore you to use your skills to make the world a better place. There are numerous volunteer organizations that use OSINT analysis to help men, women, and children out of crisis situations. You can choose what kind of analyst you want to be.

It is never okay to do the following:

- Publish a person's private information to the Internet without consent.
- Hunt predators without the backing of law enforcement.
- Monitor *anyone* who is not approved as a subject of interest in a legitimate case (not an ex, mother, father, boss, etc.).
- Use active reconnaissance techniques.

Never Stop Learning

If I had never had the insatiable urge to keep learning, I would have never taken the blind (and some would say crazy) leap into cybersecurity in my late 30s; and if I had never begun studying cybersecurity at Penn State, I would have never been introduced to OSINT. Of course, you don't have to begin an entirely new career to keep learning just to be open to new experiences and ideas.

Learn from yourself.   Use your wins, your missteps, and even your mistakes as learning experiences. It can be easy to fall into the trap of imposter syndrome while standing next to your heroes, but *you belong here*. Continue to find new techniques and methods, set new goals to achieve, and try new things.

Learn from others.   Because of the nature of the technology profession, there is the undying stigma that everyone must always be an expert, know every answer, and be a lone wolf. However, you are more valuable as an analyst when you can admit your faults, share ideas, and ask people for help. It would be brilliant to say I wrote this book all on my own, but it would be resoundingly false. My support system of brilliant and kind experts that teach me new things every day is in perpetual development. More important, I maintain relationships with people who think differently than I do, who are not afraid to (kindly) educate me, and who want to see me succeed. Find your support system and when the time comes, be someone else's.

Always Maintain Good OPSEC

Ensure during your analysis that you understand any potential enemies and the data trail you may leave behind. Focus on maintaining privacy through VPNs, VMs, research accounts, etc. A case can be ruined, and your safety and the safety of others can be in jeopardy extremely quickly, so be fully prepared ahead of time and at all times.

> "Sorry, boss, but there's only two men I trust. One of them's me. The other's not you."
>
> —*Nicholas Cage as Cameron Poe in Con-Air*

As you begin to put these methodologies into practice, remember that in the age of information, the power of open source intelligence is only limited by our imagination and willingness to learn.

Index